Cultural Rights and Wrongs in Transitional Justice

Cultural Rights and Wrongs in Transitional Justice

COLIN LUOMA
Brunel University of London

OXFORD
UNIVERSITY PRESS

OXFORD
UNIVERSITY PRESS

Great Clarendon Street, Oxford, OX2 6DP,
United Kingdom

Oxford University Press is a department of the University of Oxford.
It furthers the University's objective of excellence in research, scholarship,
and education by publishing worldwide. Oxford is a registered trade mark of
Oxford University Press in the UK and in certain other countries.

Published in the United States of America by Oxford University Press
198 Madison Avenue, New York, NY 10016, United States of America.

British Library Cataloguing in Publication Data
Data available

Library of Congress Control Number: 2025937549

ISBN 978–0–19–891137–1

DOI: 10.1093/oso/9780198911371.001.0001

The manufacturer's authorised representative in the EU for product safety is
Oxford University Press España S.A., Parque Empresarial San Fernando de Henares,
Avenida de Castilla, 2 – 28830 Madrid (www.oup.es/en or product.safety@oup.com).
OUP España S.A. also acts as importer into Spain of products made by the manufacturer.

for my grandmothers

ACKNOWLEDGEMENTS

Several people have been instrumental to the completion of this project. First, I am grateful for the support, flexibility, and expertise of the team at Oxford University Press and the peer reviewers who significantly enhanced and improved this book. I also want to thank the many people who in some way, large or small, contributed to the development of the ideas in this book. This includes my brilliant colleagues at Brunel Law School, former colleagues at Minority Rights Group International, and the various academic peers who in some way engaged with my work in constructive and meaningful ways. I am especially thankful to Alexandra Xanthaki, my PhD supervisor, colleague, mentor, and good friend. From the beginning, Alexandra believed in my potential as a scholar and helped nurture this project in a way only she can. Her unique combination of intellectual brilliance, resilience, kindness, humour, and humility has been instrumental to my development as a researcher and my capacity to do this type of work.

Long before I was interested in transitional justice or human rights, my parents, Richard and Cynthia, instilled in me the basic principle that every person is entitled to the full measure of human dignity. They provided me with the emotional security to write this book, offering me the sanctuary of home and staying close despite the many oceans, mountains, and rivers between us. Likewise, I am indebted to my siblings and their partners (Cory, Katie, Kelli, Katie, and Olivier) for inspiring me in many ways, while also reminding me to not take myself too seriously.

My life has been enriched beyond all measure by the presence of my four children (Theodore, Thomas, Vashti, and Sullivan). Their arrivals, all of which occurred during the lifecycle of this project, have been the most welcome of interruptions.

Above all, I need to thank my partner, Stephanie, for the far too many personal and professional sacrifices she has made on this journey; for her selflessness, tolerance, and patience; for taking the risks and shouldering the burdens; for unconditional love and support throughout this project; and for making all this possible—whatever this thing is or will ever be, it is because of you.

Writing this book has taken the better part of seven years. In this time, my life has changed in innumerable ways. I have moved, changed jobs, had children, and lost loved ones. Thinking about the ideas in this book has been one of the more consistent aspects of my life. For it to still feel like an unfinished project feels both natural and discomforting. I simply hope I have done it justice. All errors are, of course, my own.

CONTENTS

TABLE OF CASES

INTERNATIONAL COURT OF JUSTICE

INTERNATIONAL CRIMINAL COURT

INTERNATIONAL CRIMINAL TRIBUNAL FOR THE FORMER YUGOSLAVIA

INTER-AMERICAN COURT OF HUMAN RIGHTS

EUROPEAN COURT OF HUMAN RIGHTS

DOMESTIC COURTS

TABLE OF LEGAL INSTRUMENTS AND DOCUMENTS

INTERNATIONAL CONVENTIONS AND TREATIES

DECLARATIONS, RESOLUTIONS, RECOMMENDATIONS, GUIDELINES AND GENERAL COMMENTS

UNESCO DOCUMENTS

UN STUDIES AND REPORTS

DOMESTIC LEGISLATION

INTRODUCTION

> We can love what we are, without hating what—and who—we are not. We can thrive in our own tradition, even as we learn from others, and come to respect their teachings.[1]
>
> —*Kofi Annan, former Secretary-General of the United Nations*

1. Culture, Conflict, and Peace

Kofi Annan spoke these words while accepting the Nobel Peace Prize on behalf of himself and the United Nations ('UN') in 2001. In his speech, Annan reflected on the tumultuousness of the twentieth century and emphasized the need to respect and protect human dignity and diversity in order to stave off the worst and most violent aspects of the human experience. His comments on the day were undoubtedly coloured by the 11 September terrorist attacks carried out a mere few months earlier. He blamed the notion that different religions and cultures were inherently in conflict with one another for what he called 'endless enmity and conflict'. In the same vein, he reinforced the value of respecting the 'many cultures, traditions and memories' that embody our collective humanity.[2]

Three years after securing the Nobel Peace Prize, Annan, in his capacity as UN Secretary-General, issued a report on the rule of law and transitional justice in conflict and post-conflict societies.[3] This was in response to the UN Security Council's request that the international body leverage its experience and expertise to highlight key issues and lessons learned in connection with

[1] UN Press Release, '"We Can Love What We Are, Without Hating What—And Who—We Are Not," Secretary-General Says in Nobel Lecture', UN Doc SG/SM/8071 (10 December 2001) <https://press.un.org/en/2001/sgsm8071.doc.htm> accessed 31 December 2024.

[2] ibid.

[3] UN Secretary-General, *The Rule of Law and Transitional Justice in Conflict and Post-Conflict Societies*, UN Doc S/2004/616 (23 August 2004).

Cultural Rights and Wrongs in Transitional Justice. Colin Luoma, Oxford University Press. © Colin Luoma 2025.
DOI: 10.1093/oso/9780198911371.001.0001

the promotion of justice and the rule of law in such contexts. The Secretary-General's 2004 report constituted a consolidation of the UN's early understanding of transitional justice and subsequently emerged as one of the most important early articulations of the international norms, guidelines, and standards applicable to the concept.[4]

Among other things, it set forth a definition of transitional justice that continues to be the most well-cited in the discourse.[5] It also delineated what came to be known as the transitional justice 'toolbox', namely the standard processes and mechanisms used by transitional societies to reckon with episodes of past large-scale harm.[6] These include 'prosecutions, reparations, truth-seeking, institutional reform, vetting and dismissals, or a combination thereof'.[7] The Secretary-General's report was instrumental in institutionalizing and mainstreaming transitional justice in the UN, leading to the promulgation of a host of standards and norms meant to guide States and international actors in designing and implementing transitional justice policy.

What seemed evident in his Nobel Peace Prize lecture was Annan's appreciation for the critical role that culture, cultural identities, and cultural heritage play both in the instigation of conflict and in the maintenance of peace, security, and global order. He celebrated the fact that people of all different cultures live among one another and cautioned against the devastating tendency to engage in the othering of different groups. The subsequent UN Secretary-General report, however, did little to integrate culture and cultural rights as essential considerations for how post-conflict and divided societies should attempt to address their painful and violent pasts or how to ensure peaceful futures.[8] This has had long-lasting ramifications; indeed, in the twenty years since the seminal report, cultural rights are still rarely positioned as an integral component of transitional justice thinking or praxis.

At its most fundamental level, transitional justice is premised on the idea that something must be done in the aftermath of mass violence or large-scale

[4] Leena Grover, 'Transitional Justice, International Law and the United Nations' (2019) 88 Nordic Journal of International Law 359, 370–71.

[5] UN Secretary-General, *The Rule of Law and Transitional Justice in Conflict and Post-Conflict Societies* (n 3) para 8.

[6] Lisa J Laplante, 'Transitional Justice and Peace Building: Diagnosing and Addressing the Socio-economic Roots of Violence Through a Human Rights Framework' (2008) 2(3) The International Journal of Transitional Justice 331, 333.

[7] UN Secretary-General, *The Rule of Law and Transitional Justice in Conflict and Post-Conflict Societies* (n 3) para 8.

[8] The report did stress that 'due regard must be given to indigenous and informal traditions for administering justice or settling disputes': ibid para 36.

abuses.[9] What exactly that something can and should be is at the heart of this book. For most of the field's history, the answer to this question has mostly revolved around the legal redress of a limited set of bodily integrity crimes in societies emerging from recent periods of repressive rule or armed conflict.[10] Issues of culture—including large-scale violations of cultural rights, local and Indigenous cultural traditions, and culturally diverse responses to mass harm—have been largely excluded from the purview of transitional justice agendas. This narrow approach arguably impacts the very legitimacy of the field and justifies a more critical and thorough evaluation of the role of cultural rights in transitional justice.

2. Transitional Justice: An Expanding Enterprise

In its third decade as a cognisable field, transitional justice has become ubiquitous. It is unquestionably the dominant international framework for addressing past periods of large-scale harm.[11] For States, civil society, and victims alike, it has evolved into a sort of default response to dealing with violent and difficult pasts. The language, goals, and tools of transitional justice are now commonly invoked in a wide variety of contexts and among different stakeholders. The field's rapid expansion and consolidation is evidenced, in part, by the establishment of a specialized academic journal, a dedicated UN Special Rapporteur, several transitional justice-focused NGOs, the publication of a wide breadth of literature across several academic disciplines, and the proliferation of transitional justice mechanisms in seemingly every corner of the world. Far from a cottage industry, one can hardly wade into any context without some mention of transitional justice.

Once a relatively exceptional and narrow project (albeit imbued with some quite lofty goals), transitional justice is now employed in contexts far beyond the political dilemmas and corresponding bodily integrity violations that exemplified the field during its genesis. This is reflected in an increasingly diverse

[9] Martha Minow, *Between Vengeance and Forgiveness: Facing History after Genocide and Mass Violence* (Beacon University Press 1998) 4.

[10] James Cavallaro and Sebastián Albuja, 'The Lost Agenda: Economic Crimes and Truth Commissions in Latin America and Beyond' in Kieran McEvoy and Lorna McGregor (eds), *Transitional Justice from Below: Grassroots Activism and the Struggle for Change* (Hart Publishing 2008) 121.

[11] Jennifer Balint, Julie Evans, and Nesam McMillan, 'Rethinking Transitional Justice, Redressing Indigenous Harm: A New Conceptual Approach' (2014) 8(2) International Journal of Transitional Justice 194, 194.

set of mechanisms, the contexts in which they operate, and the types of harms they are charged with tackling. Transitional justice programming is now routinely initiated in settings with no discernible transition to peace or liberal democracy.[12] In addition to the orthodox transitional justice toolbox, several other mechanisms and approaches are utilized to confront difficult and violent legacies. These measures are also addressing a greater variety of wrongdoing, including some degree of large-scale cultural harm.[13]

The rapid expansion and mainstreaming of transitional justice, perhaps quite predictably, has been accompanied by increased scrutiny and critique. For the past twenty years, we have been interrogating what Rosemary Nagy calls the 'when, to whom and for what transitional justice applies'.[14] Scholars are consistently contesting the boundaries, goals, and conceptual underpinnings of transitional justice, resulting in a sizeable body of scholarship analysing the field's cracks and shortcomings.[15] While transitional justice has long been critiqued and problematized, this relatively recent line of scholarship has mounted many theoretical and empirical challenges to the field. The most stringent criticism is aimed at the perception that transitional justice measures consistently fail to confront the full range of issues facing post-conflict and divided societies, including, most prominently, economic and social rights.[16]

In this regard we find ourselves in an interesting moment in the history of the field. Calls for transitional justice to do increasingly more for more people, and to do it better, do not seem to be abating. It is now being asked to confront an increasingly diverse array of harms in disparate and complementary ways,

[12] Transitional justice mechanisms have been employed in ongoing conflicts (eg Colombia), in societies transitioning from one authoritarian regime to another (eg Chad), and in ostensibly peaceful, liberal democracies (eg Canada). Padraig McAuliffe, 'Transitional Justice's Expanding Empire: Reasserting the Value of the Paradigmatic Transition' (2012) 2(2) Journal of Conflictology 32, 36–38.

[13] For example, truth and reconciliation commissions in Norway, Sweden, and Finland are all charged with accounting for the legacies of assimilationist policies directed towards Indigenous Peoples and minorities located within these States.

[14] Rosemary Nagy, 'Transitional Justice as Global Project: Critical Reflections' (2008) 29(2) Third World Quarterly 275, 276.

[15] Dustin Sharp describes this as the field's 'critical turn'. Dustin N Sharp, 'What Would Satisfy Us? Taking Stock of Critical Approaches to Transitional Justice' (2019) 13(3) International Journal of Transitional Justice 570, 570.

[16] See, eg, Rubén Carranza, 'Plunder and Pain: Should Transitional Justice Engage with Corruption and Economic Crimes?' (2008) 2(3) International Journal of Transitional Justice 310; Zinaida Miller, 'Effects of Invisibility: In Search of the "Economic" in Transitional Justice' (2008) 2(3) International Journal of Transitional Justice 266; Ismael Muvingi, 'Sitting on Powder Kegs: Socioeconomic Rights in Transitional Societies' (2009) 3(2) International Journal of Transitional Justice 163; Dustin N Sharp, 'Addressing Economic Violence in Times of Transition: Towards a Positive-Peace Paradigm for Transitional Justice' (2011) 35 Fordham International Law Journal 780; Juan Carlos Ochoa-Sánchez, 'Economic and Social Rights and Transitional Justice: A Framework of Analysis' (2019) 18 Journal of Human Rights 522.

including violations that extend beyond recent memory. On one hand, this has brought more victims and forms of wrongdoing within the reach of extraordinary justice and redress. For example, there is a growing interest in using the tools and frameworks of transitional justice to engage with historical injustices and their ongoing legacies, especially as they relate to colonialism, settler colonialism, and the transatlantic slave trade. For those of us who are sympathetic to a more egalitarian, holistic, and consequential version of transitional justice, this would seem to be a positive development.

On the other hand, there is a risk that we are asking transitional justice to do far too much, transforming it into a 'theory of everything', a burden that no transitional justice process is prepared to shoulder.[17] Indeed, it is not clear to what extent transitional justice is meaningfully meeting its initial, narrowly stated goals.[18] As transitional justice has expanded and globalized, its effectiveness is routinely called into question, and we do not have a wealth of evidence demonstrating that transitional justice measures have necessarily accomplished what they have set out to achieve in the scope of holding actors accountable, improving lives, fostering peace, or ensuring the non-recurrence of violations.[19] Pablo De Grieff, the former UN Special Rapporteur on the promotion of truth, justice, reparation and guarantees of non-recurrence ('UN SRTJ'), has gone so far as to state that '[t]here is no transitional country that can legitimately claim great successes in this field'.[20] Perhaps this is why some have suggested that transitional justice is in a period of crisis.[21]

3. Overlooking Culture

Societies devastated from years of armed conflict, authoritarian rule, or severe societal divisions are often forced to grapple with various demands, resource constraints, and competing expectations. Justice in these contexts is multifaceted and at best only partially achievable, and only then through sustained and long-term interventions. The types of wrongdoing subject to a transitional justice response and the manner in which they are confronted are highly

[17] Naomi Roht-Arriaza, 'Reparations and Economic, Social, and Cultural Rights' in Dustin N Sharp (ed), *Justice and Economic Violence in Transition* (Springer 2014) 111.

[18] Dustin N Sharp, *Re-Thinking Transitional Justice for the 21st Century* (Cambridge University Press 2018) 14.

[19] Erin Baines, 'Spirits and Social Reconstruction after Mass Violence: Rethinking Transitional Justice' (2010) 190 (436) African Affairs 409, 413.

[20] Pablo De Greiff, 'Theorizing Transitional Justice' (2012) 51 Nomos 31, 35.

[21] Maja Davidovic, 'Transform or Perish? The Crisis of Transitional Justice' (2020) 20(2) Conflict, Security and Development 293.

context-dependent and should be principally responsive to the needs and priorities of victims.[22] At the same time, the field's history demonstrates a general trend, whereby certain categories of wrongdoing and modalities of justice have been prioritized in transitional justice policy, often without meaningful consideration of culture or cultural rights.

While the boundaries, goals, and underlying theories behind transitional justice are routinely challenged, this has yet to lead to a robust engagement with cultural rights or wrongs. Cultural issues are minimized and underappreciated, and sometimes go unnoticed altogether in post-conflict and divided societies. In the aftermath of periods of prolonged armed conflict or authoritarian rule, the need to reckon with large-scale bodily integrity atrocities typically overshadows less visible and more subtle forms of cultural wrongdoing. At the same time, these cultural harms often drive conflict, are committed during conflict, and persist long after conflict has subsided. Groups often use violence to destroy cultures and use their own cultures and cultural practices to justify egregious acts of violence against others. In those cases where culture does not directly contribute to or constitute violence, it is always a factor in conflict and broader societal divisions.[23] Even in ostensibly peaceful democracies attempting to confront their legacies of colonial wrongdoing, cultural rights are not respected and addressed in the same manner as other rights.

Unlike other rights categories, cultural rights have been consistently and uniquely overlooked in transitional justice discourse and programming. This treatment is at odds with how we have begun to understand culture, particularly in its broadest conception as a 'way of life'.[24] In her inaugural thematic report as UN Special Rapporteur in the field of cultural rights ('UN SRCR'), Alexandra Xanthaki described culture as a wide-ranging and essential aspect of humanity:

> Culture is much more than the sum of products. It is a process and a way of life. It permeates all spheres of life and is as essential to human experience

[22] This book uses the term 'victims' to encompass direct, indirect, and communal victims who suffered harm through past wrongdoing in post-conflict and divided societies. It also recognizes that depending on the context, the dividing lines between victims, survivors, and perpetrators is not always clear. See Alessandro Chechi, 'The Return of Cultural Objects Displaced during Colonialism. What Role for Restorative Justice, Transitional Justice and Alternative Dispute Resolution?' (2023) 6(1) International Journal of Restorative Justice 95, 103.

[23] Michelle Lebaron, 'Culture and Conflict' in Guy Burgess and Heidi Burgess (eds), *Beyond Intractability* (Conflict Information Consortium, University of Colorado, Boulder, July 2003).

[24] Laura Pineschi, 'Cultural Diversity as a Human Right? General Comment No. 21 of the Committee on Economic, Social and Cultural Rights' in Silvia Borelli and Federico Lenzerini (eds), *Cultural Heritage, Cultural Rights, Cultural Diversity: New Developments in International Law* (Martinus Nijhoff Publishers 2012) 51.

as air, water, shelter and security. It is at the core of being human: it is how people assign meaning to their lives and understand their human, natural and manufactured environment, as individuals and collectives.[25]

The essentialness of culture to human existence and well-being is incongruent with cultural rights' subordinated positionality on the peripheries of transitional justice theory and practice. Mass cultural harm is still not seen as being as grave as other forms of wrongdoing. Cultural traditions and justice practices are regularly ignored, denigrated, or relegated as secondary solutions to dealing with violent and unjust legacies.[26] And the cultural violence that underpins episodes of large-scale harm tends to go unacknowledged and unaddressed. This persistent marginalization of cultural issues provides the animus for the need to understand how and why cultural rights have been so divorced from our collective thinking around transitional justice.

It is in this general milieu that this book takes on the challenge of evaluating the specific role of cultural rights, and culture more generally, in this rapidly burgeoning yet deeply contested enterprise. It seizes upon the opportunity to take stock of the role of cultural rights in transitional justice at a time when increasing interactions between them seem inevitable. By interrogating the role of cultural rights in the field and rethinking the fundamental tenets of the transitional justice project in ways that accommodate further engagement with cultural rights, it both seeks to address an existing 'cultural rights gap' and encourages a cultural rights-based approach to doing justice in times of transition. In doing so, it provides the first in-depth analysis of cultural rights in the transitional justice discourse.

4. A Cultural Rights-based Approach to Transitional Justice

This book articulates and ultimately advances the case for a cultural rights-based approach to transitional justice—something that the field currently does not embrace. A cultural rights-based approach to transitional justice is one that addresses large-scale past cultural wrongdoing on the same footing

[25] Report of the Special Rapporteur in the field of cultural rights, Alexandra Xanthaki, 'Cultural Rights: An Empowering Agenda', UN Doc A/HRC/49/54 (22 March 2022) para 9.

[26] Sharp, *Re-Thinking Transitional Justice for the 21st Century* (n 18) 12; see also Christine Bell and Catherine O'Rourke, 'Does Feminism Need a Theory of Transitional Justice? An Introductory Essay' (2007) 1(1) The International Journal of Transitional Justice 23, 25.

as violations of civil, political, economic, and social rights. It requires that cultural rights are protected, respected, and fulfilled in the design, implementation, and operation of transitional justice initiatives. And it encourages and accommodates the use of cultural practices and interventions as a meaningful way to confront large-scale past harm in post-conflict and divided societies.

A cultural rights-based approach envisions utilizing and embracing the suite of cultural rights protections developed under international human rights law that safeguard the cultural identities, traditions, and practices of individuals and groups. These standards, underpinned by binding and non-binding international instruments, are available for transitional justice policymakers and practitioners to employ in various ways. Not only should they influence the design and implementation of transitional justice programming, but, when possible and appropriate, mechanisms should explicitly link wrongdoing to violations of these international norms. Framing cultural wrongs through the language of human rights not only strengthens the normative standing of cultural rights but also empowers victims to hold States legally, morally, and politically accountable for their transgressions against culture.

To be sure, embracing a cultural rights-based approach will not serve as a panacea to the many shortcomings of transitional justice. Notwithstanding, it has the potential to make the transitional justice project more meaningful for more people. This is already starting to come to fruition in practice, with a growing number of mechanisms treating cultural rights as more integral to the transitional justice project.[27] In this vein, this book seeks to highlight and evaluate attempts to respect and address cultural rights as examples of best practice for transitional justice stakeholders.

5. Methodology and Positionality

5.1 Methodology

Much of the research in this book is the product of my doctoral studies conducted at Brunel University of London between February 2018 and October 2021. My doctoral research focused on the role of transitional justice in relation to large-scale Indigenous cultural rights violations in settler colonial States. This book builds upon and expands this study by looking more broadly at the treatment of cultural rights within the scope of the transitional justice

[27] In particular, see positive examples of transitional justice practice discussed in Chapter 5.

field. It is principally a theoretical study, analysing how culture and cultural rights relate to transitional justice principles, concepts, and theories. Although transitional justice has rapidly become the dominant international framework for responding to past periods of mass violence and large-scale human rights abuses, it is often repeated that it has been undertheorized for much of its history.[28] In this way, it contributes to addressing some of the theoretical gaps and challenges that persist in the transitional justice field.

This research employs a theoretical analysis to examine the underlying beliefs, biases, and assumptions embedded in the field's mainstream theory in ways that challenge and ultimately seek to accommodate a cultural rights-based approach to transitional justice. It seeks to bridge the theoretical divide between transitional justice and cultural rights, exploring how and why transitional justice has developed in ways that marginalize cultural rights and examining the gaps and potential for future interaction between these two areas. It critiques narrow transitional justice approaches and offers a theoretical lens for understanding how the field can reorient itself to better engage with cultural rights in post-conflict and divided societies. By interrogating and retheorizing some of the field's core concepts, it contends that a more significant engagement with cultural rights is both possible and justified in transitional justice. In this vein, it is squarely an intervention in what Dustin Sharp calls the '"fourth generation of transitional justice", characterized in part by its increasing willingness to grapple with issues that continue to sit at the periphery of transitional justice concern'.[29]

Transitional justice is also a heavily under-empiricized field, but this research does not seek to make an empirical contribution. Its purpose is not to evaluate the effectiveness of any particular transitional justice mechanism or prescribe how societies should seek to redress the myriad wrongs they have suffered. Instead, building off a growing body of critical transitional justice scholarship, it challenges the field's mainstream theory and approaches for largely ignoring cultural rights and marginalizing the violent experiences of groups who have sustained large-scale cultural harm. In doing so, it seeks to position cultural rights and cultural wrongs within the wider contestations concerning the idea and application of transitional justice.

While primarily a theoretical project, this book also contains normative aspects in the sense that it describes, critiques, and compares how transitional

[28] Susanne Buckley-Zistel and others, 'Transitional Justice Theories: An Introduction' in Susanne Buckley-Zistel and others (eds), Transitional Justice Theories (Routledge 2014) 2.

[29] Dustin N Sharp, 'Interrogating the Peripheries: The Preoccupations of Fourth Generation Transitional Justice' (2013) 26 Harvard Human Rights Journal 149, 157.

justice mechanisms engage with cultural rights across various settings. This approach uses qualitative research methods to understand how transitional justice has engaged with these categories of rights in practice. The corpus of this material includes relevant transitional justice outputs, as well as the scholarly texts, articles, and reports of non-governmental and intergovernmental organizations analysing these outputs. As transitional justice is a global, interdisciplinary field, this review extends beyond the confines of international human rights law and is informed by transitional justice scholarship in various fields, including sociology, political science, anthropology, history, memory studies, and philosophy, among other disciplines.[30]

5.2 Positionality

I am writing about cultural rights and transitional justice from the position of someone whose life, liberty, socio-economic status, and cultural identity remains stable and unthreatened. At all times relevant to this research, I have enjoyed the full benefits of being a member in the dominant culture of the societies I have lived in. I do not fully understand the worldviews, cultural identities, or lived experiences of other groups, including those who have experienced large-scale violations of their cultural rights justifying a transitional justice response. While this restricts my ability to comprehend other cultures, I acknowledge that there are many ways of knowing and living in this world. As a result, I approached this research narrowly and primarily through the lens of transitional justice theory and the international human rights regime applicable to culture.

6. Notes on Terminology

6.1 Cultural rights

Authors have long struggled with defining cultural rights in the human rights arena, acknowledging the difficulty of articulating their scope and content. Since cultural rights are inherently tied to the definition of culture, it is

[30] Christine Bell, 'Transitional Justice, Interdisciplinarity and the State of the "Field" or "Non-Field"' (2009) 3(1) International Journal of Transitional Justice 5.

impossible to grasp the nature of these rights without first understanding what culture means.[31] However, culture is one of the most complicated words in the English language.[32] Hundreds of different definitions of culture have been proffered across various disciplines.[33] It is perhaps unsurprising then that there is no universally endorsed definition of culture, and hence, cultural rights.[34]

The definitional evolutions associated with the term 'culture' have been discussed exhaustively elsewhere.[35] While initially understood quite narrowly, culture is now conceived of, in its broadest sense, as the entire 'way of life' of a social group.[36] In a remarkably expansive construction, the Committee on Economic, Social and Cultural Rights ('CESCR') has described culture as encompassing 'all manifestations of human existence'.[37] Under this conception, culture includes, *inter alia*, values, knowledge, beliefs, language, literature, philosophy, religion, science, and technology.[38]

The substantial overlap between rights relating to culture and other human rights makes it difficult to delineate a specific list of cultural rights.[39] Select legal instruments and authors have engaged in this exercise, but all of them are imperfect and non-exhaustive.[40] This book does not seek to prescribe a list of cultural rights; instead it broadly conceives of them as those human rights that promote, protect, and preserve the rights of individuals and groups to develop and maintain their cultural identities, worldviews, and practices.[41]

[31] Elsa Stamatopoulou, *Cultural Rights in International Law: Article 27 of the Universal Declaration of Human Rights and Beyond* (Brill 2007) 5; Janusz Symonides, 'Cultural Rights: A Neglected Category of Human Rights' (2002) 50(158) International Social Science Journal 559.

[32] Raymond Williams, *Keywords: A Vocabulary of Culture and Society* (Oxford University Press 1983).

[33] Yvonne Donders, *Towards a Right to Cultural Identity?* (Intersentia 2003) 24–30.

[34] Report of the Independent Expert in the Field of Cultural Rights, UN Doc A/HRC/14/36 (22 March 2010) para 5.

[35] See, eg, Alexandra Xanthaki, 'Indigenous Cultural Rights in International Law' (2000) 2 European Journal of Law Reform 343, 348–58; Roger O'Keefe, 'The "Right to Take Part in Cultural Life" under Article 15 of the ICESCR' (1998) 47 International and Comparative Law Quarterly 904, 906–18.

[36] Xanthaki, 'Indigenous Cultural Rights in International Law' (n 35) 355–58.

[37] UN Committee on Economic, Social and Cultural Rights (CESCR), General Comment no. 21, Right of Everyone to Take Part in Cultural Life (art 15, para 1a of the Covenant on Economic, Social and Cultural Rights), UN Doc E/C.12/GC/21 (21 December 2009) para 11.

[38] Patrick Thornberry, *International Law and the Rights of Minorities* (Oxford University Press 2001) 188.

[39] Report of the Independent Expert in the Field of Cultural Rights (n 34) para 11.

[40] Stamatopoulou, *Cultural Rights in International Law* (n 31) 2–3; see also UNESCO Universal Declaration on Cultural Diversity (2 November 2001); Fribourg Declaration on Cultural Rights (2007).

[41] Yvonne Donders, 'Foundations of Collective Cultural Rights in International Human Rights Law' in Andrzej Jakubowski (ed), *Cultural Rights as Collective Rights: An International Law Perspective* (Brill 2016) 85.

6.2 Cultural wrongs and cultural harm

Cultural rights violations are tied to a corresponding State obligation or international legal norm. Conversely, the terms 'cultural wrongs' and 'cultural harm' are used interchangeably in this book to encompass the full range of attacks on the cultures, cultural practices, traditions, languages, and cultural identities of individuals and/or groups regardless of whether they violate an international human rights obligation or norm. This encompasses various infringements on culture, including but not limited to the suppression of traditional dress and language; forced assimilation and removal policies; prohibitions or restrictions on customs, practices, and rituals; destruction of cultural heritage; and denial or denigration of cultural identities. Critically, this type of wrongdoing is not conditioned on the existence of physical damage, economic loss, or other material deprivation.[42] Many of the cultural wrongs discussed in this book amount to violations of cultural rights under existing international norms and standards. However, maintaining a distinction between cultural wrongs and cultural rights violations is appropriate in certain instances, particularly with respect to harms that occurred prior to the incorporation of core cultural rights obligations under international law.

6.3 Transitional justice

There is no universally accepted meaning of transitional justice. Various definitions have been promulgated and authors have thoroughly studied how the phrase has been defined and evolved across the history of the field.[43] This book broadly conceives of transitional justice as a set of responses to the various dilemmas that arise when societies seek to reckon with legacies of large-scale past harm.[44] This understanding of transitional justice is aligned with the definition set forth in the UN Secretary-General's 2004 report as embodying 'the

[42] Federico Lenzerini, 'Reparations for Indigenous Peoples in International and Comparative Law: An Introduction' in Federico Lenzerini (ed), *Reparations for Indigenous Peoples: International and Comparative Perspectives* (Oxford University Press 2008) 15.

[43] Rosemary Nagy, 'Transitional Justice as Global Project' (n 14) 276–79.

[44] Naomi Roht-Arriaza, 'The New Landscape of Transitional Justice' in Naomi Roht-Arriaza and Javier Mariezcurrena (eds), *Transitional Justice in the Twenty-First Century: Beyond Truth versus Justice* (Cambridge University Press 2014) 2.

full range of processes and mechanisms associated with a society's attempt to come to terms with a legacy of large-scale past abuses, in order to ensure accountability, serve justice and achieve reconciliation'.[45]

Not only does this definition align with the UN's understanding of transitional justice, but it also contains certain characteristics that empower and accommodate a more meaningful engagement with cultural rights. First, it is not tethered to a specific type of transition, thus offering a certain level of flexibility in determining when and where transitional justice frameworks may apply. Second, in referencing 'large-scale past harm' instead of 'large-scale human rights violations' it does not necessarily preclude transitional justice from addressing historical wrongdoing committed before the ratification of most human rights obligations under international law.[46] Lastly, it does not explicitly restrict its application to certain categories of harm, as is the case for other definitions.[47]

6.4 Post-conflict and divided societies

Throughout this book, the phrase 'post-conflict and divided societies' is used in reference to societies that are recovering from periods of armed conflict or authoritarian rule and/or experiencing deep-rooted social, cultural, political, ethnic, or religious divisions. There is obviously significant overlap between post-conflict societies, on one hand, and divided societies, on the other. It is not difficult to imagine post-conflict contexts that are also marked by severe societal divisions. I acknowledge the breadth of this terminology, especially as it relates to divided societies, which could conceivably encompass a multitude of countries that are traditionally seen as exempt from the scope of transitional justice. This imperfect phrasing is intentional and meant to include the many countries which are considered peaceful and democratic but have legacies of large-scale past harm justifying a transitional justice response.

[45] UN Secretary-General, The Rule of Law and Transitional Justice in Conflict and Post-Conflict Societies (n 3) para 7.

[46] Evelyne Schmid and Aoife Nolan, '"Do No Harm"? Exploring the Scope of Economic and Social Rights in Transitional Justice' (2014) 8(3) International Journal of Transitional Justice 362, 381 n 99.

[47] Evelyne Schmid, 'War Crimes Related to Violations of Economic, Social and Cultural Rights' (2011) 71(3) Heidelberg Journal of International Law 523, 525.

7. Argument and Structure of the Book

This book is structured around three interrelated arguments. The first argument is that cultural rights represent a significant blind spot in the field of transitional justice. Cultural rights have not been seriously incorporated into transitional justice practice or adequately considered in transitional justice discourse. This blind spot has yet to be comprehensively interrogated, as done in this book. In furtherance of this argument, Chapter 1 surveys the marginalization of cultural rights in the field of transitional justice. In the discourse, cultural rights are largely either explicitly omitted or only discussed by virtue of being grouped in the economic, social, and cultural ('ESC') category of rights. In practical mechanisms, cultural rights are commonly backgrounded as historical context, or only discussed in the context of other rights deemed more important for post-conflict and divided societies. The few mechanisms that have engaged with cultural rights have often done so in limited and problematic ways. This has contributed to and reinforced the relegation of cultural rights as something unworthy of our collective attention in how transitional societies should seek to address past large-scale harm.

The second argument advanced in this book is that the marginalization of cultural rights is primarily attributable to certain biases, assumptions, and limitations that developed during the nascence of the field, and which became engrained in a dominant model of transitional justice that continues be replicated without sufficient consideration of cultural rights. This has made transitional justice—at least as conventionally theorized and implemented—incompatible with a cultural rights-based approach. Thus, Chapter 2 interrogates the evolutionary history and dominant theorization of transitional justice to understand the field's (non)relationship with cultural rights. The way in which transitional justice originated and evolved shaped its contours in ways that consistently neglected cultural rights. More specifically, mainstream transitional justice theory has embraced exceedingly narrow understandings of what constitutes a *transition* (transitions from authoritarianism to democracy or, alternatively, from armed conflict to peace), *justice* (top-down, internationalized, and legalistic mechanisms focused on individual and criminal accountability) and *violence* (recent, egregious bodily integrity crimes). These normative conceptions have become engrained in the conventional ways in which transitional justice is understood and operationalized, which has severely curtailed the field's ability to address cultural wrongdoing and marshal culturally diverse responses to past harm.

In this way, Chapter 2 reflects on why cultural rights have been relegated to the peripheries of transitional justice. While similar research has been conducted with respect to the omission of economic and social rights, and socio-economic considerations more generally, this book looks specifically at how the field evolved and consolidated in ways that marginalized culture and cultural rights. Thus, it positions itself within existing critical scholarship while also extending a specific line of critique to the marginalization of cultural rights.

The third argument is that transitional justice can be reconceptualized to accommodate a more robust engagement with cultural rights. Chapter 3 challenges and rethinks orthodox understandings of what can constitute a transition, justice, and violence under the dominant model of transitional justice. Transitions can be fairly broadened to include contexts beyond the paradigmatic transitions from armed conflict to peace or from dictatorship to liberal democracy. This brings a broader range of cultural wrongdoing squarely into the purview of transitional justice scrutiny, particularly as it pertains to the wrongs committed by so-called established democracies, who are increasingly called to reckon with the violent legacies of colonialism and attendant large-scale cultural harm. Dominant justice modalities can also be rethought to align with the international standards that have developed to protect and respect the cultural identities, cultural practices, traditions, and worldviews of victims and survivors. Lastly, dominant violence can be expanded to include large-scale cultural wrongdoing, harms that have equally devastating effects on victims and on transitional societies. This would include both historical harms and contemporary acts and policies which destroy, denigrate, or diminish cultural systems, practices, and identities.

Armed with a more flexible and robust theory of transitional justice, the remainder of the book articulates, justifies, and advances a cultural rights-based approach to transitional justice. Chapter 4 reflects on the extent to which transitional justice should seek to engage with cultural rights. To date, there has not been an explicit defence of the idea that transitional justice should address cultural rights violations specifically, as opposed to ESC rights violations more generally. In doing so, this book builds on existing debates concerning expanding the scope of the transitional justice, but specifically tailors the analysis to an engagement with cultural rights. Among other things, incorporating cultural rights into transitional justice agendas has the potential to strengthen the normative value of cultural rights, address root causes of conflict, respond to victim priorities, and shape more meaningful long-term reforms in post-conflict and divided societies.

Chapter 5 then proceeds to envision what a cultural rights-based approach to transitional justice might look like. It draws from recent practice which increasingly treats cultural rights as an integral part of transitional justice policy and agendas. In this sense, it moves from the level of theory to explore how transitional justice measures can respect and address cultural rights in practice. A cultural rights-based approach to transitional justice contemplates an engagement with culture tailored to the specific needs, demands, and limitations of any given post-conflict and divided society. Under such an approach, this may mean (1) confronting cultural rights violations; (2) accounting for underlying cultural violence in societies that contributes to other forms of violence; (3) accommodating local and Indigenous cultures in justice processes; (4) creating space for cultural processes, responses, and interventions; (5) engaging in memorialization; and (6) providing cultural reparations. These represent distinct but concrete ways to engage with culture and utilize a cultural rights-based approach in the scope of transitional justice praxis.

There is perhaps no area more in need of a cultural rights-based approach to transitional justice than settings where Indigenous Peoples are seeking justice for wrongdoing committed during periods of colonialization and ongoing colonial structures of oppression. Thus, Chapter 6 situates and explores the arguments advanced in this book in the specific context of Indigenous Peoples' claims for justice. While post-conflict and divided societies have traditionally neglected the experiences and perspectives of Indigenous Peoples, several recent initiatives have sought to address historical wrongdoing experienced by these groups, including their contemporary legacies. These initiatives have already begun to push the boundaries of the dominant model in significant ways.

Chapter 6 draws from numerous contexts to highlight existing approaches, practices, gaps, and limitations with respect to the intersections between transitional justice and Indigenous Peoples' cultures and cultural rights. It further underscores the important balancing act that must occur in transitional justice to ensure that cultural rights-based approaches do not distract from or dilute other core Indigenous demands and grievances. Ultimately, it illustrates the additive role that cultural rights can play in post-conflict and divided societies under a retheorized version of transitional justice.

The book concludes by reflecting on the implications of a cultural rights-based approach to transitional justice and what it might mean for future efforts by societies to reckon with past large-scale harm. Interactions between transitional justice and cultural rights only seem poised to increase, especially as States are pressed to confront wrongdoing that was previously outside the reach of transitional justice scrutiny. Yet, the many tensions, challenges, and opportunities associated with addressing and incorporating cultural rights in transitional justice are only beginning to be teased out. Accordingly, there is certainly scope to further study the potential application of transitional justice to cultural harm and do more to ensure that cultural rights are realized, violations remedied, and effective mechanisms of redress provided.

1
THE MARGINALIZATION OF CULTURAL RIGHTS IN TRANSITIONAL JUSTICE

1. Introduction

This book begins in earnest by surveying the role of cultural rights in the field of transitional justice. In many ways transitional justice and cultural rights have developed on relatively parallel tracks. Both fields emerged and gained momentum along similar timelines, with each now having migrated somewhere near the mainstream of human rights and peacebuilding.[1] This is evidenced, in part, by the fact that both transitional justice and cultural rights are now the subjects of robust academic commentary and feature prominently in the frameworks and outputs of the UN, including through dedicated special rapporteurs.[2] Yet, to date, only sparse attention has been afforded to the potential and realized intersections between transitional justice and cultural rights.[3]

Despite a range of advancements and interventions, cultural rights have long been a blind spot in the field of transitional justice, one that has yet to be thoroughly interrogated on either a theoretical or practical level.[4] This is at

[1] Kieran McEvoy, 'Beyond Legalism: Towards a Thicker Understanding of Transitional Justice' (2007) 34(4) Journal of Law and Society 411, 412 (noting the mainstreaming of transitional justice); see also Elsa Stamatopoulou, 'Monitoring Cultural Human Rights: The Claims of Culture on Human Rights and the Response of Cultural Rights' (2012) 34(4) Human Rights Quarterly 1170, 1176 (observing critical developments in the promotion and protection of cultural rights).

[2] An independent expert in the field of cultural rights (later the UN Special Rapporteur in the field of cultural rights) was established in 2009: UN Human Rights Council Resolution 10/23 (23 March 2009). A UN Special Rapporteur on the promotion of truth, justice, reparation and guarantees of non-recurrence was established in 2011: UN Human Rights Council Resolution 18/7 (29 September 2011).

[3] See, eg, *The Derry/Londonderry Report on Upholding the Human Right to Culture in Post-Conflict Societies* (Northern Ireland Human Rights Commission 2014); Colin Luoma, 'Closing the Cultural Rights Gap in Transitional Justice: Developments from Canada's National Inquiry into Missing and Murdered Indigenous Women and Girls' (2021) 39(1) Netherlands Quarterly of Human Rights 30; Sinéad Coakley and Pádraig McAuliffe, 'Picking Up the Pieces: Transitional Justice Responses to Destruction of Tangible Cultural Heritage' (2022) 40(3) Netherlands Quarterly of Human Rights 311.

[4] This book borrows the terminology of 'blindness' and 'blind spot' from scholars who have previously used it to describe transitional justice's neglect of economic and social rights. See, eg, Zinaida Miller, 'Effects of Invisibility: In Search of the "Economic" in Transitional Justice' (2008) 2(3) International Journal of Transitional Justice 266, 271; Dustin N Sharp, 'Addressing Economic

Cultural Rights and Wrongs in Transitional Justice. Colin Luoma, Oxford University Press.
DOI: 10.1093/oso/9780198911371.003.0001

odds with a demonstrated willingness by experts, policymakers, practitioners, and victims of mass harm to challenge transitional justice's preoccupation with bodily integrity crimes, and civil and political rights violations more generally. Indeed, the idea that transitional justice needs to better engage with much of the quotidian violence and injustice that underpins post-conflict and divided societies is increasingly gaining acceptance.[5] This is particularly the case with economic and social rights violations, which have attracted significant attention among transitional justice scholars and practioners.[6]

This momentum towards a more expansive version of transitional justice has yet to lead to significant and sustained engagement with cultural rights. Unlike other rights categories, cultural rights have been uniquely overlooked and diminished in transitional justice discourse and practice. This is not only antithetical to demands for the field to afford attention to violations of all rights, but also reinforces the continuing subordination of cultural rights, a bias mirrored in the human rights field.[7] In the human rights arena, it is oft-repeated that cultural rights are neglected.[8] Similarly, in the scope of transitional justice work, they once again find themselves relegated to the 'poor cousins' of other rights deemed more important.[9]

As subsequent chapters of this book will expound, cultural rights are not wholly absent from transitional justice and, indeed, are increasingly being addressed, respected, accommodated, and studied in interesting and significant ways. Select forms of cultural harm, including acts of intentional destruction of cultural property and the cultural wrongdoing inherent in the forced removals

Violence in Times of Transition: Towards a Positive-Peace Paradigm for Transitional Justice' (2011) 35 Fordham International Law Journal 780, 782; Padraig McAuliffe, 'Transitional Justice's Expanding Empire: Reasserting the Value of the Paradigmatic Transition' (2012) 2(2) Journal of Conflictology 32, 33.

[5] Lia Kent, 'Engaging with "The Everyday": Towards a More Dynamic Conception of Hybrid Transitional Justice' in Joanne Wallis and others (eds), *Hybridity on the Ground in Peacebuilding and Development: Critical Conversations* (ANU Press 2018) 145–61.

[6] See, eg, Rubén Carranza, 'Plunder and Pain: Should Transitional Justice Engage with Corruption and Economic Crimes?' (2008) 2(3) International Journal of Transitional Justice 310; Ismael Muvingi, 'Sitting on Powder Kegs: Socioeconomic Rights in Transitional Societies' (2009) 3(2) International Journal of Transitional Justice 163; Miller, 'Effects of Invisibility' (n 4); Sharp, 'Addressing Economic Violence in Times of Transition' (n 4); Juan Carlos Ochoa-Sánchez, 'Economic and Social Rights and Transitional Justice: A Framework of Analysis' (2019) 18 Journal of Human Rights 522.

[7] Guidance Note of the Secretary-General: United Nations Approach to Transitional Justice, UN Doc. ST/SG(09)/A652 (10 March 2010).

[8] Dominic McGoldrick colourfully calls cultural rights 'the failed Cinderella of the international human rights lexicon—pretty to pick sure but they don't quite make it to the ball.' Dominic McGoldrick, 'Culture, Cultures, and Cultural Rights' in Mashood A Baderin and Robert McCorquodale (eds), *Economic, Social and Cultural Rights in Action* (Oxford University Press 2007) 447.

[9] Report of the Special Rapporteur in the Field of Cultural Rights, UN Doc A/67/287 (10 August 2012) para 14.

of Indigenous children, have been the subject of transitional justice mechanisms and are analysed in the corresponding literature. Accommodating and integrating local cultures, traditions, and practices into transitional justice agendas and processes is a near consensus priority and considered best practice, even if this does not always come to fruition on the ground. Victims, civil society, and other stakeholders are also increasingly responding to difficult and violent legacies through cultural interventions, including art, photography, literature, song, theatre, and dance. More generally, large-scale cultural wrongdoing is beginning to be discussed as something worthy of the extraordinary reckoning and redress often associated with transitional justice.

These relatively recent developments, however, constitute clear exceptions to transitional justice's overall antipathy towards culture and stand in stark contrast to the historical marginalization of cultural rights in an enterprise originally designed to confront civil and political wrongs.[10] As such, this chapter explores a cultural rights gap that still largely persists in transitional justice. It begins by dissecting transitional justice discourse, examining how cultural rights are discussed and positioned in academic commentary, government statements, policy papers, and media coverage, as well as in the various reports, principles, standards, and documents developed in intergovernmental bodies and non-governmental organizations. In the discourse, cultural rights are commonly ignored, heavily backgrounded, or treated as mere context to civil and political rights violations (and to a lesser extent economic and social rights violations). Among other things, such treatment has the effect of diminishing the value and importance of human cultures in post-conflict and divided societies.

Cultural rights are likewise marginalized in transitional justice practice. This is especially the case with the redress of cultural rights violations, or cultural wrongs more generally, which is the primary focus of this chapter. Cultural rights violations have only recently found their way into transitional justice agendas or mechanisms. Even when flagrant cultural wrongdoing is central to an underlying conflict, transitional justice policies tend to overlook these specific harms or fail to meaningfully address them. When they are accounted for, it is often done through limited and problematic methods. This marginalization runs through all the orthodox mechanisms in the transitional justice toolbox. And although the wholesale neglect of cultural rights has waned in

[10] UN Office of the High Commissioner for Human Rights, 'Transitional Justice and Economic, Social and Cultural Rights', UN Doc HR/PUB/13/5 (2014).

recent practice, they are still rarely scrutinized in the same manner or on the same scale as other rights categories.

2. The Historical Marginalization of Cultural Rights in Transitional Justice Discourse

In the field's constantly growing and evolving discourse, cultural rights are routinely omitted, backgrounded, or discussed without reference to State obligations under international human rights law.[11] Historically, serious and sustained consideration was not afforded to harms that deviated from the civil and political rights that predominated during the nascence of transitional justice. The academic scholarship that helped bring the field into existence gave little to no thought to the role of culture in the transitional justice project. Ruti Teitel's *Transitional Justice*, for example, conceived of transitional justice as the collection of legal responses utilized in periods of radical political transformation, but it overlooked the broader cultural and socio-economic dimensions of the enterprise.[12] Likewise, Neil Kritz's multi-volume *Transitional Justice: How Emerging Democracies Reckon with Former Regimes* focused on the formal and legal institutions and responses by States in transitioning societies without considering cultural aspects of informal, community, and local processes.[13] These early seminal texts are indicative of the way in which transitional justice was narrowly conceived of in its early years.

In the past two decades, a body of critical scholarship has emerged interrogating the long-standing exclusion of certain issues from transitional justice scrutiny, particularly economic and social rights violations. Early advocates of more inclusive, broader approaches to transitional justice argued that the field needed to pay more attention to socio-economic matters, including subsistence rights,[14] economic development,[15] and distributive justice.[16] Yet these were certainly exceptions to the dominant transitional justice paradigm,

[11] The term 'discourse' is used to describe the knowledge relating to transitional justice, including across a vast archive of sources. See Marcos Zunino, *Justice Framed: A Genealogy of Transitional Justice* (Cambridge University Press 2019) 6.

[12] Ruti Teitel, *Transitional Justice* (Oxford University Press 2000).

[13] Neil Kritz, *Transitional Justice: How Emerging Democracies Reckon with Former Regimes* (US Institute of Peace Press 1995).

[14] Mahmood Mamdani, 'Amnesty or Impunity? A Preliminary Critique of the Report of the Truth and Reconciliation Commission of South Africa (TRC)' (2002) 32(3/4) Diacritics 33, 40–41.

[15] Laurel Fletcher and Harvey Weinstein, 'Violence and Social Repair: Rethinking the Contribution of Justice to Reconciliation' (2002) 24(3) Human Rights Quarterly 573, 580.

[16] Rama Mani, *Beyond Retribution: Seeking Justice in the Shadows of War* (Polity Press 2002).

still rather myopically focused on addressing mass violations of civil and political rights.

Critiques around transitional justice's preoccupation with civil and political rights were catalysed by the speech of Louise Arbour, then UN High Commissioner for Human Rights, at New York University in 2006.[17] Arbour directly appealed for transitional justice to engage with the underlying root causes of conflict, including violations of economic, social, and cultural rights. She advanced a case for transitional justice to reach 'beyond the crimes and abuses committed during the conflict' and to address those that 'pre-existed the conflict and caused, or contributed to it'.[18] Arbour emphasized the need to address these underlying sources of conflict, or else risk that the same conditions will 'fuel the next conflagration'.[19] While naming cultural rights, Arbour was primarily concerned with 'economic and social justice for societies in transition', explicitly calling for the integration of such rights into the transitional justice framework.[20]

This idea was embraced and institutionalized at the level of the UN, including through the Secretary-General's 2010 Guidance Note regarding the organization's approach to transitional justice, which states that '[t]transitional justice should further seek to take account of the root causes of conflicts and the related violations of all rights, including civil, political, economic, social and cultural rights'.[21] The Office of the United Nations High Commission for Human Rights ('OHCHR') further reiterated that '[t]he failure to realize economic, social and cultural rights as well as violations of these rights can be—and usually are—part of the root causes of conflict'.[22]

Arbour's speech spurred a host of scholars and experts to start seriously considering and debating the role of economic and social rights in transitional justice. The ensuing line of scholarship principally grapples with whether and how the field can more adequately address socio-economic harm and broader socio-economic issues facing post-conflict and divided societies. Several monographs and edited collections have been dedicated to these issues.[23] Moreover, the field's leading journal, the *International Journal of Transitional*

[17] Louise Arbour, 'Economic and Social Justice for Societies in Transition' Second Annual Transitional Justice Lecture hosted by the Center for Human Rights and Global Justice at New York University School of Law and by the International Center for Transitional Justice (New York University Law School, 25 October 2006).

[18] ibid at 2.

[19] Louise Arbour, 'Economic and Social Justice for Societies in Transition' (2007) 40 New York University Journal of International Law and Politics 1, 8.

[20] ibid 13.

[21] Guidance Note of the Secretary-General (n 7) 3.

[22] OHCHR, 'Transitional Justice and Economic, Social and Cultural Rights' (n 10) 1.

[23] See, eg, Dustin N Sharp (ed), *Justice and Economic Violence in Transition* (Springer 2014); Evelyne Schmid, *Taking Economic, Social and Cultural Rights Seriously in International Criminal Law*

Justice, has published a wealth of scholarship in this area, including a special issue dedicated to the nexus between transitional justice and development.[24] Indeed, the extent to which transitional justice should be concerned with economic and social issues continues to be the subject of intense debate, to the point that it perhaps can no longer be claimed that transitional justice ignores economic and social rights—at least not in theory.

Much of the critique around transitional justice's failure to engage with structural violence and socio-economic issues is also encompassed in the scholarship concerning 'transformative justice'. Transformative justice is a concept developed in response to the perceived limitations of transitional justice, with a greater emphasis placed on local agency, structural violence, and socio-economic issues.[25] Notwithstanding, as with transitional justice, the discourse on transformative justice largely overlooks cultural rights in favour of socio-economic considerations. It does not treat the redress and protection of cultural rights as essential to transforming unjust societies in the same way as it envisions addressing land rights, mass incarceration, or systemic racism, for instance. Thus, even in the more radical and progressive theories and frameworks for seeking justice and historical redress, cultural rights are notably absent.

To be sure, Arbour included cultural rights in her call for transitional justice to address the wider range of issues facing post-conflict and divided societies. But the resulting socio-economic critique, what has also been described as the field's 'ESC rights thesis',[26] has yet to be meaningfully extended to the neglect of cultural rights in transitional justice. The debates and contestations surrounding economic and social rights fall short of engaging with the particular dilemmas associated with addressing, respecting, and incorporating cultural rights in transitional justice.

Evelyne Schmid and Aoife Nolan explicitly observed the 'cultural rights gap' in 2014, remarking in a footnote that 'the particular challenges posed by

(Cambridge University Press 2015); Padraig McAuliffe, *Transformative Transitional Justice and the Malleability of Post-conflict States* (Edward Elgar Publishing 2017).

24 The International Journal of Transitional Justice 2 (2008).

25 Wendy Lambourne, 'Transformative Justice, Reconciliation and Peacebuilding' in S Buckley-Zistel and others (eds), *Transitional Justice Theories* (Routledge 2013) 19–39; Paul Gready and Simon Robins, 'From Transitional to Transformative Justice: A New Agenda for Practice' (2014) 8(3) International Journal of Transitional Justice 339; Matthew Evans, 'Structural Violence, Socioeconomic Rights, and Transformative Justice' (2016) 15(1) Journal of Human Rights 1.

26 Frank Haldemann and Rachelle Kouassi, 'Transitional Justice Without Economic, Social and Cultural Rights?' in Eibe Riedel, Gilles Giacca, and Christophe Golay (eds), *Economic, Social, and Cultural Rights in International Law: Contemporary Issues and Challenges* (Oxford University Press 2014) 499.

[cultural] rights ... have not generally been given adequate attention by transitional justice scholars and deserve further research'.[27] Pablo de Greiff agreed, observing that transitional justice 'has generally and systematically ignored claims of culture'.[28] This sentiment was further echoed by the Northern Ireland Human Rights Commission, which stated that the 'the promotion and protection of cultural rights in societies emerging from conflict is a neglected area'.[29] More recent scholarship has acknowledged this gap in interrogating the relative neglect of cultural rights in transitional justice.[30] Overwhelmingly, however, the marginalization of cultural rights is not expressly acknowledged at all. This silence has the effect of rendering culture and cultural rights invisible in discussions about how to reckon with large-scale past harm.

The invisibility of cultural rights in transitional justice discourse manifests itself in three primary and distinct ways. First, some authors will explicitly engage with the role of economic and social rights in transitional justice without referencing or considering cultural rights.[31] This literature problematizes the field's preoccupation with civil and political rights, but only in relation to the exclusion of economic and social rights. It makes no attempt to engage with the field's shortcomings with respect to cultural rights or the potential benefits of incorporating such rights. This silence arguably reinforces the relegation of cultural rights in the human rights hierarchy by implying that economic and social rights should be on the same footing as civil and political rights, but not necessarily cultural rights.

Second, other authors will explicitly acknowledge that their engagement with ESC rights in transitional justice does not account for cultural rights.[32] They quickly clarify that cultural rights remain important human rights and reiterate that economic and social rights need to be implemented in culturally

[27] Evelyne Schmid and Aoife Nolan, '"Do No Harm"? Exploring the Scope of Economic and Social Rights in Transitional Justice' (2014) 8(3) International Journal of Transitional Justice 362, 363, n 3.

[28] Pablo de Greiff, 'Preface: On Making the Invisible Visible: The Role of Cultural Interventions in Transitional Justice Processes' in Clara Ramirez-Barat (ed), *Transitional Justice, Culture, and Society: Beyond Outreach* (Social Science Research Council 2014) 12.

[29] Derry/Londonderry Report (n 3) 5.

[30] Luoma, 'Closing the Cultural Rights Gap' (n 3); Coakley and McAuliffe, 'Picking Up the Pieces' (n 3).

[31] See, eg, Carranza, 'Plunder and Pain' (n 6); Miller, 'Effects of Invisibility in Search of the "Economic" in Transitional Justice' (n 4); Muvingi, 'Sitting on Powder Kegs' (n 6); Sharp, 'Addressing Economic Violence' (n 4); Ochoa-Sánchez, 'Economic and Social Rights and Transitional Justice' (n 6).

[32] Sam Szoke-Burke, 'Not Only "Context": Why Transitional Justice Programs Can No Longer Ignore Violations of Economic and Social Rights' (2015) 50 Texas International Law Journal 465, 468; Schmid and Nolan (n 27) 363, n 3; Christine Chinkin, 'The Protection of Economic, Social and Cultural Rights Post-Conflict', Report Commissioned by the Office of the High Commissioner for Human Rights (2007) 5 <https://www2.ohchr.org/english/issues/women/docs/Paper_Protection_ESCR.pdf> accessed 31 December 2024.

appropriate ways. At the same time, they fail to frame cultural rights as an independent set of human rights with corresponding State obligations under international law. Other scholarship omits cultural rights based on their supposed underdevelopment in international law and potential to conflict with socio-economic rights.[33] The focus of this literature is on how economic and social rights fit within transitional justice frameworks, while culture is only discussed in the context of how other rights can be implemented and protected. Thus, it is not uncommon for authors to talk about cultural rights solely in connection with how they intersect with the protection, advancement, and redress of other human rights violations deemed more important for post-conflict and divided societies.

Lastly, cultural rights are routinely enumerated with economic and social rights but receive no independent attention whatsoever. A portion of the academic literature purports to engage with ESC rights in transitional justice, but in most cases this is misleading because no separate consideration is given to how cultural rights specifically fit within transitional justice agendas.[34] Instead, cultural rights are only mentioned as a by-product of being the 'C' in the ESC category of rights. The UN SRCR has highlighted this neglect more generally, observing that 'even some working in the field of what is too often simply called "economic and social rights," forget cultural rights'.[35] By being grouped into the ESC category of rights, but without any particularized treatment, cultural rights are reinforced as a 'remnant category' of rights.[36] Accordingly, whether they are overlooked or consciously neglected, cultural rights have yet to find their way to the centre of transitional justice discourse.

This neglect is apparent not only in academic scholarship, but also in UN committee and expert practice. Although the UN has developed guidelines establishing that transitional justice must seek to address violations of all rights, its standard-setting has mostly revolved around civil and political rights violations.[37] Even when engaging with ESC rights in transitional justice, UN

[33] Tafadzwa Pasipanodya, 'A Deeper Justice: Economic and Social Justice as Transitional Justice in Nepal' (2008) 2 International Journal of Transitional Justice 378, 379 n 8.

[34] See, eg, Haldemann and Kouassi, 'Transitional Justice Without Economic, Social, and Cultural Rights?' (n 26).

[35] Report of the Special Rapporteur in the Field of Cultural Rights, Cultural Rights: Tenth Anniversary Report, UN Doc A/HRC/40/53 (17 January 2019) para 55.

[36] Asbjørn Eide, 'Cultural Rights as Individual Human Rights' in Asbjørn Eide, Catarina Krause, and Allan Rosas (eds), *Economic, Social and Cultural Rights* (1st edn, Martin Nijhoff Publishers 1995) 229.

[37] Naomi Roht-Arriaza, 'Measures of Non-repetition in Transitional Justice: The Missing Link?' in Paul Gready and Simon Robins (eds), *From Transitional to Transformative Justice* (Cambridge University Press 2019) 105.

bodies are principally concerned with the subordinate position of economic and social rights, not cultural rights.

For instance, a 2011 UN Secretary-General report discussed the need for transitional justice to address root causes of conflict by engaging with economic and social rights, but makes no reference to cultural rights.[38] It further emphasized the need to promote 'the realization of economic and social rights'—not cultural rights—'through transitional justice mechanisms'.[39] Additionally, the CESCR's General Comment No. 21 on the right of everyone to take part in cultural life is silent on the various issues and challenges associated with exercising and protecting the right in post-conflict and divided societies.[40] When the CESCR has addressed the right to culture in post-conflict contexts, it tends to highlight the importance of interculturalism, a quite narrow aspect of cultural rights.[41] This illustrates the rather superficial and diminished position of cultural rights within transitional justice policy and standard-setting at the UN.

2.1 Cultural rights developments in the discourse

There are recent notable exceptions to the general marginalization of cultural rights in the discourse described above, including interventions that directly link transitional justice and culture, and to a lesser extent, cultural rights. Increasingly, culture is being considered and incorporated into transitional justice strategies.[42] This is particularly true in the case of cultural heritage, despite being historically treated outside of transitional justice work.[43] There is a growing body of academic and policy literature engaging with the international crime of the intentional destruction of cultural property,[44] the repatriation of

[38] UN Secretary-General, The Rule of Law and Transitional Justice in Conflict and Post-Conflict Societies, UN Doc S/2011/634 (12 October 2011) para 52.

[39] ibid.

[40] UN Committee on Economic, Social and Cultural Rights, General Comment No 21, Right of Everyone to Take Part in Cultural Life (Art 15, para 1a of the Covenant on Economic, Social and Cultural Rights), UN Doc E/C.12/GC/21 (21 December 2009).

[41] See, eg, UN Committee on Economic, Social and Cultural Rights, Serbia/Kosovo, Concluding Observations of the Committee, UN Doc E/C.12/UNK/CO/1 (1 December 2008) para 32.

[42] Philippe Sands and Ashrutha Rai, 'After the Dust Settles: Transitional Justice and Identity in the Aftermath of Cultural Destruction' in James Cuno and Thomas G Weiss (eds), *Cultural Heritage and Mass Atrocities* (Getty Publications 2022).

[43] Coakley and McAuliffe, 'Picking Up the Pieces' (n 3) 313.

[44] See, eg, Federico Lenzerini, 'Intentional Destruction of Cultural Heritage' in Francesco Francioni and Ana Vrdoljak (eds) *The Oxford Handbook on International Cultural Heritage Law* (Oxford University Press 2020); Luke Moffett, Dacia Viejo Rose, and Robin Hickey, 'Shifting the Paradigm on Cultural Property and Heritage in International Law and Armed Conflict: Time to Talk about Reparations?' (2020) 26 International Journal of Heritage Studies 619.

looted cultural heritage,[45] and issues surrounding transitional justice and cultural heritage more broadly.[46]

Although outside the strict scope of human rights, cultural heritage has important links to cultural rights. Both types of cultural heritage (tangible and intangible) raise human rights issues, and each needs to be preserved to respect and protect cultural rights, including the rights to cultural identity and take part in cultural life.[47] Thus, it is commonly recognized that attacks against cultural heritage are violative of cultural rights.

International responses to the destruction of cultural heritage have entered into public debate and discourse, including in popular media.[48] Much of this focuses on high-profile criminal prosecutions of individuals accused of destroying cultural heritage during periods of armed conflict or repressive rule.[49] Notorious examples include the destruction of Timbuktu's shrines and mausoleums and the widespread looting, smuggling, and destruction of cultural property by combatants in Iraq and Syria in the past two decades. This form of cultural wrongdoing is increasingly being analysed through the language and frameworks of transitional justice.[50]

The restitution of cultural property is also being increasingly studied as a measure of transitional justice.[51] There is significant pressure in many Western

[45] Padraig McAuliffe, 'Complicity or Decolonization? Restitution of Heritage from "Global" Ethnographic Museums' (2021) 15(3) International Journal of Transitional Justice 678; Alessandro Chechi, 'Repairing Historic Injustice: The Return of Indigenous Peoples' Ancestral Human Remains Through Transitional Justice' (2023) 30(4) International Journal of Cultural Property 419.

[46] See, eg, Lucas Lixinski, *Legalized Identities: Cultural Heritage Law and the Shaping of Transitional Justice* (Cambridge University Press 2021).

[47] Report of the Independent Expert in the Field of Cultural Rights, Farida Shaheed, UN Doc A/HRC/17/38 (21 March 2011) para 78; William Logan, 'Cultural Diversity, Cultural Heritage and Human Rights: Towards Heritage Management as Human Rights-based Cultural Practice' (2012) 18(3) International Journal of Heritage Studies 231, 236.

[48] See, eg, Beverly D'Silva, 'The Battle for Ukraine's Cultural Gems', BBC News (22 August 2023) <https://www.bbc.com/culture/article/20230821-the-fight-to-save-ukraines-cultural-spaces-and-heritage#:~:text=Today%2C%20intentional%20targeting%20of%20cultural,protocol%20drawn%20up%20in%201999> accessed 31 December 2024.

[49] Caroline Ehlert, *Prosecuting the Destruction of Cultural Property in International Criminal Law: With a Case Study on the Khmer Rouge's Destruction of Cambodia's Heritage* (Martinus Nijhoff Publishers 2013); Mark S Ellis, 'The ICC's Role in Combatting the Destruction of Cultural Heritage' (2017) 49 Case Western Reserve Journal of International Law 23; Moffet, Rose, and Hickey, 'Shifting the Paradigm on Cultural Property and Heritage in International Law and Armed Conflict' (n 44); Helen Walasek, 'Cultural Heritage and Memory after Ethnic Cleansing in Post-Conflict Bosnia-Herzegovina' (2019) 101 International Review of the Red Cross 273.

[50] Coakley and McAuliffe, 'Picking Up the Pieces' (n 3); Marie Wartenberg, 'Cultural Heritage—An Overlooked Component in Transitional Justice?' (2021) 12(12) International Journal on Rule of Law, Transitional Justice and Human Rights 59.

[51] For example, Justice Info, a website dedicated to covering transitional justice initiatives in various contexts, introduced a series on colonial crimes, with a special focus on the restitution of cultural heritage. Hour of Reckoning for Colonial Crimes, JusticeInfo, <https://www.justiceinfo.net/en/78778-hour-of-reckoning-for-colonial-crimes.html> accessed 31 December 2024.

societies, including in former colonial powers, to reckon with their violent histories of colonialism and imperialism and the ongoing legacies.[52] A major area of contestation concerns whether and how cultural heritage should be returned to the States and the groups from which they originated and were subsequently taken. These processes are now being framed and understood of as a component of transitional justice, even in countries that are seemingly non-transitional.[53] It is rare, however, for these processes to be discussed in reference to cultural rights standards or obligations, many of which were not in place at the time of the commission of the wrongful act.

Cultural heritage has also been studied in connection with its role in shaping narratives in post-conflict and divided societies.[54] Lucas Lixinski has examined the potential opportunities and dilemmas associated with cultural heritage in post-apartheid South Africa, the United States, and other contexts.[55] He analysed the important role that cultural heritage plays in transitional justice, including the many ways in which it can contribute to peace or, alternatively, be coopted and weaponized by governments and other policymakers.[56] While advocating for cultural heritage to play a more prominent role in transitional justice, Lixinski is also careful not to conflate cultural heritage with human rights, maintaining that '[h]uman rights law becomes simply the door through which heritage law enters the transitional justice arena'.[57]

The UN has also begun to engage with the treatment of cultural rights in transitional justice in more substantial ways. The OHCHR's report *Transitional Justice and Economic, Social and Cultural Rights* (2014) gave consideration to cultural harm in the context of Guatemala's Historical Clarification Commission (*Comision para el Esclarecimiento Historico*) and in the case law of the Inter-American Court of Human Rights ('IACtHR'); however, the vast majority of the report's analysis and findings focus on the treatment of economic and social rights violations in transitional justice measures.[58] Two

[52] McAuliffe, 'Complicity or Decolonization?' (n 45) 678.

[53] ibid; Alessandro Chechi, 'The Return of Cultural Objects Displaced During Colonialism. What Role for Restorative Justice, Transitional Justice and Alternative Dispute Resolution?' (2023) 6(1) International Journal of Restorative Justice 95; Ruth Whittaker, 'Cultural Property and Identity: Reconceptualising Restitution as a Form of Transitional Justice' in Michelle D Fabiani, Kate Burmon, and Saskia Hufnagel (eds), *Cultural Property Crime and the Law* (Routledge 2024) 201–18.

[54] Joanne McEvoy, 'Managing Culture in Post-conflict Societies' (2011) 6(1) Contemporary Social Science 55; The Derry/Londonderry Report (n 3).

[55] Lixinski, Legalized Identities (n 46); see also Lucas Lixinski, 'Cultural Heritage Law and Transitional Justice: Lessons from South Africa' (2015) 9(2) International Journal of Transitional Justice 278; Lucas Lixinski, 'Confederate Monuments and International Law' (2017) 35 Wisconsin International Law Journal 549.

[56] Lixinski, 'Legalized Identities' (n 46).

[57] Lixinski, 'Cultural Heritage Law and Transitional Justice' (n 55) 285.

[58] OHCHR, 'Transitional Justice and Economic, Social and Cultural Rights' (n 10).

reports from the former UN SRCR Farida Shaheed highlighted the role of cultural rights in two specific initiatives that are regularly considered part of the broader transitional justice toolbox: history teaching reform and memorialization initiatives.[59] Among other things, Shaheed commented on the field's cultural rights gap, noting that 'all too often, a cultural rights-based approach to transitional justice and reconciliation strategies is not rendered the attention it deserves'.[60]

Cultural rights are implicitly incorporated in the discourse with regard to the localization of transitional justice.[61] Transitional justice is routinely interrogated on how it can better accommodate and integrate local traditions and practices into its various processes. Rama Mani rightly links this to culture, calling for transitional justice to address issues of 'cultural justice', meaning that policies should be culturally sensitive and considerate of the specific culture of the post-conflict society, and transitional measures should be designed accordingly.[62] She argues that 'including culture within transitional justice would not be a panacea' but rather an imperative for post-conflict societies based on the proposition that 'culture still largely determines the societies that experience conflict, and can play an influential role in restoring justice and peace'.[63] This is especially true for countries experiencing transitions in the Global South, where culture generally carries more significance than in the Western world.[64] Thus, Mani argues, 'there is an urgent need to expand the scope of transitional justice underpinned by a holistic conceptualization of justice that incorporates culture'.[65]

Additionally, some commentators contend that transitional justice should engage with the underlying cultural attitudes that foster and ultimately enable large-scale physical atrocities to occur. Matthew Mullen argues that the field needs to make a 'paradigmatic and programmatic shift' to focus on structural

[59] Report of the Special Rapporteur in the Field of Cultural Rights, Farida Shaheed, UN Doc A/68/296 (9 August 2013); Report of the Special Rapporteur in the Field of Cultural Rights, Farida Shaheed: Memorialization Initiatives, UN Doc A/HRC/25/49 (23 January 2014).

[60] UN OHCHR, 'Integrating Cultural Rights in Transitional Justice Strategies in Post-conflict Societies' (25 March 2014) <https://www.ohchr.org/EN/NewsEvents/Pages/Integratingculturalrightsinpost-conflictsocieties.aspx> accessed 31 December 2024.

[61] See, eg, Rosalind Shaw, Lars Waldorf, and Pierre Hazan (eds), *Localizing Transitional Justice: Interventions and Priorities after Mass Violence* (Stanford University Press 2010); Kieran McEvoy and Lorna McGregor (eds), *Transitional Justice from Below: Grassroots Activism and the Struggle for Change* (Bloomsbury Publishing 2008); Paul Gready, 'Analysis: Reconceptualising Transitional Justice: Embedded and Distanced Justice' (2005) 5(1) Conflict, Security & Development 3.

[62] Rama Mani, 'Women, Art and Post-Conflict Justice' (2011) 11 International Criminal Law Review 543, 544.

[63] ibid 546–47.

[64] ibid 549.

[65] ibid 546.

and cultural violence and calls on transitional justice to address the underlying values, attitudes, and perceptions that allow for mass atrocity to occur.[66] Others have drawn close links between culture and mass violence, including through policymaking at UNESCO.[67] However, these interventions principally probe culture through the lens of other forms of violence, direct or structural, rather than treating cultural wrongdoing as its own, independent form of harm with corresponding rights and obligations.

Lastly, we have seen the steady incorporation of culture in the discourse through examinations of the role of art and performance in transitional justice. These creative processes are important tools to document events, foster dialogue, and challenge dominant narratives. The positionality of these interventions has been studied within the transitional justice literature.[68] For instance, a 2014 volume in the *Advancing Transitional Justice Series*, a joint project of the International Center for Transitional Justice ('ICTJ') and the Social Science Research Council, was dedicated to how cultural initiatives intersect with transitional justice.[69] Similarly, a 2020 special issue of the International Journal of Transitional Justice was focused on artistic and cultural projects in the field.[70] At the UN, a 2015 report of the UN SRTJ emphasized the importance of cultural interventions in transitional justice, including artistic media, museums, exhibitions, monuments, and theatres.[71] This was reiterated by the UN SRCR in her 2019 report marking the tenth anniversary of her mandate on cultural rights.[72]

These developments have worked to gradually move culture away from the peripheries and closer to the core of transitional justice thinking. However, they tend to invoke broader issues of culture, as opposed to cultural rights specifically. Cultural rights are just one component of the cultural dimension of transitional justice. While there is a sense that culture needs to play a more prominent role in transitional justice policy, the discourse does not

[66] Matthew Mullen, 'Reassessing the Focus of Transitional Justice: The Need to Move Structural and Cultural Violence to the Centre' (2015) 28 Cambridge Review of International Affairs 462, 463.

[67] UNESCO, 'The Role of Culture in Peace and Reconciliation' (April 2013) <http://www.unesco.org/new/fileadmin/MULTIMEDIA/HQ/CLT/images/PeaceReconciliationENG.pdf> accessed 24 December 2024.

[68] Paul Gready, 'Culture, Testimony, and the Toolbox of Transitional Justice' (2008) 20(1) Peace Review 41.

[69] Clara Ramirez-Barat (ed), *Transitional Justice, Culture, and Society: Beyond Outreach* (Social Science Research Council 2014).

[70] See 2020 14(1) International Journal of Transitional Justice 1–250; see also Peter D Rush and Olivera Simic (eds), *The Arts of Transitional Justice* (Springer 2014).

[71] Report of the Special Rapporteur on the Promotion of Truth, Justice, Reparation and Guarantees of Non-Recurrence, UN Doc A/HRC/30/42 (7 September 2015) para 95.

[72] Report of the Special Rapporteur in the Field of Cultural Rights (n 35) para 26.

comprehensively engage with how cultural rights, and especially cultural rights violations, fit within the scope of the field. The propriety of incorporating these rights is not debated in the same manner that economic and social rights have been and there is a dearth of discussion of whether transitional justice should address and incorporate cultural rights, how that would be best accomplished, or the theoretical and practical hurdles that would need to be overcome to do so.

3. The Historical Marginalization of Cultural Rights in Transitional Justice Practice

Perhaps unsurprisingly given their paucity in the discourse, cultural rights have been equally overlooked in practice. Historically, transitional justice programming has overwhelmingly fixated on redressing violations of civil and political rights, ordinarily in the form of large-scale physical violence. Mechanisms are designed and tasked with addressing acts of genocide, mass murder, enforced disappearances, torture, sexual violence, and other serious bodily integrity violations, but they rarely engage with other forms of harm, including endemic cultural rights violations. This neglect runs through all the traditional mechanisms in the transitional justice toolbox, as recognized by the OHCHR, which concluded there has been no 'widespread move' to include violations of cultural rights in transitional justice programming.[73] In the instances when measures have engaged with large-scale cultural harm, it is often done in limited or problematic ways. Thus, with some notable exceptions, transitional justice practice has generally failed to meaningfully engage with cultural rights violations, even when they feature prominently in underlying conflicts or societal divisions.[74]

The extent to which cultural wrongdoing has been engaged with in different transitional justice mechanisms has not been sufficiently analysed. The following thus examines the extent to which transitional justice mechanisms have addressed cultural rights violations in the context of judicial proceedings, truth commissions, and reparations programmes, the three most prominent mechanisms in the field. While this survey is by no means exhaustive, it illustrates the range of ways in which post-conflict and divided societies have generally failed to confront mass cultural wrongdoing and respect cultural rights

[73] OHCHR, Transitional Justice and Economic, Social and Cultural Rights (n 10) 1.
[74] ibid.

in their various transitional justice processes. Despite some positive developments stemming from truth commissions grappling with wrongdoing against Indigenous Peoples, cultural rights violations largely remain on the outermost margins of transitional justice practice. Thus, as with the discourse, a significant practical gap exists with respect to cultural rights and transitional justice.

3.1 Judicial proceedings

Judicial proceedings are a legitimate avenue to confront cultural rights violations in transitional justice. Historically, however, judicial bodies have focused on addressing violations of civil and political rights to the exclusion of other forms of harm, including mass cultural wrongdoing. This narrow approach has been criticized for accepting a level of impunity for ESC rights violations, several of which constitute war crimes and crimes against humanity under applicable international criminal law standards.[75] Cultural rights violations, in particular, have received sparse attention in judicial proceedings compared to all other rights categories.

Noteworthy exceptions to this neglect include efforts to establish accountability for acts of intentional destruction of cultural heritage in select international criminal tribunals and human rights courts.[76] Significant jurisprudence on these international crimes initially emerged from the International Criminal Tribunal for the former Yugoslavia ('ICTY').[77] Attacks on culture and identity were a defining feature of the conflicts in the former Yugoslavia, as the destruction of cultural heritage were part and parcel of the ethnic cleansing that was perpetrated.[78] In turn, a number of cases before the ICTY successfully prosecuted acts of intentional destruction of cultural heritage under the Court's enabling statute.[79] It found defendants guilty of war

[75] Evelyne Schmid, 'War Crimes Related to Violations of Economic, Social and Cultural Rights' (2011) 71(3) Heidelberg Journal of International Law 523; see also Arbour, 'Economic and Social Justice for Societies in Transition' (n 19) 15–16.

[76] Sands and Rai, 'After the Dust Settles' (n 42).

[77] Precedent had already been established at the Nuremberg trials when Alfred Rosenberg was tried and convicted of war crimes and crimes against humanity for the plunder of property in zones of Nazi occupation and which ultimately led to the adoption of the Hague Convention for the Protection of Cultural Property in the Event of Armed Conflict in 1954. Ana Filipa Vrdoljak, 'The Criminalisation of the Intentional Destruction of Cultural Heritage' in Tiffany Bergin and Emanuela Orlando (eds), *Forging a Socio-Legal Approach to Environmental Harms* (Routledge 2017) 237–66.

[78] Serge Brammertz and others, 'Attacks against Cultural Heritage as a Weapon of War: Prosecutions at the ICTY' (2016) 14(5) Journal of International Criminal Justice 1143, 1162; Ellis, 'The ICC's Role in Combatting the Destruction of Cultural Heritage' (n 49) 41–52.

[79] The ICTY statute criminalizes destruction and seizure of cultural property. See UN Security Council, Statute of the International Criminal Tribunal for the Former Yugoslavia (25 May 1993), Art 3(d).

crimes for destroying religious and cultural heritage sites and further confirmed that cultural destruction could amount to a crime against humanity in the form of persecution under the right circumstances.[80]

Building off the ICTY's jurisprudence, there have also been judicial decisions concerning the destruction of cultural heritage before the International Criminal Court ('ICC'). In 2017, the ICC convicted defendant Ahmad al-Faqi al-Mahdi after he pled guilty to the war crime of deliberately directing the destruction of shrines and mausoleums in Timbuktu.[81] This was a significant accomplishment for the ICC, in part because it was the first time the Court had prosecuted an individual for attacks on cultural property.[82] In its Reparations Order the ICC described the cultural harm inflicted on the local population, as well as the international community as a whole, and it explicitly tied the destruction of cultural heritage to the deprivation of identity and memory.[83]

A second case was brought in the ICC against defendant Al Hassan Ag Abdoul Aziz Ag Mohamed Ag Mahmoud, who was ultimately acquitted of the war crime of intentional destruction of cultural property after being alleged to have directed attacks against buildings dedicated to religion and historic monuments in Timbuktu.[84] However, the ICC convicted Al Hassan for contributing to the crime of persecution, which it directly linked to the cultural deprivations of the local population through the imposition of Ansar Dine's interpretation of *Sharia*, including restrictions on traditional, social, and cultural practices (such as dancing or playing or listening to music), prohibitions on taking part in traditional customs, and the destruction of cultural monuments.[85]

Aside from this limited set of international criminal prosecutions in post-conflict settings, human rights courts have also addressed the destruction of cultural property, albeit sparingly. The Human Rights Chamber for Bosnia

[80] See, eg, *Prosecutor v Radoslav Brdjanin* (Trial Judgment), Case No IT-99-36-T, International Criminal Tribunal for the former Yugoslavia (1 September 2004); *Prosecutor v Blagojevic and Jokic* (Trial Judgment), Case No IT-02-60-T, International Criminal Tribunal for the former Yugoslavia (17 January 2005); *Prosecutor v Pavle Strugar* (Trial Judgment), Case No IT-01-42-T, International Criminal Tribunal for the former Yugoslavia (31 January 2005); *Prosecutor v Kupreskic et al* (Trial Judgment), Case No IT-95-16-T, International Criminal Tribunal for the former Yugoslavia (14 January 2000); *Prosecutor v Dario Kordić and Mario Čerdez* (Trial Judgment), Case No IT-95-14/2-T, International Criminal Tribunal for the former Yugoslavia (26 February 2001) para 207.

[81] *Prosecutor v Al Mahdi*, Judgment and Sentence, International Criminal Court, Case No. ICC-01/12-01/15-171 (27 September 2016).

[82] Uzma S Bishop-Burney, 'Prosecutor v. Ahmad Al Faqi Al Mahdi' (2017) 111(1) American Journal of International Law 126, 129.

[83] *Prosecutor v Al Mahdi*, Reparations Order, International Criminal Court Case No ICC-01/12-01/15-236 (17 August 2017) para 22.

[84] *Prosecutor v Al Hassan Ag Abdoul Aziz Ag Mohamed Ag Mahmoud*, Trial Judgment, International Criminal Court Case No ICC-01/12-01/18 (28 June 2024).

[85] *Prosecutor v Al Hassan Ag Abdoul Aziz Ag Mohamed Ag Mahmoud*, Sentencing Judgment, International Criminal Court Case No ICC-01/12-01/18 (20 November 2024) para 72.

and Herzegovina adjudicated more than 15,000 total cases over the span of approximately seven years, but only a small percentage of the cases involved cultural harm.[86] The most notable concerned the destruction of mosques during the conflict and the subsequent refusal of local governments to issue the necessary permits enabling their reconstruction.[87] Importantly, however, these cases were brought under Article 9 of the European Convention on Human Rights, which protects freedom of thought, conscience, and religion, and not cultural rights per se. The Chamber's failure to directly address cultural harm within a cultural rights framework is at least partially attributable to limits in its jurisdiction, as it could only adjudicate human rights violations as provided in the European Convention (which does not contain any explicit cultural rights protections),[88] as well as alleged discrimination in contravention of certain international treaties.[89]

Some advocates have also suggested that regional human rights bodies, such as the IACtHR, could be increasingly used to address violations of ESC rights in transitional settings.[90] The IACtHR is not a transitional justice mechanism in the sense that it was not established in response to mass violence and large-scale abuses during a specific country's period of transition. At the same time, it has adjudicated claims brought against States in transitional contexts and it has arguably contributed to transitional justice objectives.[91] However, in post-conflict and post-authoritarian settings, the IACtHR has mostly addressed violations of civil and political rights. In cases where the Court has addressed cultural harm, it has done so pursuant to the legal framework that ensures civil and political rights under the American Convention on Human Rights.[92] Thus,

[86] OHCHR, Transitional Justice and Economic, Social and Cultural Rights (n 10) 27–28.

[87] See, eg, *The Islamic Community in Bosnia And Herzegovina v The Republika Srpska* (Decision on Admissibility and Merits), Case No CH/98/1062 (12 October 2001); *The Islamic Community in Bosnia and Herzegovina v The Republika Srpska* (Decision on Admissibility and Merits), Case No CH/01/7701 (22 December 2003).

[88] The European Convention does not directly provide for cultural rights, but jurisprudence from the European Court of Human Rights has protected the culture of minorities under Convention provisions, including the right to privacy and family life (Art 8). See, eg, *Chapman v United Kingdom* (Judgment, Merits), App No 27238/95, ECHR (27 January 2001).

[89] To the extent that the Chamber's jurisdiction was derived from the rights set forth in other international instruments, the complainant would have the additional hurdle of having to establish discrimination in exercising those freedoms in order to be successful. Jessica Simor, 'Tackling Human Rights Abuses in Bosnia and Herzegovina: The Convention Is Up to It; Are Its Institutions?' (1997) European Human Rights Law Review 644, 649.

[90] Haldemann and Kouassi, 'Transitional Justice Without Economic, Social and Cultural Rights?' (n 26) 505–06.

[91] Eleonora Mesquita Ceia, 'The Contributions of the Inter-American Court of Human Rights to the Development of Transitional Justice' (2015) 14 Law and Practice of International Courts and Tribunals 457.

[92] See, eg, *Case of the Plan de Sánchez Massacre v Guatemala*, Judgment (Reparations), Inter-American Court of Human Rights Series C No. 116 (19 November 2004); *Case of the Río Negro*

even in cases involving large-scale cultural harm, human rights courts tend to resort to the legal provisions applicable to other rights categories.

While these modest attempts to address cultural harm are noteworthy, they have not led to a wider adjudication of cultural rights violations through judicial processes. Most cultural wrongs do not amount to criminal offences under the implementing statutes of international or hybrid courts. Thus, perpetrators who commit serious and systematic cultural wrongs that do not otherwise fit within the strict confines of cultural heritage destruction will likely evade judicial accountability, at least at the international level. Moreover, jurisdictional limitations often weaken the ability of human rights bodies to treat cultural harm as violative of cultural rights protections, as was the case in the Human Rights Chamber for Bosnia and Herzegovina and the IACtHR. The challenges are even more pronounced for historical cultural violations, which face jurisdictional hurdles under the doctrine of temporality and general obstacles in presenting evidence for wrongs committed decades, if not centuries, beforehand.

3.2 Truth commissions

In comparison to other transitional justice measures, truth-seeking bodies have demonstrated a willingness to reach beyond the traditional remit of bodily integrity violations to address broader forms of harm, including violations of ESC rights.[93] These bodies seek to discover not only what happened during periods of violence or repression, but also why it occurred in the first place.[94] Particularly with respect to historical injustices, where criminal prosecutions are highly unlikely or jurisdictionally impossible, they can represent an important avenue for victims to establish accountability and a historical record for years of human rights abuses.[95] At least in principle, these bodies

Massacres v Guatemala, Judgment (Preliminary objection, merits, reparations and costs) Inter-American Court of Human Rights Series C No 250 (4 September 2012).

[93] UN OHCHR, Transitional Justice and Economic, Social and Cultural Rights (n 10) 17; see also M Florencia Librizzi, 'Challenges of the Truth Commissions to Deal with Injustice against Indigenous Peoples' in Wilton Littlechild and Elsa Stamatopoulou (eds), *Indigenous Peoples' Access to Justice, Including Truth and Reconciliation Processes* (Institute for the Study of Human Rights, Columbia University 2014) 183.

[94] Lisa J Laplante, 'Transitional Justice and Peace Building: Diagnosing and Addressing the Socioeconomic Roots of Violence through a Human Rights Framework' (2008) 2 International Journal of Transitional Justice 331, 334.

[95] Lisa J Laplante, 'On the Indivisibility of Rights: Truth Commissions, Reparations, and the Right to Develop' (2007) 10 Yale Human Rights and Development Law Journal 141, 146.

possess a high degree of flexibility, making them well-positioned mechanisms to address cultural rights violations.[96]

Despite this flexibility, truth commissions have largely sought to account for civil and political rights violations.[97] Rarely do they engage with cultural rights violations, and in some cases truth-seeking bodies do not account for cultural harm even when it features prominently in the underlying conflict.[98] For instance, Peru's Truth and Reconciliation Commission (the *Comisión de la Verdad y Reconciliación del Perú*) was tasked with accounting for two decades of violence during the military dictatorship of President Alberto Fujimori.[99] Peru's internal conflict disproportionately impacted Indigenous Peoples, including their cultural identities. Yet, and despite a relatively broad mandate, Peru's Truth and Reconciliation Commission still focused on civil, political, and economic rights violations, including principally assassinations, torture, forced disappearances, and forced displacements.[100] Entire Indigenous communities were targeted for violence, but the Truth and Reconciliation Commission did not adequately account for the collective cultural harm they experienced, instead focusing on individual civil and political rights violations.[101]

While other truth commissions have engaged with cultural harm, it is often done in limited and problematic ways. This problematic treatment falls into three main categories. First, some truth commissions discuss cultural harm solely as historical background to other rights violations. For instance, the Solomon Islands Truth and Reconciliation Commission ('Solomon Islands TRC') observed that certain ethnic groups were forced to abandon their distinct cultural traditions and customs and individuals were prevented from speaking their native languages during the civil conflict that ran from 1998

[96] ICTJ, 'Indigenous Voice and Truth Commissions' Summary Materials: International Seminar (22–23 March 2010) <https://www.ictj.org/sites/default/files/IPTC-March-2010-Meeting-Summary-Materials.pdf> accessed 1 February 2025.

[97] Ochoa-Sánchez, 'Economic and Social Rights and Transitional Justice' (n 6).

[98] Coakley and McAuliffe reviewed the 33 truth commissions in the United States Institute of Peace's Truth Commission Digital Collection and determined that no commission was tasked with addressing the destruction of tangible cultural heritage. Coakley and McAuliffe, 'Picking Up the Pieces' (n 3) 313–14.

[99] *Comisioín de la Verdad y Reconciliacioín, Informe Final de la Comisioín de la Verdad y Reconciliacioín*, Vol 1 (2004) <http://www.cverdad.org.pe/ingles/ifinal/index.php> accessed 24 December 2024.

[100] César Rodríguez-Garavito and Yukyan Lam, 'Addressing Violations of Indigenous Peoples' Territory, Land, and Natural Resource Rights During Conflicts and Transitions' in ICTJ (ed), *Strengthening Indigenous Rights through Truth Commissions: A Practitioner's Resource* (ICTJ 2012) 30–31.

[101] Jeff Corntassel and Cindy Holder, 'Who's Sorry Now? Government Apologies, Truth Commissions, and Indigenous Self-determination in Australia, Canada, Guatemala, and Peru' (2008) 9(4) Human Rights Review 465, 482.

to 2000.[102] The Solomon Islands TRC acknowledged these cultural abuses as background context to the wider conflict but did not identify any specific cultural rights violations. Instead, it limited its inquiry to physical and property harms.[103] Thus, even though its mandate was arguably broad enough to encompass the redress of large-scale violations of cultural rights, the Solomon Islands TRC opted to prioritize civil, political, and economic rights violations in its final report.

Likewise, Kenya's Truth, Justice and Reconciliation Commission ('Kenya TJRC') found that the government consistently failed to recognize the unique cultures of minorities and Indigenous Peoples and that land dispossession made it impossible for these communities to engage in their culture.[104] However, the TJRC ultimately prioritized bodily integrity violations, including political assassinations, extra-judicial killings, massacres, unlawful detention, torture, ill-treatment, and sexual violence, and to a lesser extent land rights and socio-economic rights.[105] This approach arguably contributes to cultural rights being viewed as less important for transitional societies, relegated to historical context rather than being seen as instrumental to conflict.[106] Even when cultural rights abuses are acknowledged in truth commissions, they are commonly rendered 'invisible' in this manner. Zinaida Miller has explained an analogous dynamic with respect to socio-economic rights in transitional justice:

> Silence occurs not only through the literal absence but also through the tendency either to mention inequality or structural violence as a problem and then to ignore it or to background structural factors in favor of more obvious concerns about physical violence.[107]

The second method of problematic treatment concerns truth-seeking bodies engaging with cultural harm, but only to the extent that they are inseparable from other human rights violations. Timor-Leste's Commission for Reception,

[102] Solomon Islands Truth and Reconciliation Commission, Confronting the Truth for a Better Solomon Islands: Final Report, Vol 1 (February 2012) 172–73.

[103] The Solomon Islands TRC focused on six rights categories of harm: (1) killings, (2) abduction/illegal detention, (3) torture/ill-treatment, (4) sexual violence, (5) property violation, and (6) forced displacement: ibid, Vol 2, 336.

[104] Kenya Truth, Justice and Reconciliation Commission, Report of the Truth, Justice and Reconciliation Commission, Vol. 2C (3 May 2013) paras 210, 216.

[105] Kituo Cha Sheria, Summary of the Truth, Justice and Reconciliation Commission (TJRC) Report (2014) <https://kituochasheria.or.ke/wp-content/uploads/2022/09/TJRC-Report-2013-GS-with-isbn1.pdf> accessed 24 December 2024.

[106] Carranza, 'Plunder and Pain' (n 6) 311–12.

[107] Miller, 'Effects of Invisibility' (n 4) 273.

Truth, and Reconciliation (*Comissão de Acolhimento, Verdade e Reconciliação de Timor-Leste,* or 'CAVR') was tasked with examining violations of a broad range of human rights standards, including the rights and freedoms contained in the ICESCR.[108] The CAVR observed that 'Indonesian practice in such areas as education, health and land rights violated the norms and integrity of East Timorese culture' in violation of the ICESCR.[109] At the same time, the CAVR acknowledged that, due to resource limitations, it only considered cultural rights violations 'to the extent that they [were] inseparable from violations of social and economic rights'.[110] While acknowledging regret over the omission, the CAVR still took an exclusionary approach regarding culture, implicitly contributing to the long-standing misconception that cultural rights are not 'real rights' or are mere luxuries compared to their seemingly more important counterparts.

Guatemala's Historical Clarification Commission stressed the value and importance of cultural identities and practices to Indigenous Mayan communities and ultimately concluded that their cultural rights were violated.[111] Among other things, they were prevented from honouring their cultural and religious rites, forced to conceal their ethnic and cultural identity, and prohibited from transmitting their culture to subsequent generations.[112] But the Historical Clarification Commission positioned cultural harm primarily in the context of other forms of violence committed against Indigenous Peoples during the country's civil war. For example, the final report described how egregious acts of physical violence were also used to wage attacks on the cultural identities of Mayan communities:

> The massacres, scorched earth operations, forced disappearances and executions of Mayan authorities, leaders and spiritual guides, were not only an attempt to destroy the social base of the guerrillas, but above all, to destroy the cultural values that ensured cohesion and collective action in Mayan communities.[113]

[108] Commission for Reception, Truth and Reconciliation in East Timor, *Chega! The Final Report of the Timor-Leste Commission for Reception, Truth and Reconciliation* (2005) chapter 2, para 15. <https://www.etan.org/etanpdf/2006/CAVR/07.9-Economic-and-Social-Rights.pdf> accessed 24 December 2024.
[109] ibid chapter 7.9, para 12.
[110] ibid.
[111] Guatemala Memory of Silence, *Report of the Commission for Historical Clarification: Conclusions and Recommendations* (1999) para 88 <https://hrdag.org/wp-content/uploads/2013/01/CEHreport-english.pdf> accessed 24 December 2024.
[112] ibid paras 32, 62–64, 88.
[113] ibid para 32.

While the Historical Clarification Commission's findings represent one of the more robust attempts to account for cultural harm committed during armed conflict, its analysis was carried out almost entirely through the prism of bodily integrity violations and not as an independent form of violence with corresponding State obligations under international law. Moreover, even with its recognition of mass cultural wrongdoing perpetrated against Mayan communities, the Historical Clarification Commission's investigation still overwhelmingly focused on bodily integrity violations—extrajudicial executions, enforced disappearances, torture, forced displacement, rape and sexual violence, genocide, and other forms of systemic physical violence.[114]

The most serious and meaningful attempts to address cultural rights in transitional justice practice have occurred through truth commissions with a specific mandate to investigate wrongdoing committed against Indigenous Peoples. Two of the earliest such bodies focused on abuses committed against Indigenous children in Australia and Canada. Australia's National Inquiry into the Separation of Aboriginal and Torres Strait Island Children from Their Families was formed to investigate the State-sanctioned removal of 100,000 Indigenous Australian children from their families and communities between 1910 and 1970.[115] Likewise, Canada's Truth and Reconciliation Commission ('Canada's TRC') was established to compile a historical record of the Indian residential school system and legacy, including systematic harms, intergenerational consequences, and the impact on human dignity.[116] In both contexts, Indigenous children were forced through law and policy to abandon their Indigenous cultural identities and practices through forced removals, resulting in cultural loss that has devastated Indigenous communities in those countries across generations.

Despite an overriding focus on culture and cultural harm, neither Australia's National Inquiry nor Canada's TRC employed rights-based language to situate the cultural harm of forced removals within the framework of international human rights law. International human rights law was not entirely absent from the final reports of these commissions, but the cultural harm inflicted through assimilationist policies and practices was not framed as violative of specific

[114] UNPFII, Study on the Rights of Indigenous Peoples and Truth Commissions and Other Truth-Seeking Mechanisms on the American Continent, UN Doc E/C.19/2013/13 (14 September 2013) para 27.

[115] Report of the National Inquiry into the Separation of Aboriginal and Torres Strait Islander Children from Their Families: Bringing Them Home (1997).

[116] Truth and Reconciliation Commission of Canada, 'The Legacy' in *Honouring the Truth, Reconciling the Future: Summary of the Final Report of the Truth and Reconciliation Commission of Canada* (2015).

international obligations regarding Indigenous cultures.[117] These bodies did not expound on applicable cultural rights standards, frame such harm as violations of State commitments, or explicitly link any State action to a violation of a specific cultural protection. Nor did they confront the other myriad forms of cultural harm inflicted on Indigenous Peoples.

Canada's TRC, in particular, has been extremely influential and has served as a blueprint for other truth-seeking initiatives in countries attempting to reckon with their own violent histories with Indigenous Peoples.[118] Truth-seeking bodies in Greenland,[119] Norway,[120] and Sweden[121] have each delivered their final reports detailing the devastating cultural loss inflicted through assimilationist policies implemented against Indigenous Peoples and minority groups in these countries. In each case, these bodies were empowered by mandates to specifically investigate cultural wrongs associated with assimilation or modernization policies. A similar truth commission is currently under way in Finland,[122] as well as a second truth commission in Sweden focused on the Indigenous Sami people.[123]

3.3 Reparations

Cultural harm also does not feature prominently in reparations initiatives. Indeed, a general scepticism exists towards expanding reparations measures beyond the realm of civil and political rights violations.[124] There are many reasons for this, including the fact that reparations flowing from violations of

[117] See Nicola Henry, 'From Reconciliation to Transitional Justice: The Contours of Redress Politics in Established Democracies' (2015) 9(2) International Journal of Transitional Justice 199, 201.

[118] Franck Petit, 'Jean-Pierre Massias: "The Canadian Commission is a New Model for Transitional Justice"' JusticeInfo (23 July 2019) <https://www.justiceinfo.net/en/41980-jean-pierre-massias-canadian-commission-new-model-for-transitional-justice.html> accessed 24 December 2024.

[119] Greenland's Reconciliation Commission, 'We Understand the Past; We Take Responsibility for the Present; We Are Working for a Better Future' (December 2017).

[120] Commission to Investigate the Norwegianisation Policy and Injustice against the Sámi and Kvens/Norwegian Finns (1 June 2023) <https://www.stortinget.no/globalassets/pdf/sannhets--og-forsoningskommisjonen/rapport-til-stortinget-fra-sannhets--og-forsoningskommisjonen.pdf> accessed 24 December 2024.

[121] Truth and Reconciliation Commission for Kvens, Tornedalians and Lantalaiset (15 November 2023).

[122] Truth and Reconciliation Commission Concerning the Sámi People <https://sdtsk.fi/en/home/> accessed 31 December 2024.

[123] Truth Commission for the Sámi People <https://sanningskommissionensamer.se/en/about-the-commision/#:~:text=The%20Truth%20Commission%20for%20the%20Sami%20People&text=The%20Commission%20will%20survey%20and,consequences%20for%20the%20Sami%20people> accessed 31 December 2024.

[124] Naomi Roht-Arriaza, 'Reparations and Economic, Social, and Cultural Rights' in Dustin N Sharp (ed), *Justice and Economic Violence in Transition* (Springer 2014) 109–110.

ESC rights often invoke more long-term, sustained commitment, including at times, significant financial resources. These violations are more often systemic, rather than isolated acts of wrongdoing, making their repair less palatable for States and other actors who do have the political will to engage in reparations on such a large scale. Moreover, even when reparations are implemented, they often disregard local and cultural practices and dynamics.[125]

Select truth commissions have recommended reparations focused on the cultures of particular victim groups. In Guatemala, for example, the Historical Clarification Commission recommended that a National Reparation Programme be created to provide redress for human rights violations during the country's armed conflict.[126] Among other things, the recommended programme included 'cultural reparation measures' aimed at restoring the culture and identities of the Mayan peoples.[127] Unfortunately, the reparative measures in Guatemala have not been widely implemented.[128] Similarly, in Peru, the Truth and Reconciliation Commission recommended a set of collective and symbolic reparations aimed at Indigenous communities, albeit without explicitly linking them with specific cultural abuses.[129] These included a national apology, renaming of schools, arranging for a national day of remembrance for Indigenous victims, and providing intercultural educational opportunities.[130] Most of these initiatives have also stalled.[131]

Reparations can also be ordered through judicial proceedings; however, courts have been equally reluctant to link monetary reparations to cultural harm. When survivors of Canada's residential school system originally sought damages through domestic litigation, the only cognisable injuries were individual acts of physical and sexual violence, leaving the collective cultural harm suffered by generations of children nonjusticiable.[132] This gap was partially addressed through the Indian Residential Schools Settlement Agreement, which included monetary reparations to survivors in the form of a 'common experience payment' that was not linked to any specific harm.[133] However, to claim

[125] Lieselotte Viaene and Eva Brems, 'Transitional Justice and Cultural Contexts: Learning from the Universality Debate' (2010) 28(2) Netherlands Quarterly of Human Rights 199, 217–18.

[126] Historical Clarification Commission (n 111) 50.

[127] Ruth Rubio-Marín and others, 'Indigenous Peoples and Reparations Claims: Tentative Steps in Peru and Guatemala', ICTJ Research Brief (2009) 4.

[128] Roht-Arriaza, 'Reparations and Economic, Social, and Cultural Rights' (n 124) 118.

[129] Ruth Rubio-Marín and others, 'Indigenous Peoples and Reparations Claims' (n 127) 1–2.

[130] ibid 2.

[131] ibid.

[132] Leslie Thielen-Wilson, 'Troubling the Path to Decolonization: Indian Residential School Case Law, Genocide, and Settler Illegitimacy' (2014) 29(2) Canadian Journal of Law & Society/La Revue Canadienne Droit et Société 181, 182.

[133] Indian Residential Schools Settlement Agreement, <http://www.residentialschoolsettlement.ca/settlement.html> accessed 1 February 2025.

anything beyond the common experience payment, the claimant needed to establish physical or sexual abuse through a separate process—thus diminishing the impact of the cultural harm inflicted through the residential schools.[134]

Exceptions to the marginalization of cultural rights in court-ordered monetary reparations can be found in the case law of the IACtHR. For instance, in the *Case of Plan de Sánchez Massacre v Guatemala,* the Court's judgment accounted for the fact that the massacre of more than 268 Indigenous people by the Guatemalan military 'gravely affected the identity and values of the members of the Maya-Achí people'.[135] The IACtHR explicitly connected the ordered reparations to the cultural harm that occurred, ordering them 'as compensation for the non-pecuniary damage resulting from the need to preserve the traditional culture of the victims and their descendants'.[136] The Court awarded 20,000 USD to each victim, partially to compensate damages incurred to their culture.[137] In the context of symbolic reparations, it also required Guatemala to publicly acknowledge its responsibility for the massacre with members of the Mayan community and to publicly honour the memory of deceased, many of whom were Mayan.[138]

Likewise, in the *Case of Río Negro Massacres v Guatemala,* the IACtHR ordered Guatemala to design and implement 'a programme for the rescue of the Maya Achí culture'.[139] Relying on its finding that State actions had harmed the cultural integrity of the Río Negro community, the Court ordered a reparations programme focused on 'the rescue, promotion, dissemination and conservation of the ancestral customs and practices, based on the values, principles and philosophies of the Maya Achí people'.[140] Regrettably, these measures have largely not been implemented and the redress of cultural rights violations through reparations remains highly uncertain. While the above-referenced exceptions exist, reparations in transitional justice praxis remain principally concerned with compensating individuals for violations of their civil and political rights.

[134] Marie Wilson, 'The Truth and Reconciliation Commission of Canada' in Wilton Littlechild and Elsa Stamatopoulou (eds), *Indigenous Peoples' Access to Justice, Including Truth and Reconciliation Processes* (Institute for the Study of Human Rights, Columbia University 2014) 129.

[135] Case of the Plan de Sánchez Massacre (n 92) para 81.

[136] Separate opinion of Judge Sergio Garcia Ramirez in the judgment on reparations in the *Case of Plan de Sánchez Massacre v Guatemala* (19 November 2004) para 15.

[137] *Case of Plan de Sánchez Massacre v Guatemala* (n 92) para 88.

[138] Significantly, the Court also ordered that Guatemala 'take into account the traditions and customs of the members of the affected communities' in conducting this public act of remembrance: ibid para 101.

[139] *Case of the Río Negro Massacres* (n 92) para 285.

[140] ibid.

A unique and long-standing reparations (and truth-telling) mechanism can be found in the Waitangi Tribunal, a quasi-judicial body established to address Māori grievances for breaches of the Waitangi Treaty by the Pakeha (white settlers) and the colonial government of Aotearoa New Zealand.[141] While principally a mechanism to settle land claims, the tribunal has occasionally addressed the cultural harm perpetrated against Māori through breaches of the Waitangi Treaty. For instance, the Tribunal's *Taranaki* report detailed how settler colonial land policies forced upon the Māori stripped the land of meaning and culture, leaving a vibrant Māori society broken.[142] Moreover, many of the tribunal's decisions discuss the cultural heritage of the Māori people at length.[143] Notwithstanding, the tribunal has been criticized for only being able to make recommendations, none of which are binding on the State.[144]

Perhaps the most significant area of development in the realm of reparations and cultural rights concerns the return of cultural objects and/or human remains. States are increasingly pressured to return plundered cultural objects and human remains to marginalized groups or their origin countries. These acts are commonly framed as a form of reparations in connection with the loss of culture.[145] These initiatives have increasingly been framed as measures of transitional justice and the transitional justice legal architecture has been consistently invoked in the policy and practice of restituting cultural objects and/or human remains.[146] This is very much in furtherance of addressing transitional justice's ambivalence towards accounting for colonial wrongs and the ongoing effects.[147]

141 Catherine J Iorns Magallanes, 'Reparations for Maori Grievances in Aotearoa New Zealand' in Federico Lenzerini (ed), *Reparations for Indigenous Peoples: International and Comparative Perspectives* (Oxford University Press 2008) 536–37.

142 The Taranaki Report Kaupapa Tuatahi, Waitangi Tribunal Report (1996) 274–75 <https://forms.justice.govt.nz/search/Documents/WT/wt_DOC_68453721/Taranaki%201996.compressed.pdf> accessed 1 February 2025.

143 Robert K Paterson, 'Protecting Taonga: The Cultural Heritage of the New Zealand Maori' (1999) 8(1) International Journal of Cultural Property 108.

144 Valmaine Toki, 'The Issues of the Criminal Justice System and of Resources in Aoteoroa/New Zealand' in Wilton Littlechild and Elsa Stamatopoulou (eds), *Indigenous Peoples' Access to Justice, Including Truth and Reconciliation Processes* (Institute for the Study of Human Rights, Columbia University 2014) 83.

145 Ana Filipa Vrdoljak 'Reparations for Cultural Loss' in Federico Lenzerini (ed), *Reparations for Indigenous Peoples: International and Comparative Perspectives* (Oxford University Press 2008) 198.

146 Whittaker, 'Cultural Property and Identity' (n 53); Thérèse O'Donnell, 'The Restitution of Holocaust Looted Art and Transitional Justice: The Perfect Storm or the Raft of the Medusa?' (2011) 22(1) European Journal of International Law 49.

147 McAuliffe, 'Complicity or Decolonization?' (n 45) 681.

In a quite prominent case, in 2018 France committed itself to a restitution policy providing for the return of various cultural objects taken without consent from several countries in Africa during the colonial period.[148] More commonly, ad hoc initiatives have returned cultural heritage to countries or communities of origin. For instance, in 2002, forty-eight Aymara textiles were returned to their original community in Bolivia after they had been taken in the 1970s and ended up in the possession of private collectors.[149] In 2019 the Swedish history museum agreed to return twenty-five human skulls to the Sami people in a repatriation ceremony.[150] Similarly, Aborigine human remains housed in the Birmingham Museum & Art Gallery in the United Kingdom were returned to traditional custodians in 2016.[151]

More often than not, however, former colonial powers use political and legal tools to evade their responsibility to restitute stolen cultural heritage.[152] Nonetheless, as nations and institutions continue to confront colonial-era injustices, restitution is likely to become an essential component of transitional justice praxis. While the legal frameworks applicable to restitution and reparation processes are particularly weak at the international level, there is room to acknowledge the importance of cultural rights in such endeavours, especially in demonstrating the importance of cultural objects and human remains to the cultural identities and cultural continuity of affected communities.

[148] Sarr-Savoy Report on the Restitution of African Cultural Heritage, Toward a New Relational Ethics (November 2018) <https://www.about-africa.de/images/sonstiges/2018/sarr_savoy_en.pdf> accessed 24 December 2024.

[149] Report of the Expert Mechanism on the Rights of Indigenous Peoples, Repatriation of Ceremonial Objects, Human Remains and Intangible Cultural Heritage under the United Nations Declaration on the Rights of Indigenous Peoples, UN Doc A/HRC/45/35 (21 July 2020) para 56.

[150] Jon Henley, 'Swedish Museum to Return Exhumed Skulls of 25 Sami People', *The Guardian* (7 August 2019) <https://www.theguardian.com/world/2019/aug/07/swedish-museum-to-return-exhumed-skulls-of-25-sami-people#:~:text=The%20skulls%20of%2025%20Sami,by%20the%20country's%20indigenous%20community> accessed 24 June 2025.

[151] University of Birmingham, 'Aboriginal Remains Returned to Ancestral Home' (18 October 2016) <https://www.birmingham.ac.uk/news-archive/2016/aboriginal-remains-returned-to-ancestral-home> accessed 24 December 2024.

[152] Report of the Special Rapporteur on the Promotion of Truth, Justice, Reparation and Guarantees of Non-recurrence, Fabián Salvioli, Transitional Justice Measures and Addressing the Legacy of Gross Violations of Human Rights and International Humanitarian Law Committed in Colonial Contexts, UN Doc A/76/180 (19 July 2021) paras 63–69.

2
UNDERSTANDING THE MARGINALIZATION OF CULTURAL RIGHTS IN TRANSITIONAL JUSTICE

1. Introduction

Why have cultural rights traditionally existed on the outermost margins of the transitional justice project? While this book does not seek to provide a definitive answer to this question, it does begin to think through some of the reasons why considerations of culture have not been central to the remit of the field. Understanding the rationale for their subordinated position in transitional justice is necessary to address and rectify the marginalization of cultural rights and to imagine what a cultural rights-based approach to transitional justice may ultimately look like.[1]

Although several factors contribute to the marginalization of cultural rights, it can primarily be traced to certain conceptual constraints that developed during the field's evolutionary history and which are now embedded in a dominant model of transitional justice.[2] The dominant model connotes the orthodox way in which transitional justice has been theorized and implemented, including the field's many underlying assumptions, biases, and preoccupations. It is principally characterized by the use of a limited set of mechanisms (most prominently criminal trials and truth commissions) in response to egregious and recent acts of physical violence (e.g. genocide, war crimes, torture, forced disappearances, sexual violence, etc.) in societies transitioning away from armed conflict or authoritarian rule.[3] Even as the field has globalized and

[1] The specific contours of a cultural rights-based approach to transitional justice are described in chapter 5 of this book.

[2] Similarly, James Cavallaro and Sebastián Albuja describe a 'dominant script' of transitional justice. James Cavallaro and Sebastián Albuja, 'The Lost Agenda: Economic Crimes and Truth Commissions in Latin America and Beyond' in Kieran McEvoy and Lorna McGregor (eds), *Transitional Justice from Below: Grassroots Activism and the Struggle for Change* (Hart Publishing 2008) 126.

[3] Dustin N Sharp, *Re-thinking Transitional Justice for the Twenty-First Century: Beyond the End of History* (Cambridge University Press 2018) 15.

Cultural Rights and Wrongs in Transitional Justice. Colin Luoma, Oxford University Press.
DOI: 10.1093/oso/9780198911371.003.0002

expanded into disparate settings, transitional justice is still most often understood and applied within the confines of this familiar, monolithic paradigm, often to the exclusion of economic, social, and especially cultural rights.[4]

Three core features of the dominant model make transitional justice incompatible with a serious and sustained engagement with cultural rights, namely what have traditionally been conceived as: (1) a transition, (2) justice, and (3) violence. Exceedingly narrow understandings of these concepts have been crystallized in mainstream transitional justice theory, restricting the field's scope of application and hindering its development. In large part, how we interpret these concepts determines where, when, how, and to what transitional justice applies.[5] Therefore, understanding why cultural rights have been largely positioned outside of mainstream transitional justice begins with interrogating how the concepts of transition, justice, and violence have been traditionally understood under the dominant model.

It should be said that the shift away from some of the more dogmatic ideas around transition, justice, and violence is already occurring. Transitional justice mechanisms continue to be employed in numerous contexts outside of the paradigmatic cases, including in ostensibly peaceful Western democracies that many suggest are quintessentially non-transitional.[6] At least in theory, blueprint, ready-to-export justice models have been widely criticized in both scholarly and practical circles.[7] And undoubtedly, the field has expanded its conceptual parameters to encompass a wider range of harm. Yet, many of the original biases, assumptions, and preoccupations of the dominant model have been difficult to shed, making transitional justice, as commonly theorized and implemented, particularly unsuitable for addressing complex, intersecting, and intergenerational forms of cultural harm, respecting traditional and customary justice processes, and accommodating culturally diverse responses to mass wrongdoing.

[4] *See* Roger MacGinty, 'Indigenous Peace-making versus the Liberal Peace' (2008) 43(2) Cooperation and Conflict 139, 144; Rosemary Nagy, 'Transitional Justice as Global Project: Critical Reflections' (2008) 29(2) Third World Quarterly 275, 275; Zinaida Miller, 'Effects of Invisibility: In Search of the "Economic" in Transitional Justice' (2008) 2(3) International Journal of Transitional Justice 266, 271.

[5] Nagy evaluates the 'when, to whom and for what' of transitional justice to interrogate and critique its standardization. Nagy, 'Transitional Justice as Global Project' (n 4) 276.

[6] Padraig McAuliffe, 'Transitional Justice's Expanding Empire: Reasserting the Value of the Paradigmatic Transition' (2012) 2(2) Journal of Conflictology 32, 34–38.

[7] See, eg, Makau Mutua, 'What Is the Future of Transitional Justice?' (2015) 9 International Journal of Transitional Justice 1, 5; see also UN Secretary-General, The Rule of Law and Transitional Justice in Conflict and Post-Conflict Societies, UN Doc S/2004/616 (23 August 2004) para 36.

2. The Origins and Evolutions of Transitional Justice

The evolutionary history of transitional justice has been comprehensively rehearsed elsewhere in the academic literature. Ruti Teitel's *Transitional Justice Genealogy*[8] and Paige Arthur's *How Transitions Reshaped Human Rights: A Conceptual History of Transitional Justice*[9] have been particularly influential in tracing and elucidating the conceptual and intellectual history of the field. The manner in which transitional justice grew, evolved, and consolidated has had a major influence on dominant theory and practice, and in turn on the field's long-standing marginalization of cultural rights. Thus, to understand the marginalized position of cultural rights in transitional justice, one must appreciate how the field came into existence, developed, and consolidated in ways largely divorced from considerations of culture and cultural rights.

Despite the scholarly work done to pin down the inception of the transitional justice field, its origins remain contested.[10] Acknowledging the difficulty of identifying a specific starting point, Arthur explains that '[w]here to start a history of the field of transitional justice is no easy question to answer'.[11] Some scholars persuasively argue that practices dating back hundreds if not thousands of years fit within our modern understanding of transitional justice. Trials and practices in ancient Greece,[12] the international criminal trial of Peter von Hagenach in 1474,[13] the exile of Napoleon Bonaparte and post-civil war amnesties in the United States,[14] and war crimes tribunals in the early twentieth century[15] have all been cited as examples of what could arguably be conceived as transitional justice practice. Proponents of this view reason that transitional justice is hardly a new phenomenon, but rather an enduring exercise where societies across space and time have sought to deal with past abuses in various ways.[16] However, while the general idea of a public reckoning

[8] Ruti G Teitel, 'Transitional Justice Genealogy' (2003) 16 Harvard Human Rights Journal 69.

[9] Paige Arthur, 'How Transitions Reshaped Human Rights: A Conceptual History of Transitional Justice' (2009) 31 Human Rights Quarterly 321.

[10] Marcos Zunino, *Justice Framed: A Genealogy of Transitional Justice* (Cambridge University Press 2019) 9–14.

[11] Arthur, 'How Transitions Reshaped Human Rights' (n 9) 327.

[12] Jon Elster, *Closing the Books: Transitional Justice in Historical Perspective* (Cambridge University Press 2004) 3–23.

[13] Jeremy Sarkin and Tetevi Davi, 'Examining the Criticisms Levelled Against Transitional Justice: Towards an Understanding of the State of the Field' (2017) 11(1) *Human Rights and International Legal Discourse* 7, 11.

[14] Andrew G Reiter, 'The Development of Transitional Justice' in Olivera Simic (ed), *An Introduction to Transitional Justice* (2nd edn, Routledge 2021) 30.

[15] Gary Bass, *Stay the Hand of Vengeance: The Politics of War Crimes Tribunals* (Princeton University Press 2014).

[16] Zunino, *Justice Framed* (n 10) 10.

with the past was encompassed in historical justice processes, the transitional justice paradigm clearly did not exist in antiquity in the way that it does today. Thus, even though these historical practices may constitute the roots of transitional justice practice, few argue that the modern field began at this time.

The prevailing view is that even though antecedents of transitional justice existed in the distant past, the contemporary history of the field emerged after the Second World War.[17] Most of the discourse locates transitional justice in this period, with the Nuremberg and Tokyo trials marking the start of the phenomenon.[18] In her influential genealogy of transitional justice, Teitel describes the post-Second World War period as the field's first generation.[19] This initial phase was exclusively international and legalistic, characterized by international actors imposing individual criminal accountability for the mass physical violence committed during the Holocaust.[20] In this sense, transitional justice was initially seen as strictly retributive and narrowly focused on holding individual criminals to account for their bodily integrity crimes.

This is an important era because certain ideas became entrenched in how transitional justice is understood and operationalized even today. These include the primacy of legal responses to past wrongdoing, the prioritization of international criminal prosecutions in post-conflict environments, and a paramount commitment to justice for violations of civil and political rights after the cessation of conflict.[21] The public reckoning in the aftermath of the horrors of the Holocaust is also symptomatic of the type of 'atrocity justice' that began to define transitional justice at the end of the twentieth century.[22] Transitional justice was thus originally conceived as a strictly backward-looking process, with the goal of establishing individual criminal accountability through international law. Even though this first phase is now considered overly narrow and legalistic, its legacy strongly influenced the field, to the point that retributive

[17] Even Jon Elster, who traces the field's antecedents to antiquity, agrees that the modern history begins in the post-war period. Elster, *Closing the Books* (n 12) 47; see also Patricia Lundy and Mark McGovern, 'Whose Justice? Rethinking Transitional Justice from the Bottom Up' (2008) 35(2) Journal of Law and Society 265, 268.

[18] Pádraig McAuliffe, 'From Molehills to Mountains (and Myths?): A Critical History of Transitional Justice Advocacy' (2011) 22 Finnish Yearbook of International Law 1, 18; Miller, 'Effects of Invisibility' (n 4) 269; Kora Andrieu, 'Transitional Justice: A New Discipline in Human Rights' (2010) Online Encyclopedia of Mass Violence 18, 22.

[19] Teitel, 'Transitional Justice Genealogy' (n 8) 72–74.

[20] ibid.

[21] ibid; see also Bronwyn Anne Leebaw, 'The Irreconcilable Goals of Transitional Justice,' (2008) 30 Human Rights Quarterly 95, 99.

[22] Dustin N Sharp, 'Emancipating Transitional Justice from the Bonds of the Paradigmatic Transition' (2015) 9 International Journal of Transitional Justice 150, 159.

justice in the form of international criminal prosecutions is arguably still seen as the 'gold standard'.[23]

Transitional justice practice might have originated in these post-war international tribunals, but a distinct discourse around the phenomenon did not emanate until some forty years later when a number of States, primarily in Latin America and Eastern Europe, underwent democratic transitions in the late 1980s and early 1990s.[24] These so-called third-wave transitions were premised on dictatorships transitioning towards democratization, strengthening the rule of law, and ensuring the legal redress of a limited set of civil and political rights violations.[25] In this phase, transitional justice was primarily fixated on the set of dilemmas surrounding how States should deal with the civil and political rights violations committed by prior authoritarian regimes.

The transition at issue was essentially a political one and transitional justice measures were seen as a way to bridge the divide between a prior repressive past and a new democratic one.[26] In turn, the mechanisms employed were principally tailored to what was considered to be the most effective way to provide justice for these abuses, as well as to enable the specific political transition to take place.[27] In almost all cases this meant that civil and political rights violations were prioritized and ESC rights violations were marginalized.

For example, Argentina's transitional justice policy was narrowly centred on addressing the thousands of people who were kidnapped, tortured, and forcibly disappeared during the country's military dictatorship.[28] Its pioneering transitional justice mechanism, the National Commission on the Disappearance of Persons (*Comisión Nacional sobre la Desaparición de Personas*), and its resulting *Nunca Más* report investigated and documented the circumstances surrounding these physical abuses.[29] Similarly, Chile's National Commission for Truth and Reconciliation (*Comisión Nacional de Verdad y Reconciliación*) possessed a narrow mandate restricting it to investigating bodily integrity

[23] Nicola Henry, 'From Reconciliation to Transitional Justice: The Contours of Redress Politics in Established Democracies' (2015) 9(2) International Journal of Transitional Justice 199, 212.

[24] Lauren Marie Balasco, 'The Transitions of Transitional Justice: Mapping the Waves from Promise to Practice' (2013) 12(2) Journal of Human Rights 198, 199–200.

[25] Samuel Huntington, *The Third Wave: Democratization in the Late Twentieth Century* (University of Oklahoma Press 1991).

[26] Arthur, 'How "Transitions" Reshaped Human Rights' (n 9) 339; *see also* Eric A Posner and Adrian Vermeule. 'Transitional Justice as Ordinary Justice' (2004) 117(3) Harvard Law Review 761, 768.

[27] Dustin N Sharp, 'Addressing Economic Violence in Times of Transition: Towards a Positive-Peace Paradigm for Transitional Justice' (2011) 35 Fordham International Law Journal 780, 787.

[28] Sharp, *Re-Thinking Transitional Justice for the 21st Century* (n 3) 33.

[29] *Nunca Más: The Report of the Argentine National Commission on the Disappeared* (1986) <http://www.desaparecidos.org/nuncamas/web/english/library/nevagain/nevagain_001.htm> accessed 1 February 2025.

violations: 'disappearances after arrest, executions, and torture leading to death committed by government agents or people in their service, as well as kidnappings and attempts on the life of persons carried out by private citizens for political reasons.'[30] The Argentinian and Chilean truth commissions typified transitional justice during this period, where violations of civil and political rights violations were foregrounded and the underlying cultural and structural violence that enabled these 'dirty wars' was overlooked.[31]

In this second generation, transitional justice also moved beyond its sole focus on the individualized criminal accountability embodied by the post-war tribunals and towards more collective forms of justice, particularly with truth commissions becoming a favoured mechanism.[32] Beyond the adjudication of criminal liability, it attempted to place the abuses of a prior regime in a broader historical context.[33] This shift also took place in the context of the 'peace versus justice' dilemma faced by many States debating how to grapple with abuses of former regimes while also maintaining a tenuous state of peace.[34] Criminal punishment was often eschewed in favour of amnesties deemed necessary to facilitate a successful move away from authoritarian rule.[35] When criminal liability was pursued, national prosecutions ordinarily supplanted international tribunals. Thus, Teitel maintains that transitional justice in its second generation became more restorative, provisional, and complex.[36] At the same time, it remained overwhelmingly focused on violations of civil and political rights, to the exclusion to other forms of harm.[37] A further key aspect of this phase was the idea that transitional justice should advance the goal of 'nation-building' in post-conflict and post-authoritarian societies.[38] Accountability for egregious human rights abuses was coupled with questions of how to properly engage in a process of national healing and reconciliation.[39] Truth commissions and other initiatives were thus focused on creating new and often imagined national narratives in the wake of conflict.[40]

[30] Government of Chile, Supreme Decree No 355 (25 April 1990) para 9 <https://reparations.qub.ac.uk/assets/uploads/Chile90-Report-24-27.pdf> accessed 1 February 2025.

[31] Lisa J Laplante, 'Transitional Justice and Peace Building: Diagnosing and Addressing the Socioeconomic Roots of Violence through a Human Rights Framework' (2008) 2(3) International Journal of Transitional Justice 331, 335.

[32] Teitel 'Transitional Justice Genealogy' (n 8) 78.

[33] ibid 77–78.

[34] ibid 81–85.

[35] ibid 82.

[36] ibid 78.

[37] Nagy, 'Transitional Justice as Global Project' (n 4) 284–85.

[38] Teitel, 'Transitional Justice Genealogy' (n 8) 76–78.

[39] ibid.

[40] Kora Andrieu, 'Civilizing Peacebuilding: Transitional Justice, Civil Society and the Liberal Paradigm' (2010) 41(5) Security Dialogue 537, 542.

This proved to be the most formative period for the field. Most commentators agree that the contemporary conceptualization of transitional justice is firmly grounded in these democratic transitions and the initial boundaries of the field were largely defined by them.[41] It was during this time that the term 'transitional justice' first emerged as a way to describe and understand the various strategies and practices intended to address past violence and human rights abuses.[42] Because transitional justice was viewed through the lens of these political transitions, the field ultimately coalesced around the idea that it was mainly, if not exclusively, an instrument of democratization.[43] As a strictly postcolonial project, it was not envisaged that transitional justice would respond to the violent and unjust legacies of colonialism.[44] Instead, it was inherently narrow, legalistic, and seen mostly as a framework to address acts of physical violence in societies recently transitioning from authoritarian rule to increased democracy. This became the first paradigmatic transitional justice case.

Then, beginning in the mid-1990s, transitional justice became equally associated with international responses to mass atrocities in countries emerging from sustained periods of intrastate armed conflict.[45] The ICTY, the International Criminal Tribunal for Rwanda ('ICTR'), the hybrid criminal tribunal in Sierra Leone ('SCSL'), and the ICC were all established as judicial responses to genocide, war crimes, and crimes against humanity committed during protracted armed conflicts and accompanying serious violations of international criminal law.[46] While these transitions from armed conflict to peace are commonly grouped in with the third-wave democratic transitions, they arguably represent a separate evolution in the field. Reverting back to Teitel's first generation, the focus again became individualized criminal accountability for humanity's worst crimes.[47] As a result, transitions from armed conflict to peace emerged as the second paradigmatic case of transitional justice.[48]

41 Arthur, 'How "Transitions" Reshaped Human Rights' (n 9); Sharp, 'Emancipating Transitional Justice from the Bonds of the Paradigmatic Transition' (n 22); Zunino, Justice Framed (n 10) 9-14.

42 Henry, 'From Reconciliation to Transitional Justice' (n 23) 206.

43 Arthur, 'How Transitions Reshaped Human Rights' (n 9) 359.

44 Sarah Maddison and Laura J Shepherd, 'Peacebuilding and the Postcolonial Politics of Transitional Justice' (2014) 2(3) Peacebuilding 253, 257.

45 Sharp, 'Addressing Economic Violence in Times of Transition' (n 27) 791.

46 Andrieu, 'Transitional Justice: A New Discipline in Human Rights' (n 18) 5.

47 Sharp, 'Emancipating Transitional Justice from the Bonds of the Paradigmatic Transition' (n 22) 159–61.

48 McAuliffe, 'Transitional Justice's Expanding Empire' (n 6) 34; Stephen Winter, 'Towards a Unified Theory of Transitional Justice' (2013) 7(2) International Journal of Transitional Justice 224, 227.

In the twenty-first century, transitional justice initiatives have proliferated significantly.[49] Indeed, it has been said that 'no region of the world has escaped the reach of transitional justice'.[50] What was once seen as a form of extraordinary justice is now quite commonplace,[51] with Kieran McEvoy commenting that transitional justice has become 'something which is normal, institutionalized and mainstream'.[52] International criminal tribunals, national prosecutions, and truth commissions continue to multiply, along with an expanding list of other mechanisms including reparations programmes, institutional reform, formal apologies, and memorialization initiatives, among others. The initiation of some form of transitional justice is now presumed in the wake of mass wrongdoing (at least in the paradigmatic cases) to the point that it is seldom a question of whether transitional justice will be implemented in the aftermath of large-scale past harm, but rather one of how it should be done.[53]

The institutionalization and normalization of transitional justice illustrates just how quickly the field has developed in a brief period of time. As Christine Bell notes, the term 'transitional justice' was not even used until the mid-1990s and it arguably did not emerge as a cognisable 'field' until after 2000.[54] From this perspective, the field's growth is extraordinary. Yet, despite its development as a normative, default response to mass atrocity, it remains quite predictable in where, when, and how it operates, including what types of harms it seeks to confront. It largely remains tethered to the paradigmatic transitions, employing a limited set of mechanisms to address acts of recent egregious physical violence in societies transitioning from authoritarianism or armed conflict. This dominant model of transitional justice has been the primary way in which transitional justice has been conceptualized and implemented, much to the detriment of respecting, addressing, and incorporating cultural rights.

Building off Teitel's genealogy, Dustin Sharp argues that we are currently experiencing a 'fourth generation' of transitional justice, characterized by

[49] Teitel, 'Transitional Justice Genealogy' (n 8) 71.
[50] Tricia Olsen, Leigh Payne, and Andrew Reiter, *'Transitional justice in balance': Comparing Processes, Weighing Efficacy* (US Institute of Peace 2010) 38.
[51] Lieselotte Viaene and Eva Brems, 'Transitional Justice and Cultural Contexts: Learning from the Universality Debate' (2010) 28(2) Netherlands Quarterly of Human Rights 199, 200.
[52] Kieran McEvoy, 'Beyond Legalism: Towards a Thicker Understanding of Transitional Justice' (2007) 34(4) Journal of Law and Society 411.
[53] Nagy 'Transitional Justice as Global Project' (n 4) 276.
[54] Christine Bell, 'Transitional Justice, Interdisciplinarity and the State of the "Field" or "Non-Field"', (2009) 3(1) International Journal of Transitional Justice 5, 7.

an 'increasing willingness to interrogate some of the boundaries and blind spots of the field'.[55] The ways in which transitional justice is conducted have long been problematized. Jeremy Sarkin and Tetevi Davi suggest that 'almost every aspect and every component of every [transitional justice] mechanism in every place has been the subject of criticism and differences of opinion to varying degrees'.[56] However, only recently have the concepts and goals underpinning transitional justice been the subject of consistent scrutiny. Bell views this as an inevitable part of the field's 'coming of age', with 'increased claims for inclusion in it, and pressure to reframe the field to include increasingly broad agendas and issues'.[57] Indeed, there is now a significant body of critical scholarship challenging the field's propensity to push certain elements to the margins. The most strident critiques are directed at an uneven balance between global and local approaches, the marginalization of socio-economic issues, the failure to account for root causes of conflict, the replication of rote justice models, a lack of responsiveness to issues of gender, and the neocolonial and imperial nature of transitional justice, particularly on the African continent.[58]

This evolutionary history provides some context for how transitional justice developed in ways removed from consideration of cultural rights. Modern conceptions and manifestations of transitional justice have been heavily influenced by how the field originated and evolved over its still relatively brief lifespan.[59] Even as transitional justice has been increasingly endorsed by States, civil society, the UN, academia, and donors, moving squarely into the mainstream of post-conflict agendas, the field has not deviated too far from its original attributes and goals.[60] This is especially true with respect to the following three core concepts discussed in detail below: transition, justice, and violence.

[55] Sharp, *Re-Thinking Transitional Justice for the 21st Century* (n 3) 15; see also Dustin N Sharp, 'Interrogating the Peripheries: The Preoccupations of Fourth Generation Transitional Justice' (2013) 26 *Harvard Human Rights Journal* 149, 149.

[56] Sarkin and Davi, 'Examining the Criticisms Levelled Against Transitional Justice' (n 13) 7.

[57] Bell, 'Transitional Justice, Interdisciplinarity and the State of the "Field" or "Non-Field"' (n 54) 13.

[58] Dustin N Sharp, 'What Would Satisfy Us? Taking Stock of Critical Approaches to Transitional Justice' (2019) 13(3) *International Journal of Transitional Justice* 570, 570–71; Sarkin and Davi, 'Examining the Criticisms Levelled Against Transitional Justice' (n 13) 11.

[59] Arthur, 'How Transitions Reshaped Human Rights' (n 9) 324–26.

[60] Sharp, *Re-thinking Transitional Justice for the Twenty-First Century* (n 3) 8-13.

3. Dominant Transitions

The first half of the transitional justice phraseology strongly suggests that the field is fundamentally tied to the idea of a transition.[61] The dilemmas associated with confronting violent and unjust legacies have been studied under various banners, including reparative justice,[62] transformative justice,[63] and reparations politics,[64] among others. However, it is the *transitional* lexicon that ultimately emerged as the dominant way to talk about reckoning with large-scale past human rights abuses.[65] While some may suggest that the field has outgrown the transitional terminology,[66] others maintain that it is a fundamental premise behind the project.[67] The act of a transition is often viewed as the differentiating factor between transitional and 'ordinary' justice.[68] Put differently, transitional justice's extraordinary character is not solely attributable to the scale of harm it seeks to confront, but also to its aim to aid some sort of change. Thus, the concept of a transition is inherently teleological in that its purpose is for a society to reach some desired endpoint.[69]

A transition has been variously described as a journey,[70] a shift from one state or condition to another,[71] or a movement from some starting point to a final destination.[72] In between these stages is a finite period of time, a so-called rupture point, where transitional justice is supposedly possible.[73] These rare

[61] Jennifer Matsunaga, 'Two Faces of Transitional Justice: Theorizing the Incommensurability of Transitional Justice and Decolonization in Canada' (2016) 5(1) Decolonization: Indigeneity, Education & Society 24, 28.

[62] See, eg, Rama Mani, *Beyond Retribution: Seeking Justice in the Shadows of War* (Polity Press 2002).

[63] See, eg, Wendy Lambourne, 'Transformative Justice, Reconciliation and Peacebuilding' in Susanne Buckley-Zistel and others (eds), *Transitional Justice Theories* (Routledge 2013) 19-39; see also Paul Gready and Simon Robins, 'From Transitional to Transformative Justice: A New Agenda for Practice' (2014) 8(3) International Journal of Transitional Justice 339.

[64] John Torpey, *Making Whole What Has Been Smashed: On Reparations Politics* (Harvard University Press 2006).

[65] Andrew Woolford, 'Transition and Transposition: Genocide, Land and the British Columbia Treaty Process' (2011) 4(2) New Proposals: Journal of Marxism and Interdisciplinary Inquiry 67, 68; Sharp, *Re-Thinking Transitional Justice for the 21st Century* (n 3) 75.

[66] Lars Waldorf, 'Cuddled, Loved and Mutilated: Transitional Justice as Transitional Object' (2019) 2 Responsibility to Protect Student Journal 6; Zunino, *Justice Framed* (n 10) 4.

[67] Joanna R Quinn, 'Whither the Transition of Transitional Justice' (2014) 8 Interdisciplinary Journal of Human Rights 63, 64.

[68] Henry, 'From Reconciliation to Transitional Justice' (n 23) 207; but see Posner and Vermeule, 'Transitional Justice as Ordinary Justice' (n 26).

[69] Maddison and Shepherd, 'Peacebuilding and the Postcolonial Politics of Transitional Justice' (n 44) 259.

[70] Fionnuala Ní Aoláin and Colm Campbell, 'The Paradox of Transition in Conflicted Democracies' (2015) 27 Human Rights Quarterly 172, 173.

[71] Maddison and Shepherd, 'Peacebuilding and the Postcolonial Politics of Transitional Justice' (n 44) 259.

[72] Sharp, 'Addressing Economic Violence in Times of Transition' (n 27) 800.

[73] Harry Hobbs, 'Locating the Logic of Transitional Justice in Liberal Democracies: Native Title in Australia' (2016) 39 University of New South Wales Law Journal 512, 521.

periods are presumed exceptional, a deviation from the normal course, but the exact duration is not made explicit.[74] The conventional understanding of a transition further implies a clean break away from a prior era and the beginning of a new one.[75] Mainstream transitional justice theory, in turn, has been predicated on this specific period of time in which extraordinary measures can be employed to facilitate a society towards some final destination.[76]

However, it has never been clearly articulated what exactly amounts to a transition, or what societies are purportedly transitioning to or from.[77] Commentators have long noted the 'elusive'[78] and 'slippery'[79] nature of the term. Bell directly observes its unbounded scope, noting that 'little attempt has been made to define a concept of a transition that would place limitations on when transitional justice can legitimately be applied'.[80] The absence of a clear definition and the resulting conceptual confusion complicates the settings in which transitional justice may be pursued, especially in non-paradigmatic cases where subnational groups often suffer from 'slow violence' at the hands of 'peaceful' democratic States.[81]

What is accepted as a 'transition' determines when and where transitional justice operates. Dominant transitions have historically been limited to movements from dictatorship to liberal democracy or, alternatively, from armed conflict to peace.[82] These are understood as 'clear-cut cases' of transitional justice.[83] They are 'clear-cut' because of how transitional justice was theorized during the nascence of the field, when situations considered deserving of extraordinary justice measures were restricted to the paradigmatic cases. In such cases, the starting point of the transitional justice process begins when repressive rule or mass violence is brought to a halt.[84] Thus, acceptable transitional

[74] Sharp, 'Addressing Economic Violence in Times of Transition' (n 27) 800.

[75] Kimberley Theidon, 'Editorial Note' (2009) 3(3) The International Journal of Transitional Justice 1, 1.

[76] Nagy, 'Transitional Justice as Global Project' (n 4) 280.

[77] Christine Bell and Catherine O'Rourke, 'Does Feminism Need a Theory of Transitional Justice? An Introductory Essay' (2007) 1(1) The International Journal of Transitional Justice 23, 35.

[78] McAuliffe, 'Transitional Justice's Expanding Empire' (n 6) 33.

[79] Naomi Roht-Arriaza, 'The New Landscape of Transitional Justice' in Naomi Roht-Arriaza and Javier Mariezcurrena (eds), *Transitional Justice in the Twenty-First Century* (Cambridge University Press 2006) 1.

[80] Bell, 'Transitional Justice, Interdisciplinarity and the State of the "Field" or "Non-Field"' (n 54) 23.

[81] Pauline Wakeham, 'The Slow Violence of Settler Colonialism: Genocide, Attrition, and the Long Emergency of Invasion' (2022) 24(3) Journal of Genocide Research 337.

[82] Kazuo Ohgushi, 'A Critical Note on "Hypercritical" Studies of Transitional Justice' (2015) 79 The Journal of Social Science 83, 84.

[83] Quinn, 'Whither the Transition of Transitional Justice' (n 67) 70.

[84] Nagy 'Transitional Justice as Global Project' (n 4) 280.

settings have long been wedded to the two paradigmatic cases associated with its most formative years.

On its face, this would not seem necessarily to contribute to the marginalization of culture or cultural rights. However, a preoccupation with the paradigmatic transitions has diminished the purported relevance of transitional justice in many other settings, including in established Western democracies with minority groups and Indigenous Peoples who have experienced and who may still be experiencing devastating forms of large-scale cultural harm under the oppression of majority-controlled governments and ongoing colonial structures and policies. As described more fully in Chapter 6 of this book, cultural rights remain critically important to Indigenous Peoples' ways of life and their unique identities as culturally distinct peoples. Perhaps as a consequence, large-scale cultural wrongdoing has featured prominently in colonial encounters, particularly in policies to assimilate Indigenous Peoples into mainstream societies and gain permanent access to their territories and resources.

Dogmatic conceptions of a 'transition' have enabled many Western nations to avoid reckoning with their own violent histories. The United States, for example, has supported numerous transitional justice initiatives across traditional post-conflict and post-authoritarian settings in the Global South, but rejects its application to its own affairs.[85] In discussing the United States' foreign policy on transitional justice, Annie Bird notes that '[w]henever a new [transitional justice] mechanism is established or investigation is begun, the United States will invariably work to ensure that it does not claim jurisdiction or authority over US nationals'.[86] It has also consistently rebuked calls for a historical reckoning with its violent relationships with African-Americans. Legislation has been proposed for thirty-five years in the United States Congress with the objective of studying and developing reparations proposals for African-Americans based on the institution of slavery, racial discrimination, and its lingering effects.[87] Notwithstanding, the bill has never gained much traction and there is not sufficient political will to seriously proceed with the contemplated reparative measures.

The US and other established democracies free of armed conflict are deemed to be already at the destination of the transitional justice journey. As a result,

[85] Jean Galbraith, 'The Trump Administration Revokes the ICC Prosecutor's US Visa Shortly Before the ICC Pre-Trial Chamber Declines to Authorize an Investigation into War Crimes in Afghanistan' (2019) 113(3) The American Journal of International Law 625.

[86] Annie R Bird, *US Foreign Policy on Transitional Justice* (Oxford University Press 2015) 3.

[87] H.R.40, Commission to Study and Develop Reparation Proposals for African Americans Act 118th Congress (2023–2024) <https://www.congress.gov/bill/118th-congress/house-bill/40> accessed 1 February 2025.

victims of large-scale cultural harm in these States are not afforded recourse through the same frameworks as victims of mass physical atrocities and brutal episodes of political repression elsewhere. Thus, these countries have been historically shielded from having to meaningfully reckon with their own history of human rights abuses, including mass violations of cultural rights.[88]

Recent transitional justice practice largely conforms to the conventional theorization of what constitutes a bona fide transition. This means that transitional justice mechanisms are overwhelmingly implemented in post-authoritarian and post-conflict States, usually located in the Global South.[89] Truth-seeking bodies in Gambia (2017) and Tunisia (2019), for instance, were tasked with addressing violations committed during sustained periods of dictatorship.[90] Transitional justice mechanisms also continue to proliferate in traditional post-conflict contexts, including in Côte d'Ivoire (2014)[91] and Burundi (2014).[92] Further transitional justice initiatives are being contemplated or initiated in other paradigmatic settings, including Sri Lanka,[93] Northern Ireland,[94] and Fiji.[95] These types of 'clear-cut' transitions continue to dominate the transitional justice landscape.

This not only limits the societies subject to transitional justice scrutiny, but also restricts the types of harm most likely to be confronted. For example, cultural harm is likely to be more prominent in the case of established Western democracies seeking to address the wrongdoing associated with colonialism

[88] Colin Luoma, 'Closing the Cultural Rights Gap in Transitional Justice: Developments from Canada's National Inquiry into Missing and Murdered Indigenous Women and Girls' (2021) 39(1) Netherlands Quarterly of Human Rights 30, 32.

[89] Matt James and Michelle Bonner, 'The Three R's of Seeking Transitional Justice: Reparation, Responsibility, and Reframing in Canada and Argentina' (2011) 2(3) The International Indigenous Policy Journal 1, 2.

[90] The Truth and Dignity Commission was tasked with investigating and accounting for civil and political rights violations that occurred between 1955 and 2013, including enforced disappearance, extrajudicial execution, torture, death due to torture, and excessive use of force. See Republic of Tunisia, Organic Law on Establishing and Organizing Transitional Justice (2013) < https://ihl-databases.icrc.org/en/national-practice/organic-law-no-2014-17-relating-provisions-relating-transitional-justice-and > accessed 24 December 2024; The Gambia Truth, Reconciliation and Reparations Commission Act (2017), <https://www.moj.gm/downloads > accessed 24 December 2024.

[91] Hienzo Florence-Audrey Kouame, *Reconciliation in Côte d'Ivoire: A Case Study of the Implementation of Transitional Justice in Post-conflict States* (Ethics International Press 2024)

[92] Astrid Jamar, 'Accounting for Which Violent Past? Transitional Justice, Epistemic Violence, and Colonial Durabilities in Burundi' (2022) 14(1) Critical African Studies 73.

[93] International Commission of Jurists, 'Sri Lanka: New Bill to Establish "Commission for Truth, Unity and Reconciliation" Lacks Credibility and Unlikely to Bring Accountability (12 January 2024) <https://www.icj.org/sri-lanka-new-bill-to-establish-commission-for-truth-unity-and-reconciliation-lacks-credibility-and-unlikely-to-bring-accountability/> accessed 24 December 2024.

[94] Northern Ireland, Independent Commission for Reconciliation and Information Recovery <https://icrir.independent-inquiry.uk/> accessed 24 December 2024.

[95] Parliament of the Republic of Fiji, Fiji Truth and Reconciliation Commission Bill 2024 (Bill No 19 of 2024) <https://www.parliament.gov.fj/wp-content/uploads/2024/10/Bill-No.-19-Fiji-Truth-and-Reconciliation-Commission-Bill-2024.pdf> accessed 1 February 2025.

and their ongoing relationships with Indigenous Peoples and minority groups. These contexts often lack the type of recent mass bodily integrity crimes that drive transitional justice agendas in post-conflict and post-authoritarian contexts, and ultimately end up overshadowing and sidelining cultural harm. Thus, treating established Western democracies as non-transitional works to exclude such harm from the scope of the field.

Gradually, cohesive attempts to grapple with large-scale human rights abuses have occurred outside the paradigmatic transitions. Measures in the transitional justice toolbox are increasingly employed in established democracies, States experiencing ongoing armed conflict, and authoritarian States with no perceptible shift towards democracy.[96] It is plain that transitional justice, as currently conceived and implemented, is not constrained to societies transitioning to liberal democracy or peace.[97] Yet, in practice, the transitional justice label is often not applied.[98] For instance, Canada does not treat any of its investigatory or justice processes, including its signature Truth and Reconciliation Commission, as forms of transitional justice.[99] These contexts are only starting to be taken seriously as transitional justice cases. So while the field has reached beyond its narrowest conception of what constitutes a transition, its application outside the paradigmatic cases is in its infancy and remains uncertain.[100]

4. Dominant Justice

The ways in which 'justice' has been historically conceived of determine the modality of transitional justice measures and how they are implemented. Justice in the dominant model is principally theorized as a set of short-term corrective measures aimed at facilitating the paradigmatic transitions,[101] the idea being that by confronting past human rights abuses, one can hope to move a State towards peace or democracy.[102] From the outset, this meant international actors employing a limited suite of Western legal or quasi-legal

[96] McAuliffe, 'Transitional Justice's Expanding Empire' (n 6).

[97] Thomas Obel Hansen, 'Transitional Justice: Toward a Differentiated Theory' (2011) 13 *Oregon Review of International Law* 1, 2–3.

[98] Maddison and Shepherd, 'Peacebuilding and the Postcolonial Politics of Transitional Justice' (n 44) 254.

[99] Matsunaga, 'Two Faces of Transitional Justice' (n 61) 29.

[100] See, eg, Michael Phillips, 'Justice-Seeking in Settler States: A Model for Thinking about "Justice" in Transitional Societies' in Claudio Corradetti, Nir Eisikovits, and Jack Volpe Rotondi (eds), *Theorizing Transitional Justice* (Ashgate Publishing 2015); James and Bonner, 'The Three R's of Seeking Transitional Justice' (n 89).

[101] Arthur, 'How "Transitions" Reshaped Human Rights' (n 9) 355.

[102] Balasco, 'The Transitions of Transitional Justice' (n 24) 200.

mechanisms centred on holding perpetrators to account for acts of political violence or mass physical atrocities.

This chapter maintains that there are five characteristics of justice in the dominant model that complicate transitional justice's engagement with cultural rights. Specifically, justice under mainstream theory is overwhelmingly State-centric, internationalized, legalistic, criminalizing, and individualistic. Each of these characteristics hinder the field from incorporating, accommodating, and addressing cultural rights in more direct and meaningful ways.

4.1 State-centric justice

Transitional justice is traditionally associated with building unity at the State level.[103] Mainstream theory suggests that one of the primary objectives of transitional justice is to advance some degree of 'nation-building' in post-conflict and post-authoritarian societies.[104] In post-genocide Rwanda, for example, transitional justice agendas discarded ethnic distinctions in favour of a uniform Rwandan identity.[105] Similarly, in post-apartheid South Africa, transitional justice policy advanced a multicultural, democratic, and imagined national identity commonly referred to as the 'rainbow nation'.[106] Will Kymlicka observes that in both cases, nation-building 'was used to delegitimize inherited ethnic and racial identities'.[107] Australia has been observed to take a similar approach in its reconciliation policies directed towards improving relationships with Indigenous Peoples, with the goal to 'replace past division with a new, shared sense of nationhood', a 'harmonious and integrated society'.[108] The goal is for a new, national identity to be adopted to weaken societal divisions and overcome past violence and oppression, replacing the plurality that is often inherent in post-conflict and divided societies.

Nation-building ambitions can pose a particular risk to cultural rights, and especially the cultural rights of minorities and Indigenous Peoples, whose

[103] Sharp, 'Addressing Economic Violence in Times of Transition' (n 27) 789.

[104] Teitel, 'Transitional Justice Genealogy' (n 8) 76; Andrieu, 'Civilizing Peacebuilding' (n 40) 541.

[105] African Peer Review Mechanism, Country Review Report of the Republic of Rwanda (June 2006) para 153 <https://www.eisa.org/aprm/pdf/Countries_Rwanda_APRM_Report.pdf> accessed 24 December 2024.

[106] Ereshnee Naidu, 'Symbolic Reparations and Reconciliation: Lessons from South Africa' (2012) 19 Buffalo Human Rights Law Review 251.

[107] Will Kymlicka, 'Transitional Justice, Federalism, and the Accommodation of Minority Nationalism' in Paige Arthur (ed), *Identities in Transition: Challenges for Transitional Justice in Divided Societies* (Cambridge University Press 2011) 304.

[108] Maddison and Shepherd, 'Peacebuilding and the Postcolonial Politics of Transitional Justice' (n 44) 268.

cultural identities may not easily align with a newly constructed national identity. Governments, especially in multi-ethnic States, often force subnational groups to adopt the dominant, majority culture, leading to the destruction of minority cultural identity.[109] Culture, through cultural heritage and cultural expressions, is also used to advance a singular cultural narrative post-conflict, which can serve as 'a source of ongoing cultural contestation' in post-conflict and divided societies.[110]

Among other things, a focus on building a uniform, national identity rejects the 'aspirations of difference' maintained by minorities and Indigenous Peoples.[111] It also chips away at the rich cultural diversity that is protected under international standard-setting.[112] Indeed, promoting a homogeneous identity as part of a nation-building strategy has the potential to ostracize and marginalize minority communities. By eroding sub-national cultural identities, such an approach can also risk further conflict.[113]

4.2 International (Western) justice

It is routinely noted that mainstream transitional justice is preoccupied with Western concepts and methods of justice.[114] The concept of justice in the dominant model has been overwhelmingly rooted in Western ideals often incompatible with the cultures, priorities, and worldviews of victims and transitional societies. Historically, a host of international professionals, NGOs, and donor networks in the West have been the primary influencers and implementers of transitional justice, rather than local populations and grassroots movements.[115] In turn, conventional strategies have tended to impose top-down,

[109] William Logan, 'Cultural Diversity, Cultural Heritage and Human Rights: Towards Heritage Management as Human Rights-Based Cultural Practice' (2012) 18(3) International Journal of Heritage Studies 231.

[110] *The Derry/Londonderry Report on Upholding the Human Right to Culture in Post-Conflict Societies* (Northern Ireland Human Rights Commission 2014).

[111] Damien Short, 'Reconciliation, Assimilation, and the Indigenous Peoples of Australia' (2003) 24(4) International Political Science Review 491, 506.

[112] CESCR, General Comment No 21, Right of Everyone to Take Part in Cultural Life (Art. 15, Para. 1a of the Covenant on Economic, Social and Cultural Rights), UN Doc E/C.12/GC/21 (December 2009) para 40.

[113] Logan, 'Cultural Diversity, Cultural Heritage and Human Rights' (n 109) 237.

[114] Nagy, 'Transitional Justice as Global Project' (n 4) 275–76; Khanyisela Moyo, 'Mimicry, Transitional Justice and the Land Question in Racially Divided Former Settler Colonies' (2015) 9 International Journal of Transitional Justice 70; Lundy and McGovern, 'Whose Justice?' (n 17) 99, 101.

[115] Gready and Robins, 'From Transitional to Transformative Justice' (n 63) 340; Dustin N Sharp, 'Addressing Dilemmas of the Global and the Local in Transitional Justice' (2014) 29 Emory International Law Review 71, 73.

Westernized, and paternalistic forms of transitional justice.[116] As the field globalized, these traditional approaches were replicated in successive transitional settings, often without sufficient consideration of the culturally specific particularities and needs of different populations.[117]

A central problem with transposing rote international approaches is the tendency to be unresponsive to the cultural values, traditions, and practices of the transitional society at issue. This has been evident in practice. In some cases, international criminal tribunals were placed far from actual sites of violence, largely staffed with international personnel, and unattuned to local customs and practices.[118] This diminished local ownership over the trials, ultimately resulting in prosecutions that were at best insensitive to local cultures and traditions, and at worst completely ignorant of them.[119] Other transitional justice mechanisms have been designed and implemented without adequate participation or consultation with victim communities and without incorporating their traditions, customs, and worldviews.[120] This has led to a perceived lack of legitimacy for modes of justice that advanced the ideals of Western societies in non-Western States or societies.[121]

International top-down approaches that fail to provide for local participation, agency, and ownership over justice processes are now routinely criticized in the literature.[122] The dominant model's predisposition towards Western ideals of justice has led scholars to label transitional justice as 'neocolonial',[123] 'colonizing',[124] and potentially falling prey to the same 'saviour/savage dynamic' that plagues the human rights field.[125] Despite these critiques, transitional

[116] Augustine SJ Park, 'Remembering the Children: Decolonizing Community-Based Restorative Justice for Indian Residential Schools' (2016) 19(4) Contemporary Justice Review 424, 427–28.

[117] Cavallaro and Albuja, 'The Lost Agenda' (n 2) 125.

[118] For example, the ICTY and the ICTR both barred nationals of those States from holding senior positions within the courts. Sharp, *Re-Thinking Transitional Justice for the 21st Century* (n 3) 45.

[119] With respect to the ICTR, Mutua contends that it 'orbited in space, suspended from political reality and removed from both the individual and the national psyches of the victims as well as the victors in the Rwanda conflict'. Mutua, 'What Is the Future of Transitional Justice?' (n 7) 6.

[120] Hobbs, 'Locating the Logic of Transitional Justice in Liberal Democracies' (n 73) 523.

[121] Rama Mani, 'Dilemmas of Expanding Transitional Justice, or Forging the Nexus Between Transitional Justice and Development' (2008) 2(3) International Journal of Transitional Justice 253, 257; Viaene and Brems, 'Transitional Justice and Cultural Contexts' (n 51) 201–02.

[122] See, eg, Sharp, 'Addressing Dilemmas of the Global and the Local in Transitional Justice' (n 116); Pierre Hazan, Rosalind Shaw, and Lars Waldorf (eds) *Localizing Transitional Justice: Interventions and Priorities after Mass Violence* (Stanford University Press 2020); Kieran McEvoy, 'Beyond Legalism' (n 52); Lundy and McGovern, 'Whose Justice?' (n 17).

[123] Abdullahi Ahmed An-Na'im, 'Editorial Note: From the Neocolonial "Transitional" to Indigenous Formations of Justice' (2013) 7 The International Journal of Transitional Justice 197.

[124] Stephanie Vielle, 'Transitional Justice: A Colonizing Field' (2012) 4(3) Amsterdam Law Forum 58

[125] Nagy, 'Transitional Justice as Global Project' (n 4) 275.

justice measures still tend to resort to Western modes of doing justice, even when promising a culturally appropriate justice response.

Local and Indigenous justice models are almost by default relegated as secondary solutions to dealing with violent and unjust legacies.[126] Not only does this fail to accommodate cultural diversity and cultural rights, but the wrongs targeted for redress are overwhelmingly civil and political rights violations. State governments and international elites still define most transitional justice agendas, often without sufficient consideration of what these communities need or desire of the process. This has led to a situation where international bodies, national governments, and other stakeholders determine what type of harm should be addressed and the modalities for doing so. Under the Western tradition, this often translates to an overriding emphasis on violations of civil and political rights, with little consideration paid to other forms of harm, including cultural rights violations.[127]

4.3 Legalistic justice

A further feature of dominant justice is the primacy placed on law and legal solutions to the dilemmas facing transitional societies.[128] The field's reliance on internationalized responses is partially attributable to an early preoccupation with international law and legalistic approaches more generally.[129] As originally envisioned, transitional justice was inherently legalistic.[130] Early transitional justice advocates (often lawyers) prioritized the legal tools seen as essential to holding former regimes accountable for past abuses, securing a democratic future, and ensuring compliance with international human rights standards. This is reflected in many of the initial definitions of transitional justice, which incorporated some legal or human rights law components.[131] These legalistic and rights-based understandings of justice took root and have been foregrounded ever since.[132]

[126] Sharp, *Re-Thinking Transitional Justice for the 21st Century* (n 3) 12; Bell and O'Rourke, 'Does Feminism Need a Theory of Transitional Justice?' (n 77) 25.

[127] Naomi Roht-Arriaza, 'Reparations and Economic, Social, and Cultural Rights' in Dustin N Sharp (ed), *Justice and Economic Violence in Transition* (Springer 2014) 110.

[128] Henry, 'From Reconciliation to Transitional Justice' (n 23) 207.

[129] McEvoy, 'Beyond Legalism' (n 52); Bell, 'Transitional Justice, Interdisciplinarity and the State of the "Field" or "Non-Field"' (n 54) 10.

[130] Lars Waldorf, 'Anticipating the Past: Transitional Justice and Socio-Economic Wrongs' (2012) 21(2) *Social and Legal Studies* 171, 179.

[131] Teitel, 'Transitional Justice Genealogy' (n 8) 69.

[132] Vielle, 'Transitional Justice: A Colonizing Field' (n 125) 58.

The influence of legalism on the field has significantly shaped the forms of justice pursued in transitional justice programming,[133] which have been described as 'difficult to disrupt'.[134] Among other things, it has impeded considerations of non-legal forms of justice that can better align with the cultural values, practices, and worldviews of disparate victim communities.[135] For instance, Canada's National Inquiry into Missing and Murdered Indigenous Women and Girls ('MMIWG Inquiry') has been critiqued for adopting a legalistic approach that relied too heavily upon formal hearings with witness testimony, as opposed to Indigenous laws and protocols. This arguably upheld the 'colonial status quo' of truth-seeking rather than radically transforming it in a culturally responsive way.[136] Many authors have thus rightly argued that the law needs to be decentred in transitional justice processes and have critiqued rights-based approaches for reinforcing colonial power structures.[137] Despite this, law continues to be the preferred justice response to confronting past large-scale harm.

4.4 Criminal justice

Closely related to the field's legalistic bent is a long-standing preoccupation with criminal justice. Transitional justice is commonly seen as tantamount to ensuring accountability for international crimes and criminal punishment is often prioritized as the best solution to large-scale wrongdoing.[138] Thus, criminal law has been a preferred justice option in the dominant model, which fully embraces the Western tradition of ensuring legal accountability for criminal wrongdoing.[139] Several decades after the Nuremberg and Tokyo trials, many still view justice for societies in transition primarily through the lens of criminal proceedings, where war criminals are put on trial for their heinous crimes.[140]

[133] Henry, 'From Reconciliation to Transitional Justice' (n 23) 212–14.

[134] Bell 'Transitional Justice, Interdisciplinarity and the State of the "Field" or "Non-Field"' (n 54) 22.

[135] Vielle, 'Transitional Justice: A Colonizing Field' (n 125) 63–65.

[136] Jenna Walsh, 'The National Inquiry into the Missing and Murdered Indigenous Women and Girls of Canada: A Probe in Peril' (2012) 8 Indigenous Law Bulletin 1, 7.

[137] Jeff Corntassel, 'Re-envisioning Resurgence: Indigenous Pathways to Decolonization and Sustainable Self-Determination' (2012) 1(1) Decolonization: Indigeneity, Education & Society 86, 92–93; Rosemary Nagy, 'The Scope and Bounds of Transitional Justice and the Canadian Truth and Reconciliation Commission' (2013) 7(1) International Journal of Transitional Justice 52, 53–54.

[138] Colleen Murphy, *The Conceptual Foundations of Transitional Justice* (Cambridge University Press 2017) 7.

[139] Henry, 'From Reconciliation to Transitional Justice' (n 23) 212; Wendy Lambourne, 'Transitional Justice and Peacebuilding after Mass Violence' (2009) 3(1) *International Journal of Transitional Justice* 28, 30.

[140] Henry, 'From Reconciliation to Transitional Justice' (n 23) 212.

This preoccupation strongly implies that anything short of courtroom justice is considered an inadequate response to large-scale human rights abuses.[141] As a result, many of the signature transitional justice mechanisms have been criminal courts in the form of ad hoc international criminal tribunals, hybrid criminal courts, and, most famously, the ICC. Many cultural rights violations, and particularly historical cultural wrongdoing, do not necessarily amount to international crimes or are excluded from implementing statutes of international and domestic judicial bodies. Thus, the dominant model's preoccupation with criminal justice complicates the redress of these specific violations.

4.5 Individual justice

The final characteristic of dominant justice that has historically marginalized cultural rights is the supreme emphasis placed on individual culpability, violations, and remedies. The primacy of individualism is another bias inherited from the parent field of human rights. Even today, several States still refuse to officially recognize collective human rights.[142] Thus, taking the lead from the field of human rights, transitional justice has prioritized naming and shaming individual perpetrators of mass violence against individual victims. This focus on individual accountability further elevated the legalistic and criminalistic approaches detailed above.

In the democratic transitions of the 1980s and 1990s, protecting individual rights was seen as the best way to respond to periods of political repression.[143] Stephanie Vielle comments that the mainstream liberal approach to transitional justice 'conceives of the individual as the basic and irreducible unit of society, and finds it difficult to accommodate practices that do not correspond with this view'.[144] On a theoretical level, scholars have often failed to consider approaches that diverge from the traditional individualistic frameworks embodied in the paradigmatic transitions.[145]

Accordingly, most transitional justice measures focus on violence against individuals rather than the collective and often intergenerational violence

[141] Sharp, *Re-Thinking Transitional Justice for the 21st Century* (n 3) 10.

[142] Alexandra Xanthaki, 'The UN Declaration on the Rights of Indigenous Peoples and Collective Rights: What's the Future for Indigenous Women?' in Stephen Allen and Alexandra Xanthaki (eds), *Reflections on the UN Declaration on the Rights of Indigenous Peoples* (Hart Publishing 2011) 414.

[143] Arthur, 'How Transitions Reshaped Human Rights' (n 9) 339.

[144] Vielle, 'Transitional Justice: A Colonizing Field' (n 125) 60.

[145] ibid.

perpetrated against groups, including through mass cultural wrongdoing.[146] For instance, truth commissions have traditionally assumed that individuals are the sole rights-bearers and thus only evaluated violations of individual human rights.[147] These bodies prioritize the culpability of individual actors, while the collective harm is overlooked.[148] This neglects not only the collective nature of various forms of cultural wrongdoing, but also collective remedies necessary for their redress.

5. Dominant Violence

Lastly, the dominant model embraces an exceedingly thin understanding of what types of violence are subject to transitional justice scrutiny.[149] In a March 2017 workshop amongst prominent transitional justice experts, Camilo Sanchez questioned the tendency of transitional justice to address only select forms of violence: 'Why do not all sorts of violence matter equally? Why do we get always stuck with some forms of violence, but not others?'[150] This was a comment on the dominant model's penchant for excluding certain forms of harm based on a deeply engrained preoccupation with what type of violence is worthy of attention and redress in transitional justice.

The transitional justice field privileges a limited set of civil and political rights violations, in the form of recent and egregious acts of physical violence, while neglecting many of the broader underlying injustices embedded in transitional societies.[151] This fixation on bodily integrity harms has excluded other, subtler but equally significant forms of violence from consistent consideration, including mass cultural harm. Inheriting the biases and hierarchies from the parent field of human rights, mainstream transitional justice relegates cultural rights violations as less grave, less justiciable, and less important for transitional societies.[152]

[146] Matsunaga, 'Two Faces of Transitional Justice' (n 61) 201.

[147] Deborah J Yashar, 'Indigenous Rights and Truth Commissions: Reflections for Discussion' in International Center for Transitional Justice, *Strengthening Indigenous Rights through Truth Commissions: A Practitioner's Resource* (ICTJ 2012) 7.

[148] César Rodríguez-Garavito and Yukyan Lam, 'Addressing Violations of Indigenous Peoples' Territory, Land, and Natural Resource Rights During Conflicts and Transitions' in ICTJ (ed), *Strengthening Indigenous Rights through Truth Commissions: A Practitioner's Resource* (ICTJ 2012) 19.

[149] Nagy, 'Transitional Justice as Global Project' (n 4) 284–86; Miller 'Effects of Invisibility' (n 4) 267.

[150] Laurel Fletcher and Harvey Weinstein, '"North-South" Dialogue: Bridging the Gap in Transitional Justice—Workshop Transcript' (2018) 36(2) Berkeley Journal of International Law 218, 238.

[151] Sharp, *Re-thinking Transitional Justice for the Twenty-First Century* (n 3) 20.

[152] ibid 37.

Historical violence, including colonial-era cultural harm, is also rarely engaged with in transitional justice and its enduring impacts and legacies on livelihoods and cultures are routinely underrecognized.[153] Recent and extraordinary bodily harm is foregrounded, while much of the everyday cultural harm that runs through societies is deemed a problem for development actors and long-term political reforms. This predominant focus on contemporary, discrete bodily integrity violations has worked to significantly limit the scope of transitional justice's application to equally devastating cultural wrongdoing.

5.1 Bodily integrity harm

It is often acknowledged that transitional justice has focused almost exclusively on acts of physical violence and violations of civil and political rights more generally.[154] These commonly include acts of genocide, mass killings, torture, forced disappearances, and sexual violence. These bodily integrity violations derive from acts of direct physical violence.[155] Judicial proceedings, truth commissions, reparations, and other measures in the transitional justice toolbox have traditionally prioritized the redress of these bodily integrity violations.[156] In turn, the common understanding of violence subject to transitional justice treatment has narrowly focused on this limited suite of harms.[157]

The early, signature transitional justice cases that helped legitimize the field focused almost exclusively on bodily integrity harms, and on civil and political rights more generally. For instance, Argentina's National Commission on the Disappearance of Persons was singularly centred on forced disappearances during the country's period of military rule.[158] While this narrow approach arguably made sense in the context of the conflict,[159] it also sidestepped other structural and cultural causes of the political violence experienced in

[153] Maddison and Shepherd, 'Peacebuilding and the Postcolonial Politics of Transitional Justice' (n 44) 254.

[154] Rubén Carranza, 'Plunder and Pain: Should Transitional Justice Engage with Corruption and Economic Crimes?' (2008) 2(3) The International Journal of Transitional Justice 310, 310; Miller, 'Effects of Invisibility' (n 4) 268; Ismael Muvingi, 'Sitting on Powder Kegs: Socioeconomic Rights in Transitional Societies' (2009) 3(2) International Journal of Transitional Justice 163, 166; Louise Arbour, 'Economic and Social Justice for Societies in Transition' (2007) 40 International Law and Politics 1, 4–5.

[155] Matthew Evans, 'Structural Violence, Socioeconomic Rights, and Transformative Justice' (2016) 15(1) Journal of Human Rights 1, 3–4.

[156] ICTJ, *Strengthening Indigenous Rights through Truth Commissions: A Practitioner's Resource* (2012) 1 <https://www.ictj.org/sites/default/files/ICTJ-Truth-Seeking-Indigenous-Rights-2012-English.pdf> accessed 24 December 2024.

[157] Sharp, 'Addressing Economic Violence in Times of Transition' (n 27) 792.

[158] Nunca Más (n 29).

[159] Sharp, *Re-Thinking Transitional Justice for the 21st Century* (n 3) 33.

the country.[160] In South Africa, the harm at the centre of apartheid was socio-economic violence against black South Africans propagated by institutionalized racial segregation. Despite this, the South African TRC narrowly defined victims as only those who suffered egregious bodily harm, at the same time sidelining ESC rights violations.[161] Critically, it also only acknowledged individual victims, ignoring the collective harm that was central to the system of apartheid.[162] For Mahmood Mamdani, the South African TRC's narrow focus on individual bodily integrity violations helped to 'dehistoricize and decontextualize the story of apartheid'.[163]

The Argentinian and South African cases are emblematic of the narrow approach to conceptualizing violence as bodily integrity harm in post-authoritarian and post-conflict environments. While the dominant model foregrounds these civil and political rights violations, it relegates violations of ESC rights, including many of the social injustices, institutional inequalities, and cultural wrongdoing that plague post-conflict and divided societies.[164] Bodily integrity violations fit comfortably within the scope of the dominant model, while forms of cultural harm (forced assimilation, prohibition of dress and customs, suppression of languages, restrictions on cultural practices, etc.) are seen as less egregious and less deserving of an extraordinary justice response.

The hierarchy of harm in transitional justice was also exemplified in some of the tepid responses to the landmark *Al Mahdi* verdict at the ICC, even among some of the most prominent human rights institutions. The Office of the Prosecutor at the ICC made a strategic decision to bring a single charge against Al Mahdi, namely the war crime of intentionally directing attacks against religious and historic buildings. The International Federation for Human Rights celebrated the conviction of Al Mahdi, but also remarked that 'a focus solely on cultural damage should not overshadow horrific violence against individuals'.[165] Likewise, Amnesty International noted that the positive development

160 Laplante, 'Transitional Justice and Peace Building' (n 31).

161 Truth and Reconciliation Commission of South Africa Report (1999) <https://www.justice.gov.za/trc/report/> accessed 24 December 2024.

162 Mahmood Mamdani, 'Amnesty or Impunity? A Preliminary Critique of the Report of the Truth and Reconciliation Commission of South Africa (TRC)' (2002) 32 (2) *Diacritics* 33, 45–46.

163 ibid 57.

164 See Gready and Robins, 'From Transitional to Transformative Justice' (n 63) 342.

165 FIDH, 'Mali: The Hearing of Al Mahdi before the ICC is a Victory, But Charges Must Be Expanded' (30 September 2015) <https://www.fidh.org/en/issues/international-justice/international-criminal-court-icc/mali-the-hearing-of-abou-tourab-before-the-icc-is-a-victory-but> accessed 1 February 2025.

'should not let us lose sight of the fact that hundreds of civilians were murdered, tortured and raped during the 2012 conflict in Mali'.[166]

This overriding emphasis on a narrow set of civil and political rights violations in transitional justice stems from four main factors. First, it derives from conceptualizing transitions as ones to either peace or liberal democracy. Adherence to the paradigmatic transitions has restricted the field's focus to what are perceived to be the most egregious abuses committed during prior periods of armed conflict or repression.[167] In these specific transitions, doing justice was equated with engaging with short-term political violence, rather than cultural abuses or structural violence. From the outset, this meant addressing serious individual violations of civil and political rights.[168] Under conventional transitional justice theory, engaging with these violations is seen as the best way to progress a society towards a more peaceful and democratic future. Because the political transition was the dominant lens through which transitional justice was initially theorized, civil and political rights violations have been foregrounded.

Second, conventional understandings of violence under the dominant model have also been heavily influenced by the field's privileging of criminal law and individual violations.[169] It is those acts that rise to the level of international crimes, most often acts of physical violence, that normally take precedence in transitional justice frameworks.[170] Yet, as discussed, many cultural rights violations do not constitute crimes under international criminal law. Relatedly, transitional justice has generally kept to addressing individual rights violations, without engaging with the structural and cultural injustices underpinning transitional societies.[171] This near exclusive focus on individual rights relegates other human rights abuses, including mass cultural wrongdoing.[172]

Third, transitional justice has been indelibly shaped by the field of human rights. Because of this, transitional justice theory has tended to inherit many of

166 Amnesty International, 'Landmark ICC Verdict against Al-Mahdi Must Be First Step to Broader Justice in Mali Conflict' (27 September 2016) <https://www.amnesty.org/en/latest/news/2016/09/landmark-icc-verdict-against-almahdi-must-be-first-step-to-broader-justice-in-mali-conflict-2/> accessed 1 February 2025.

167 Sharp, 'Addressing Economic Violence in Times of Transition' (n 27) 800.

168 Roger Duthie, 'Toward a Development-Sensitive Approach to Transitional Justice' (2008) 2(3) International Journal of Transitional Justice 292, 294–95.

169 Frank Haldemann and Rachelle Kouassi, 'Transitional Justice without Economic, Social and Cultural Rights?' in Eibe Riedel and others (eds), *Economic, Social, and Cultural Rights: Contemporary Issues and Challenges* (Oxford University Press 2014) 498.

170 Evans, 'Structural Violence, Socioeconomic Rights, and Transformative Justice' (n 155) 4.

171 Jennifer Balint and Julie Evans, 'Transitional Justice and Settler States', The Australian and New Zealand Critical Criminology Conference (2011) 3.

172 ICTJ, *Strengthening Indigenous Rights through Truth Commissions* (n 156) 1.

the limitations and biases that persist in the human rights discourse.[173] Within the broader human rights discipline, civil and political rights have long been elevated over ESC rights, with cultural rights in particular being the most neglected category of rights, often viewed as less important and less justiciable compared to all other rights categories.[174] This hierarchy is maintained by Western States, civil society, and technocrats, who still do not treat cultural rights with equal significance under international law.

During the genesis of transitional justice, civil and political rights were deemed real justiciable rights, whereas ESC rights were seen as mere aspirations.[175] Sharp observes that even the largest human rights organizations at the time were reluctant to recognize violations outside of civil and political rights.[176] As such, it was perhaps inevitable that transitional justice ideologies would inherit the biases and hierarchies from its parent field.[177] These prejudices have squarely carried over to transitional justice and have contributed to the invisibility of cultural rights.[178]

A hierarchy of suffering, favouring civil and political rights violations over ESC rights violations, has set the standard of violence to be confronted in transitional justice. Transitional justice policymakers are more likely to view bodily integrity violations or political repression as violative of human rights, rather than deep-seated racism, inequality, or cultural harm.[179] Mani suggests that this bias aligns with the Western liberal model of justice which 'tends to favour freedom and liberty over equality'.[180] Seemingly exceptional violations are prioritized, while the everyday harms are left on the margins.[181] Bodily integrity violations are not only treated as more important than other forms of harm, but more amenable to disposition through transitional justice. Carranza argues that 'civil and political rights violations are seen not only as justiciable but also as susceptible to being redressed through transitional justice' while other rights violations 'are considered non-justiciable and therefore better addressed

[173] Miller, 'Effects of Invisibility' (n 4) 268.

[174] Janusz Symonides, 'Cultural Rights: A Neglected Category of Human Rights' (1998) 50(158) International Social Science Journal 559.

[175] Amanda Cahill-Ripley, 'Foregrounding Socioeconomic Rights in Transitional Justice: Realising Justice for Violations of Economic and Social Rights' (2014) 32(2) Netherlands Quarterly of Human Rights 183, 188.

[176] Sharp, *Re-Thinking Transitional Justice for the 21st Century* (n 3).

[177] Miller, 'Effects of Invisibility' (n 4) 277; Carranza, 'Plunder and Pain' (n 154) 315; Haldemann and Kouassi, 'Transitional Justice without Economic, Social and Cultural Rights?' (n 169) 501.

[178] See Miller, 'Effects of Invisibility' (n 4).

[179] Sharp, 'Addressing Economic Violence in Times of Transition' (n 27) 801.

[180] Mani, *Beyond Retribution* (n 62) 151.

[181] Jennifer Balint, Julie Evans, and Nesam McMillan, 'Rethinking Transitional Justice, Redressing Indigenous Harm: A New Conceptual Approach' (2014) 8(2) International Journal of Transitional Justice 194, 199.

by a catch-all reference to development programs'.[182] Thus, the field of transitional justice squarely embraces the established hierarchy that positions civil and political rights above ESC rights.[183] While left unaddressed by the existing literature, such a rationale would be even more persuasive with respect to cultural rights— as the most neglected rights in the human rights arena.[184]

Lastly, a thin conception of violence is also attributable to the 'gross violations standard' under international law. In international fora, transitional justice is commonly discussed as only applicable to gross violations of human rights.[185] This is principally reflected in UN standard-setting. For instance, the UN Sub-Commission on Prevention of Discrimination and Protection of Minorities' study concerning the right to restitution, compensation, and rehabilitation for victims of gross violations of human rights and fundamental freedoms (the 'Van Boven Principles') was limited to 'gross violations of human rights and fundamental freedoms'.[186] Additionally, the Basic Principles and Guidelines on the Right to a Remedy and Reparation for Victims of Gross Violations of International Human Rights Law and Serious Violations of International Humanitarian Law ('Basic Principles and Guidelines') impose a duty on States to investigate 'gross violations of international human rights law'.[187] This 'gross violations' standard is reflected in a number of other transitional justice principles, scholarship, and practical mandates.[188]

There is no consensus on what constitutes gross violations, but Federico Lenzerini observes that it involves widespread and systematic violations as well as a particularly significant underlying value that is breached.[189] The Van Boven Principles suggest that the word 'gross' indicates the serious character of the violations, but it is also related to the type of human right that is being violated.[190] It states that gross violations should not be 'understood in a fixed

[182] Carranza, 'Plunder and Pain' (n 154) 315.
[183] Katie Boyle, 'Reconceptualising Socio-economic Rights in the Transitional Justice Discipline' (2016) 20(2) Law, Social Justice and Global Development Journal 1, 2–3.
[184] Symonides, 'Cultural Rights: A Neglected Category of Human Rights' (n 174).
[185] Nagy, 'Transitional Justice as Global Project' (n 4) 284.
[186] UN Sub-Commission on Prevention of Discrimination and Protection of Minorities, Study Concerning the Right to Restitution, Compensation and Rehabilitation for Victims of Gross Violations of Human Rights and Fundamental Freedoms: Final Report Submitted by Mr. Theo van Boven, Special Rapporteur, UN Doc E/CN.4/Sub.2/1993/8 (2 July 1993) para 8.
[187] UN General Assembly, Basic Principles and Guidelines on the Right to a Remedy and Reparation for Victims of Gross Violations of International Human Rights Law and Serious Violations of International Humanitarian Law, UN Doc A/RES/60/147 (21 March 2006) para 4.
[188] See, eg, UN Secretary-General, The Rule of Law and Transitional Justice in Conflict and Post-Conflict Societies (n 7); Guidance Note of the Secretary-General: United Nations Approach to Transitional Justice (10 March 2010).
[189] Federico Lenzerini, 'Reparations for Indigenous Peoples in International and Comparative Law: An Introduction' in Federico Lenzerini (ed), *Reparations for Indigenous Peoples in International and Comparative Law* (Oxford University Press 2008) 4–5.
[190] Van Boven Principles (n 187) para 8.

and exhaustive sense', but in the end only 'genocide; slavery and slavery-like practices; summary or arbitrary executions; torture and cruel, inhuman or degrading treatment or punishment; enforced disappearance; arbitrary and prolonged detention; deportation or forcible transfer of population; and systematic discrimination' fall under the category of 'gross violations'.[191] This narrow construction is further reflected in the Updated Set of Principles for the Protection and Promotion of Human Rights Through Action to Combat Impunity (the 'Joinet/Orentlicher Principles'), where gross violations of human rights are limited to bodily integrity violations, in the form of torture, enforced disappearances, or extra-legal, arbitrary, or summary executions.[192]

Thus, while not explicitly defined, 'gross violations' have been equated with serious and systematic violations of civil and political rights. At a minimum, it implies that gross human rights abuses do not encompass large-scale violations of cultural rights. In turn, most transitional justice mechanisms were designed to address these bodily integrity violations, which were deemed graver and more serious than cultural wrongdoing.[193] Undeniably, violations of cultural rights can constitute gross human rights violations; notwithstanding, they are not treated with the same sense of gravity as other violations in the field of transitional justice.

5.2 Recent violence

Dominant violence is not only limited by the character of the harm, but also temporally.[194] Transitional justice programming has almost exclusively engaged with contemporary violence or repressive events.[195] Conventional theory tends to focus on acts of violence immediately preceding the transition at issue. It follows that signature transitional justice mechanisms, such as judicial tribunals and truth commissions, have ordinarily failed to address historical harms either through jurisdictional limitations, restrictive mandates, or a lack of political will.[196]

[191] ibid. para 13.

[192] UN Commission on Human Rights, Report of the Independent Expert to Update the Set of Principles to Combat Impunity, UN Doc E/CN.4/2005/102/Add.1 (8 February 2005) principal 26(a).

[193] Andrieu, 'Civilizing Peacebuilding' (n 40) 543.

[194] Robyn Green, 'Unsettling Cures: Exploring the Limits of the Indian Residential School Settlement Agreement' (2012) 27(1) Canadian Journal of Law and Society 129, 140.

[195] Balint, Evans, and McMillan, 'Rethinking Transitional Justice, Redressing Indigenous Harm' (n 181) 201.

[196] ibid.

The exceedingly narrow temporal theorization of violence is most acute in the field's nonengagement with colonial wrongdoing. It is often repeated that transitional justice has failed to address colonial crimes and legacies.[197] From the very beginning, transitional justice was positioned as an extraordinary response to recent acts of mass physical violence, such as the horrors of the Holocaust. Initially, at least, no such extraordinary processes were instituted in response to the many atrocities that were commissioned by States actively participating in colonialism and/or the transatlantic slave trade. Sarah Maddison and Laura Shepherd have remarked on this disparity, claiming that the crimes of the Holocaust were not necessarily exceptional, noting that genocidal campaigns had also been carried out by settler colonial powers against Indigenous Peoples in the Americas, Oceania, and elsewhere.[198] Yet, these historical harms were not considered the proper subjects of transitional justice and corresponding mechanisms were not marshalled in response to large-scale abuses in these contexts until well into the twenty-first century.

Even when transitional justice measures have the flexibility to examine historical abuses, they rarely venture beyond contemporary violations that can be substantiated by individual witnesses, survivors, and written records.[199] Only a handful of mechanisms have sought to address historical harm dating back beyond recent memory.[200] Instead, most measures concentrate on recent instances of physical violence, even when the root causes of conflict can be traced much further back.[201] As a consequence, historical harms are not commonly included in the dominant conceptions of violence and their ongoing impacts are essentially elided by mainstream approaches.[202]

It is perhaps ironic that transitional justice, an enterprise focused on confronting past wrongdoing, is reticent to challenge historical violence and injustice, particularly those wrongs stemming from colonialism. The field's reluctance to robustly engage with the socio-economic and cultural legacies of colonialism and slavery can be juxtaposed against its embrace of recent

[197] See, eg, Bill Rolston and Fionnuala Ní Aoláin, 'Colonialism, Redress and Transitional Justice: Ireland and Beyond' (2018) 7 State Crime Journal 329; Theresa Mair, 'Transforming Transitional Justice to Address Colonial Crime: The Nama's and Herero's Claim for Justice for Germany's Colonial Genocide in Namibia' in Norman Weiß (ed), *Transitional* Justice: Theoretical and Practical Approaches (Verlag Potsdam 2022) 73.

[198] Maddison and Shepherd, 'Peacebuilding and the Postcolonial Politics of Transitional Justice' (n 44) 261.

[199] ICTJ, 'Strengthening Indigenous Rights through Truth Commissions' (n 156).

[200] See, eg, Report of the Truth and Justice Commission of Mauritius (November 2011) <https://www.usip.org/sites/default/files/ROL/TJC_Vol1.pdf> accessed 24 December 2024.

[201] Balint and Evans, 'Transitional Justice and Settler States' (n 171) 4.

[202] ibid.

bodily integrity violations.[203] In Rwanda, for example, there were a number of international and domestic prosecutions of suspected *génocidaires*, as well local Gacaca proceedings, all of which sought to address acts of genocide, mass killings, and sexual violence committed during the 1994 genocide against the Tutsi. The deeper roots of the genocide, including Belgian colonial policies that worked to destroy Rwandan culture and governance systems, were omitted from any consideration in formal transitional justice processes.[204]

Thus, for countries emerging from periods of authoritarian rule or armed conflict, the overwhelming focus has been on addressing recent civil and political rights violations without accounting for other underlying harms, such as the cultural harm brought about through colonialism. This is the case even when such harm is a significant root cause of the physical violence or repression. Historical harms, including their contemporary impacts on transitional societies, are seldom the target of transitional justice and it is rightly argued that the field is 'relatively presentist in its concerns'.[205]

A preoccupation with recent violence is also attributable to the nature of transitions under the dominant model. Linking transitional justice to a specific rupture point limits the temporal focus to a relatively brief period of time preceding the transition.[206] Not only does this work to exclude deep-seated structural and cultural injustices,[207] but it also bars consideration of historical abuses that remain in the collective memories of victims and which continue to shape their lives.[208] Dominant theory further assumes that a violent or repressive past can be neatly separated from a new peaceful or democratic future, but it overlooks the fact that historical harm is inextricably intertwined with contemporary forms of violence, which is particularly the case in the context of colonialism and settler colonialism.[209] This narrow temporal framework impedes the recognition and redress of historic harms, as well as their ongoing legacies which continue to exact various forms of cultural harm on post-conflict and divided societies.[210]

[203] Zinaida Miller, 'Transitional Justice, Race, and the United States', Just Security (30 June 2020) <https://www.justsecurity.org/71040/transitional-justice-race-and-the-united-states/> accessed 1 February 2025.

[204] Noam Schimmel, 'A Postcolonial Reflection on the Rwandan Genocide against the Tutsi and Statement of Solidarity with Its Survivors' (2021) 4(2) Journal of Victimology and Victim Justice 179.

[205] Balint, Evans, and McMillan, 'Rethinking Transitional Justice, Redressing Indigenous Harm' (n 181) 201.

[206] Sharp, 'Addressing Economic Violence in Times of Transition' (n 27) 800-01.

[207] Balint, Evans, and McMillan, 'Rethinking Transitional Justice, Redressing Indigenous Harm' (n 181) 201.

[208] ICTJ, 'Strengthening Indigenous Rights through Truth Commissions' (n 156) 1.

[209] Balint, Evans and McMillan, 'Rethinking Transitional Justice, Redressing Indigenous Harm' (n 181) 200–01.

[210] ibid.

On occasion, transitional justice mechanisms in established Western democracies have sought to engage with more distant wrongs, but many still tend to focus on relatively recent, discrete events, as opposed to broader colonial-era harms.[211] For example, Canada's TRC was saddled with a narrow directive and a finite timeframe in that it was only empowered to address a single aspect of the broader campaign of colonial violence against Indigenous Peoples in Canada—the Indian residential school system and its legacy.[212] The Indian residential school system was undoubtedly instrumental to the suffering of Indigenous Peoples in Canada, but it was only one component among many other violently anti-Indigenous policies and actions taken by the government. The TRC's narrow focus sidelined more distant forms of cultural harm, as well as their ongoing impacts on Indigenous communities. It also isolated the wrongs of the Indian residential schools from the rest of the colonial and contemporary violence experienced by Indigenous Peoples, which tacitly permitted the majority settler society to position this wrongdoing as a historical mistake, something that it could put firmly in the past.[213]

The example of Canada's TRC demonstrates the rather narrow temporal approach to violence which leaves unaddressed much of the colonial violence that occurred decades, if not centuries, earlier. By focusing solely on recent acts of violence, transitional justice tends to push historical wrongdoing, including mass cultural harm, outside the scope of the field.[214] Accordingly, the dominant conception of violence, both in its typology and its timing, has traditionally placed cultural abuses beyond the reach of transitional justice. This limits the potential of transitional justice and arguably stymies its capacity to be holistic and transformative.[215]

[211] Maddison and Shepherd, 'Peacebuilding and the Postcolonial Politics of Transitional Justice' (n 44) 254.

[212] 'Indian Residential Schools Settlement Agreement, Schedule N, Mandate for the Truth and Reconciliation Commission (8 May 2006) <http://www.residentialschoolsettlement.ca/settlement.html> accessed 27 July 2021.

[213] Jeff Corntassel, Chaw-win-is, and T'lakwadzi, 'Indigenous Storytelling, Truth-Telling, and Community Approaches to Reconciliation' (2009) 35 English Studies in Canada 137, 144–45.

[214] Maddison and Shepherd, 'Peacebuilding and the Postcolonial Politics of Transitional Justice' (n 44) 254.

[215] Report of the Special Rapporteur on the Promotion of Truth, Justice, Reparation and Guarantees of Non-Recurrence, Fabián Salvioli, Transitional Justice Measures and Addressing the Legacy of Gross Violations of Human Rights and International Humanitarian Law Committed in Colonial Contexts, UN Doc A/76/180 (19 July 2021) para 7.

3

(RE)THEORIZING THE RELATIONSHIP BETWEEN TRANSITIONAL JUSTICE AND CULTURAL RIGHTS

1. Introduction

Dogmatic and inflexible understandings of what constitutes a transition, justice, and violence under dominant transitional justice theory have hindered the field from consistently and adequately engaging with cultural rights. The transitional justice enterprise was clearly not designed or theorized as an avenue to confront or remedy mass cultural harm or to accommodate culturally diverse responses to difficult and violent legacies.[1] While mainstream theory is ill-suited to engage with cultural rights, this chapter argues that transitional justice can be retheorized in ways that empower it to respect, protect, and address cultural rights in more meaningful ways.

For much of the field's history, transitional justice has been chronically undertheorized.[2] Transitional justice practice arguably applies across too many disparate contexts for a general theory to apply and, indeed, the idea that it operates under a common theory has been repeatedly rejected.[3] As a result, there is no consensus on what should constitute transitional justice, its goals, its purpose, where it should be applied, or what issues are properly within its scope.[4] This has led to much contestation regarding the nature, character, and remit of the transitional justice project.

[1] See generally, Pablo de Greiff, 'Preface: On Making the Invisible Visible: The Role of Cultural Interventions in Transitional Justice Processes' in Clara Ramirez-Barat (ed), *Transitional Justice, Culture, and Society: Beyond Outreach* (Social Science Research Council 2014) 1.

[2] Susanne Buckley-Zistel and others, 'Transitional Justice Theories: An Introduction' in Susanne Buckley-Zistel and others (eds), *Transitional Justice Theories* (Routledge 2014) 2; Pablo De Greiff, 'Theorizing Transitional Justice' (2012) 51 Nomos 31, 32.

[3] Thomas Obel Hansen, 'Transitional Justice: Toward a Differentiated Theory' (2011) 13 *Oregon Review of International Law* 1; Buckley-Zistel and others, 'Transitional Justice Theories' (n 2) 4; Paige Arthur, 'How Transitions Reshaped Human Rights: A Conceptual History of Transitional Justice' (2009) 31 Human Rights Quarterly 321, 359.

[4] See Nicola Henry, 'From Reconciliation to Transitional Justice: The Contours of Redress Politics in Established Democracies' (2015) 9(2) International Journal of Transitional Justice 199.

Cultural Rights and Wrongs in Transitional Justice. Colin Luoma, Oxford University Press. © Colin Luoma 2025.
DOI: 10.1093/oso/9780198911371.003.0003

Significant theoretical work has been done to challenge the dominant theory closely associated with the field's origins. Transitional justice is now seemingly being rethought in nearly every conceivable context, including in connection with how it relates to local justice practices,[5] civil society,[6] specific countries,[7] minorities,[8] Indigenous Peoples,[9] women,[10] and the environment.[11] In much the same way, this book seeks to (re)theorize the relationship between transitional justice and culture. It challenges the many implicit biases, assumptions, and preoccupations in mainstream transitional justice theory and praxis that have contributed to the marginalization of cultural rights, and it rethinks the way culture relates to the enterprise more generally.[12]

This theoretical exercise involves a reimagining of the same three core concepts—transition, justice, and violence—whose narrow conventional interpretations have largely given rise to the field's marginalization of cultural rights. These concepts are interrogated and retheorized in order to weaken the conceptual barriers contributing to the general neglect of culture in the sphere of transitional justice. By interrogating each of these concepts in different ways, this book aims at arriving at alternative ways of thinking about and doing transitional justice in relation to culture and cultural rights. Indeed, unmoored from its initial conceptual boundaries, transitional justice has the flexibility to respect cultural rights, confront large-scale cultural rights violations, and empower cultural interventions in the wake of mass harm.

With respect to what constitutes a 'transition', settings demanding a transitional justice response can be expanded beyond situations where wars end or political regimes change. While there is arguably still value in retaining the idea of a bona fide 'transition' underpinning the application of transitional justice, these situations can be fairly broadened to include less obvious but

[5] Lars Waldorf, 'Mass Justice for Mass Atrocity: Rethinking Local Justice as Transitional Justice' (2006) 79(1) Temple Law Review 1.

[6] Paul Gready and Simon Robins, 'Rethinking Civil Society and Transitional Justice: Lessons from Social Movements and "New" Civil Society' (2017) 21(7) The International Journal of Human Rights 956.

[7] Joseph Geng Akech, 'Rethinking Transitional Justice in South Sudan: Critical Perspectives on Justice and Reconciliation' (2020) 14(3) International Journal of Transitional Justice 585.

[8] Farah Mihlar, 'Contending with Identity and Minority Rights in Transitional Justice: The Case Study of Sri Lanka' (2024) 28(1) The International Journal of Human Rights 1592.

[9] Jennifer Balint, Julie Evans, and Nesam Millan, 'Rethinking Transitional Justice, Redressing Indigenous Harm: A New Conceptual Approach' (2014) 8(2) International Journal of Transitional Justice 194.

[10] Christine Bell and Catherine O'Rourke, 'Does Feminism Need a Theory of Transitional Justice? An Introductory Essay' (2007) 1(1) The International Journal of Transitional Justice 25.

[11] Janine Natalya Clark, 'Re-thinking Memory and Transitional Justice: A Novel Application of Ecological Memory' (2021) 14(4) Memory Studies 695.

[12] This retheorization does not employ a specific theoretical framework, but instead draws from various perspectives, including postcolonial theory, settler-colonial theory, and liberalism.

still viable transitions in settings outside of the paradigmatic cases, including in established democracies with legacies of large-scale cultural harm. The singular endpoint of negative peace or liberal democracy does not align with the endemic and ongoing cultural harm present in many societies. This analysis focuses primarily on established democracies, considered ostensibly peaceful and democratic, but often with a history of cultural wrongdoing both at home and abroad.

Established democracies, undergoing admittedly less discernable, but equally significant, transitions, are plagued with many of the same issues as post-conflict societies seeking to grapple with unresolved legacies of large-scale harm. Conceiving of transitions more broadly to include, *inter alia*, moves from 'unjust to just relations' validates the application of transitional justice frameworks in established democracies, while also retaining the *raison d'être* of the transitional justice project.[13] Alternatively, adhering to a narrow understanding of a transition under dominant theory would effectively shield numerous countries from being forced to formally reckon with large-scale cultural wrongdoing.

Dominant justice modalities can also be rethought to align with the international standards that have developed to protect the diverse cultures, traditions, and worldviews of victims and survivors in transitional societies. Doing justice in periods of transition can and should increasingly deviate from top-down measures imposing individual accountability for mass bodily integrity crimes. A preoccupation with nation-building can be discarded in favour of a more nuanced approach that respects and fosters the cultural identities of victims and survivors in multicultural societies. Moreover, justice modalities can align with the diverse traditions and worldviews that exist in post-conflict and divided societies. This may at times present a rather uncomfortable deviation for many regarding how justice is typically understood under conventional Western thought.[14]

Lastly, dominant violence can be expanded to include large-scale cultural harm. Violence has long been theorized to extend beyond the physical.[15] Post-conflict and divided societies are afflicted by various and intersecting forms of violence, including direct, structural, and cultural forms. Thus, violence is

[13] Balint, Evans, and McMillan, 'Rethinking Transitional Justice, Redressing Indigenous Harm' (n 9) 214; Harry Hobbs, 'Locating the Logic of Transitional Justice in Liberal Democracies: Native Title in Australia' (2016) 39 University of New South Wales Law Journal 512, 513.

[14] Dustin N Sharp, *Rethinking Transitional Justice for the Twenty-First Century: Beyond the End of History* (Cambridge University Press 2018) xii.

[15] Johan Galtung, 'Violence, Peace, and Peace Research' (1969) 6(3) Journal of Peace Research 167.

pursued not only through physical means but also culturally, ranging from the slow erosion of traditional ways of life to more explicit, culturally genocidal policies. Thus, cultural wrongdoing represents its own form of violence deserving of the public reckoning traditionally reserved for mass bodily integrity crimes.

Violence in transitional justice can be retheorized to encompass a wide range of cultural harm, including the destruction of tangible cultural heritage and policies of cultural assimilation, among other forms of wrongdoing. This also includes historical cultural harm, as well as contemporary practices and policies which continue to destroy, denigrate, or diminish cultural heritage, systems, practices, and identities. This retheorization does not require a radical reimagining of the field's underlying principles and objectives; rather, it merely pushes the conceptual boundaries of transitional justice ever so slightly in furtherance of the enterprise being more flexible and responsive to the demands of a diverse set of victims in disparate settings.

2. Rethinking Dominant Transitions

Orthodox interpretations of what constitute a transition have worked to foreclose the application of transitional justice in many settings, despite the presence of large-scale past harm. While transitional justice mechanisms have migrated into diverse contexts, there is still resistance to fully embracing transitions outside of the paradigmatic cases.[16] This has been the case with most established democracies, especially in the West. This chapter focuses on rethinking 'transitions' in the context of established democracies because many of these States have a history of committing large-scale cultural harm through the violent policies and practices of colonialism, settler colonialism, and the transatlantic slave trade. And while some democracies have embraced the language and conceptual tools of transitional justice in their efforts to address such historical wrongdoing, less theoretical work has been done to understand how the concept of a 'transition' can be understood in these contexts.[17]

[16] Dustin N Sharp, 'Addressing Economic Violence in Times of Transition: Toward a Positive-Peace Paradigm for Transitional Justice' (2011) 35 Fordham International Law Journal 780, 782.

[17] Important and notable exceptions include Stephen Winter, 'Towards a Unified Theory of Transitional Justice' (2013) 7(2) International Journal of Transitional Justice 224; Joanna Quinn, 'Whither the Transition of Transitional Justice' (2014) 8 Interdisciplinary Journal of Human Rights Law 63; Hobbs, 'Locating the Logic of Transitional Justice' (n 13); Hansen, 'Transitional Justice: Toward a Differentiated Theory' (n 3).

In contrast to the repressive and war-torn nations ordinarily subject to transitional justice processes, most established democracies are perceived as relatively stable, democratic, and ostensibly 'peaceful'. As such, authors and practitioners often reject the idea that transitional justice should be theorized in these quintessentially 'non-transitional' arenas.[18] Padraig McAuliffe, for instance, calls historical reckoning in these contexts 'far removed from that of a paradigmatic transition'.[19] It follows that attempts to reckon with mass wrongdoing in these settings have traditionally been treated outside the parameters of transitional justice.[20] Instead, such endeavours are commonly framed as acts of State redress,[21] redress politics,[22] or symbolic justice.[23]

2.1 Debunking the myth of the peaceful and liberal Western democratic state

Even under mainstream transitional justice theory, established democracies can arguably be regarded as transitional cases. The prevailing assumption is that these countries have already reached the endpoint of the transitional justice process.[24] As ostensibly peaceful and liberal States, they are deemed to be in no need of the extraordinary justice reserved for post-authoritarian or post-conflict States.[25] Yet, it is highly questionable whether established democracies have actually reached the end goals posited under the field's dominant theory. While superficially liberal and democratic, some States still possess virulently colonial, racist, and/or anti-Indigenous characteristics that need to be transitioned away from to realize a just and peaceful society.[26]

[18] Padraig McAuliffe, 'Transitional Justice's Expanding Empire: Reasserting the Value of the Paradigmatic Transition' (2011) 2(2) Journal of Conflictology 32, 36; see also Glen Sean Coulthard, *Red Skin, White Masks: Rejecting the Colonial Politics of Recognition* (University of Minnesota Press 2014) 108.

[19] McAuliffe, 'Transitional Justice's Expanding Empire' (n 18) 36.

[20] Hansen, 'Transitional Justice: Toward a Differentiated Theory' (n 3) 44.

[21] Winter, 'Towards a Unified Theory of Transitional Justice' (n 17).

[22] Henry, 'From Reconciliation to Transitional Justice' (n 4).

[23] Wendy Lambourne, 'Transformative Justice, Reconciliation and Peacebuilding' in Susanne Buckley-Zistel and others (eds), *Transitional Justice Theories* (Routledge 2013) 46.

[24] Colin Luoma, 'Closing the Cultural Rights Gap in Transitional Justice: Developments from Canada's National Inquiry into Missing and Murdered Indigenous Women and Girls' (2021) 39(1) Netherlands Quarterly of Human Rights 30, 41.

[25] See Rosemary Nagy, 'Transitional Justice as Global Project: Critical Reflections' (2008) 29(2) Third World Quarterly 275, 276–77.

[26] Andrew Woolford, 'Transition and Transposition: Genocide, Land and the British Columbia Treaty Process' (2011) 4(2) New Proposals: Journal of Marxism and Interdisciplinary Inquiry 67.

Indeed, the supposed peaceful nature of established democracies has been strenuously challenged in the literature.[27] Settler-colonial theory, for instance, demonstrates how democratic settler-colonial nations promote the narrative of a peaceful and benevolent State, yet their ultimate objective is the elimination and ultimate replacement of Indigenous Peoples on their own lands.[28] The CANZUS (Canada, Australia, New Zealand, United States) nations are almost universally accepted as liberal democracies. However, Indigenous Peoples and minority groups in these countries do not necessarily experience the same democratic and liberal society that the majority populations may enjoy. These countries have an international reputation for being peaceful and democratic, but they are neither liberal or peaceful with respect to their relationship with subnational groups.[29] For example, Taiaiake Alfred argues that Canada, 'operating in the guise of a liberal democratic state[,] is, by design and culture, incapable of just and peaceful relations with Indigenous peoples'.[30] The illiberal nature of the CANZUS States' relationship with Indigenous Peoples is perhaps most starkly exemplified by the fact they were the only countries to affirmatively vote in 2007 against the adoption of the UN Declaration on the Rights of Indigenous Peoples ('UNDRIP'), the signature international instrument setting out the minimum standards for the survival, dignity, and well-being of Indigenous Peoples.[31]

Mainstream theory and dominant transitional justice practice promotes a false narrative, essentially that developing nations in the Global South are the ones with pervasive human rights abuses, while established Western democracies are models of peace and liberalism.[32] Thomas Hansen rightly suggests this 'implies a moral differentiation' where mainly poor nations 'are seen as having endemic problems with gross violations of human rights', while 'consolidated democracies, mainly in the West, are implied to be free of such mess'.[33] Even referring to States as 'established democracies', 'consolidated democracies', 'mature democracies', or 'liberal democracies' infers that they are somehow liberated from the repression and systemic human rights abuses that afflict

[27] See, eg, Paulette Regan, *Unsettling the Settler Within: Indian Residential Schools, Truth Telling, and Reconciliation in Canada* (UBC Press 2010).

[28] Alissa Macoun and Elizabeth Strakosch, 'The Ethical Demands of Settler Colonial Theory' (2013) 3(4) Settler Colonial Studies 426, 433.

[29] Quinn, 'Whither the Transition of Transitional Justice' (n 17) 69.

[30] Gerald Taiaiake Alfred, 'Restitution Is the Real Pathway to Justice for Indigenous Peoples,' in Gregory Younging and others (eds), *Response, Responsibility, and Renewal: Canada's Truth and Reconciliation Journey* (Aboriginal Healing Foundation 2009) 184.

[31] Sheryl R Lightfoot, *Global Indigenous Politics: A Subtle Revolution* (Routledge 2016) 4.

[32] Hobbs, 'Locating the Logic of Transitional Justice' (n 13) 522.

[33] Hansen, 'Transitional Justice: Toward a Differentiated Theory' (n 3) 46.

so-called illiberal States.[34] These labels work to evade discussions of both the colonial and contemporary violence perpetrated against Indigenous Peoples, racial and ethnic minorities, migrants, and other marginalized groups within these ostensibly 'peaceful' societies.

Authoritarian and conflict-affected nations do not hold a monopoly on the commission of serious and systemic human rights abuses—the very subject of most transitional justice endeavours.[35] Anne Orford pleads for the recognition of 'the everydayness and bureaucratisation of genocide and of massive human rights violations in the liberal democratic state'.[36] Zinaida Miller further observes that '[t]he assumption that stability is less dangerous, violent, or threatening than instability in an ostensibly liberal democratic state is just that: an assumption—and often one tilted towards the privileged.'[37] While established democracies are less associated with the repression and violence that characterized many of the early transitional justice contexts, large-scale wrongdoing remains pervasive, making them appropriate cases for transitional justice responses.[38] The seeming stability of many established democracies masks the fact that the status quo is often radically and inherently violent for certain groups, especially culturally. Cultural harm may not be readily apparent on the surface in the same manner as mass physical violence, but it can run through these societies in ways that have devastating and long-lasting impacts on victims. Reflexively denominating established democracies as liberal and benevolent societies ignores the nature of pervasive cultural wrongdoing that continues to negatively affect the lives of Indigenous Peoples, minorities, and other marginalized groups in a similarly repressive and violent manner as the paradigmatic transitional justice cases.[39]

A fundamental problem with rigidly adhering to a thin conception of what constitutes a transition is that many established democracies are not held to account for their own large-scale human rights abuses through transitional

[34] Jennifer Matsunaga, 'Two Faces of Transitional Justice: Theorizing the Incommensurability of Transitional Justice and Decolonization in Canada' (2016) 5(1) Decolonization: Indigeneity, Education & Society 24, 29.

[35] Fionnuala Ní Aoláin and Colm Campbell, 'The Paradox of Transition in Conflicted Democracies' (2005) 271 Human Rights Quarterly 172, 174; Matt James and Michelle Bonner, 'The Three R's of Seeking Transitional Justice: Reparation, Responsibility, and Reframing in Canada and Argentina' (2011) 2(3) The International Indigenous Policy Journal 1, 24.

[36] Anne Orford, 'Commissioning the Truth' (2006) 15(3) Columbia Journal of Gender and Law 851, 863.

[37] 'Zinaida Miller, 'Transitional Justice, Race and the United States', *Just Security* (30 June 2020) <https://www.justsecurity.org/71040/transitional-justice-race-and-the-united-states/.> accessed 24 December 2024.

[38] James and Bonner, 'The Three R's of Seeking Transitional Justice' (n 35).

[39] *See* Woolford, 'Transition and Transposition' (n 26) 69.

justice frameworks.[40] These abuses, dating back to colonial encounters, are well documented and many authors have consistently and strenuously disputed the myth that these established democracies are peaceful.[41] If large-scale human rights abuses are widespread in established democracies, but these societies are not treated as transitional, the field arguably confines itself to the violence, strife, and corruption of the Global South.[42] This lends credence to critiques that transitional justice is a neocolonial enterprise, essentially a tool used by powerful countries in the West to 'solve' the problems of poorer nations.[43] Indeed, many established democracies in the West tend to support post-conflict initiatives in the developing world, but balk at any notion that they themselves should be the subject of such extraordinary processes.[44] Thus, conventional approaches to where and when transitional justice applies are not only a creation of the West, but continue to be propagated by Western democracies in ways that shield them from scrutiny over their own wrongdoing.

2.2 Challenging dominant transitions in established democracies

Even if we assume that established democracies are both peaceful and liberal, the application of transitional justice in these States raises fundamental questions regarding the meaning of a transition.[45] In the first instance, it must be considered whether the terminology of a 'transition' should be discarded altogether. It is perhaps reasonable to believe that the field should no longer be understood as a process whereby societies must move from a defined origin to a desired endpoint. It is arguably more accurate to think about transitional justice as a way to work through difficult pasts, rather than linking it to specific change.[46] There is support for this among commentators, with Paige Arthur noting that some 'have dismissed the relevance of the word "transitional" as

[40] Henry, 'From Reconciliation to Transitional Justice' (n 4) 215.
[41] For a discussion on the 'peacemaker myth' in Canada, see generally Regan, *Unsettling the Settler Within* (n 27).
[42] Nagy, 'Transitional Justice as Global Project' (n 25) 275.
[43] Abdullahi Ahmed An-Na'im, 'Editorial Note: From the Neocolonial Transitional to Indigenous Formations of Justice' (2013) 7 International Journal of Transitional Justice 197.
[44] Balint, Evans, and McMillan, 'Rethinking Transitional Justice, Redressing Indigenous Harm' (n 9) 195.
[45] Sharp, *Re-Thinking Transitional Justice for the 21st Century* (n 14) 86.
[46] Frank Haldemann and Rachelle Kouassi, 'Transitional Justice without Economic, Social and Cultural Rights?' in Eibe Riedel and others (eds), *Economic, Social, and Cultural Rights: Contemporary Issues and Challenges* (Oxford University Press 2014) 500.

a kind of syntactical error'.[47] Christine Bell, for one, advocates for 'relabelling' the concept of transitional justice as 'contending with the past' to more appropriately describe the breadth and scope of the field.[48]

I suggest there is still some value in retaining the transitional concept as a differentiating factor between transitional and ordinary justice, even in contexts outside the paradigmatic cases.[49] Conceptualizing the field around a transition benefits from linking the tools and processes developed during its formation to the disparate contexts in which transitional justice mechanisms now operate. Further, on a practical level, experience has shown that transitional justice measures are less impactful when implemented in societies lacking the political will to genuinely reckon with and move beyond periods of large-scale human rights abuses.[50] At the same time, this does not rationalize overly restrictive interpretations of what constitutes a transition, which are especially problematic as transitional justice mechanisms have migrated into diverse settings.[51]

It is worth noting that the goal of a clean and successful transition envisioned in mainstream theory is seldom realized in practice. The transitional terminology is quite optimistic in that it assumes that societies will ultimately achieve a better, more peaceful, and more liberal future.[52] However, this is rarely the case; or, at a minimum, transitions to these desired destinations are more commonly conditional or incomplete.[53] Dustin Sharp observes that a 'fundamental problem with the historic and narrow conception of transitions is that it is simply empirically inaccurate'.[54] Thus, the idea of a 'transition' being either towards liberal democracy or peace has rarely lived up to the conceptual constraints imposed on the field.

Moreover, liberal democracy, typically viewed as an unqualified good, has actually been the source of harm in some contexts.[55] The establishment of

[47] Arthur, 'How Transitions Reshaped Human Rights' (n 3) 325; Marcos Zunino, *Justice Framed a Genealogy of Transitional Justice* (Cambridge University Press 2019) 4.

[48] Christine Bell, 'The Fabric of Transitional Justice: Binding Local and Global Political Settlements' University of Edinburgh School of Law, Research Paper Series No 2016/22 (2016) 19 <https://www.politicalsettlements.org/wp-content/uploads/2016/10/Bell-Transitional-Justice-Ch-1-2016.pdf> accessed 24 December 2024.

[49] Sarah Maddison and Laura Shepherd, 'Peacebuilding and the Postcolonial Politics of Transitional Justice' (2014) 2 Peacebuilding 253, 259.

[50] See, eg, Gabrielle Lynch, *Performances of Injustice: The Politics of Truth, Justice and Reconciliation in Kenya* (Cambridge University Press 2018).

[51] Hansen, 'Transitional Justice: Toward a Differentiated Theory' (n 3) 47.

[52] Kora Andrieu, 'Transitional Justice: A New Discipline in Human Rights' Online Encyclopedia of Mass Violence (2010) 3.

[53] Hansen, 'Transitional Justice: Toward a Differentiated Theory' (n 3) 4–5.

[54] Sharp, *Re-Thinking Transitional Justice for the 21st Century* (n 14) 78–79.

[55] Woolford, 'Transition and Transposition' (n 26) 69–70.

liberal democracy in settler-colonial States, for example, has its foundations in the genocide and mass dispossession of Indigenous Peoples and, in some countries, was built on the backs of enslaved African people.[56] Therefore, democratization is not always the desired endpoint of a transitional process, but arguably the origin of violence that a society needs to move past.[57] More generally, the liberal democracy model assumes that distinct cultural groups will, among other things, eventually assimilate into wider society to be treated equally with other citizens of the liberal State.[58] This is fundamentally at odds with a cultural rights-based approach.

2.3 Reconceptualizing transitions in established democracies

Sceptics of treating established democracies as transitional argue that there is a risk to expanding the concept of transition beyond the paradigmatic cases.[59] Even staunch supporters of more robust forms of transitional justice acknowledge the inherent difficulty in labelling efforts to address historical injustices in established democracies as transitional.[60] The concern is that an overly expanded theorization of what constitutes a transition would discredit the entire project, rendering it 'conceptually barren'.[61] These critics contend that transitional justice does not operate in established democracies because no transition is actually taking place.[62]

McAuliffe, in particular, cogently advocates for the retention of an orthodox conception of transition in the field.[63] He argues that the efficacy of transitional justice measures can be best evaluated within the context of the paradigmatic transitions and maintains that labelling certain contexts transitional, such as established democracies, is a 'convenient fiction' and one that 'risks conceptual incoherence'.[64] He distinguishes between the paradigmatic cases of transitional justice and the mere use of transitional justice mechanisms in settings outside of post-conflict and post-authoritarian settings.[65] Instead of extending

[56] Maddison and Shepherd, 'Peacebuilding and the Postcolonial Politics of Transitional Justice' (n 49) 265.
[57] ibid.
[58] Alfred, 'Restitution Is the Real Pathway to Justice for Indigenous Peoples' (n 30) 184–85.
[59] Padraig McAuliffe, 'Transitional Justice's Expanding Empire' (n 18); Priscilla B Hayner, *Unspeakable Truths: Transitional Justice and the Challenge of Truth Commissions* (2nd edn, Routledge 2010) 17; Nagy, 'Transitional Justice as Global Project' (n 25) 281.
[60] Nagy, 'Transitional Justice as Global Project' (n 25) 281.
[61] Hobbs, 'Locating the Logic of Transitional Justice' (n 13) 526.
[62] See Coulthard, *Red Skin, White Masks* (n 18) 108.
[63] McAuliffe, 'Transitional Justice's Expanding Empire' (n 18).
[64] ibid 33, 40.
[65] ibid 33–34.

the theoretical apparatus of transitional justice to what McAuliffe deems 'non-transitional circumstances', he suggests treating such 'humanitarian projects' separately from the mechanisms employed in dominant practice.[66]

In distinguishing established democracies from the paradigmatic cases, McAuliffe suggests that problems faced by established democracies are 'less intractable', in part because there are 'decades between the wrongdoing and the application of [transitional justice].'[67] Such a strict temporal outlook, however, ignores the ongoing nature of violence in many established democracies. A central tenet of settler-colonial theory, for example, is that settler colonialism is a 'structure', not an 'event'.[68] The colonial invasion occurred at some fixed time in the past, but settler colonialism continues to manifest contemporary harms into the present day.[69] In these contexts, such harms cannot be easily relegated to distant wrongdoing because the systems and structures that sustain such violence continue unabated, exerting violence day after day. Additionally, centuries after the arrival of colonial powers, the relationship between many established Western democracies and Indigenous Peoples remains fractured and volatile, suggesting a level of intractability on par with the field's paradigmatic transitions.

In traditional postcolonial contexts, colonial systems and structures also remain long after formal decolonization, recreating colonial harms.[70] Postcolonial theorist Edward Said emphasized that colonial powers impose their own language and culture, while also using culture to exoticize and denigrate the culture of the colonized.[71] Even after decolonization, the dominance of colonial languages, knowledge systems, and cultural norms often persists, marginalizing the culture and heritage of the former colonies. This cultural hegemony does not disappear the moment colonial rule is brought to a halt, in a neat and simplistic way. This calls into question the neat temporal distinction between a repressive, violent past and a liberal, peaceful future in the postcolonial context.

Glen Coulthard identifies a related risk to applying the 'transitional label' to established democracies. He argues that in established democracies, there is 'no clear or formal transition from an authoritarian past to a democratic

[66] ibid 40.
[67] ibid 36.
[68] Patrick Wolfe, 'Settler Colonialism and the Elimination of the Native' (2006) 8(4) Journal of Genocide Research 387, 388.
[69] Elisabeth Paquette, 'Reconciliation and Cultural Genocide: A Critique of Liberal Multicultural Strategies of Innocence' (2020) 35(1) Hypatia 143, 145.
[70] Aníbal Quijano, 'Coloniality and Modernity/Rationality' (2007) 21(2) Cultural Studies 168, 170.
[71] Edward Said, *Orientalism* (Routledge and Kegan Paul 1978).

present', and thus a transition must be manufactured. This has the effect of allocating wrongdoing to the 'dust bins of history' despite the presence of ongoing structural and cultural violence.[72] Coulthard thus suggests that this 'conceptual revision' is necessary 'to apply transitional justice mechanisms to quintessentially nontransitional circumstances'.[73]

From a semantical perspective, however, a transition does not dictate a specific origin, change, or endpoint.[74] This is supported by the UN's definition, which describes transitional justice without tying it to an identifiable transition.[75] At the same time, the conceptual expansion of what constitutes a transition should not be considered an unrestrained exercise. If no transition is present in a society, then by definition it should not be analysed through the lens of transitional justice.[76] Admittedly, the transitions at issue in post-conflict or post-authoritarian societies are more obvious, even if uncertain.[77] Established democracies ordinarily do not experience an obvious rupture point akin to the termination of conflict or a political regime change. There is no clean or obvious break with the past, where a 'new dawn' can be realized.[78]

However, such a remarkable break with the past rarely exists even in the paradigmatic cases. Pablo De Grieff remarks that 'there is no such thing as a radical new beginning'.[79] A transition in established democracies does not need to be a complete departure from past wrongdoing, just as paradigmatic transitions have not been complete departures from authoritarian rule or armed conflict. In this vein, Stephen Winter contends there are few 'posttransitional utopias'.[80] Instead, transitions can be rightly understood as slight but perceptible departures from the past.[81] Instead of discarding established democracies as less than ideal cases for transitional justice, this book agrees with Sharp that the concept of a transition needs to be reconceptualized to 'capture[] the complex realities of an expanding field'.[82] Broadening our understanding of a transition, tailored to specific transitional contexts, does not risk conceptual

72 Coulthard, *Red Skin, White Masks* (n 18) 108.
73 ibid.
74 Dustin N Sharp, 'Emancipating Transitional Justice from the Bonds of the Paradigmatic Transition' (2015) 9(1) International Journal of Transitional Justice 150, 155.
75 UN Secretary-General, The Rule of Law and Transitional Justice in Conflict and Post-Conflict Societies, UN Doc S/2004/616 (23 August 2004) para 8.
76 Quinn, 'Whither the Transition of Transitional Justice' (n 17) 67.
77 ibid.
78 Balint, Evans, and McMillan, 'Rethinking Transitional Justice, Redressing Indigenous Harm' (n 9) 200.
79 Pablo de Greiff, 'Transitional Justice and Development' in Bruce Currie-Alder and others (eds), *International Development: Ideas, Experience & Prospects* (Oxford University Press 2014) 412–13.
80 Winter, 'Towards a Unified Theory of Transitional Justice' (n 17) 227.
81 Hobbs, 'Locating the Logic of Transitional Justice' (n 13) 521.
82 Sharp, 'Emancipating Transitional Justice' (n 74) 157.

coherence unless we remain dogmatically moored to the narrow transitions of the paradigmatic cases.[83]

Some scholars have begun to articulate alternative conceptions of what could constitute a 'transition' in the context of established democracies. Winter contends that transitional justice can take place in these States assuming there is a 'radical change' signifying a transition.[84] Using the Waitangi process in New Zealand as evidence of a genuine transition, Winter argues that such a move constitutes the 'normative shift' that justifies a transitional response.[85] Relying on the same 'normative shift' standard, Harry Hobbs argues that a transition can be found in 'the gradual development of an Indigenous rights consciousness among non-Indigenous Australian society'.[86] Other authors analysing dilemmas in established democracies have reformulated transitions as encompassing 'transformative structural political changes',[87] 'the process of deepening substantive democracy'[88] or shifts from 'unjust relations to just relations'.[89]

One viable way to encourage and enable further engagement with cultural rights is to conceive of transitions in established democracies as gradual but perceptible shifts away from unjust relationships (between the State and subnational groups within it, or between the State and its former colonies) and towards a more just relationship with these constituencies. These unjust relationships cause severe divisions within States and are the source of harm, animosity, and conflict between former colonial powers and postcolonial societies.[90] Broadening our understanding of a transition to include meaningful progress to more just relations (among other retheorizations) can support a transitional response in established democracies without rendering the term 'transitional' meaningless.

Under this theorization, a discernable normative shift in how a State approaches its relationship with subnational groups or its former colonies is sufficiently transitional, even if that change is gradual and invariably incomplete. Whether any given transition is likely to be realized is also not dispositive of the conceptual application of the transitional justice lens. Because all

[83] ibid 157–59.
[84] Winter, 'Towards a Unified Theory of Transitional Justice' (n 17) 226.
[85] ibid 230.
[86] Hobbs, 'Locating the Logic of Transitional Justice' (n 13) 521.
[87] Maddison and Shepherd, 'Peacebuilding and the Postcolonial Politics of Transitional Justice' (n 49) 269.
[88] Hobbs, 'Locating the Logic of Transitional Justice' (n 13) 513.
[89] Balint, Evans, and McMillan, 'Rethinking Transitional Justice, Redressing Indigenous Harm' (n 9) 214.
[90] ibid.

transitions are protracted and uncertain, transitional justice frameworks can be rightly invoked in States that are ostensibly peaceful and liberal, but which may be undergoing normative transitions with respect to their history of cultural wrongdoing.[91] While arguably stretching the limits of the concept, such transitions can be understood as gradual, with incremental progress occurring over a long period of time, without defeating the idea.[92]

It follows that we should not uncritically denominate established democracies as some sort of 'non-transitional finished product' incapable of undergoing a substantive transition, even if they are treated as peaceful and stable.[93] This theorization is buttressed by the fact that, in practice, the field has already started to move beyond a strict reliance on the paradigmatic transitions.—This generally aligns with what Joanna Quinn describes as a 'definitional creep' regarding transitional justice characterized by a 'loosening of a once narrow definition'.[94] Accordingly, the field has already started to show a willingness to embrace broader and more flexible conceptions of transitions justifying an extraordinary justice response. This has the potential to bring a greater range of cultural wrongdoing into the remit of transitional justice initiatives.

3. Rethinking Dominant Justice

Mainstream transitional justice theory promotes an exceedingly narrow conception of justice which hinders a meaningful engagement with cultural rights. Justice under the dominant model is characterized by an overriding focus on nation-building and Western ideals of justice that are overwhelmingly legalistic, criminalizing, and individualistic. The field's bias towards these justice characteristics has largely dictated how transitional justice programming has been designed and implemented across the world.

Dominant justice can be challenged and rethought in ways that specifically empower transitional justice to more adequately address, incorporate, and respect cultural rights. There has been no shortage of theoretical work interrogating the concept of 'justice', reaching back to some of the earliest philosophers.[95] Modern seminal work from political philosophers has theorized

[91] Even paradigmatic transitions, such as the Argentinian case, took decades to be realized. Sharp, *Re-Thinking Transitional Justice for the 21st Century* (n 14) 84–85.

[92] See Ní Aoláin and Campbell, 'The Paradox of Transition in Conflicted Democracies' (n 35).

[93] Matsunaga, 'Two Faces of Transitional Justice' (n 34) 29.

[94] Quinn, 'Whither the Transition of Transitional Justice' (n 17) 66–67.

[95] Rama Mani notes that '[j]ustice is a universal concept that has been debated for millennia by political thinkers and philosophers around the world'. Rama Mani, *Beyond Retribution: Seeking Justice in the Shadows of War* (Polity 2002) 4.

justice around 'fairness'[96] or on the basis of 'entitlements'.[97] These understandings of justice diverge significantly, but they both embrace the importance of individual rights and liberties. These theorizations can be quite incompatible in some non-Western societies, where group membership and solidarity can take precedence over individual liberties.[98]

Justice has also long been theorized outside the strict confines of law and retributive measures, including in the transitional justice field.[99] The narrow focus of early transitional justice mechanisms and thinking has been challenged in ways that have advanced different conceptions of justice, including restorative justice, distributive justice, and transformative justice. This book does not contribute to the philosophical debates around the meaning of justice. Rather, it merely seeks to illustrate a certain level of theoretical flexibility in the concept that enables transitional justice to move beyond the conventional limits, biases, and preoccupations that have largely thwarted a serious engagement with cultural rights. These conceptual barriers have, in the words of Rama Mani, caused justice to be 'addressed in a skewed, partial and piecemeal manner'.[100] Notwithstanding, justice in post-conflict and divided societies can and should increasingly be understood as inclusive, local, cultural, and collective, and thus more amenable to robust interaction with cultural rights.

3.1 Inclusive justice

The nation-building ambitions at the heart of mainstream transitional justice theory can be particularly detrimental for the cultural rights of minorities and Indigenous Peoples within a transitional society. Transitional justice measures tend to focus on solidifying the legitimacy of the State rather than empowering communities themselves.[101] These subnational groups, however, often have little interest in legitimizing the State, including its ongoing structures of colonialism or oppression.[102] In this manner, the rebuilding of societies in

[96] John Rawls, *A Theory of Justice* (Harvard University Press 1971).
[97] Robert Nozick, *Anarchy, State and Utopia* (Blackwell 1794).
[98] Mani, *Beyond Retribution* (n 95) 48.
[99] Erin Baines, 'Spirits and Social Reconstruction after Mass Violence: Rethinking Transitional Justice' (2010) 190 (436) *African Affairs* 409, 415.
[100] Mani, *Beyond Retribution* (n 95) 4.
[101] Courtney Jung, 'Canada and the Legacy of the Indian Residential Schools: Transitional Justice for Indigenous Peoples in a Non-Transitional Society' in Paige Arthur (ed), *Identities in Transition: Challenges for Transitional Justice in Divided* Societies (Cambridge University Press 2010) 241.
[102] See Coulthard, *Red Skin, White Masks* (n 18) 106–07.

transitional justice can at times obscure rather than redress the harm at the centre of conflict and division.

One of the central problems with the nation-building function of transitional justice is that it is only effective if the State promotes a national identity inclusive of all groups within it.[103] However, the overriding goal of national unity often falls short of accounting for the rights of victims and survivors to maintain their distinct cultural identities.[104] Mono-national approaches can be at odds with the lived experiences of victims who suffer severe wrongdoing at the hands of the State.[105] This is most glaring in the reconciliation frameworks that have come to prominence in transitional justice practice and discourse, especially in established democracies.[106] There is a significant body of literature dissecting the concept of reconciliation as a goal of transitional justice, including a significant amount of scholarship focusing on the incompatibility between the reconciliation concept and the inherent rights and worldviews of Indigenous Peoples.[107] Reconciliation discourses and policies, in particular, jeopardize the ability to effectuate justice because the reconciliation paradigm is premised on legitimizing the State, often itself the driver of the underlying harm.[108] Reconciliation projects can also unintentionally reinforce assimilationist agendas that are antithetical to the exercise and realization of cultural rights. For instance, Damien Short contends that in Australia, reconciliation

[103] Will Kymlicka, 'Transitional Justice, Federalism, and the Accommodation of Minority Nationalism' in Paige Arthur (ed) *Identities in Transition: Challenges for Transitional Justice in Divided Societies* (2011) 304.

[104] Damien Short, 'Reconciliation, Assimilation, and the Indigenous Peoples of Australia' (2003) 24(4) *International Political Science Review* 491, 496; Matsunaga, 'Two Faces of Transitional Justice' (n 34) 30.

[105] International Center for Transitional Justice, 'Strengthening Indigenous Rights through Truth Commissions: A Practitioner's Resource' (2012) <https://www.ictj.org/sites/default/files/ICTJ-Truth-Seeking-Indigenous-Rights-2012-English.pdf> accessed 1 February 2025.

[106] Kyle Powys Whyte, 'On Resilient Parasitisms, or Why I'm Skeptical of Indigenous/Settler Reconciliation' (2018) 14(2) Journal of Global Ethics 277, 280.

[107] See, eg, Sarah Maddison and others (eds), *The Limits of Settler Colonial Reconciliation Non-Indigenous People and the Responsibility to Engage* (Springer 2018); Rauna Kuokkanen, 'Reconciliation as a Threat or Structural Change? The Truth and Reconciliation Process and Settler Colonial Policy Making in Finland' (2020) 21 Human Rights Review 293; Esme G Murdock, 'Unsettling Reconciliation: Decolonial Methods for Transforming Social-Ecological Systems' (2018) 27 Environmental Values 513; Short, 'Reconciliation, Assimilation, and the Indigenous Peoples of Australia' (n 104); Deborah McGregor, 'Reconciliation and Environmental Justice' (2018) 14(2) Journal of Global Ethics 222; Henry, 'From Reconciliation to Transitional Justice' (n 4); Dirk Moses, 'Official Apologies, Reconciliation, and Settler Colonialism: Australian Indigenous Alterity and Political Agency' (2011) 15(2) Citizenship Studies 145; Rosemary Nagy, 'Truth, Reconciliation and Settler Denial: Specifying the Canada–South Africa Analogy' (2012) 13(3) Human Rights Review 349; Jeff Corntassel, Chaw-win-is, and T'lakwadzi, 'Indigenous Storytelling, Truth-Telling, and Community Approaches to Reconciliation' (2009) 35 English Studies in Canada 137.

[108] Balint, Evans and McMillan, 'Rethinking Transitional Justice, Redressing Indigenous Harm' (n 9) 200–01.

processes have not accommodated 'indigenous aspirations of difference'.[109] When transitional justice policies seek to strengthen the dominant national identity, they risk alienating the separate and often vulnerable cultural identities of subnational groups.[110]

While reconciliation does not have an agreed-upon definition,[111] it is often conceived as possessing an element of restoring relationships.[112] When applied to most postcolonial and settler-colonial contexts, reconciliation projects erroneously assume that an amicable or friendly time period existed sometime in the past.[113] However, relations between the colonizer and the colonized have been anything but amicable at any time in the past. Instead, these relations are characterized by genocide, land theft, massive resource extraction, coercion, broken promises, forced assimilation, cultural imperialism, and institutional abuse, leaving a long trail of victims across multiple generations.[114] Courtney Jung observes this in the settler-colonial context by noting that '[a]s we look to the past, there does not seem to be a moment in which settler-Indigenous relations were such that they might serve as a model for a just future'.[115]

To be rights-respecting, transitional justice must deviate from its preoccupation with nation-building and move towards more inclusive forms of justice that respect the needs of victims and survivors to exist together peacefully, but also accommodate a base level of cultural separation in certain cases. At a minimum, nation-building should not be pursued if it excludes, diminishes, or marginalizes cultural identities.[116] Much value is rightly placed on respecting and protecting cultural identities, in part because they give individuals and communities a sense of belonging. This sense of belonging is, in turn, closely connected to human dignity, which constitutes the premise behind the entire theory of all human rights.[117] This is also key to ensuring the non-recurrence of violations.

[109] Short, 'Reconciliation, Assimilation, and the Indigenous Peoples of Australia' (n 104) 506.

[110] Kymlicka, 'Transitional Justice, Federalism, and the Accommodation of Minority Nationalism' (n 103) 304.

[111] Brandon Hamber and Gráinne Kelly, 'Beyond Coexistence: Towards a Working Definition of Reconciliation' in Joanna R Quinn (ed), Reconciliation(s): Transitional Justice in Postconflict Societies (McGill-Queen's University Press 2009): 286–310.

[112] Linda Radzik and Colleen Murphy, 'Reconciliation' in Edward N. Zalta and Uri Nodelman (eds) *Stanford Encyclopedia of Philosophy* (2003).

[113] Some scholars suggest the use of the term 'conciliation' in the context where just and peaceful relations did not exist in some previous time period: ibid.

[114] Courtney Jung, 'Reconciliation: Six Reasons to Worry' (2018) 14(2) Journal of Global Ethics 252, 253.

[115] ibid.

[116] ICTJ, 'Strengthening Indigenous Rights through Truth Commissions' (n 105).

[117] Yvonne Donders, *Towards a Right to Cultural Identity?* (Intersentia 2002).

3.2 Bottom-up justice

Justice can be reconceptualized to accommodate local ownership, governance, and control over transitional justice policy and mechanisms. Top-down international justice modalities have largely proven ineffective and are routinely identified as a primary reason why transitional justice measures often fail to be transformative. Fortunately, the field has already begun to reach beyond this orthodox understanding of justice. A 'focus on the local' is now a repeated mantra in the field.[118] At least rhetorically, there is a clear shift away from 'checklist' or 'blueprint' forms of justice and towards increasingly understanding and prioritizing localized and contextualized approaches, even if that means broadening the scope of what was previously considered to be transitional justice.[119] The importance of building upon local ownership, priorities, practices, and values is now almost universally endorsed as a key to successful interventions.[120] All of this points to a general willingness to question dominant international justice modalities and to try to strike a better balance between global standards and local practices.[121]

Local ownership, governance, and control at all stages of transitional justice programming (conception, design, decision-making, implementation, and management) is critical to respecting cultural rights. Among other things, this ensures a certain level of cultural autonomy over justice processes.[122] Perhaps it goes without saying that if local people are in charge of transitional justice choices, it is much more likely that they will not infringe on the cultures, traditions, customs, and worldviews of that society. International and national actors can provide valuable technical and financial assistance in support of transitional justice mechanisms and play an important role in mediating conflicts that arise, particularly between subnational groups and the State.[123] However, bottom-up justice demands a shift in the conventional power dynamic, with affected communities having ownership over the design and implementation of justice processes that address legacies of harm perpetrated against them, with States and international actors playing a supporting role.

118 Lauren Marie Balasco, 'The Transitions of Transitional Justice: Mapping the Waves from Promise to Practice' (2013) 1 Journal of Human Rights 198, 205.

119 Lieselotte Viaene and Eva Brems, 'Transitional Justice and Cultural Contexts: Learning from the Universality Debate' (2010) 28(2) Netherlands Quarterly of Human Rights 199, 212.

120 UN Secretary-General, The Rule of Law and Transitional Justice in Conflict and Post-Conflict Societies, UN Doc. S/2004/616 (23 August 2004) para 36.

121 Sharp, *Re-Thinking Transitional Justice for the 21st Century* (n 14) 39-40.

122 Jeremie Bracka, 'Reckoning with Colonial Legacies of Harm: Victoria's Yoorrook Justice Commission' (2024) 18(2) International Journal of Transitional Justice 325, 332.

123 Hobbs, 'Locating the Logic of Transitional Justice' (n 13) 517–18.

This has proven to be a difficult balance to strike, as the field is both State-centric and rooted in international frameworks, institutions, and experts, which does not necessarily lend itself easily to deferring to local expertise or grassroots movements.[124]

Ensuring local governance over transitional justice agendas not only aligns with the respect of cultural rights in justice processes, but also has the potential to lead to a more serious engagement with cultural rights violations. Many cultural harms, such as cultural erasure, destruction of cultural heritage, and prohibition of languages, exist in the lived memories of victims and survivors in post-conflict and divided societies. Bottom-up approaches are more likely to address such wrongdoing, as local decisionmakers appreciate and/or have experienced the devastating impacts of this wrongdoing in their own lives and their own communities. In contrast, if mechanisms are principally designed and administered by States, or by international experts, the tendency will be for civil and political rights to be foregrounded—a bias that remains in Western legal thought. Local ownership, governance, and control ensures that outsiders do not dictate the type of harms subject to remedy and redress.

3.3 Cultural justice

In addition to accommodating bottom-up approaches, justice can be reconceived in a way that better recognizes and incorporates its cultural dimensions. Mani argues that 'there is an urgent need to expand the scope of [transitional justice] underpinned by a holistic conceptualisation of justice that incorporates culture'.[125] She calls for transitional justice to address issues of 'cultural justice', meaning that policies should be culturally sensitive and considerate of the specific culture of the post-conflict society, and transitional measures should be designed accordingly.[126] Mani further contends that 'including culture within transitional justice would not be a panacea' but rather an imperative for post-conflict and divided societies, based on the proposition that 'culture still largely determines the societies that experience conflict, and can play an influential role in restoring justice and peace'.[127] Mani's idea

[124] Dustin N Sharp, 'Addressing Dilemmas of the Global and the Local in Transitional Justice' (2014) 29 Emory International Law Review 71, 73.

[125] Rama Mani, 'Women, Art and Post-Conflict Justice' (2011) 11 International Criminal Law Review 543, 564.

[126] ibid, 544.

[127] ibid, 546–47.

of cultural justice is essential to respecting, protecting, and fulfilling cultural rights in transitional justice.

Justice can be retheorized to accommodate culturally diverse worldviews, customs, traditions, and practices. Dominant justice approaches have not traditionally accommodated local or Indigenous alternatives very well.[128] Instead, they are often rooted in Western modes of accountability or truth-telling that do not necessarily translate across different cultures. This often promotes a form of justice wholly foreign to the very groups it purports to serve. Local and Indigenous conceptions of justice are highly developed, but often contradict the widely accepted Westernized forms utilized in transitional justice.[129] Indeed, authors consistently note the fundamental differences between mainstream and local approaches to truth, healing, and justice.[130] For Indigenous Peoples, for example, community healing, cultural revitalization, decolonization, and redistribution of land take precedence over the more retributive modes of justice characterized in Western ideologies and embodied in the dominant model of transitional justice.[131]

Locally owned, governed, and controlled justice models are more likely to embrace the unique traditions, customs, and practices of victims and local solutions in ways that make transitional justice more compatible with the cultures of affected communities. But even international and national institutions are obliged to respect the cultural practices and protocols of victims and survivor communities in transitional justice. As a corollary, cultural justice demands that local mechanisms should also not be analysed under the same lens and held up to the same norms as international or Western processes.[132] Conventional standards and protocols may need to give way to more culturally appropriate processes.

As one example, cultural justice may dictate a departure from transitional justice's long-standing reliance on written and archival sources to document violations and inform policy choices.[133] The field's use of written sources does not comport with the traditions of many groups, especially those whose histories are passed down orally and across generations. Mainstream transitional

[128] An-Na'im, 'Editorial Note: From the Neocolonial Transitional to Indigenous Formations of Justice' (n 43) 197.

[129] McGregor, 'Reconciliation and Environmental Justice' (n 107) 229.

[130] Rosemary Nagy, 'The Scope and Bounds of Transitional Justice and the Canadian Truth and Reconciliation Commission' (2013) 7(1) International Journal of Transitional Justice 52, 60; see also Robyn Green, 'Unsettling Cures: Exploring the Limits of the Indian Residential School Settlement Agreement, (2012) 27(1) Canadian Journal of Law and Society 129, 135–36.

[131] Green, 'Unsettling Cures' (n 130) 136.

[132] Baines, 'Spirits and Social Reconstruction after Mass Violence' (n 99) 414.

[133] ICTJ, 'Strengthening Indigenous Rights through Truth Commissions' (n 105).

justice models, influenced by Western law, prioritize these written sources of proof, while dismissing oral traditions as unreliable.[134] Oral accounts of violent and unjust experiences are treated as untrustworthy in dominant justice models simply because they do not align with standards of Western record-keeping.[135] Written records, however, may also be seen by victims not as a way to effectuate justice, but rather as fundamentally tools of colonialism, used to describe, itemize, and ultimately subjugate people.[136]

Respecting, protecting, and fulfilling cultural rights in transitional justice may require, at times, what Sharp calls an 'uncomfortable degree of legal pluralism for many Western human rights lawyers'.[137] This is particularly the case with respect to shifts away from the legalistic roots of the field. While legal responses are still touted as first-rate solutions to addressing past large-scale harm, law has also been the genesis of violence and wrongdoing for many communities.[138] Colonialism replaced local and Indigenous laws and epistemologies with Eurocentric legal systems and ideologies.[139] Law has also been consistently used to oppress and subjugate communities, particularly in the context of colonialism. As a result, some authors have called for a general decentring of the law in transitional justice, including a departure from rights-based discourses.[140] Utilizing cultural rights-based approaches, including local and Indigenous laws and protocols, arguably works to combat cultural loss.[141]

3.4 Collective justice

States have generally hesitated to afford greater cultural rights protections to minority and Indigenous populations within their borders for fear of recognizing collective rights and jeopardizing national unity.[142] Historically, there

[134] Chris Cunneen, 'Colonialism and Historical Injustice: Reparations for Indigenous Peoples' (2005) 15 Social Semiotics 59, 69

[135] ibid.

[136] ibid 68–69.

[137] Sharp, *Re-Thinking Transitional Justice for the 21st Century* (n 14) xii.

[138] Cunneen, 'Colonialism and Historical Injustice' (n 134) 68.

[139] Eve Tuck and K Wayne Yang, 'Decolonization Is Not a Metaphor' (2012) 1 Decolonization: Indigeneity, Education & Society 1, 6–7; Adam J Barker, 'The Contemporary Reality of Canadian Imperialism: Settler Colonialism and the Hybrid Colonial State' (2009) 33(3) The American Indian Quarterly 325, 341.

[140] See, eg, Jeff Corntassel, 'Re-envisioning Resurgence: Indigenous Pathways to Decolonization and Sustainable Self-Determination' (2012) 1(1) Decolonization: Indigeneity, Education & Society 86. =

[141] Augustine SJ Park, 'Remembering the Children: Decolonizing Community-Based Restorative Justice for Indian Residential Schools' (2016) 19(4) Contemporary Justice Review 424, 438–40.

[142] Elsa Stamatopoulou, *Cultural Rights in International Law: Article 27 of the Universal Declaration of Human Rights and Beyond* (Brill 2007); Janusz Symonides, 'Cultural Rights: A Neglected Category of Human Rights' (1998) 50(158) International Social Science Journal 559.

has been a concern that the promotion of minority and Indigenous cultures may result in conflicts relating to language, religion, and ethnicity, possibly leading to violence or secessionist sentiments.[143] Thus, from a political standpoint, some States are incentivized to ignore the cultural rights of the most marginalized groups. This is especially true in post-conflict and divided societies, where peaceful coexistence between groups is often fragile and tenuous.

Most transitional justice measures focus on individual accountability and individual remedies, rather than collective violence committed against groups and corresponding measures of collective redress.[144] Cultural rights violations, however, are not easily reduced to issues of individual or criminal accountability.[145] These violations often impact the individual as well as the group as a whole.[146] A fixation on individual victims neglects the broader cultural contexts in which these abuses take place and can pervert both the causes and consequences of large-scale harm. It also may miss opportunities to provide collective remedies to victims of large-scale cultural harm. When collective harm is pushed to the margins, States evade responsibility for a wide array of wrongdoing, including intergenerational cultural harm that demands some degree of collective redress.

Critically, there is also no legal impediment to recognizing and pursuing redress for collective cultural rights violations. The status of collective cultural rights under international law is now clear. Cultural rights can be collective in nature and groups can be rightsholders per se. Even though Article 15(a)(1) of the ICESCR uses the language 'the right of everyone ... to take part in cultural life', thus presumably denoting individual rights,[147] the CESCR later interpreted the term 'everyone' to include either the individual or the collective.[148] Moreover, in the context of Indigenous Peoples, the adoption of the UNDRIP solidified the position of Indigenous Peoples' collective cultural rights under international law, affirming in Article 1 that '[i]ndigenous peoples

[143] Athanasios Yupsanis, 'The Concept and Categories of Cultural Rights in International Law: Their Broad Sense and the Relevant Clauses of the International Human Rights Treaties' (2009) 37 Syracuse Journal of International Law and Commerce 207; Elsa Stamatopoulou, 'Monitoring Cultural Human Rights: The Claims of Culture on Human Rights and the Response of Cultural Rights' (2012) 34(4) Human Rights Quarterly 1170, 1176.

[144] Jennifer Matsunaga, 'Two Faces of Transitional Justice' (n 34) 30; ICTJ, 'Strengthening Indigenous Rights through Truth Commissions' (n 105).

[145] Jung, 'Canada and the Legacy of the Indian Residential Schools' (n 101) 237–38.

[146] ibid.

[147] Roger O'Keefe, 'The "Right to Take Part in Cultural Life" under Article 15 of the ICESCR' (1998) 47(4) The International and Comparative Law Quarterly 904, 917.

[148] UN Committee on Economic, Social and Cultural Rights (CESCR), General Comment no 21, Right of Everyone to Take Part in Cultural Life (art 15, para 1a of the Covenant on Economic, Social and Cultural Rights), UN Doc E/C.12/GC/21 (21 December 2009) para 7.

have the right to the full enjoyment, as a collective or as individuals'.[149] The UNDRIP further provides for Indigenous Peoples' access to and prompt decisions through procedures and remedies vis-à-vis infringements of Indigenous Peoples' individual and collective rights.[150]

Dominant justice is certainly focused on the individual, but it can be reimagined to recognize collective harm and provide collective redress to victims of large-scale cultural wrongs. Among other things, this could help change the narrative around the nature of underlying conflicts, who constitutes a victim, and what harm is ultimately confronted.[151] Good practice in this regard can be derived from the Historical Clarification Commission in Guatemala and the Truth and Reconciliation Commission in Peru, each of which provided recommendations for the provision of collective reparations.[152]

4. Rethinking Dominant Violence

The types of violence justifying a transitional justice response have traditionally been limited to recent and egregious acts of mass bodily integrity harm, and violations of civil and political rights more generally. Violence under dominant theory is conceptually constrained by both (a) the character of the harm—seemingly exceptional bodily integrity violations, and (b) when it occurs—immediately preceding the transition at issue or in the relatively recent past. This preoccupation with recent, bodily integrity harm has proven incompatible with confronting the violent and unjust legacies associated with mass cultural wrongdoing.

Violence in mainstream discourse and in everyday parlance usually connotes a level of physicality. For instance, the World Health Organization defines violence as

> the intentional use of physical force or power, threatened or actual, against oneself, another person, or against a group or community, that either results in or has a high likelihood of resulting in injury, death, psychological harm, maldevelopment, or deprivation.[153]

[149] UN Declaration on the Rights of Indigenous Peoples, adopted by the UN General Assembly, UN Doc A/RES/61/295 (13 September 2007) Art 1.
[150] ibid Art 40.
[151] Jung, 'Canada and the Legacy of the Indian Residential Schools' (n 101) 237–38.
[152] See section 3.3 in chapter 1 of this book.
[153] Etienne Krug et al (eds), *World Report on Violence and Health* (World Health Organization 2002) 5.

Thus, we tend to appreciate violence as something that is inherently physical, whether threatened or realized. Notwithstanding, alternative conceptions of violence have long been proffered outside of the realm of the physical. Johan Galtung's groundbreaking work on peace and violence is arguably the starting point to retheorizing violence in the field of transitional justice.[154] Acknowledging that 'there are obviously many types of violence', Galtung defined violence, in part, as 'any avoidable insult to basic human needs, and, more generally, to sentient life of any kind, defined as that which is capable of suffering pain and enjoying well-being'.[155] For him, violence not only harmed the body, but the mind and spirit.[156] Galtung also famously posited a violence triangle as a conceptual framework for understanding violence, which includes direct, structural, and cultural violence.[157]

Cultural violence was defined by Galtung as 'those aspects of culture, the symbolic sphere of our existence—exemplified by religion and ideology, language and art, empirical science and formal science (logic, mathematics)—that can be used to justify or legitimize direct or structural violence'.[158] He went on to explain that cultural violence makes other forms of violence 'feel right—or at least not wrong'.[159] It motivates actors to commit direct violence, facilitates structural violence, and produces the necessary emotions and attitudes for widespread atrocities to take place.[160] Galtung's articulation and theorization of cultural violence has been extremely influential, including in the field of transitional justice, with practical mechanisms referring to the conception and incorporating it into their outputs.[161]

Galtung's theorization of violence has been instrumental to understanding the various interrelated dimensions of violence outside of the strict domain of physical harm. However, he only conceived of cultural violence as a causal factor in other forms of violence (direct and structural), rather than understanding and treating attacks on culture as an independent form of violence. This book relies on Galtung's theorization, while also challenging his narrow conception of cultural violence as principally a driver of direct and structural

[154] Galtung, 'Violence, Peace, and Peace Research' (n 15); Johan Galtung, 'Cultural Violence' (1990) 27(3) Journal of Peace Research 291.
[155] Johan Galtung and Dietrich Fischer, *Johan Galtung: Pioneer of Peace Research* (Springer 2013) 35.
[156] ibid.
[157] Galtung, 'Violence, Peace, and Peace Research' (n 15); Galtung, 'Cultural Violence' (n 154).
[158] Galtung, 'Cultural Violence' (n 154) 291.
[159] ibid.
[160] Matthew Mullen, 'Reassessing the Focus of Transitional Justice: The Need to Move Structural and Cultural Violence to the Centre' (2015) 28(3) Cambridge Review of International Affairs 462, 463.
[161] For example, see Canada's National Inquiry into Missing and Murdered Indigenous Women and Girls, *Reclaiming Power and Place: The Final Report of the National Inquiry into Missing and Murdered Indigenous Women and Girls* (2019) 77.

violence.[162] Cultural wrongs are inextricably interrelated with direct physical violence and structural violence, but they can also be inherently violent in their own right.

Further inspiration in this regard is drawn from the work of Rafael Lemkin, whose contributions to human rights and the concept of genocide have been discussed comprehensively elsewhere.[163] Critically, Lemkin did not understand violence against culture as inherently less egregious than direct violence.[164] Instead, he believed that the destruction of cultural symbols, traditions, language, and institutions was as devastating as physical annihilation. As the 'father of the genocide convention',[165] Lemkin conceived of the crime as inherently cultural, an attack on people and their cultural identities as much as anything else.[166] Regrettably, cultural genocide was negotiated out of the final text of the 1948 Genocide Convention. This was largely the result of lobbying by Western States who wanted to narrow the definition to avoid culpability for their own large-scale cultural wrongdoing.[167]

Among other things, the theoretical work of Galtung and Lemkin demonstrates that understanding violence to include cultural harm does not represent a radical reimagining of the concept. The transitional justice field has coalesced around the idea that it is principally responsible for responding to recent acts of mass physical violence, but there are few conceptual barriers to conceiving of violence more broadly to encompass the various forms of cultural wrongdoing that wreak havoc on societies in equally destructive and enduring ways. This is even the case for cultural abuses that occurred in the distant past, but have legacies that have caused suffering across generations. The following analysis thus challenges orthodox interpretations of violence under the dominant model and retheorizes it in relation to cultural wrongdoing.

[162] Dáire McGill, 'Different Violence, Different Justice? Taking Structural Violence Seriously in Post-conflict and Transitional Justice Processes' (2017) 6(1) State Crime Journal 79, 81.

[163] See, eg, John Cooper, *Raphael Lemkin and the Struggle for the Genocide Convention* (Palgrave Macmillan 2008); Samantha Power, *'A Problem from Hell': America and the Age of Genocide* (Basic Books 2002); Philippe Sands, *East West Street: On the Origins of Genocide and Crimes Against Humanity* (Knopf 2016).

[164] Fiona Greenland and Fatma Müge Göçek, 'Introduction' in Fiona Greenland and Fatma Müge Göçek (eds), *Cultural Violence and the Destruction of Human Communities New Theoretical Perspectives* (Routledge 2020) 2.

[165] A Dirk Moses, 'Rafael Lemkin, Culture and the Concept of Genocide' in Donald Bloxham and A Dirk Moses (eds), *The Oxford Handbook of Genocide Studies* (2012) 19.

[166] Leora Bilsky and Rachel Klagsbrun, 'The Return of Cultural Genocide?' (2018) 29(2) European Journal of International Law 373, 374.

[167] Pauline Wakeham, 'The Slow Violence of Settler Colonialism: Genocide, Attrition, and the Long Emergency of Invasion' (2022) 24(3) Journal of Genocide Research 337, 344.

4.1 Understanding cultural wrongs as violence

The types of violence subject to transitional justice scrutiny can be rethought to recognize the complex and myriad ways in which victims experience harm and injustice in post-conflict and divided societies. The field's fixation with civil and political rights violations ignores the fact that the human rights abuses that underlie many transitions go well beyond violations of bodily integrity. Nonetheless, this preoccupation severely complicates the field's ability to address various forms of violence, including cultural wrongdoing. Cultural harm can take many forms, but here I focus on two specific abuses to demonstrate how attacks on culture can and should be increasingly understood as violence in the transitional justice sphere: (1) the destruction and weaponization of tangible cultural heritage and (2) assimilationist policies, including the forced removals of children. A focus on these violations is not meant to minimize the violent nature of the various other ways in which culture is destroyed, denigrated, and eroded. Rather, it uses these two clear-cut examples to demonstrate the inherently violent nature of cultural harm, on par with the bodily integrity violations prioritized in dominant transitional justice theory and practice.

4.1.1 Destruction and weaponization of tangible cultural heritage

The most visible cultural wrongs committed during armed conflict are acts of intentional destruction of cultural heritage. In protracted periods of violent conflict, combatants regularly seek to destroy the cultural institutions, symbols, and heritage of their enemies.[168] The prevalence of these abuses is explained by the fact that cultural heritage, like culture in general, is a crucial part of identity for individuals and groups. As the 2003 UNESCO Declaration concerning the Intentional Destruction of Cultural Heritage confirms, cultural heritage 'is an important component of the cultural identity of communities, groups and individuals, and of social cohesion'.[169] Unfortunately, the intentional destruction of cultural heritage seems to have only escalated in recent conflicts.[170] For example, research suggests that in just the first six months of

[168] William Logan, 'Cultural Diversity, Cultural Heritage and Human Rights: Towards Heritage Management as Human Rights-Based Cultural Practice' (2012) 18(3) International Journal of Heritage Studies 231.

[169] UNESCO Declaration concerning the Intentional Destruction of Cultural Heritage (adopted 17 October 2003) UNESCO Doc 38 C/25, Preamble.

[170] Helen Walasek, 'Cultural Heritage and Memory after Ethnic Cleansing in Post-Conflict Bosnia-Herzegovina' (2019) 101 International Review of the Red Cross 273, 274.

Russia's invasion of Ukraine in 2022, more than 400 objects of cultural heritage in Ukraine were damaged or partially destroyed.[171]

In his seminal article 'Violence, Peace, and Peace Research', Galtung rhetorically questioned whether the destruction of things was violence.[172] In his view, such destruction constituted a sort of 'psychological violence' both in the sense that it portends a threat of harm to an actual person and by destroying material things that are dear to persons.[173] Other scholars have conceptualized the loss of access to or the destruction of cultural heritage as a form of violence.[174] The former UN SRCR Karima Bennoune, in an expert report submitted to the ICC during the reparations phase of the *Al Mahdi* trial, described the violent impacts of cultural heritage destruction as:

> attacking cultural diversity and cultural rights; erasing memory of current and past events, civilizations and peoples; erasing evidence of the presence of minorities, other people, philosophies, religions and beliefs; or deliberating targeting or terrorizing individuals and groups on the basis of their cultural, ethnic or religious affiliation, or their way of life and beliefs.[175]

In the Reparations Order in the *Al Mahdi* case, the ICC connected the destruction of cultural heritage with violations of cultural rights, by stating that the attacks on Timbuktu's cultural heritage 'not only destroyed and damaged physical structures' but also '"diminished the link and identity the local community had" with such valuable cultural heritage'.[176]

Tangible cultural heritage can also be weaponized in post-conflict and divided societies to oppress or denigrate certain groups. This risk is especially acute when cultural heritage is employed by the dominant national or ethnic group to impose a homogenous identity on subnational groups.[177] These tactics threaten ambitions to move towards peaceful, multicultural, and tolerant

[171] Alla Kravchenko et al, 'Crime against Memory or Cultural Genocide? On the Destruction of the Cultural Heritage of Ukraine during Russian Aggression in the XXI Century' (2022) 10(2) European Journal of Transformation Studies 206.

[172] Galtung, 'Violence, Peace and Peace Research' (n 15) 170.

[173] ibid.

[174] See, eg, George Nicholas and Claire Smith, 'Considering the Denigration and Destruction of Indigenous Heritage as Violence' in Veysel Apaydin (ed), *Critical Perspectives on Cultural Memory and Heritage: Construction, Transformation and Destruction* (UCL Press 2020) 131–54.

[175] Brief by Ms Karima Bennoune, UN Special Rapporteur in the Field of Cultural Rights, *The Prosecutor v Ahmad Al Faqi Al Mahdi*, ICC-01/12-01/15 (21 April 2017).

[176] *Prosecutor v Al Mahdi*, Reparations Order, International Criminal Court Case No ICC-01/12-01/15-236 (17 August 2017) para 19.

[177] Report of the Independent Expert in the Field of Cultural Rights, UN Doc A/HRC/17/38 (21 March 2011) para 11.

societies after periods of large-scale harm. In other circumstances, cultural violence can take the form of symbols or monuments that glorify a legacy of subordination, discrimination, marginalization, and violence against minorities, Indigenous Peoples, and other marginalized groups, or otherwise promote hateful ideologies.[178] This has the effect of further eroding social trust and cohesion in post-conflict and divided societies.

The destruction and weaponization of tangible cultural heritage produces violence on the souls and identities of individuals and communities. When these physical representations of culture are destroyed or weaponized, it weakens group identities and disrupts these groups' sense of self and where they came from.[179] These may also have knock-on effects on culture that are equally violent. For instance, the destruction of tangible cultural heritage may prevent victims from transmitting and/or receiving traditional knowledge or engaging with cultural practices that are intimately tied to this tangible heritage.

4.1.2 Assimilationist policies

Assimilationist policies, including the forced removals of children, the banning of languages and dress, and restrictions on cultural and spiritual practices have been pursued by States to exact cultural harm on Indigenous Peoples and minorities. These measures can be overt, but often they are insidious, working to fracture the social and communal bonds that allow communities to exist and flourish as culturally distinct groups. Assimilationist policies and ideologies have been particularly devastating in colonial and settler-colonial contexts.[180] Indigenous Peoples have been routinely targeted by State-sanctioned policies of assimilation which sought to rupture the cultural bonds of Indigenous communities and absorb them into mainstream society. Scholar Bonita Lawrence describes the intergenerational impact of this violence in her own life:

> For many years, I have witnessed the result of these policies, as my family, friends, and many of my Aboriginal students have struggled with our lack of knowledge about our heritage due to our parents' silence, the fact that our languages were beaten out of our grandparents' generation, that we may have

[178] See, eg, Lucas Lixinski, 'Confederate Monuments and International Law' (2017) 35 Wisconsin International Law Review 549.

[179] Sinéad Coakley and Pádraig McAuliffe, 'Picking Up the Pieces: Transitional Justice Responses to Destruction of Tangible Cultural Heritage' (2022) 40(3) Netherlands Quarterly of Human Rights 311, 318.

[180] Lynette Russell, 'Settler Colonial Studies: Eliminating the Native and Creating the Nation' (2020) 23(1) Postcolonial Studies 153, 155.

> been cut off from access to the land for generations, that we may know little of our own ceremonies, and that our indigeneity is ultimately validated or denied by government cards that certify 'Indian' status.[181]

These policies have arguably been the most effective tools used by colonial and settler-colonial governments to eliminate Indigenous Peoples and dispossess them of their lands.[182]

Under settler-colonial theory, for instance, Indigenous Peoples do not need to be killed physically to sustain settler colonialism, but rather culturally, spiritually, and socially.[183] The violence behind assimilationist policies directed at Indigenous Peoples is displayed in the still popular slur that 'the only good Indian is a dead Indian',[184] which Wolgang Mieder argues has both physical and cultural components:

> on the literal level it justified the actual mass slaughter of Indians by the military, and, on a more figurative level, it promoted the belief that Indians could only be 'good' persons if they became Christians and took on the civilization of their white oppressors. Then they might be 'good', but as far as their native Indian culture was concerned, they would, in fact, be dead.[185]

Likewise, the racist adage 'kill the Indian, save the man' was a policy mantra for governments who established boarding and residential schools for Indigenous children in North America, not for the purposes of physically eliminating them but to kill them culturally, including by separating them from their families, Christianizing them, suppressing their native tongue, and denigrating their cultural identities.[186]

Colonizing States and majority populations convince themselves that their assimilative actions are good and righteous within their own cultures.[187] Dominant cultures are elevated as superior and inevitable, while also used to

[181] Bonita Lawrence and Enakshi Dua, 'Decolonizing Antiracism' (2005) 32(4) Social Justice 120, 121.

[182] Augustine SJ Park, 'Settler Colonialism and the Politics of Grief: Theorising a Decolonising Transitional Justice for Indian Residential Schools' (2015) 16(3) Human Rights Review 273, 278.

[183] ibid.

[184] The quote is generally attributed to General Philip Sheridan, a general in the United States Army during the so-called 'Indian Wars'. Andrew R Hutton, *Phil Sheridan and His Army* (University of Nebraska Press 1985).

[185] Wolfgang Mieder, '"The Only Good Indian Is a Dead Indian": History and Meaning of a Proverbial Stereotype' (1993) 106 Journal of American Folklore 38, 42.

[186] Ward Churchill, *Kill the Indian, Save the Man: The Genocidal Impact of American Indian Residential Schools* (City Lights 2004).

[187] Whyte, 'On Resilient Parasitisms' (n 106) 284.

delegitimize other cultures, which are then framed as backwards and uncivilized. As a consequence, minority cultural practices and expressions are commonly banned. Later, strict bans on cultural expressions come to be no longer seen as acceptable; but instead of granting colonized communities the cultural autonomy to revive their own traditions, they exist as nostalgic memories or are coopted by mainstream societies in ways that are divorced from their original meaning, rendering them performative.[188]

Forced assimilation aligns with Galtung's conception of cultural violence in that it legitimizes structural and direct violence against marginalized communities. These policies have been found to have a close nexus with socio-economic disparities, pervasive discrimination, poorer health outcomes, and higher incarceration rates, among other negative impacts.[189] But forced assimilation also constitutes a direct form of violence against culture. Calling assimilation 'disruptive and heartless', Alan Wolfe conceives it as 'a form of symbolic violence'.[190] For Wolfe, when dominant groups impose their language, traditions, and values on non-dominant groups, it exerts something akin to 'the actual violence of war'.[191]

The examples of tangible cultural heritage destruction and forced cultural assimilation illustrate just two ways in which wrongs against culture produce violence on the lives of individuals and communities. These can lead to severe infringements on human dignity, including through the denigration and/or erasure of identities, traditions, and ways of life. They also work to remove the very thing that binds communities together.[192] Such harm can be as destructive as the physical violence or political persecution that was emblematic of the paradigmatic cases.[193] While much of the standard-setting around transitional justice has focused on violations of civil and political rights, there is nothing in the UN's definition, its legal framework, or broader standard-setting that would exclude large-scale cultural harm from the field's remit. This supports a conceptual broadening of the violence subject to transitional justice to include particularly devastating cultural rights abuses, wrongs which are every bit as serious and grave as the bodily integrity crimes favoured in the dominant model.

188 Coulthard, *Red Skin, White Masks* (n 18) 71–72.
189 *See* David K Androff, 'Adaptations of Truth and Reconciliation Commissions in the North American Context: Local Examples of a Global Restorative Justice Intervention' (2012) 13(2) Advances in Social Work 408, 414.
190 Alan Wolfe, *An Intellectual in Public* (University of Michigan Press 2005) 11.
191 ibid.
192 Pok Yin S Chow, *Cultural Rights in International Law and Discourse: Contemporary Challenges and Interdisciplinary Perspectives* (Brill Nijhoff 2018) 1.
193 ICTJ, 'Strengthening Indigenous Rights through Truth Commissions' (n 105).

4.2 Treating distant harm as violence

Violence can also be expanded temporally to encompass harms (cultural or otherwise) dating back beyond recent memory. Some transitional justice scholars argue that attempts to address historical injustices fall outside the purview of the field.[194] On the other hand, authors also routinely critique transitional justice's reluctance to engage with historical wrongdoing, including in connection with colonialism.[195] Hakeem Usuf notes that '[p]aradoxically, transitional justice has averted its gaze from, or has been slow at best, to address the extensive harm caused by colonialism.'[196] Others criticize mechanisms that create an artificial divide between a colonial past and a supposedly peaceful present, effectively maintaining the status quo while foreclosing any consideration of continuing harm.[197]

The Declaration produced at the 2001 World Conference against Racism, Racial Discrimination, Xenophobia and Related Intolerance in Durban, South Africa (the 'Durban Declaration') articulated a clear need to reckon with historical abuses as a condition of justice:

> We emphasize that remembering the crimes or wrongs of the past, wherever and whenever they occurred, unequivocally condemning its racist tragedies and telling the truth about history, are essential elements for international reconciliation and the creation of societies based on justice, equality and solidarity.[198]

The Durban Declaration went on to state that these historical injustices 'had undeniably contributed to the poverty, marginalization and social exclusion, instability, and insecurity affecting so many people in distinct parts of the world.'[199]

[194] McAuliffe, 'Transitional Justice's Expanding Empire' (n 18) 136.

[195] Tuck and Yang, 'Decolonization Is Not a Metaphor' (n 139); Esme G Murdock, 'Storied with Land: Transitional Justice on Indigenous Lands' (2018) 14(2) *Journal of Global Ethics* 232; Leanne Betasamosake Simpson, 'Land and Reconciliation: Having the Right Conversations', *Watershed Sentinel* (23 November 2017) <https://watershedsentinel.ca/article/land-reconciliation/> accessed 1 February 2025.

[196] Hakeem O Yusuf, 'Transitional Justice and Colonialism' in Cheryl Lawther, Luke Moffett, and Dov Jacobs (eds), *Research Handbook on Transitional Justice* (Edward Elgar 2023).

[197] See, eg, Park, 'Settler Colonialism and the Politics of Grief' (n 182) 276; Jeff Corntassel, Chaw-win-is, and T'lakwadzi, 'Indigenous Storytelling, Truth-Telling, and Community Approaches to Reconciliation' (n 107) 145; Maddison and Shepherd, 'Peacebuilding and the Postcolonial Politics of Transitional Justice' (n 49) 254; Jennifer Henderson and Pauline Wakeham (eds), *Reconciling Canada: Critical Perspectives on the Culture of Redress* (University of Toronto Press 2013).

[198] Durban Declaration and Plan of Action, Adopted at the World Conference Against Racism, Racial Discrimination, Xenophobia and Related Violence (8 September 2001) para 106.

[199] ibid para 158.

The temporal limitations of dominant violence in transitional justice have been specifically observed by UN special procedures in the context of colonialism and the transatlantic slave trade. In 2021, Fabián Salvioli, former UN SRTJ, produced a report on transitional justice in colonial contexts.[200] Salvioli explicitly linked the field's non-engagement with colonial wrongdoing with its preoccupation with bodily integrity violations.[201] Furthermore, in 2019, Tendayi Achiume, former UN Special Rapporteur on contemporary forms of racism, racial discrimination, xenophobia and related intolerance, presented a report on reparations for racial discrimination rooted in slavery and colonialism.[202] Among other things, Achiume noted the 'historic racial injustices of slavery and colonialism that remain largely unaccounted for today, but which nevertheless require restitution, compensation, satisfaction, rehabilitation and guarantees of non-repetition.'[203]

Mainstream transitional justice treats historic wrongdoing and injustice as something less relevant for post-conflict and divided societies. Historical harms, particularly those associated with colonialism and the transatlantic slave trade, have ongoing and enduring impacts on individuals and communities. Such wrongdoing cannot be relegated to distant history. Yusuf again problematizes transitional justice's neglect of colonial wrongdoing partly on account of postcolonial societies still being indelibly shaped by the impact of colonialism.[204] Colonialism is not historic injustice; it remains in the economic, political, and cultural fabrics of postcolonial societies. Colonialism also reinvents itself and evolves in ways that continue to exert violence on colonized and formerly colonized peoples.[205] Thus, victims in colonial and postcolonial contexts may not always view harms strictly as historical injustices, but rather as abuses that have been taking place over centuries in a continuous and often uninterrupted manner.

[200] Report of the Special Rapporteur on the Promotion of Truth, Justice, Reparation and Guarantees of Non- Recurrence, Fabián Salvioli, Transitional Justice Measures and Addressing the Legacy of Gross Violations of Human Rights and International Humanitarian Law Committed in Colonial Contexts, UN Doc A/76/180 (19 July 2021).

[201] ibid para 5.

[202] Report of the Special Rapporteur on contemporary forms of racism, racial discrimination, xenophobia and racial intolerance, UN Doc A/74/321 (21 August 2019).

[203] ibid para 6(a).

[204] Hakeem Yusuf, 'Colonialism and the Dilemmas of Transitional Justice in Nigeria' (2018) 12(2) International Journal of Transitional Justice 257–59.

[205] John Borrows, *Freedom and Indigenous Constitutionalism* (University of Toronto Press 2016) 142.

Settler-colonial theory, for instance, would suggest that the colonial violence experienced by Indigenous Peoples remains institutionalized in modern laws, policies, and practices. Thus, it is not strictly historical or contemporary—it is both.[206] In the Canadian context, Paulette Regan aptly describes colonial violence against Indigenous Peoples as being 'woven into the fabric of Canadian history in an unbroken thread from past to present'.[207] Settler-colonial States continue to maintain colonial policies and practices into the present day even though they are violent and anti-Indigenous.[208] Eve Tuck and K. Wayne Yang maintain that this colonial violence 'is not temporally contained in the arrival of the settler but is reasserted each day of occupation'.[209] Thus, these injustices continue to negatively impact the lived experiences of Indigenous Peoples.[210]

For many victims, engaging solely with contemporary violence (defined in the Western tradition) may be wholly inadequate.[211] By treating colonial violence as strictly historical, and not as an ongoing structure, it masks and downplays the cultural harm that continues to plague colonized and formerly colonized people and societies.[212] States will also use transitional justice policies to position their wrongdoing as historical to avoid present-day obligations.[213] For example, Canada's TRC narrowly focused on the Indian residential schools, the last of which closed in 1996. This effectively isolated the rest of the colonial and contemporary violence experienced by Indigenous Peoples and tacitly permitted Canada to position its wrongdoing as a historical mistake, something that it could put firmly in the past.[214]

Yet, neither the formative transitional justice literature nor the standard-setting at the UN dictates how far back in time transitional justice can reach. Instead, as Zinaida Miller argues, they 'allude to an open-ended and flexible conception of temporality, reliant only on the importance of the past and the need for a peaceful future'.[215] Moreover, addressing distant wrongdoing does

[206] Sophie Rigney, 'The Hopes and Discontents of Indigenous-Settler Reconciliation' (2017) 11(2) International Journal of Transitional Justice 359, 359.

[207] Regan, *Unsettling the Settler Within* (n 27) 6.

[208] Whyte, 'On Resilient Parasitisms' (n 106) 279.

[209] Tuck and Yang, 'Decolonization Is Not a Metaphor' (n 139) 5.

[210] Maddison and Shepherd, 'Peacebuilding and the Postcolonial Politics of Transitional Justice' (n 49) 264.

[211] ICTJ, 'Strengthening Indigenous Rights through Truth Commissions' (n 105).

[212] Jung, 'Reconciliation: Six Reasons to Worry' (n 114) 259.

[213] Zinaida Miller, 'Temporal Governance: The Times of Transitional Justice' (2021) 21(5) International Criminal Law Review 848, 858.

[214] Corntassel, Chaw-win-is, and T'lakwadzi, 'Indigenous Storytelling, Truth-Telling, and Community Approaches to Reconciliation' (n 107) 144–45.

[215] Miller, 'Temporal Governance' (n 213) 849.

not risk conceptual soundness if we are to conceive of transitions as gradual processes often occurring over a considerable period of time. Addressing historical cultural wrongs may encounter legal and political challenges, but on a conceptual level there is theoretical flexibility for the transitional justice field to confront such abuses in a similar manner as more recent harms.

4
JUSTIFYING AN ENGAGEMENT WITH CULTURAL RIGHTS

1. Introduction

This book has illustrated the marginalization of cultural rights in the transitional justice field, analysed the reasons behind this treatment, and challenged mainstream theory in ways that accommodate a more serious and robust engagement with culture. Freed from the dogmatic approaches of the field's dominant theory, transitional justice possesses the conceptual flexibility to respect and protect cultural rights and redress their violations in a similar manner as other rights categories. Of course, a different question altogether is whether transitional justice should seek to engage with such rights. What exactly is the value of expanding its traditional parameters in order to bring culture more squarely within the field's remit? Should transitional justice programming be all that concerned with issues of culture, especially considering the many demands that are placed on it? And what are the potential risks in doing so—both conceptually and practically? These questions have yet to be considered in the literature in a comprehensive manner.

Issues of prioritization are commonly debated in nearly every transitional justice setting. Post-conflict and divided societies seeking to grapple with legacies of large-scale harm must be willing to compromise and be selective about what issues to address and what mechanisms to employ. Numerous factors may influence the prioritization of issues in any given transitional justice policy, including the nature of the underlying conflict, political agendas, victim demands, resource constraints, and influence from various stakeholders, including international actors. These prioritization dilemmas also often take place in the context of severe fragility and a lack of overall institutional capacity, especially in societies emerging from protracted periods of armed conflict. This often leads to transitional justice mechanisms being overburdened, underfunded, and encumbered by expectations that are rarely met.[1]

[1] Lars Waldorf, 'Between Transition and Transformation Legal Empowerment as Collective Reparations' in Paul Gready and Simon Robins (eds), From Transitional to Transformative Justice (Cambridge University Press 2019) 148–49.

Cultural Rights and Wrongs in Transitional Justice. Colin Luoma, Oxford University Press. © Colin Luoma 2025.
DOI: 10.1093/oso/9780198911371.003.0004

Notwithstanding, culture remains omnipresent in post-conflict and divided societies and to not engage with issues of culture presents certain risks.[2] Indeed, there are compelling justifications for transitional justice to incorporate, address, and engage with cultural rights in more meaningful ways. First, a normative case is made, grounded in the well-established principle that human rights are universal, indivisible, interdependent, and interrelated.[3] Cultural rights are as important to human dignity as other rights and States have not only a moral obligation to respect them and address their violations, but well-established legal duties as well. This includes ensuring the right to an adequate, effective, and prompt remedy for violations of cultural rights under international law.[4] Treating cultural rights on par with other rights categories in transitional justice has the potential to reinforce their normative value in the broader protection and fulfilment of human dignity.

Second, an instrumental justification is advanced. Cultural wrongs are at the heart of many conflicts and societal divisions, serving as their own mode of violence, but also constituting root causes of related and intersecting forms of violence.[5] Cultural wrongs should be accounted for and addressed in transitional justice to close an existing impunity gap around attacks against culture, but also to tackle underlying drivers of structural and direct violence in post-conflict and divided societies. Moreover, respecting and protecting cultural rights through transitional justice processes can help move societies towards more inclusive, tolerant, and peaceful futures and, ultimately, help ensure the non-recurrence of future violations.

Third, respecting, protecting, and addressing cultural rights often aligns with victim priorities. Transitional justice agendas should be responsive to what victims expect and want. Victims in traditional post-conflict and post-authoritarian settings may tend to prioritize the redress of civil, political, economic, or social rights, rather than cultural rights. But this is not necessarily the case in other contexts, including in established democracies plagued by deep societal divisions and legacies of large-scale cultural harm. This is especially true with respect to minority and Indigenous groups, whose distinct

[2] Michelle Lebaron, 'Culture and Conflict' in Guy Burgess and Heidi Burgess (eds), *Beyond Intractability* (Conflict Information Consortium, University of Colorado, Boulder, July 2003).

[3] The Vienna Declaration and Programme of Action, adopted by the World Conference on Human Rights in Vienna (25 June 1993) para 5.

[4] See generally UN General Assembly, Basic Principles and Guidelines on the Right to a Remedy and Reparation for Victims of Gross Violations of International Human Rights Law and Serious Violations of International Humanitarian Law, UN Doc A/RES/60/147 (21 March 2006).

[5] National Inquiry into Missing and Murdered Indigenous Women and Girls, *Reclaiming Power and Place: The Final Report of the National Inquiry into Missing and Murdered Indigenous Women and Girls* (3 June 2019) 327.

cultural identities are marginalized in post-conflict and divided societies and who tend to centre some of their broader justice claims on cultural dislocation, restitution, and revitalization.

Finally, incorporating and addressing cultural rights in transitional justice can shape more truthful narratives regarding underlying conflicts and potentially set better agendas for post-transitional reforms. Transitional justice mechanisms have the power to challenge and upend dominant narratives and highlight the need for States to engage in more substantive, long-term reforms around culture. By placing culture at the centre of transitional scrutiny, States and other stakeholders may be encouraged to tackle systemic cultural wrongdoing and inequalities through legislation and policy in ordinary domestic justice systems and development initiatives.

This case for a cultural rights-based approach to transitional justice draws on and extends a critical strand of transitional justice scholarship focused on the field's failure to incorporate economic and social rights, but which has yet to independently justify the inclusion of cultural rights. And while there is some overlap in the proffered rationales between bringing socio-economic and cultural rights more squarely into transitional justice thinking and praxis, many of the arguments made here are uniquely tailored to cultural rights. In this way, the case set out seeks to disaggregate the specific justifications for incorporating cultural rights from broader debates about the inclusion of ESC rights.

None of this is to suggest that transitional justice should reflexively seek to incorporate cultural rights or necessarily prescribe how this should be accomplished. This decision-making is context-dependent and will be influenced by a multiplicity of factors. There are also persuasive pragmatic reasons to be quite cautious about expanding the traditional parameters of transitional justice beyond what we can reasonably expect the project to accomplish. These practical concerns are not spurious, but they are perhaps mitigated in the context of incorporating cultural rights, which do not necessarily implicate the same resource concerns applicable to economic and social rights.

2. The Normative Case

An increased engagement with cultural rights in transitional justice is justified on a normative level through the repeatedly affirmed principle that all human rights are universal, indivisible, interdependent, and interrelated.[6]

[6] The Vienna Declaration and Programme of Action (n 3) para 5.

Universality means that all people are afforded equal human rights.[7] The principles of indivisibility, interdependence, and interrelatedness dictate that there is no hierarchy of rights. Rights are interdependent when their realization requires the realization of other rights, whereas interrelatedness denotes a certain level of mutuality or connection between rights.[8] While cultural relativism has undeniably challenged the universality of human rights, a strict hierarchy along rights categories has been firmly rejected, at least in theory.[9]

This well-established tenet of international human rights law is commonly invoked as a rationale to address the full spectrum of violations within transitional justice, and not simply the civil and political wrongs that tend to be prioritized.[10] In the human rights field, strict demarcations between rights categories have been gradually dismantled and the indivisible nature of all rights is now endorsed.[11] This consensus is demonstrated by, among other things, an overwhelming majority of States adopting the Vienna Declaration and Programme of Action in 1993, which declares that '[a]ll human rights are universal, indivisible and interdependent and interrelated'.[12] The Maastricht Guidelines on Violations of Economic, Social and Cultural Rights, adopted in 1997, further provide that 'it is now undisputed that all human rights are indivisible, interdependent, interrelated and of equal importance for human dignity'.[13]

Cultural rights, like all human rights, are essential to the protection of human dignity. Culture is how we assign meaning to our lives. It shapes the ways in which we live, care for one another, and carry out our daily endeavours. The close nexus between cultural rights and human dignity has been reinforced in UN treaty monitoring practice, with the CESCR stating that '[t]he full promotion of and respect for cultural rights is essential for the maintenance of human

[7] Report of the Special Rapporteur in the Field of Cultural Rights, Universality, Cultural Diversity and Cultural Rights, UN Doc A/HRC/73/227 (25 July 2018) para 2.

[8] Daniel Whelan, 'Indivisible Human Rights' (2010) 9 Global Issues Series 3, 3–4.

[9] Alexandra Xanthaki, 'When Universalism Becomes a Bully: Revisiting the Interplay Between Cultural Rights and Women's Rights' (2019) 41(3) Human Rights Quarterly 701, 716.

[10] Most authors make a normative argument solely in connection with economic and social rights, but without including cultural rights. See, eg, Paul Gready and Simon Robins, 'From Transitional to Transformative Justice: A New Agenda for Practice' (2014) 8(3) International Journal of Transitional Justice 339; Rubén Carranza, 'Plunder and Pain: Should Transitional Justice Engage with Corruption and Economic Crimes?' (2008) 2 International Journal of Transitional Justice 310; Lisa J Laplante, 'Transitional Justice and Peace Building: Diagnosing and Addressing the Socioeconomic Roots of Violence through a Human Rights Framework' (2008) 2(3) International Journal of Transitional Justice 331.

[11] Peter Uvin, *Human Rights and Development* (Kumarian Press 2004) 38–39.

[12] Vienna Declaration (n 3) para 5.

[13] International Commission of Jurists (ICJ), Maastricht Guidelines on Violations of Economic, Social and Cultural Rights (26 January 1997) para 4.

dignity and positive social interaction between individuals and communities in a diverse and multicultural world'.[14] Because cultural rights constitute a crucial piece of the international human rights framework, with a wide range of protections, including those imposing binding obligations, States are just as responsible for remedying violations of cultural rights as they are for all other rights violations.

The interrelation and interdependence of cultural rights with other rights categories is demonstrated by the fact that violations of cultural rights often lead to infringements on civil, political, economic, and/or social rights.[15] Likewise, the protection of cultural rights indirectly protects civil, political, economic, and social rights.[16] For example, land rights are commonly protected through enforcing the right to culture, including the rights of minorities to enjoy their culture under Article 27 of the International Covenant on Civil and Political Rights ('ICCPR').[17] At the same time, land rights can be a necessary vehicle for individuals and groups to realize their cultural rights, including maintaining their cultural identities and engaging in their cultural practices.[18]

Despite the consensus around the interrelation, interdependence, and indivisibility of all human rights at a conceptual level, a categorical hierarchy has been inherited by transitional justice. Cultural rights are still very much considered a luxury compared to other rights, only deemed appropriate to address after more serious violations have been confronted.[19] Indeed, the perception is that cultural rights are something that should be addressed and protected only after society has sought justice for mass physical violence and achieved basic minimum standards of socio-economic well-being.[20] Put another way, cultural rights must come after 'bread and water'.[21] At best, they have been treated as ancillary rights; at worst they are seen as mere aspirations, rather than binding

[14] CESCR, General Comment No. 21, Right of everyone to take part in cultural life (art 15, para 1a of the Covenant on Economic, Social and Cultural Rights), UN Doc E/C.12/GC/21 (21 December 2009) para 11.

[15] Report of the Special Rapporteur in the Field of Cultural Rights, UN Doc A/HRC/31/59 (3 February 2016) para 5.

[16] Theo van Boven, 'Categories of Rights' in Daniel Moeckli and others (eds), *International Human Rights Law* (3rd edn, Oxford University Press 2018) 140–41.

[17] Beatriz Garcia and Lucas Lixinski, 'Beyond Culture: Reimagining the Adjudication of Indigenous Peoples' Rights in International Law' (2020) 15 Intercultural Human Rights Law Review 127.

[18] Joanna Gibson, 'Community Rights to Culture' in Stephen Allen and Alexandra Xanthaki (eds), *Reflections on the UN Declaration on the Rights of Indigenous Peoples* (Hart Publishing 2011) 434.

[19] Julie Ringelheim, 'Cultural Rights' in Daniel Moeckli and others (eds), *International Human Rights Law* (3rd edn, Oxford University Press 2018) 279.

[20] Athanasios Yupsanis, 'The Concept and Categories of Cultural Rights in International Law: Their Broad Sense and the Relevant Clauses of the International Human Rights Treaties' (2009) 37 Syracuse Journal of International Law and Commerce 207, 236.

[21] Elsa Stamatopoulou, 'Monitoring Cultural Human Rights: The Claims of Culture on Human Rights and the Response of Cultural Rights' (2012) 34(4) Human Rights Quarterly 1170, 1172.

State obligations. Far from being treated as indivisible, they are commonly subordinated behind all other rights considered more important for post-conflict and divided societies seeking to address legacies of large-scale past harm.

This hierarchy is implicitly embraced by some authors, who advocate for a more narrow conception of transitional justice that prioritizes redress for civil and political rights violations.[22] Cultural rights violations are typically viewed as less egregious, less grave, and less worthy of an extraordinary response.[23] Even scholars sympathetic to a further engagement between transitional justice and cultural rights have noted a certain uneasiness that arises when prioritizing cultural issues in contexts where populations cannot meet their basic needs.[24] This tends to position culture as a secondary, perhaps even a tertiary right, and as something that is inherently dispensable in the broader project of seeking justice for societies in transition.

This runs counter to the indivisibility principle and has been critiqued in the transitional justice literature. Louise Arbour comments on the 'unhelpful categorization of rights' between civil and political rights versus ESC rights in transitional justice.[25] Lisa Laplante further criticizes the rights pecking order in transitional justice responses, suggesting that the practical, everyday experiences of survivors demonstrate the impossibility of separating rights into categories.[26] More generally, the subordination of cultural rights in transitional justice is wholly incongruent with the fact that they constitute an integral part of the human rights framework.

The normative case for the general inclusion of ESC rights in transitional justice has gained traction at the UN. In 2012, the Human Rights Council adopted a resolution stressing that the full range of human rights should be addressed in transitional justice contexts 'in order to promote, *inter alia*, the rule of law and accountability'.[27] Additionally, in 2014, the OHCHR's report on *Transitional Justice and Economic, Social and Cultural Rights* emphasized that all rights are universal, indivisible, interdependent, and interrelated.[28] In

[22] See, eg, Lars Waldorf, 'Anticipating the Past: Transitional Justice and Socio-Economic Wrongs' (2012) 21(2) Social and Legal Studies 171.

[23] Sinéad Coakley and Pádraig McAuliffe, 'Picking Up the Pieces: Transitional Justice Responses to Destruction of Tangible Cultural Heritage' (2022) 40(3) Netherlands Quarterly of Human Rights 311, 319.

[24] ibid.

[25] Louise Arbour, 'Economic and Social Justice for Societies in Transition' (2007) 40 International Law and Politics 1, 3.

[26] Lisa J Laplante, 'On the Indivisibility of Rights: Truth Commissions, Reparations, and the Right to Development' (2018) 10 Yale Human Rights and Development Journal 141, 142.

[27] Human Rights and Transitional Justice, Resolution 21/15 adopted by the UN Human Rights Council, UN Doc. A/HRC/RES/21/15 (11 October 2012).

[28] United Nations Human Rights Office of the High Commissioner, Transitional Justice and Economic, Social and Cultural Rights, HR/PUB/13/5 (2014) 7.

many ways, this seems to signal a natural extension of a well-accepted principle of human rights law into the domain of transitional justice. And while the indivisibility of rights is overwhelmingly invoked in calls for the field to account for socio-economic issues, this argument can be rightly extended to justify the field's engagement with cultural rights.

While the idea that all human rights should be on equal normative footing in transitional justice policy is gaining acceptance, the practical implementation of this principle has proved challenging. Lars Waldorf argues that even though States have committed to the indivisibility of human rights, 'it has yet to become anything approaching customary international law'.[29] Even accepting that all human rights should be treated equally, he rightly maintains that this 'offers no guidance on which rights to prioritize in the context of fragile transitions and limited resources'.[30] Paul Gready and Simon Robins agree with this sentiment, suggesting that treating all rights as universal, interdependent, and indivisible has not been transformative in part because there is 'no decision-making mechanism for the selection, prioritization or sequencing of interventions'.[31]

While most transitional justice agendas are faced with sequencing and prioritization challenges under significant resource constraints, it seems misguided to automatically demote cultural rights to default lesser rights, not worthy of consideration in transitional settings based on arbitrary categorical distinctions. Of course, one should accept the possibility, even likelihood, that some rights violations will go unaddressed in any given transitional justice setting. This is part of the political compromise that sits at the heart of the transitional justice enterprise.[32] But the decision as to what rights to address and incorporate should not be based on a human rights hierarchy that has been rebuffed.[33] Instead, transitional justice policies should prioritize rights violations on a case-by-case basis, engaging with cultural rights when featuring prominently in the underlying conflict and when prioritized by victims. To do otherwise would add credence to old delusions around cultural rights not being 'real rights' and would undermine the indivisibility principle more generally.

[29] Waldorf, 'Anticipating the Past' (n 22) 174.

[30] ibid.

[31] Gready and Robins, 'From Transitional to Transformative Justice' (n 10) 345.

[32] Colleen Murphy, *The Conceptual Foundations of Transitional Justice* (Cambridge University Press 2017).

[33] Dustin N Sharp, 'Emancipating Transitional Justice from the Bonds of the Paradigmatic Transition' (2015) 9(1) International Journal of Transitional Justice 150, 160.

Still others question the justiciability of cultural rights in transitional justice processes.[34] Rights are justiciable if they can be scrutinized and adjudicated before courts or other judicial and quasi-judicial bodies.[35] Transitional justice has largely viewed civil and political rights violations as being justiciable and capable of redress, while other rights are deemed non-justiciable, and thus better left to post-transitional development policies.[36] Waldorf argues that the redress of civil and political rights is more suitable for transitional justice processes because these rights are more amenable to 'naming and shaming'.[37] Frank Haldemann and Rachelle Kouassi further criticize proponents of a more expansive version of transitional justice for not seriously engaging with the judicial enforceability of ESC rights.[38]

These debates harken back to long-standing misconceptions about the non-justiciability of ESC rights.[39] However, as Evelyne Schmid and Aoife Nolan assert, old assumptions about the nature of ESC rights, including their non-justiciability, have been disproven in practice.[40] Cultural rights are now widely recognized as being real, justiciable rights with corresponding State obligations under international human rights law.[41] Cultural rights violations have been adjudicated, including through criminal and human rights courts, and they are included in human rights treaties. Some cultural rights protections represent binding legal duties, with certain core obligations that require immediate implementation by States.[42] These include guaranteeing non-discrimination in connection with the right to take part in cultural life, respecting the right to one's cultural identity, and protecting the right of everyone to engage in their own cultural practices.[43]

While many cultural rights obligations are progressive in nature, this does not preclude the monitoring and adjudication of how States meet their

[34] Frank Haldemann and Rachelle Kouassi, 'Transitional Justice without Economic, Social, and Cultural Rights?' in Eibe Riedel and others (eds), *Economic, Social, and Cultural Rights in International Law: Contemporary Issues and Challenges* (Oxford University Press 2014) 503–04.

[35] Yvonne Donders, *Towards a Right to Cultural Identity?* (Intersentia 2002) 18.

[36] Carranza, 'Plunder and Pain' (n 10) 315.

[37] Waldorf, 'Anticipating the Past' (n 22) 173.

[38] Haldemann and Kouassi, 'Transitional Justice without Economic, Social, and Cultural Rights?' (n 34) 504.

[39] See Evelyne Schmid and Aoife Nolan, '"Do No Harm"? Exploring the Scope of Economic and Social Rights in Transitional Justice' (2014) 8(3) International Journal of Transitional Justice 362, 378.

[40] ibid.

[41] Donders, *Towards a Right to Cultural Identity?* (n 35) 18; Jackbeth K Mapulanga-Hulston, 'Examining the Justiciability of Economic, Social and Cultural Rights' (2002) 6(4) The International Journal of Human Rights 29, 42–43.

[42] CESCR, General Comment No. 21 (n 14) para 55.

[43] ibid, para 48.

obligations in taking reasonable steps to realize these rights.[44] Thus, contrary to such antiquated misunderstandings, cultural rights contain several positive and negative State obligations capable of judicial enforcement. Perhaps more important, the question of their justiciability only becomes limiting if we are to blindly accept the dominant theory of justice in the field, preoccupied with legal institutions, actors, and responses, rather than the more flexible justice approaches articulated in the previous chapter of this book.

The continuous, intersecting, and interrelated forms of violence sustained by victims in diverse societies necessitate a holistic approach to transitional justice, one that treats all rights as universal, interdependent, interrelated, and indivisible, rather than blindly prioritizing acts of physical violence or socio-economic inequalities.[45] In treating physical violence, political repression, or socio-economic wrongdoing as violative of human rights, but failing to do so for acts of cultural harm, transitional justice will contribute to a sort of back-sliding, reinforcing the canard that cultural rights are aspirational, rather than concrete and often enforceable State legal obligations. On the other hand, the redress of cultural harm in transitional justice practice, including framing such harm as violative of State human rights commitments and with specific references to applicable instruments, can ultimately strengthen the normative value of cultural rights under international law.[46]

3. The Instrumental Case

Cultural wrongdoing is both a distinct type of violence and a root cause of other forms of direct and structural violence plaguing post-conflict and divided societies. In many transitional justice cases, cultural harm is at the root of mass violence and deep societal divisions. This is especially the case for Indigenous Peoples and minority groups, whose cultures suffer from colonial-era cultural harms that continue to persist and new cultural wrongs that are constantly evolving and emerging in our increasingly globalized world.[47]

[44] UN Office of the High Commission on Human Rights, 'Key Concepts on ESCRs—Can Economic, Social and Cultural Rights Be Litigated at Courts?' <https://www.ohchr.org/en/human-rights/economic-social-cultural-rights/escr-vs-civil-political-rights> accessed 1 February 2025.

[45] Gready and Robins, 'From Transitional to Transformative Justice' (n 10) 344.

[46] Evelyne Schmid, 'Socio-Economic and Cultural Rights and Wrongs after Armed Conflicts: Using the State Reporting Procedure before the United Nations Committee on Economic, Social and Cultural Rights More Effectively' (2013) 31(3) Netherlands Quarterly of Human Rights 241, 245–46.

[47] Alexandra Xanthaki, 'Indigenous Cultural Rights in International Law' (2000) 2 European Journal of Law Reform 343, 343.

Experts and international bodies now generally acknowledge that transitional justice must move beyond the violent consequences of conflicts and begin dealing with their underlying causes.[48] This so-called instrumental case posits that the root causes of violence need to be identified and accounted for in transitional justice processes in order to ensure the non-recurrence of future conflict.[49] Although this argument has previously been developed, articulated, and debated almost exclusively in the context of socio-economic harm and inequality, it is equally applicable to cultural rights.

While the causation of conflict is context-specific and often highly contested, it is clear that human rights abuses can and do lead to violent conflict.[50] This causal connection has long been recognized in international law. For instance, the Preamble to the Universal Declaration on Human Rights declared that 'disregard and contempt for human rights have resulted in barbarous acts'.[51] Even earlier, the UN Charter identified the prevention of violent conflict as one of its primary purposes.[52] However, links between human rights and violent conflict tend to focus on violations of civil, political, and economic rights that precede mass violence, while consistently overlooking cultural considerations. This is at odds with the fact that cultural rights violations drive conflict, are committed during conflict, and persist long after conflict has subsided. Even when cultural wrongdoing does not directly provoke physical violence, issues of culture always factor into and influence conflict.[53]

Some scholars have suggested that the 'instrumental case' has less relevance when applied to cultural wrongdoing. For instance, Sinéad Coakley and Padraig McAuliffe contend that 'war is not fought over cultural differences'.[54] Instead, these authors rightly reinforce the strong nexus between conflict and inequalities among groups. This has support among experts and international bodies. For example, a 2018 joint report from the UN and World Bank

[48] Arbour, 'Economic and Social Justice for Societies in Transition' (n 25) 3; Guidance Note of the Secretary-General: United Nations Approach to Transitional Justice (10 March 2010) para 9; OHCHR, Transitional Justice and Economic, Social and Cultural Rights (n 28) 1.

[49] Schmid and Nolan, '"Do No Harm"?' (n 39) 375; Arbour, 'Economic and Social Justice for Societies in Transition' (n 25) 8; Ismael Muvingi, 'Sitting on Powder Kegs: Socioeconomic Rights in Transitional Societies' (2009) 3(2) International Journal of Transitional Justice 163; Zinaida Miller, 'Effects of Invisibility: In Search of the "Economic" in Transitional Justice' (2008) 2(3) International Journal of Transitional Justice 266, 288.

[50] See, eg, Oskar NT Thoms and James Ron, 'Do Human Rights Violations Cause Internal Conflict' (2007) 29 Human Rights Quarterly 674.

[51] United Nations General Assembly, Universal Declaration of Human Rights (10 December 1948), Preamble.

[52] United Nations, Charter of the United Nations (24 October 1945) Art 1.

[53] Lebaron, 'Culture and Conflict' (n 2).

[54] Coakley and McAuliffe, 'Picking up the Pieces' (n 23) 319.

identified one of the largest precipitators of violent conflict to stem from 'perceptions of exclusion and injustice, rooted in inequalities across groups'.[55]

At the same time, we must guard against automatically dismissing cultural harm as a root cause of violent conflict or other forms of mass wrongdoing. There does not seem to be a consensus among social scientists as to what drives violent conflict.[56] And, undoubtedly, violence is a complex phenomenon, caused and influenced by numerous factors in any given context. Violence is often framed as being religious, ethnic, or political in nature, but when one digs deeper, cultural rights can be found at the heart of many conflicts.[57] Rama Mani and Thomas Weiss draw close links between cultural loss and mass atrocity, arguing that we have overlooked the 'profound processes and consequences of cultural collapse and the horror that lurks with the dissolution of the unifying glue of spirituality, ethics, and values'.[58] Mani finds it unsurprising that attacks on culture serve as a prelude to egregious acts of physical violence, stating:

> People whose cultural values, mores and traditions have been denigrated, sapped and uprooted for generations, whose creativity has been truncated, whose ability to express dissent and alternatives have been stifled, are more susceptible to blind persuasion and violence.[59]

Of course, this is not meant to suggest that culture bears some unique responsibility for all violent conflict, but cultural loss, denigration, and destruction create the necessary conditions for the instigation of violent conflict. This has regrettably come to fruition in various contexts. We have observed cultural rights violations lead to periods of violent conflict and deep societal divisions. For example, the war in Kosovo was preceded by numerous cultural rights violations, including the prohibition of the Albanian language and the closing of Albanian schools and cultural institutions.[60] Restrictions to contested cultural

[55] UN and World Bank, *Pathways for Peace: Inclusive Approaches to Preventing Violent Conflict* (World Bank 2018) 98.

[56] Thoms and Ron, 'Do Human Rights Violations Cause Internal Conflict' (n 50) (arguing that violations of civil and political rights are more directly linked to violence); but see Paul Collier, *Economic Causes of Civil Conflict and their Implications for Policy* (World Bank 2006) <https://documents.worldbank.org/en/publication/documents-reports/documentdetail/272561468780312524/economic-causes-of-civil-war-and-their-implications-for-policy> accessed 1 February 2025.

[57] UNESCO, 'The Role of Culture in Peace and Reconciliation' Background Note (April 2013) (on file with author).

[58] Rama Mani and Thomas G Weiss, 'Can Culture Prevent Massacres?' (2011) 17 Global Governance: A Review of Multilateralism and International Organizations 417, 422.

[59] Rama Mani, 'Women, Art and Post-Conflict Justice' (2011) 11 International Criminal Law Review 543, 551.

[60] See UN General Assembly, 'Situation of Human Rights in Kosovo' A/RES/50/190 (6 March 1996).

sites between Israelis and Palestinians have led to increased tensions and contributed to prolonged conflict in the region.[61] Prior to the Syrian civil war, government-imposed barriers on Kurdish cultural celebrations, commemorative events, and language contributed to hostilities.[62] Furthermore, division and violence in Cameroon in recent years can be primarily traced to the denial of language rights among Anglophone communities.[63]

This idea that cultural wrongs, specifically, can lead to mass physical violence has been acknowledged at the international level. According to UNESCO, societies are particularly susceptible to falling into violent conflict when the cultures, traditions, and beliefs of vulnerable groups are marginalized, rejected, or ignored.[64] The drafters of the Fribourg Declaration were '[c]onvinced that violations of cultural rights give rise to identity-related tensions and conflicts which are one of the principal cause(s) of violence, wars and terrorism'.[65] Beyond this, a number of scholars,[66] UN mandate holders,[67] and intergovernmental bodies[68] have commented on the linkages between deprivation of culture and violent conflict.

Outside the paradigmatic contexts of dictatorships or armed conflict, the links between cultural wrongdoing and mass human rights abuses are even more apparent. It is instructive to look at settler colonial States in this regard. In the context of settler colonialism, settlers use violence to destroy Indigenous cultures and rely on their own sense of cultural superiority to justify and perpetrate other forms of violence against Indigenous Peoples. Apart from being its own form of violence, the denial of cultural rights can lead to or justify both structural and physical violence.[69] This includes ideologies and assimilationist policies derived from beliefs in the superiority of the majority culture.[70] In

[61] Janet Blake, 'Taking a Human Rights Approach to Cultural Heritage Protection', (2011) 4(2) Heritage & Society 199, 206.

[62] Human Rights Watch, *Group Denial: Repression of Kurdish Political and Cultural Rights in Syria* (2009) <https://www.hrw.org/sites/default/files/reports/syria1109web_0.pdf> accessed 1 February 2025.

[63] Elena Frogameni, 'Cameroon's Anglophone Crisis: The Dangers of Language Conflict on Display', Oxford Political Review (14 August 2024) <https://oxfordpoliticalreview.com/2024/08/14/cameroons-anglophone-crisis-the-dangers-of-language-conflict-on-display/> accessed 24 December 2024.

[64] UNESCO, 'The Role of Culture in Peace and Reconciliation' (n 57).

[65] Fribourg Declaration on Cultural Rights (2007), para 3.

[66] See, eg, Matthew Mullen, 'Reassessing the Focus of Transitional Justice: The Need to Move Structural and Cultural Violence to the Centre' (2015) 28(3) Cambridge Review of International Affairs 462, 463; Stamatopoulou, 'Monitoring Cultural Human Rights' (n 21) 1175.

[67] See, eg, Report of the Special Rapporteur in the Field of Cultural Rights, UN Doc A/HRC/31/59 (3 February 2016) para 5.

[68] UNESCO, 'The Role of Culture in Peace and Reconciliation' (n 57).

[69] National Inquiry into Missing and Murdered Indigenous Women and Girls, *Reclaiming Power and Place* (n 5) 416.

[70] ibid 77.

some contexts, cultural loss has been linked to higher rates of poverty, substance abuse, domestic violence, incarceration, and suicide.[71] It has also been found to contribute to increased rates of physical violence against Indigenous Peoples.[72]

In turn, neglecting the cultural abuses underpinning deeply divided societies can reinforce a status quo that is inherently violent. Narrowly focusing on a limited set of civil, political, or socio-economic rights violations in transitional justice may hinder the realization of a more just and peaceful long-term existence for victims and survivors. Even in the paradigmatic settings, cultural violence can persist long after the cessation of conflict or repression.[73] Indeed, many decades after the commission of mass physical atrocities, cultural loss often remains in the social fabric of communities.

The premise behind the instrumental case is that root causes of conflict must be addressed or you risk fuelling the 'next conflagration'.[74] The same rationale applies to the respect of cultural rights in transitional justice processes. Cultural rights remain particularly vulnerable in post-conflict societies, even long after violence has ceased.[75] When cultural rights are not respected and promoted after conflict, States run the risk of renewed violence.[76] Cultural rights scholars have long recognized the intimate connection between cultural rights and the maintenance of peace. Elsa Stamatopoulou notes that 'avoiding the respect of cultural rights can only lead to frustrations in society and the instigation of conflict' and that 'states have learned hard lessons' in this regard.[77] Yvonne Donders similarly notes that violence is particularly a risk when cultural identities are restricted, oppressed, or jeopardized.[78]

The denial of cultural rights can and has been used to sow division among groups and facilitate further human rights violations in transitional periods.[79] Culture can be weaponized in ways that foster feelings of victimhood and is used to demarcate differences among groups, perpetrate myths, and increase

[71] David K Androff, 'Adaptations of Truth and Reconciliation Commissions in the North American Context: Local Examples of a Global Restorative Justice Intervention' (2012) 13(2) Advances in Social Work 408, 414; Gerald Taiaiake Alfred, 'Colonialism and State Dependency' (2009) 5(2) International Journal of Indigenous Health 42, 49.

[72] National Inquiry into Missing and Murdered Indigenous Women and Girls, Reclaiming Power and Place, Executive Summary of the Final Report (3 June 2019) 23.

[73] Mullen, 'Reassessing the Focus of Transitional Justice' (n 66) 463.

[74] Arbour, 'Economic and Social Justice for Societies in Transition' (n 25) 8.

[75] See Mullen, 'Reassessing the Focus of Transitional Justice' (n 66).

[76] *The Derry/Londonderry Report on Upholding the Human Right to Culture in Post-Conflict Societies* (Northern Ireland Human Rights Commission 2014).

[77] Stamatopoulou, 'Monitoring Cultural Human Rights' (n 21) 1175.

[78] Donders, *Towards a Right to Cultural Identity?* (n 35).

[79] Elsa Stamatopoulou, *Cultural Rights in International Law* (Brill 2007); see also *The Derry/Londonderry Report* (n 76).

hostilities.[80] Violent conflict also has the tendency to produce memorials and practices that work to impede on the cultural rights of certain groups and contribute to or reignite tensions.[81] These violations prove particularly challenging for post-conflict and divided societies.

On the flipside, culture is equally essential for promoting and sustaining peace in post-conflict and divided societies. A mutual respect for cultural rights between groups has shown the ability to gradually build multicultural, tolerant, and cohesive post-conflict societies.[82] The close relationship between culture and peace is perhaps unsurprising, as it is well accepted that the protection of culture is indispensable for the values of human dignity, self-respect, and identity.[83] Accordingly, it has been said that culture has the power to increase unity, foster peace, and promote reconciliation in transitional periods.[84]

4. Responding to Victim Priorities

It is axiomatic that transitional justice strategies and programming should be responsive to what victims and survivors actually want and expect.[85] Too often, however, transitional justice policy is far removed from local priorities, undermining its effectiveness and legitimacy among victims of large-scale harm.[86] As detailed earlier, a recurring critique of transitional justice centres on the lack of deference given to local populations and grassroots movements. The recent endorsement of local agency and ownership over transitional justice processes has been accompanied by the sentiment that the field needs to be more responsive to victim priorities and understanding these priorities is essential to implementing effective transitional justice policies.[87]

[80] Judith Marie Barsalou and Victoria Baxter, *The Urge to Remember: The Role of Memorials in Social Reconstruction and Transitional Justice* (United States Institute of Peace 2007); see also Ziya Meral, 'A Duty to Remember? Politics and Morality of Remembering Past Atrocities' (2012) 5(1) International Political Anthropology 29.

[81] Ereshnee Naidu-Silverman, *The Contribution of Art and Culture in Peace and Reconciliation Processes in Asia* (Centre for Culture and Development 2015) 9.

[82] *The Derry/Londonderry Report* (n 76).

[83] Stamatopoulou, *Cultural Rights in International Law* (n 79) 107–08.

[84] *The Derry/Londonderry Report* (n 76).

[85] Lieselotte Viaene and Eva Brems, 'Transitional Justice and Cultural Contexts: Learning from the Universality Debate' (2010) 28(2) Netherlands Quarterly of Human Rights 199, 212.

[86] Patricia Lundy and Mark McGovern, 'Whose Justice? Rethinking Transitional Justice from the Bottom Up' (2008) 35(2) Journal of Law and Society 265, 266; Dustin N Sharp, 'Addressing Dilemmas of the Global and the Local in Transitional Justice' (2014) 29 Emory International Law Review 71, 73–74.

[87] Simon Robins, 'Whose Voices? Understanding Victims' Needs in Transition: Nepali Voices: Perceptions of Truth, Justice, Reconciliation, Reparations and the Transition in Nepal by the International Centre for Transitional Justice and the Advocacy Forum, March 2008' (2009) 2(1) Journal of Human Rights Practice 320, 320.

However, until recently, little research had been dedicated to determining what exactly those priorities are. Indeed, despite the emergence of transitional justice as a sort of default response to mass violence, it remains a highly under-empiricized field.[88] There is a sort of incongruity at play, where it is seen as imperative that transitional justice policies respond to the needs of victims, but the empirical research identifying those needs remains conspicuously scarce.[89] Indeed, we have very little data to draw from in order to understand what victims desire and the limited findings available are difficult to apply across disparate transitional justice contexts.

The available empirical studies provide some guidance on the issues that victims tend to prioritize in traditional post-conflict settings. For instance, research into the priorities of victims of Nepal's Maoist insurgency demonstrates that they emphasize immediate, everyday economic and social needs over the punishment of perpetrators.[90] In Northern Uganda, victims identified health, peace, education, and livelihood concerns as their main priorities.[91] Studies in Kenya,[92] Sierra Leone,[93] and the Democratic Republic of the Congo[94] have yielded similar results. Among other things, this research suggests that victims in post-conflict societies often prioritize the redress of structural violence and everyday injustices over the legal redress and criminal punishment of perpetrators of large-scale human rights abuses.[95]

Evaluating local priorities is, of course, a context-specific endeavour. Some degree of caution must be exercised in seeking to apply such findings across different sets of victims in diverse transitional settings. In post-conflict societies emerging from years of sustained armed conflict, it may be more logical for victims to prioritize immediate, unmet socio-economic needs. Likewise, in conventional post-authoritarian settings, it may make sense that civil and political rights violations may be prioritized.[96]

[88] Dustin N Sharp, Re-Thinking Transitional Justice for the 21st Century (Cambridge University Press 2018) 13.

[89] Viaene and Brems, 'Transitional Justice and Cultural Contexts' (n 85) 212.

[90] Robins, 'Whose Voices?' (n 87) 325.

[91] Phuong Pham and others, *When the War Ends: A Population-based Survey on Attitudes about Peace, Justice, and Social Reconstruction in Northern Uganda* (UC Berkeley, Human Rights Center, December 2007) 23.

[92] Simon Robins, Kenya: 'To Live as Other Kenyans Do': A Study of the Reparative Demands of Kenyan Victims of Human Rights Violations (ICTJ 2011) 21–32.

[93] Gearoid Millar, 'Local Evaluations of Justice through Truth Telling in Sierra Leone: Postwar Needs and Transitional Justice' (2011) 12(4) Human Rights Review 515, 524–29.

[94] Patrick Vinck and Phuong Pham, 'Ownership and Participation in Transitional Justice Mechanisms: A Sustainable Human Development Perspective from Eastern DRC' (2008) 2(3) International Journal of Transitional Justice 398, 403.

[95] Waldorf, 'Anticipating the Past' (n 22) 175.

[96] Sharp, *Re-Thinking Transitional Justice for the 21st Century* (n 88) 33.

However, in some post-conflict and divided societies, culture is paramount for victims even among a litany of bodily integrity and socio-economic violations. This was exemplified in the ICC's Reparations Order in the *al-Mahdi* case, which noted:

> The importance of cultural heritage to communities is illustrated by the fact that the communities themselves often request that the protection of their cultural landmarks be prioritised, even in situations of violence where human life is at risk.[97]

The Reparations Order further recited a quote from former UNESCO Director for Legal Protection of Cultural Heritage, Lyndel Prott, when she was asked why UNESCO prioritized protecting cultural heritage when other urgent humanitarian concerns were present. Prott responded by saying:

> We are often asked the question, 'Why protect monuments when people are dying?' The reason is, the people who are dying ring us up and say, 'Please protect our monuments.' If people feel that strongly about their heritage, we don't feel the international community can simply stand back and say, 'It's not important. As long as you're not dying, that's all that counts.'[98]

Thus, too often, States, international actors, and policymakers take for granted what victims desire out of transitional justice processes. For Indigenous victims, community healing, cultural revitalization, decolonization, and land redistribution take precedence over the retributive modes of justice characterized in Western ideologies and embodied in the dominant model of transitional justice.[99] Again, insufficient empirical research has been dedicated to Indigenous priorities in transitional justice. Studies from other disciplines, however, demonstrate the significance placed on cultural loss by Indigenous communities. In Canada, a study on Indigenous mental health found that between 33 and 38 per cent of Indigenous Peoples think about issues of historical

[97] *Prosecutor v Al Mahdi*, Reparations Order, International Criminal Court Case No. ICC-01/12-01/15-236 (17 August 2017) para 18.

[98] Marion Forsyth, 'Casualties of War: The Destruction of Iraq's Cultural Heritage as a Result of US Action During and After the 1991 Gulf War' (2004) 14 DePaul Journal of Art, Technology & Intellectual Property Law 73, 106.

[99] Robyn Green, 'Unsettling Cures: Exploring the Limits of the Indian Residential School Settlement Agreement' (2012) 27(1) Canadian Journal of Law and Society 129, 136.

loss related to land, language, and culture every single day.[100] Further research into historical trauma among American Indians reveals that cultural losses, including the erosion of native language and traditional familial ties, were frequently identified by Indigenous Peoples as harms closely associated with their historical trauma.[101] Indigenous elders and knowledge holders also commonly note how the most challenging issues in Indigenous communities are not legal, political, or financial, but relate to the destruction of culture, language, spiritual rituals, and family institutions.[102] In turn, emphasis is placed on redressing these wrongs and restoring a sense of cultural identity for their communities.[103]

To be sure, Indigenous individuals suffer from significant disparities in their physical, economic, and social well-being in comparison to their mainstream counterparts.[104] However, Taiaiake Alfred argues there is little evidence to suggest that providing Indigenous Peoples with monetary reparations or economic development programmes improves their well-being.[105] In the face of numerous and multifaceted human rights violations, there are consistent calls for transitional justice to engage in and promote forms of cultural resurgence and revitalization, key Indigenous concepts of healing.[106] The concept of resurgence in this context involves, *inter alia*, reconnecting with culture.[107] These broader forms of redress, including cultural and language revitalization, better align with Indigenous priorities and worldviews compared to many of the dominant justice approaches preoccupied with individualized accountability and remedies.[108]

[100] Laurence J Kirmayer, Gregory M Brass, and Gail Guthrie Valaskakis, 'Conclusion: Healing/Invention/Tradition' in Laurence J Kirmayer and Gail Guthrie Valaskakis (eds), *Healing Traditions: The Mental Health of Aboriginal Peoples in Canada* (UBC Press 2014) 454.

[101] Les B Whitbeck and others, 'Conceptualizing and Measuring Historical Trauma among American Indian People' (2004) 33(4) American Journal of Community Psychology 119, 121–22.

[102] See, eg, Eva McKay, 'If They Read What You Are Writing, This Is the Teachings, This Is Some of the Teachings that We Want Them to Read About' in Peter McCaskill and others (eds), *In the Words of Elders: Aboriginal Cultures in Transition* (University of Toronto Press 1999).

[103] Alfred, 'Colonialism and State Dependency' (n 71) 45.

[104] Androff, 'Adaptations of Truth and Reconciliation Commissions in the North American Context' (n 71) 414.

[105] Alfred, 'Colonialism and State Dependency' (n 71) 44.

[106] See, eg, Jeff Corntassel, 'Re-envisioning Resurgence: Indigenous Pathways to Decolonization and Sustainable Self-Determination' (2012) 1(1) Decolonization: Indigeneity, Education & Society 86; Augustine SJ Park, 'Remembering the Children: Decolonizing Community-Based Restorative Justice for Indian Residential Schools' (2016) 19(4) Contemporary Justice Review 424, 438–39.

[107] Corntassel, 'Re-envisioning Resurgence' (n 106) 97.

[108] Green, 'Unsettling Cures' (n 99) 135–36.

5. Correcting Narratives and Promoting Long-term Cultural Reforms

The final justification advanced for an increased engagement with cultural rights in transitional justice is grounded in its potential to promote longer-term, substantive reforms. Sidelining cultural rights in transitional justice can promote a distorted narrative around conflict and societal divisions, one which could potentially limit the range of future policy options undertaken by States.[109] Backgrounding cultural rights in favour of redressing civil and political rights violations positions cultural harm as something that is isolated and discrete. This can certainly be the case, but more often such harm is structural and systematic, requiring substantial and often radical reforms. By directly confronting cultural harm, and treating it as violative of human rights norms, transitional justice frameworks can help promote more substantial future reforms aimed at restoring and protecting human cultures.[110]

Transitional justice is recognized as a powerful narrator of difficult histories, including the origins and nature of conflict.[111] The types of harm confronted in mechanisms help to determine the way conflict is understood and remembered. Holistic approaches, accounting for a wider range of violence, arguably promote a more inclusive, truthful account of the nature and scale of human rights abuses committed in the past and why they occurred in the first place.[112] Conversely, when transitional justice narrowly focuses on a certain category of rights (commonly, civil and political rights violations), it generally misrepresents the true dynamics behind post-conflict and divided societies. For example, in South Africa, the TRC narrowly defined victims as only those who suffered egregious bodily harm, while ignoring the social, economic, and cultural harm caused by apartheid.[113] This allowed a fictional narrative to develop, one that was divorced from the everyday discrimination and inequality faced by black South Africans.[114] Apartheid thus became a story about racism and the bodily integrity harms suffered by individuals, rather than the structural violence inherent in apartheid.[115]

109 See Miller, 'Effects of Invisibility' (n 49) 280–84.
110 See Laplante, 'Transitional Justice and Peace Building' (n 10) 342.
111 Miller, 'Effects of Invisibility' (n 49) 266–67.
112 Carranza, 'Plunder and Pain' (n 10) 320.
113 Rosemary Nagy, 'Transitional Justice as Global Project: Critical Reflections' (2008) 29(2) Third World Quarterly 275, 284; Mahmood Mamdani, 'Amnesty or Impunity? A Preliminary Critique of the Report of the Truth and Reconciliation Commission of South Africa (TRC)' (2002) 32(3/4) Diacritics 33, 45–46.
114 Mamdani, 'Amnesty or Impunity?' (n 113) 34.
115 Miller, 'Effects of Invisibility' (n 49) 280–81.

Dustin Sharp argues that transitional justice's near-exclusive emphasis on civil and political rights has become unacceptable in part because it promotes a simpler, one-dimensional narrative of conflict, when in reality most conflicts 'are a messy mix of political, social, economic, and cultural factors'.[116] Grievous human rights abuses can rarely be traced to a single causal origin; rather, they are brought about and influenced by numerous factors in any given context.[117] Thus, divorcing transitional justice from such a large segment of issues, such as systemic cultural harm, allows myths to form regarding the true origins and nature of conflict or societal divisions.[118]

By focusing solely on bodily integrity harm, or socio-economic abuses and inequalities, transitional justice measures fail to acknowledge the true scope of violence perpetrated against victims. As noted earlier, when survivors of Canada's residential school system sought damages through domestic litigation, the only cognisable injuries were individual acts of physical and sexual violence, leaving the collective cultural harm suffered by generations of Indigenous Peoples unaccounted for.[119] In this sense, the story became about children that were killed, tortured, or abused at these schools, rather than the State-sanctioned colonial campaign to disconnect Indigenous children from their families and their culture. Canada's TRC later sought to rectify this by foregrounding the destruction of Indigenous culture at the centre of the Indian Residential School System.[120]

As detailed in previous chapters of this book, established democracies often embrace international reputations as benevolent, human rights-abiding countries.[121] The mass human rights abuses committed through colonialism, settler colonialism, and the transatlantic slave trade are commonly overlooked, effectively written out of history. In some established democracies, mass cultural harm was perpetrated with the same voracity and scope as bodily integrity violations in the third-wave transitions in the 1980s and 1990s. Yet, these cultural abuses are ordinarily not accounted for in the dominant histories and narratives about these nations. Transitional justice measures can work to correct these narratives and increase public awareness in the process, arguably the first step in engaging in more meaningful, long-term reforms at the domestic level.

116 Sharp, *Re-Thinking Transitional Justice for the 21st Century* (n 88) 22.
117 Thoms and Ron, 'Do Human Rights Violations Cause Internal Conflict' (n 50) 676.
118 Miller, 'Effects of Invisibility' (n 49) 268.
119 Leslie Thielen-Wilson, 'Troubling the Path to Decolonization: Indian Residential School Case Law, Genocide, and Settler Illegitimacy.' (2014) 29(2) Canadian Journal of Law and Society 181, 182.
120 Truth and Reconciliation Commission of Canada, Honouring the Truth, Reconciling for the Future: Summary of the Final Report of the Truth and Reconciliation Commission of Canada (2015) 1.
121 See Paulette Regan, *Unsettling the Settler Within: Indian Residential Schools, Truth Telling, and Reconciliation in Canada* (UBC Press 2010).

One of the most relevant and achievable things a transitional justice mechanism can do when confronting past colonial violence is to set the record straight, particularly in the face of public denial.[122] Expanding dominant understandings of violence to include cultural harm extends the logic of transitional justice to established democracies and makes these abuses visible to greater society.[123] For example, prior to Canada's Truth and Reconciliation Commission, polling in 2008 found that only 51 per cent of non-Indigenous Canadians had heard or read something about the Indian residential schools. After the Truth and Reconciliation Commission completed its work, polling in 2016 found that approximately 66 per cent of non-Indigenous Canadians had heard or read something about the Indian residential schools.[124]

The way in which conflict is remembered and narrated has important implications beyond simply producing a truthful account. Transitional mechanisms not only tell a story about what happened in the past, but also help shape the issues that need to be resolved in the future.[125] As Zinaida Miller rightly asserts, the 'post-conflict vocabulary is limited by the mechanisms that deploy it'.[126] Thus, the story that is told through transitional programming has the potential to help set an agenda for post-transitional recovery, including through legislative and development policies at the national level.

Excluding or backgrounding cultural rights violations in transitional justice hinders the range of possible policy options available to States.[127] By ignoring the cultural underpinnings of conflict, it limits the ability of various stakeholders to advocate for longer-term cultural reforms, particularly at the national level. In the absence of accounting for cultural harm, framed as human rights violations, it is easier for States to reject the legitimate grievances of victims.[128] New governments may come into power and claim to address past injustices, while maintaining the status quo of deep-seated cultural inequality.[129]

122 Priya Pillai, 'Truth Commissions and Colonial Atrocities: Moving the Needle Further Towards State Responsibility?' OpinioJuris (27 April 2019) <http://opiniojuris.org/2019/04/27/truth-commissions-and-colonial-atrocities-moving-the-needle-further-towards-state-responsibility/> accessed 1 February 2025.

123 See Rosemary Nagy, 'The Scope and Bounds of Transitional Justice and the Canadian Truth and Reconciliation Commission' (2013) 7(1) International Journal of Transitional Justice 52, 72.

124 Canadian Public Opinion on Aboriginal Peoples, Indian Residential Schools and the Truth and Reconciliation Commission <https://www.environicsinstitute.org/docs/default-source/project-documents/public-opinion-about-aboriginal-issues-in-canada-2016/indian-residential-schools-and-the-trc.pdf?sfvrsn=25b66577_2#:~:text=Awareness%20of%20the%20TRC%20varies,education%20level%20and%20household%20income.> accessed 1 February 2025.

125 Miller, 'Effects of Invisibility' (n 49) 280–84.

126 ibid 284.

127 See Sharp, 'Addressing Dilemmas of the Global and the Local in Transitional Justice' (n 86) 792.

128 Laplante, 'Transitional Justice and Peace Building' (n 10) 342.

129 Miller, 'Effects of Invisibility' (n 49) 283.

In turn, victims may fairly come to see transitional justice as a new manifestation of the same oppressive system.

Conversely, when cultural rights violations, and the cultural roots of other forms of violence, are accounted for in transitional justice processes, they are more likely to be the subject of future policy-making.[130] Lisa Laplante argues that by viewing underlying harms 'not as unchangeable facts of life but as consequences of conscious policy decisions that fail to protect fundamental rights', transitional justice mechanisms can help promote these types of reforms.[131] Their inclusion could generate a level of awareness and understanding regarding cultural marginalization that could potentially put pressure on governments and non-State actors to begin taking more substantive steps to address these issues.[132]

6. Pragmatic Objections

Conceptual reasons to retain a narrower version of transitional justice have certainly been advanced, but the most compelling objections tend to be practical ones. Some scholars argue that expanding the reach of transitional justice outside core civil and political rights violations will inevitably strain already overburdened mechanisms and saddle them with unreasonable expectations.[133] This pragmatic argument is a serious and compelling challenge to the idea that the field should increasingly engage with cultural rights. Indeed, given the scale of cultural wrongdoing in various contexts, it is difficult to imagine how transitional justice, still a limited and extraordinary form of justice, could possibly remedy such harm.

It is often suggested that expanding transitional justice outside the redress of civil and political rights requires additional resources and expertise. Louise Arbour alluded to this challenge in her initial call for transitional justice to tackle ESC rights violations, acknowledging the 'significant leap' necessary for transitional justice to embrace a broader range of harm.[134] Rama Mani, despite her push for a more holistic conception of justice in post-conflict and divided societies, also acknowledged the 'dilemma' inherent in broadening the scope of harm subject to transitional scrutiny:

130 Laplante, 'Transitional Justice and Peace Building' (n 10) 342.
131 ibid.
132 See Nagy, 'The Scope and Bounds of Transitional Justice' (n 123) 65.
133 See, eg, Waldorf, 'Anticipating the Past' (n 22) 179.
134 Arbour, 'Economic and Social Justice for Societies in Transition' (n 25) 2.

> the patterns of social injustice are so wide, their victims so many, their impact and consequences so far ranging for the individuals and communities that it is difficult at first glance to envisage how to encompass them within the finite range of the targeted measures of transitional justice, be they trials, truth commissions or institutional reforms.[135]

Mani further remarks that 'existing transitional justice mechanisms are already overcharged, their responsibilities too heavy, public expectations too unrealistic and finances already too lean.'[136] Thus, even proponents of 'thicker'[137] forms of justice have been cognisant of the practical limitations of transitional justice mechanisms on the ground.

Waldorf, in particular, has articulated an apt and forceful objection to overburdening transitional justice mechanisms through forcing socio-economic considerations into their remit. For him, practical considerations will hinder the ability of transitional justice to address socio-economic rights violations, in part because post-conflict mechanisms are already overstretched, underfunded, and lack the necessary expertise.[138] Waldorf maintains that there is a real danger that the inclusion of socio-economic considerations will raise already inflated expectations of what transitional justice can accomplish.[139] He ultimately reinforces a narrow conception of transitional justice as 'inherently short-term, legalistic and corrective', with institutional inequality better left to post-transitional efforts made by the new democratic regime.[140]

These practical limitations have been echoed by others sceptical of the capacity of transitional justice to meaningfully veer into the realm of broad socio-economic reform and issues of development. McAuliffe calls it 'startlingly ambitious' and indeed suggests it is possible for post-conflict societies to transition peacefully without accounting for ESC wrongs.[141] Pablo De Grieff generally agrees, remarking that advocates of an expansive version of transitional justice are 'much too focused on socioeconomic distribution', suggesting

[135] Rama Mani, 'Dilemmas of Expanding Transitional Justice, or Forging the Nexus Between Transitional Justice and Development' (2008) 2(3) The International Journal of Transitional Justice 253, 255.

[136] ibid.

[137] Kieran McEvoy, 'Beyond Legalism: Towards a Thicker Understanding of Transitional Justice' (2017) 34(4) Journal of Law and Society 411.

[138] Waldorf, 'Anticipating the Past' (n 22) 179.

[139] ibid.

[140] ibid.

[141] Padraig McAuliffe, 'Structural Causes of Conflict and the Superficiality of Transition' in Claudio Corradetti and others (eds), Theorizing Transitional Justice (Ashgate Publishing 2015) 94.

that there is no supporting evidence that mechanisms can achieve this.[142] He plainly states that employing transitional justice in response to development deficits in transitional societies is not a serious argument.[143]

To date, pragmatic objections to an expansive version of transitional justice have focused on the potential pitfalls present in seeking to remedy systemic violations of economic and social rights and the push for the field to engage in broader forms of distributive justice and development in post-conflict and divided societies. However, when applied to the prospect of incorporating cultural rights, including addressing large-scale cultural rights violations, such objections do not carry the same force. As illustrated below, transitional justice's engagement with culture does not raise the same level of practical concern associated with the redress of economic and social rights violations, and socio-economic issues more generally.

First, there is an assumption that addressing civil and political rights violations is inherently simpler and cheaper than remedying other wrongs, including cultural rights violations, which require sustained and resource-intensive interventions.[144] However, addressing large-scale cultural rights violations is not a long-term or resource-intensive endeavour by default, just as addressing civil and political rights is not necessarily a cheap, short-term project. Conceiving of the redress of civil and political rights violations as an inherently short-term venture while describing the remedy of cultural rights violations as long-term is misguided.[145]

Undoubtedly, broad structural reforms require massive resources. However, the same can be true with respect to responses to mass physical violence. For instance, the international criminal tribunals employed in post-genocide Rwanda and the former Yugoslavia can hardly be described as short-term, temporary, or limited. Thus, addressing civil and political rights violations through measures focused on accountability and reinforcing the rule of law are not necessarily short-term or low-cost. Indeed, the reform of abusive policies or institutions that infringe on cultural rights would be unlikely to be more resource-intensive than a number of measures focused on providing legal redress of mass civil and political rights violations.[146]

142 Laurel Fletcher and Harvey Weinstein, '"North-South" Dialogue: Bridging the Gap in Transitional Justice—Workshop Transcript' (2018) 36(2) Berkeley Journal of International Law 218, 223.

143 ibid.

144 Arbour, 'Economic and Social Justice for Societies in Transition' (n 25) 11.

145 Schmid and Nolan, '"Do No Harm"' (n 39) 374–75.

146 Arbour, 'Economic and Social Justice for Societies in Transition' (n 25) 12.

Second, the pragmatic objection erroneously assumes that cultural rights violations are inherently structural, rather than discrete.[147] We know that cultural wrongdoing can be and often is systemic violence, requiring a radical transformation at governmental and/or societal levels to redress it. Notwithstanding, discrete violations of cultural rights also occur. Consider, for example, the destruction of tangible cultural heritage during periods of armed conflict. These abuses can be remedied through transitional justice measures on equal footing with other rights violations, without reaching beyond their capacity. A further example is the return of cultural objects or human remains, many of which are housed in museums and other institutions outside their country and/or community of origin.[148] Objects and remains can be restituted and repatriated in ways that do not require broad-based, systemic reform. Thus, like other rights violations, responses to cultural rights violations can be broad or narrow, and would not necessarily overburden the resources or expectations of transitional justice measures.

Lastly, even if we accept that the redress of long-standing economic inequality and structural violence would unduly burden already overtaxed transitional justice mechanisms, the same does not necessarily apply to the redress of cultural rights violations. States will often rely on the progressive nature of ESC rights as a pretext for not adhering to their international human rights obligations in resource-constrained settings.[149] Notwithstanding, cultural harm is not as closely aligned with development projects compared to economic and social rights violations.[150] Remedying cultural wrongs, even systemic ones, does not necessarily entail economic development and redistribution of resources in the same way that violations of socio-economic rights might. Furthermore, political leaders and other stakeholders might hesitate to implement radical economic reforms, but may be more willing to engage in broad cultural reforms that do not necessarily put as much strain on State resources.[151] In this way, addressing cultural rights may be more politically feasible.

We also must consider the fact that transitional justice can exist outside of the fragile, post-conflict settings which most strongly implicate resource concerns.

147 Schmid and Nolan, '"Do No Harm"' (n 39) 371–74.

148 EMRIP, Repatriation of Ceremonial Objects, Human Remains and Intangible Cultural Heritage under the United Nations Declaration on the Rights of Indigenous Peoples, UN Doc A/HRC/45/35 (21 July 2020) para 12.

149 Laplante, 'On the Indivisibility of Rights' (n 26) 150.

150 Sam Szoke-Burke, 'Not Only "Context": Why Transitional Justice Programs Can No Longer Ignore Violations of Economic and Social Rights' (2015) 50 Texas International Law Journal 465, 468.

151 See generally Sharp, *Re-Thinking Transitional Justice for the 21st Century* (n 88) 30–31.

Established democracies are usually not saddled with the same budgetary constraints as most post-conflict and post-authoritarian societies. For example, the United States allocated more than 816 billion USD dollars for its defence budget, alone, in 2023.[152] Moreover, according to the World Bank, 2023 gross domestic product for Australia and Canada exceeded 1.7 trillion USD and 2.1 trillion USD, respectively.[153] Joanna Quinn argues that these countries 'should be held to higher scrutiny, for their relative wealth should provide them with significantly more capacity to right any wrongs that might exist'.[154] These established democracies have the necessary resources, expertise, and institutional capacity at their disposal to tackle all manner of harms, and are in a unique position to grapple with deeply embedded cultural injustices. There is no financial impediment explaining why these countries cannot marshal the resources necessary to address cultural harm in more substantial ways.

[152] United States Senate Committee on Armed Services, Summary of the Fiscal Year 2023—National Defense Authorization Act <https://www.armed-services.senate.gov/imo/media/doc/fy23_ndaa_agreement_summary.pdf> accessed 1 February 2025.

[153] The World Bank Group, 'GDP (Current US$)—World Bank Open Data' <https://data.worldbank.org/indicator/NY.GDP.MKTP.CD> accessed 24 December 2024.

[154] Joanna Quinn, 'Whither the Transition of Transitional Justice' (2014) 8 Interdisciplinary Journal of Human Rights Law 63, 69.

5
A CULTURAL RIGHTS-BASED APPROACH TO TRANSITIONAL JUSTICE

1. Introduction

In 2014, former UN SRCR Farida Shaheed noted that 'all too often, a cultural rights-based approach to transitional justice and reconciliation strategies is not rendered the attention it deserves'.[1] So far, this book has discussed in considerable detail the extent to which transitional justice has and can engage with this distinct category of rights and whether there is value in such an endeavour. It now seeks to think through, articulate, and advance a cultural rights-based approach to transitional justice, one that positions culture at the centre of transitional thinking and praxis.

A cultural rights-based approach to transitional justice is one that addresses large-scale past cultural wrongdoing on the same footing as violations of civil, political, economic, and social rights. It requires that cultural rights standards are protected, respected, and fulfilled in the design, implementation, and operation of transitional justice initiatives. And it encourages using and incorporating cultural practices and interventions as a methodology to confront large-scale past harm and to encourage social reconstruction in post-conflict and divided societies. Critically, this approach is principally guided by the international standards and norms that have developed around the pursuit of transitional justice and the protection of cultural rights.

What exactly this will look like in any given transitional justice context will be governed by a multitude of factors, none of which could possibly lead to a uniform approach. In fact, a cultural rights-based approach inherently eschews a single authoritative way to do transitional justice; instead, it demands

[1] UN OHCHR, 'Integrating Cultural Rights in Transitional Justice Strategies in Post-conflict Societies' <https://www.ohchr.org/EN/NewsEvents/Pages/Integratingculturalrightsinpost-conflictsocieties.aspx> accessed 1 February 2025.

Cultural Rights and Wrongs in Transitional Justice. Colin Luoma, Oxford University Press. © Colin Luoma 2025.
DOI: 10.1093/oso/9780198911371.003.0005

the flexibility to respond to the diverse needs of victims and survivors in post-conflict and divided societies. As the examples in this chapter demonstrate, there is great diversity in the ways in which cultural rights can be respected, addressed, and incorporated in transitional justice processes.

A cultural rights-based approach relies upon and is guided by international human rights law and rights discourses around culture. This perhaps seems inconsistent with retheorizing transitional justice in a way that sheds many of the same biases, priorities, and preoccupations inherited from its parent field of human rights.[2] At the same time, a cultural rights-based approach, rooted in international human rights standards, can be used to hold States legally, morally, and politically accountable for cultural wrongdoing and can also protect, strengthen, and promote cultural rights in transitional justice processes. When employed in harmony with local laws, protocols, traditions, and methodologies, it represents a key tool for confronting cultural harm.

After briefly clarifying and justifying the utility of a cultural rights-based approach in transitional justice, this chapter interrogates the possibilities and limitations of such an approach by examining some of the primary ways in which transitional justice is likely to engage with cultural rights. These include (1) confronting cultural rights violations, (2) accommodating local and Indigenous cultures, (3) employing and accommodating artistic and cultural initiatives, (4) memorialization, and (5) cultural reparations.[3] For each of these broad categories, this chapter draws on examples from across the world to ground a cultural rights-based approach in transitional justice practice. These examples not only illustrate the close nexus between culture and the scope and aims of transitional justice, but arguably demonstrate the viability of adopting a cultural rights-based approach to addressing legacies of past large-scale harm.

2. Clarifying and Justifying a Cultural Rights-based Approach

A cultural rights-based approach to transitional justice envisages incorporating and relying on the existing corpus of international law that protects the rights of individuals and groups to access, develop, participate in, enjoy, and benefit from their cultures. Transitional justice agendas, policies, and initiatives should

[2] Dustin N Sharp, *Re-thinking Transitional Justice for the Twenty-First Century* (Cambridge University Press 2018) 37.

[3] A focus on these processes is by no means intended to marginalize the myriad other ways in which transitional justice can embrace a cultural rights-based approach.

be guided and informed by these hard-earned cultural rights protections under international human rights law. Human rights are a commonly used vehicle to advocate for a host of social justice issues in our globalized society.[4] In the professed 'age of human rights',[5] denominating State action as violative of human rights standards has become an increasingly utilized and persuasive tactic.[6] The UN OHCHR describes a human rights-based approach as

> a conceptual framework that is normatively based on international human rights standards and operationally directed to promoting and protecting human rights. It seeks to analyze obligations, inequalities and vulnerabilities and to redress discriminatory practices and unjust distributions of power that impede progress and undercut human rights.[7]

A signature of a human rights-based approach is an emphasis on the accountability of the State by drawing attention to its international legal obligations. Victims and survivors are positioned as rightsholders, which empowers them to demand that the State respect, protect, and fulfil their fundamental human rights, including by ensuring adequate redress and remedies for associated violations. In turn, a cultural rights-based approach to transitional justice requires that mechanisms would not only increasingly elucidate applicable cultural rights standards, but also would ideally judge State conduct against international legal commitments.[8]

Transitional justice has its foundation in the field of human rights, considered by many to be an arm of the human rights movement.[9] Most transitional justice

[4] See, eg, UN OHCHR, 'Applying a Human-Rights Based Approach to Climate Change Negotiations, Policies and Measures' <https://www.uncclearn.org/wp-content/uploads/library/infonotehrba1.pdf> accessed 23 June 2025; UN OHCHR, 'Principles and Guidelines for a Human Rights Approach to Poverty Reduction Strategies', HR/PUB/06/12 <https://www.ohchr.org/Documents/Publications/PovertyStrategiesen.pdf> accessed 1 February 2025; see also Ineke Boerefijn, 'A Human-Rights Based Approach of Violence Against Women' (2007) 4 International Studies Journal 181.

[5] Kofi Annan, 'The Age of Human Rights', Project Syndicate (26 September 2000) <https://www.project-syndicate.org/commentary/the-age-of-human-rights-2000-09> accessed 1 February 2025.

[6] Frank Haldemann and Rachelle Kouassi, 'Transitional Justice without Economic, Social and Cultural Rights?' in Eibe Riedel and others (eds), *Economic, Social, and Cultural Rights: Contemporary Issues and Challenges* (Oxford University Press 2014) 502.

[7] UN OHCHR, 'Applying a Human-Rights Based Approach to Climate Change Negotiations, Policies and Measures' (n 4).

[8] Brenda L Gunn, 'Engaging a Human Rights Based Approach to the Murdered and Missing Indigenous Women and Girls Inquiry' (2017) 2(2) Lakehead Law Journal 90, 95.

[9] Makau Mutua, 'What Is the Future of Transitional Justice' (2015) 9 International Journal of Transitional Justice 1, 3; see also Jennifer Balint and Julie Evans, 'Transitional Justice and Settler States' The Australian and New Zealand Critical Criminology Conference (2011) 2; Ismael Muvingi, 'Sitting on Powder Kegs: Socioeconomic Rights in Transitional Societies' (2009) 3(2) International Journal of Transitional Justice 163, 166.

professionals already rely on human rights law as a core normative framework for addressing past violations of civil and political rights.[10] Cultural rights, on the other hand, are less frequently viewed through a human rights lens in transitional justice.[11] This, of course, is reflective of the historically subordinated position of cultural rights in the broader human rights hierarchy.

Several authors question the reliance that transitional justice places on human rights law. Many of the same reasons that contributed to transitional justice's marginalization of cultural rights were inherited from the parent field of human rights, where cultural rights are often viewed as rights of lesser priority. The parallelism in the treatment of cultural rights in these two fields is unsurprising, as it is well accepted that developments in one area of international law often influence and promote similar developments in a separate field.[12] Another central challenge to rights-based approaches in transitional justice focuses on the tendency for human rights to rely heavily on individualized remedies rather than broader, collective forms of justice.[13] This critique is especially salient in the context of Indigenous Peoples, where human rights-based approaches invoke additional dilemmas, with authors maintaining that such an approach is not a viable vehicle to meeting Indigenous demands around self-determination, land, and culture.[14] Still others argue that human rights-based approaches can both protect human rights and support Indigenous self-determination.[15]

[10] Evelyne Schmid and Aoife Nolan, '"Do No Harm"? Exploring the Scope of Economic and Social Rights in Transitional Justice' (2014) 8(3) International Journal of Transitional Justice 362, 364–65.

[11] Evelyne Schmid, 'Socio-Economic and Cultural Rights and Wrongs after Armed Conflicts: Using the State Reporting Procedure before the United Nations Committee on Economic, Social and Cultural Rights More Effectively' (2013) 31(3) Netherlands Quarterly of Human Rights 241, 243.

[12] See, eg, Alexander Orakhelashvili, 'The Interaction between Human Rights and Humanitarian Law: Fragmentation, Conflict, Parallelism, or Convergence?' (2008) 19(1) European Journal of International Law 161.

[13] Rosemary Nagy, 'The Scope and Bounds of Transitional Justice and the Canadian Truth and Reconciliation Commission' (2013) 7(1) International Journal of Transitional Justice 52, 60–61; see also Nicola Henry, 'From Reconciliation to Transitional Justice: The Contours of Redress Politics in Established Democracies' (2015) 9(2) International Journal of Transitional Justice 199, 214.

[14] Patrick Macklem, *The Sovereignty of Human Rights* (Oxford University Press 2015).; Karen Engle, *The Elusive Promise of Indigenous Development: Rights, Culture, Strategy* (Duke University Press 2010); Andrew Erueti, *The UN Declaration on the Rights of Indigenous Peoples: A New Interpretative Approach* (Oxford University Press 2022); Jeff Corntassel and Cindy Holder, 'Who's Sorry Now? Government Apologies, Truth Commissions, and Indigenous Self-Determination in Australia, Canada, Guatemala, and Peru' (2008) 9 Human Rights Review 465, 472; Courtney Jung, 'Canada and the Legacy of the Indian Residential Schools: Transitional Justice for Indigenous People in a Nontransitional Society' in Paige Arthur (ed), *Identities in Transition: Challenges for Transitional Justice in Divided Societies* (Cambridge University Press 2010) 217.

[15] James Anaya, 'Divergent Discourses about International Law, Indigenous Peoples, and Rights over Lands and Natural Resources: Toward a Realist Trend' (2005) 16 Colorado Journal of International Environmental Law and Policy 237, 241–43.

The ways in which international human rights law has evolved in recent years have arguably diluted these otherwise cogent critiques. While civil and political rights still tend to be prioritized, cultural rights are no longer wholly neglected in the human rights arena. There is now a suite of cultural rights protections, developed under international human rights law, that can be referenced, relied upon, and incorporated in transitional justice policy and programming. These protections are scattered throughout various universal and regional instruments, taking the form of binding treaties and soft law declarations and recommendations, and clarified by various interpretations by human rights bodies.[16]

The most important cultural rights protection is the right of everyone to take part in cultural life contained in Article 15(1)(a) of the ICESCR. It is the cornerstone legal protection for cultural rights in the field of international human rights law, in no small part because of the relatively large number of States that have ratified the treaty.[17] Pursuant to the right to take part in cultural life, States have the positive obligation to adopt specific measures aimed at ensuring the right of everyone to freely choose their own cultural identity, as well as the negative obligation to refrain from interfering with the right to take part in cultural life.[18] These obligations are largely programmatic, in the sense that States must take steps to progressively realize them.[19] However, certain core obligations must be immediately implemented regardless of the financial situation of the State.[20]

Beyond the ICESCR, a number of other binding human rights treaties protect the right to culture. The International Convention on the Elimination of all Forms of Racial Discrimination ('ICERD') contains an overarching non-discrimination provision with respect to the enjoyment of cultural rights, including 'the right to equal participation in cultural activities'.[21] Other treaties protect the cultural rights of specific categories of individuals, including

[16] This fragmentation has contributed to some confusion in conceptualizing cultural rights. Janusz Symonides, 'Cultural Rights: A Neglected Category of Human Rights' 50(158) International Social Science Journal 559, 560; see also Alexandra Xanthaki, 'Indigenous Cultural Rights in International Law' (2000) 2 European Journal of Law Reform 343, 344.

[17] As of June 2025, 173 countries are parties to the ICESCR. See UN Treaty Collection, International Covenant on Economic, Social and Cultural Rights <https://treaties.un.org/Pages/ViewDetails.aspx?src=TREATY&mtdsg_no=IV-3&chapter=4> accessed 1 February 2025.

[18] UN CESCR, General Comment No. 21, Right of Everyone to Take Part in Cultural Life (Art 15, para 1a of the Covenant on Economic, Social and Cultural Rights), UN Doc E/C.12/GC/21 (21 December 2009) para 48–49.

[19] International Covenant on Economic, Social and Cultural Rights (1966) 993 UNTS 3, Art 2.1.

[20] CESCR, General Comment No 21 (n 18) para 55.

[21] International Convention on the Elimination of All Forms of Racial Discrimination (1963) 660 UNTS 195, Art 5(e)(vi).

the Convention on the Elimination of All Forms of Discrimination against Women ('CEDAW') (prohibiting discrimination against women with respect to the 'right to participate in ... all aspects of cultural life'),[22] the International Convention on the Protection of the Rights of All Migrant Workers and Members of Their Families ('ICMW') (protecting the cultural identities of migrant workers and their families and ensuring non-discrimination with respect to their right to access and participate in cultural life),[23] the Convention on the Rights of the Child ('CRC') (ensuring the right of children to participate and enjoy their own culture, use their own language, and receive an education aimed at the development of their own cultures, languages, and values),[24] and the Convention on the Rights of Persons with Disabilities ('CRPD') (providing for the right of disabled individuals to participate in 'cultural life, recreation, leisure and sport').[25] Not only should these standards influence the design, operation, and implementation of transitional justice programming, but, when possible and appropriate, mechanisms should explicitly link wrongdoing to violations of these international norms.

Other critics of the outsized role of human rights in transitional justice point to the purported incompatibility between the universal nature of human rights and the prioritization of local and Indigenous justice traditions and processes. Abdullahi An-Na'im argues that local and Indigenous justice practices are deemed unacceptable because they are inconsistent with universal human rights norms mandated by the international community, so much so that the 'possibility of an indigenous alternative conception of justice is not taken seriously at a theoretical or empirical level'.[26] Thus, for An-Na'im, transitional justice's predominant focus on universal human rights renders the field 'neocolonial'.[27]

Notwithstanding, and as discussed in Chapter 3 of this book, justice can be increasingly conceived to include local and Indigenous laws, protocols, and practices that significantly diverge from Western formulations of law and justice. Transitional justice can respect culturally diverse modes of justice while still protecting fundamental rights and peremptory norms of international law. International human rights law and non-Western cultural

[22] Convention on the Elimination of All Forms of Discrimination Against Women (1981) 1249 UNTS 13, Art. 13.

[23] International Convention on the Protection of the Rights of All Migrant Workers and Members of their Families (2003) 2220 UNTS 3, Arts 17.1, 31, and 43.1(g).

[24] Convention on the Rights of the Child (1990) 1577 UNTS 3, Art 29, 30.

[25] Convention on the Rights of Persons with Disabilities (2008) 2515 UNTS 3, Art 30.

[26] Abdullahi Ahmed An-Na'im, 'Editorial Note: From the Neocolonial "Transitional" to Indigenous Formations of Justice' (2013) 7 The International Journal of Transitional Justice 197, 197.

[27] ibid.

practices can be balanced and reconciled in transitional justice, even if there will be at times challenging cases to negotiate. Perhaps equally important is the fact that victims themselves often invoke the language and principles of international human rights law in their justice claims. Accordingly, there is a particular power and salience in employing human rights-based approaches in transitional justice.

There is certainly a risk associated with an overreliance on the strict application of universal human rights standards to effectuate justice for societies in transition. Despite these risks, there are several reasons to embrace a cultural rights-based approach. First, it provides a normative framework to delineate the cultural rights of individuals and groups that States are expected to respect, protect, and fulfil. Under a cultural rights-based approach, these rights are positioned as legal requirements to be adhered to by governments, as opposed to policy choices or aspirations. In turn, it empowers transitional justice measures to treat cultural harm as violative of State international legal commitments, triggering an obligation to provide a remedy and an effective mechanism of redress to victims.[28] On a normative level, a cultural rights-based approach can also reinforce the indivisibility, interrelation, and interdependence between cultural rights violations and other serious violations of human rights.

Second, international human rights standards provide critical guidance in the design, development, operation, and implementation of transitional justice policy and programming. As rightsholders, victims are entitled to be active participants in the formation of transitional justice measures and should principally be the ones to determine how States and other actors are held to account for violations of their cultural rights.[29] Cultural rights standards can set the minimum requirements for what needs to be adhered to in transitional justice programming in order to respect cultural identities, diversity, and practices and to ultimately ensure a peaceful transition.[30] These standards can serve as important guideposts for designing and implementing transitional justice measures.

[28] See UN General Assembly, Basic Principles and Guidelines on the Right to a Remedy and Reparation for Victims of Gross Violations of International Human Rights Law and Serious Violations of International Humanitarian Law, UN Doc A/RES/60/147 (21 March 2006).

[29] OHCHR, 'Applying a Human-Rights Based Approach to Climate Change Negotiations, Policies and Measures' (n 4).

[30] Amanda Cahill, 'Foregrounding Socioeconomic Rights in Transitional Justice: Realising Justice for Violations of Economic and Social Rights' (2014) 32(2) Netherlands Quarterly of Human Rights 183, 213.

Third, a cultural rights-based approach disabuses States and other actors of the delusion that cultural harm is the byproduct of policy choices of a bygone era. Instead, acts of cultural wrongdoing were and continue to constitute violations of international legal standards and State obligations. By linking cultural wrongdoing to human rights commitments, the claims of victims become perceived as more legitimate because they are framed as a breach of international human rights norms, and it puts the onus on the State to account for its actions through the lens of legal obligations as opposed to policy choices.[31] In this way it becomes more difficult for governments and majority societies to reject cultural grievances outright.

Lastly, and as discussed in the preceding chapter, by linking the destruction and denigration of cultures to right violations, as opposed to presenting it as inevitable facts of life, a cultural rights-based approach can potentially put pressure on States to engage in more substantive long-term reforms.[32] Under international human rights law, States must take affirmative steps to ensure that individuals and groups are able to access, participate in, and benefit from their cultures.[33] To the extent that transitional justice measures treat cultural harm as violative of human rights commitments, they can push States to undertake more widespread and lasting measures to guarantee cultural rights.

The temptation to resort to human rights as an exclusive route to understanding and engaging with cultural harm should certainly be avoided. Cultural wrongdoing is multifaceted, justifying a holistic approach to justice that responds to multiple layers of harm. Indigenous and local worldviews and justice processes do not need to be discarded in order to effectively leverage cultural rights protections in furtherance of justice. This also does not preclude non-rights-based responses to cultural harm, particularly local grassroots initiatives, which remain vital to successful holistic strategies. Instead, by adopting a complementary stance, a human rights-based approach helps transitional justice understand and address cultural harm more thoroughly and thoughtfully.

[31] National Inquiry into Missing and Murdered Indigenous Women and Girls, *Reclaiming Power and Place: The Final Report of the National Inquiry into Missing and Murdered Indigenous Women and Girls* (2019) 201.

[32] Lisa J Laplante, 'Transitional Justice and Peace Building: Diagnosing and Addressing the Socio-economic Roots of Violence Through a Human Rights Framework' (2008) 2(3) The International Journal of Transitional Justice 331, 342.

[33] See CESCR, General Comment No 21 (n 18).

3. Confronting Cultural Rights Violations

A cultural rights-based approach to transitional justice envisions a growing number of initiatives addressing serious, large-scale violations of cultural rights. Cultural rights violations should rightly be considered subjects for potential redress in the decision-making processes around the selection and prioritization of violations, rather than automatically being relegated as inherently less serious and grave abuses. By directly addressing cultural rights violations, including by linking them to international human rights law standards, transitional justice frameworks can contribute to increased accountability for cultural harm.

There is no prescribed methodology for States or policymakers to determine what violations to address in any given setting, but there are a number of international standards which guide the application of transitional justice and militate in favour of addressing and redressing cultural rights violations. At the level of the UN, the normative transitional justice framework is rooted in two key documents: (1) the Updated Set of Principles for the Protection and Promotion of Human Rights Through Action to Combat Impunity (the 'Joinet/Orentlicher Principles') and (2) the Basic Principles and Guidelines on the Right to a Remedy and Reparation for Victims of Gross Violations of International Human Rights Law and Serious Violations of International Humanitarian Law (the 'Basic Principles and Guidelines').[34]

The Joinet/Orentlicher Principles provide a useful framework for understanding some of the fundamental objectives and characteristics of transitional justice. In their most important contribution, they articulate the four central pillars of the field: (1) the right to justice, (2) the right to truth, (3) the right to reparation, and (4) guarantees of non-recurrence.[35] These serve as guideposts for transitional justice policymaking and, as a set of mutually reinforcing tenets, they have also birthed a wide-ranging set of measures.[36] Indeed, the traditional mechanisms and processes most commonly associated with transitional justice (criminal prosecutions, truth commissions, reparations, institutional reform, memorialization, etc.) largely seek to facilitate the realization of these rights.[37]

[34] UN Commission on Human Rights, Report of the Independent Expert to Update the Set of Principles to Combat Impunity, UN Doc E/CN.4/2005/102/Add.1 (8 February 2005); Basic Principles and Guidelines (n 28).

[35] Joinet/Orentlicher Principles (n 34).

[36] Report of the Special Rapporteur on the Promotion of Truth, Justice, Reparation and Guarantees of Non-Recurrence, UN Doc A/HRC/21/46 (9 August 2012).

[37] Marcos Zunino, *Justice Framed: A Genealogy of Transitional Justice* (Cambridge University Press 2019) 4.

Pursuant to the right to justice, States are obliged to act against perpetrators and on behalf of victims of human rights abuses.[38] The Basic Principles and Guidelines provide that States have an obligation to 'investigate violations effectively, promptly, thoroughly and impartially and, where appropriate, take action against those allegedly responsible in accordance with domestic and international law'.[39] Victims must be ensured 'equal access to an effective judicial remedy as provided for under international law', regardless of who ultimately bears responsibility for the violation(s).[40] Thus, all victims should have the opportunity to assert their rights and seek justice against their wrongdoers.[41]

3.1 Prosecuting the intentional destruction of cultural heritage at the ICC

With regard to the right of victims to seek justice for cultural rights violations, positive and evolving practice can be seen in the area of cultural heritage. The destruction of tangible cultural heritage (i.e. cultural property) is one of the very few areas where transitional justice has sought to confront cultural rights violations.[42] As discussed in Chapter 1, the *Al Mahdi* case at the ICC set an important precedent for prosecuting the destruction of tangible cultural heritage as a war crime. This case was symbolically important for the Court, in terms of legitimizing cultural heritage destruction as a war crime but also in sending a clear message about its devastating impacts and the potential legal consequences flowing from such acts.[43]

In the realm of prosecuting cultural heritage crimes, transitional justice practice and scholarship has overwhelmingly focused on the intentional destruction of tangible cultural heritage, as opposed to intangible cultural heritage.[44]

[38] UN Secretary-General, 'The Rule of Law and Transitional Justice in Conflict and Post-Conflict Societies', UN Doc S/2004/616 (23 August 2004) para 54.

[39] Basic Principles and Guidelines (n 28) para 3(b).

[40] ibid para 3(c), 12.

[41] UN Commission on Human Rights, Set of Principles for the Protection and Promotion of Human Rights through Action to Combat Impunity, UN Doc E/CN.4/Sub.2/1997/20/Rev.1 (2 October 1997) para 26.

[42] Philippe Sands and Ashrutha Rai, 'After the Dust Settles: Transitional Justice and Identity in the Aftermath of Cultural Destruction' in James Cuno and Thomas G. Weiss (eds) *Cultural Heritage and Mass Atrocities* (Getty Publications 2022) 345.

[43] Marina Lostal, 'The Misplaced Emphasis on the Intangible Dimension of Cultural Heritage in the Al Mahdi Case at the ICC' (2017) 1(2) Inter Gentes—The McGill Journal of International Law & Legal Pluralism 45, 46.

[44] See, eg, Patty Gerstenblith, 'The Destruction of Cultural Heritage: A Crime Against Property or a Crime Against People?' (2016) 15(336) John Marshall Review of Intellectual Property Law 337, 338, n 2.

Tangible cultural heritage (monuments, buildings, archaeological or historic sites, works of art, etc.) is explicitly protected under a variety of international treaties, including in Article 8 of the Rome Statute; intangible cultural heritage (traditions, customs, and expressions) is not afforded the same level of explicit protection.

The *Al Madhi* case, however, arguably opened the door for future prosecutions of the destruction of not just tangible cultural heritage but also intangible cultural heritage under the Rome Statute.[45] At the charging stage of the *Al Mahdi* case, the ICC Prosecutor issued a statement emphasizing the human element of the defendant's alleged crimes:

> Let there be no mistake: the charges we have brought against Ahmad Al Faqi Al Mahdi involve the most serious crimes; they are about the destruction of irreplaceable historic monuments, and they are about a callous assault on the dignity and identity of entire populations and their religious and historical roots.[46]

While the Prosecutor was not ultimately able to build upon the human rights nexus in cultural heritage destruction in the case due to Al Mahdi's guilty plea, the Reparations Order did note that 'cultural heritage is important not only in itself, but also in relation to its human dimension'.[47]

The ICC's signalling of a broadened approach to cultural heritage in the *Al Mahdi* case has not been universally celebrated, however. Marina Lostal argues that emphasizing the intangible aspects of cultural heritage is not an effective long-term strategy.[48] For Lostal, a focus on the human element of cultural heritage destruction is a departure from the rationale behind the criminality of destroying cultural property which existed before the human rights movement.[49] The risk is that elevating the intangible aspects of the destruction of cultural heritage may actually hinder future prosecutions, with Lostal suggesting that a 'anthropocentric reading' of the crime may result in courts 'turning a blind eye

[45] Joseph Powderly, 'Prosecuting Heritage Destruction' in James Cuno and Thomas G. Weiss (eds), *Cultural Heritage and Mass Atrocities* (Getty Publications 2022) 443.

[46] Statement of the Prosecutor of the International Criminal Court, Fatou Bensouda, following the transfer of the first suspect in the Mali investigation: 'Intentional Attacks against Historic Monuments and Buildings Dedicated to Religion Are Grave Crimes' (26 September 2015) <https://www.icc-cpi.int/news/statement-prosecutor-international-criminal-court-fatou-bensouda-following-transfer-first> accessed 1 February 2025.

[47] *Prosecutor v Al Mahdi,* Reparations Order, International Criminal Court Case No. ICC-01/12-01/15-236 (17 August 2017) para 16.

[48] Lostal, 'The Misplaced Emphasis on the Intangible Dimension of Cultural Heritage' (n 43) 51.

[49] ibid 53.

to episodes of damage and destruction that do not affect the social or cultural practices of a specific population'.[50]

Notwithstanding this critique, the ICC has seemingly leaned into an anthropogenic conception of the crime of cultural heritage destruction and has taken significant steps towards committing itself to potentially investigating and prosecuting the intentional destruction of intangible cultural heritage as a war crime. This is most evident through the Office of the Prosecutor's ('OTP') Policy on Cultural Heritage, published in 2021.[51] Among other things, the OTP has committed to addressing 'alleged crimes against or affecting cultural heritage in all stages of its work: preliminary examination, investigation, prosecution, and—when so invited—reparations'.[52] It also explicitly recognized the breadth of cultural heritage, including its tangible and intangible forms.[53] According to the OTP, the destruction of both forms of cultural heritage produces devastating losses for affected local communities, as well as the international community more broadly.[54]

Critically, the OTP expanded its conception of 'cultural heritage' beyond that of cultural property enshrined in the Rome Statute. In aiming to consider 'the broadest possible scope of criminality',[55] it construes 'cultural heritage' as both the 'products and processes' of culture.[56] In this way, it commits itself to considering the destruction of intangible cultural heritage in future prosecutions. In prioritizing the human dimension, the Policy states that cultural heritage wrongs are first and foremost, an attack on group identity and practices.[57] According to the OTP, this broadened interpretation of heritage will 'enable it to present the multifaceted nature and impact of crimes against or affecting cultural heritage'.[58]

The OTP's Policy on Cultural Heritage also makes clear the close links between cultural heritage and human rights. The Policy was developed in close collaboration with cultural rights experts, including those at UNESCO; the UN SRCR; and cultural rights scholars.[59] Despite the fact that the crime of intentional destruction of cultural heritage has not historically been associated

[50] ibid 55.
[51] The Office of the Prosecutor of the International Criminal Court, *Policy on Cultural Heritage* (June 2021) <https://www.icc-cpi.int/sites/default/files/itemsDocuments/20210614-otp-policy-cultural-heritage-eng.pdf> accessed 1 February 2025.
[52] ibid para 5.
[53] ibid para 3.
[54] ibid para 4.
[55] ibid para 30.
[56] ibid para 15.
[57] ibid para 17.
[58] ibid para 30.
[59] ibid para 21.

with the deprivation of cultural rights,[60] the OTP committed itself to 'acting with respect for cultural rights', further noting that the Rome Statute must be interpreted consistently with international human rights law.[61] It also acknowledged that attacks on cultural heritage may violate international human rights law and that the protection of cultural heritage is reflected in cultural rights, including the right to take part in cultural life and the right of minorities to enjoy their culture.[62] This is reflective of a broader shift in the field of cultural heritage away from the protection and preservation of cultural heritage on the basis of its universal value to humanity, and towards the protection of cultural heritage based on its value to the cultural identities of individuals and communities.[63]

The ICC's evolving stance on cultural heritage, as reflected in the *Al Mahdi* case and the OTP's Policy on Cultural Heritage, signals a slight shift towards a cultural rights-based approach. By recognizing the intrinsic link between cultural heritage and human identity, the Court has moved beyond a strictly property-based framework to one that acknowledges the social and cultural dimensions of heritage loss. This approach aligns with broader international human rights law, which increasingly emphasizes the close connections between cultural heritage and cultural rights. While critiques remain regarding the long-term viability of this perspective, the ICC's commitment to prosecuting crimes against both tangible and intangible heritage underscores the growing recognition of cultural heritage as an essential component of human rights and collective identity.

3.2 Reconciliation in Greenland

The Greenlandic Reconciliation Commission ('GRC') was initiated by the self-autonomous government of Greenland in 2014. While the case of Greenland is less researched and perhaps more obscure than the host of recent truth and reconciliation commissions in the Arctic, it was the first setting where a formal reconciliation commission was established in the region.[64] The GRC was

[60] Lostal, 'The Misplaced Emphasis on the Intangible Dimension of Cultural Heritage' (n 43) 51.

[61] Policy on Cultural Heritage (n 51) para 7.

[62] ibid para 28.

[63] See, eg, CESCR, General Comment No 21 (n 18) para 50; Report of the Independent Expert in the Field of Cultural Rights, Farida Shaheed, UN Doc A/HRC/17/38 (21 March 2011) paras 9–17.

[64] Elin Skaar, 'The Nordic Truth and Reconciliation Commissions: A New TRC Model for Resolving Historic and Ongoing Violations of Indigenous Rights' in Ray Aldred, John Klaasen, and Line M Skum (eds), *Cultivating Transformative Reconciliation* (Pickwick 2024) 7.

mandated to address the historical legacy of the colonial era in Greenland, but it ultimately focused on the 'modernization period' after Greenland formally became a part of the Danish Kingdom in 1953.[65]

Interestingly, Denmark refused to meaningfully engage with the reconciliation process in Greenland. Then Danish Prime Minister Helle Thorning-Schmidt reportedly stated: 'We have no need for reconciliation, however, I fully respect that that is a discussion that concerns the Greenlandic people. We will follow the discussion closely from here.'[66] As a result, the GRC elected to focus solely on reconciliation within Greenland, with four different dimensions: (1) reconciliation with one's self and one's own background (personal reconciliation); (2) reconciliation with the past (things that happened); (3) reconciliation between groups in the Greenlandic society (human relations at large); and (4) reconciliation between generations (on an individual level).[67] This internal focus evaded Denmark's status as a colonial power, and the GRC made no attempt to link past wrongdoing to Denmark's international obligations.[68]

The GRC presented its final report in December 2017 under the title 'We understand the past—We take responsibility for the present—We work for a better future'.[69] While not an official truth-seeking mechanism, it did identify a number of cultural wrongs at the heart of conflict and division in Greenlandic society. The forced removals of Greenlandic children, restrictions on traditional hunting and trapping, and the oppression of Greenlandic language all feature in the final report. The Danish modernization policy forced Greenlandic children as young as nine or ten years old to move to Nuuk or even Denmark to learn the Danish language and adopt its culture.[70] Education was noted as a specific concern for Greenlandic culture, with education systems

[65] Greenland did not achieve self-autonomy until the Self-Government Act of 2009, which granted Greenland self-governance over more areas and recognized Greenlanders as distinct peoples under the law with the right to self-determination. Act on Greenland Self-Government, Act No 473 (12 June 2009) (unofficial English translation) <https://natlex.ilo.org/dyn/natlex2/natlex2/files/download/110442/DNK110442%20Eng.pdf> accessed 24 June 2025.

[66] Arne Finne, 'Abuse and Colony Era Still Marks Greenlanders' *High North News* (25 October 2018) <https://www.highnorthnews.com/en/abuse-and-colony-era-still-marks-greenlanders> accessed 1 February 2025.

[67] Greenland's Reconciliation Commission, *We Understand the Past; We Take Responsibility for the Present; We Are Working for a Better Future* (December 2017).

[68] Astrid Nonbo Andersen, 'Lessons from the Greenlandic Reconciliation Process', JusticeInfo.Net (5 March 2020) <https://www.justiceinfo.net/en/43949-lessons-from-the-greenlandic-reconciliation-process.html> accessed 1 February 2025.

[69] GRC, *We Understand the Past* (n 67).

[70] ibid 38.

mainly running in Danish and not reflecting 'the Greenlandic culture, the Greenlandic language and the Greenlandic community'.[71] However, none of this was framed by the GRC as violative of cultural rights under international human rights law.

The GRC arguably embraced a broadened conception of violence in that it treated colonial wrongdoing on par with armed conflict. For example, the GRC observed that Danish colonialization and its resulting legacies created an 'internal war', causing self-destruction of individuals and communities.[72] Temporally, the GRC had a mandate to identify challenges in Greenlandic society as a result of colonial heritage.[73] However, it gave very little attention to the 250 years of colonization before Greenland was integrated into the Kingdom of Denmark in 1953. Thus, while tasked with addressing colonial legacies, the GRC elected to be relatively presentist in discharging its duties.

In its recommendations, the GRC addressed some of the cultural dimensions and legacies of the colonial area. It emphasized the need to narrate history from a Greenlandic perspective, in the form of a 'Greenland story—seen with our eyes', which could potentially build cultural pride in Greenlandic people.[74] The narration of this history would be grounded in local history and traditions, supported by the archives of the Danish State. The GRC further recommended legislative reform on the implementation and strengthening of Greenlandic language.[75] It also proposed for cultural reforms in the form of a Greenlandic calendar, one that reflects the culture and traditions of the Greenlandic people.[76]

Despite the important work on the GRC, in an otherwise challenging political environment, it can hardly be said that the Commission fully embraced a cultural rights-based approach to its work. Much of the harm plaguing Greenlandic society stems from the mass cultural wrongdoing perpetrated by the Danish government during its various stages of colonization. Yet, the GRC did not fully grapple with this wrongdoing, nor did it position it as a conscious choice of the Danish government in violation of its cultural rights obligations under international law.

[71] ibid 41–42.
[72] ibid 8.
[73] ibid 10.
[74] ibid 44.
[75] ibid 45.
[76] ibid 47.

4. Accommodating Local and Indigenous Cultures

A cultural rights-based approach to transitional justice respects and accommodates diverse ways of doing justice, including deferring to local and Indigenous laws, traditions, customs, and protocols. The idea that transitional justice processes must respect local and Indigenous values, traditions, and cultures is already institutionalized in transitional justice standard-setting, and is embraced, at least rhetorically, at the UN. The UN Secretary-General has long acknowledged that transitional justice programming must give 'due regard' to 'indigenous and informal traditions for administrating justice or settling disputes, to help them to continue their vital role and to do so in conformity with both international standards and local tradition'.[77] Moreover, in the context of Indigenous Peoples, the UN Expert Mechanism on the Rights of Indigenous Peoples ('EMRIP') suggests that 'transitional justice processes should be adapted to ensure cultural appropriateness and consistency with customary legal practices and concepts concerning justice and conflict resolution'.[78] International human rights law also obligates States to respect local and Indigenous cultures in the scope of their transitional justice programming. The right to take part in cultural life under Article 15(1)(a) of the ICESCR has been interpreted in ways that protect cultural justice traditions, protocols, and customs. States have a core obligation under the treaty to respect and protect the right of everyone to their own cultural practices.[79] Fulfilling the right to take part in cultural life under Article 15(1)(a) further requires that the right be realized in a way that suits a given culture or context, including by respecting the culture and cultural rights of individuals and communities.[80] Moreover, with respect to minorities and Indigenous Peoples, the right to take part in cultural life entails allowing and encouraging participation in the design and implementation of laws and policies that affect them.[81]

Indigenous Peoples benefit from special measures that flow in favour of protecting culturally appropriate justice and reconciliation practices. In the first instance, Indigenous Peoples have the right to free, prior and informed consent ('FPIC'). Their right to FPIC is mostly clearly articulated in Article 19 of the UNDRIP, which calls on States to 'consult and cooperate in good faith'

[77] UN Secretary-General, The Rule of Law and Transitional Justice in Conflict and Post-Conflict Societies (n 38) paras 16–17, 36.

[78] EMRIP, *Access to Justice in the Promotion and Protection of the Rights of Indigenous Peoples*, UN Doc A/HRC/EMRIP/2013/2 (29 April 2013) para 84.

[79] CESCR, General Comment No 21 (n 18) para 55(c).

[80] ibid para 16(e).

[81] ibid para 55(e).

with Indigenous Peoples 'in order to obtain their free, prior, and informed consent before adopting and implementing legislative or administrative measures that may affect them'.[82] Article 15(1)(a) of the ICESCR does not explicitly mention FPIC rights, but the CESCR clarified in its authoritative interpretation of the provision that 'States parties should respect the principle of free, prior and informed consent of indigenous peoples in all matters covered by their specific rights'.[83] Article 34 of UNDRIP further provides for Indigenous Peoples' 'right to promote, develop and maintain their institutional structures and their distinctive customs, spirituality, traditions, procedures, practices and, in the cases where they exist, juridical systems or customs, in accordance with international human rights standards'.[84] Article 40 of UNDRIP also gives Indigenous Peoples the right to seek a resolution of conflicts and effective remedies from the State for infringements of their individual or collective rights, with due consideration to the customs, traditions, rules, and legal systems of the Indigenous Peoples concerned.[85]

In some instances, transitional justice practice has shown flexibility in incorporating and accommodating Indigenous and local justice traditions. Good practice can be derived from transitional justice policy and programming in Timor-Leste, which principally sought to address large-scale human rights abuses committed during a brief armed conflict in 1975, as well as the numerous human rights abuses that occurred during the subsequent two decades of Indonesian colonial rule.[86] The signature formal truth-seeking body in Timor-Leste, the CAVR, demonstrated some willingness to incorporate and respect local justice traditions and protocols.

The CAVR's final report, *Chega!*, described the Commission's commitment to integrating 'customary law', particularly through its Community Reconciliation Process.[87] The Community Reconciliation Process was introduced to address less serious crimes and one of its central goals was the reconciliation and reintegration of alleged perpetrators of human rights abuses back into the community after they had fled the country fearing reprisals.[88] To facilitate this, the Community Reconciliation Process relied on a traditional process

[82] UN Declaration on the Rights of Indigenous Peoples, adopted by the UN General Assembly, UN Doc A/RES/61/295 (13 September 2007) Art 19.
[83] CESCR, General Comment No 21 (n 18) para 37.
[84] UNDRIP (n 82) Art. 34.
[85] ibid Art 40.
[86] Dionísio Babo-Soares, 'Nahe Biti: The Philosophy and Process of Grassroots Reconciliation and Justice in East Timor' (2004) 5 The Asia Pacific Journal of Anthropology 15, 16.
[87] *Chega: The Final Report of the Timor-Leste Commission for Reception, Truth, and Reconciliation*, Vol 4, p 2431 <https://chegareport.org/Chega%20All%20Volumes.pdf> accessed 1 February 2025.
[88] Babo-Soares, 'Nahe Biti' (n 86).

called *nahe biti* (literally 'stretching the mat').[89] *Nahe biti*, rooted in the distinct worldviews of Timorese society, has a long history in the country, having been used by people for thousands of years and across numerous periods of violent conflict and corruption.[90]

There is considerable diversity in the way *nahe biti* is interpreted among different communities in Timor-Leste,[91] but in its most general sense it involves bringing perpetrators and victims face-to-face on a mat. The dialogue is typically facilitated by elders or traditional leaders, with all sides presenting their perspectives, and the accused party is expected to acknowledge their wrongdoing.[92] The matters that are discussed are not to be brought into the broader community, to avoid the risk of conflict and disharmony.[93] An agreement may be reached for reparations, which could be symbolic or material.[94] In this way, *nahe biti* has elements of both retributive and restorative justice.[95] Thus, it allowed perpetrators of less serious crimes to confess publicly, engage in restitution, and be reintegrated into their communities. The ultimate aim of the *nahe biti* process is ultimately to contribute to peace and stability in the community.[96]

By integrating customary justice mechanisms such as *nahe biti* into formal transitional justice processes, Timor-Leste's CAVR exemplifies how cultural rights can be meaningfully protected, respected, and fulfilled in post-conflict settings. This approach not only fosters legitimacy and local ownership over justice initiatives but also aligns with international human rights standards, including the right of everyone to engage in their own cultural practices. Respecting Indigenous and local traditions within transitional justice frameworks ensures that justice and reconciliation efforts are not imposed from above, but rather emerge organically from within affected communities. Ultimately, when States commit to respecting cultural rights, they commit to honouring the diverse ways in which justice, healing, and peace are understood and practiced.

[89] Dustin N Sharp, 'Interrogating the Peripheries: The Preoccupations of Fourth Generation Transitional Justice' (2013) 26 Harvard Human Rights Journal 149, 165.

[90] Ellen Lutz, 'Transitional Justice: Lessons Learned and the Road Ahead' in Naomi Roht-Arriaza (ed), *Transitional Justice in the Twenty-first Century: Beyond Truth versus Justice* (Cambridge University Press 2006) 335.

[91] Babo-Soares, 'Nahe Biti' (n 86) 23.

[92] ibid 26–27.

[93] ibid 21.

[94] See Sharp, 'Interrogating the Peripheries' (n 89) 165.

[95] Wendy Lambourne, 'Transitional Justice and Peacebuilding after Mass Violence' (2009) 3(1) International Journal of Transitional Justice 28, 32.

[96] Babo-Soares, 'Nahe Biti' (n 86) 27.

5. Cultural and Artistic Interventions

A cultural rights-based approach to transitional justice protects and accommodates diverse forms of artistic and cultural initiatives designed to confront legacies of past large-scale harm. The transitional justice field, both in discourse and in practice, is increasingly engaging with and incorporating these artistic and cultural interventions.[97] While legal and quasi-legal mechanisms remain central to justice efforts, they often lack the emotional and symbolic power that artistic and cultural initiatives can provide. Art has a unique ability to engage individuals and communities in ways that formal institutions often cannot match, fostering deeper connections to historical narratives and creating spaces for healing, dialogue, and transformation.[98]

Cultural and artistic expressions can be understood as the outward manifestations of an individual's or community's cultural identity.[99] They serve multiple functions in transitional justice landscapes. They operate as powerful narrators of history, bringing visibility to previously silenced or overlooked experiences. In this way, creative work can amplify public awareness and confront prevailing narratives that so often overlook the structural and cultural violence that plagues post-conflict and divided societies. As Pablo De Greiff aptly observes, these initiatives can 'render the invisible visible', allowing communities to reclaim their narratives and challenge dominant historical accounts.[100] In contributing to a more holistic understanding of conflict and division, creative work can also help reimagine what can be done in response to past large-scale harm.[101]

Beyond truth-telling, these initiatives can further reconciliation by engaging individuals and groups in collective acts of remembrance and dialogue. They have the power to give a voice to marginalized segments of post-conflict and divided societies and encourage their participation in transitional justice processes.[102] Especially in the context of top-down mechanisms, art allows victims

[97] Olivera Simic, '"They Say That Justice Takes Time": Taking Stock of Truth Seeking in Peru, Argentina and Serbia' in Lia Kent and Melissa Demian (eds), *Transitional Justice in Law, History and Anthropology* (Routledge 2020) 144.

[98] Cynthia Cohen, 'Reimagining Transitional Justice' (2020) 14(1) International Journal of Transitional Justice 1, 2.

[99] See, eg, UNESCO Recommendation on the Safeguarding of Traditional Culture and Folklore (16 November 1989).

[100] Pablo de Greiff, 'Preface: On Making the Invisible Visible: The Role of Cultural Interventions in Transitional Justice Processes' in Clara Ramirez-Barat (ed), *Transitional Justice, Culture, and Society: Beyond Outreach* (Social Science Research Council 2014) 1.

[101] Sherin Shefik, 'Reimagining Transitional Justice through Participatory Art' (2018) 12(2) International Journal of Transitional Justice 314, 314–15.

[102] Simic, 'They Say That Justice Takes Time' (n 97) 145.

and local populations to communicate with and even challenge international and national transitional justice policymakers.[103] Furthermore, by recalling past suffering through aesthetic work, it can potentially mitigate the effects of trauma, offering victims and survivors a means to process their experiences and imagine a future beyond victimhood. Such initiatives restore dignity to victims and cultivate a culture of human rights, equality, and mutual respect.[104]

The relative power and potential of artistic and cultural initiatives has resulted in their proliferation in post-conflict and divided societies. Rama Mani and Thomas Weiss remark that '[d]iverse artistic expressions have arisen everywhere in response to acute repression and mass atrocities'.[105] These often take the form of literature, artwork, films, photography, and theatre, but they also encompass memorialization projects (discussed later in this chapter) such as exhibits in a museum, the design of a monument, or a commemoration ceremony.[106] Each of these cultural expressions are protected under the international human rights law regime.

The right to cultural expression is explicitly provided for under international human rights law, including principally through Article 15(3) of the ICESCR, which obligates States 'to respect the freedom indispensable for ... creative activity'.[107] The right to take part in cultural life under Article 15(1)(a) of the ICESCR has also been interpreted to include the right of everyone to 'seek and develop cultural knowledge and expressions and to share them with others, as well as to act creatively and take part in creative activity'.[108] It further encompasses the rights of everyone to 'be involved in creating the spiritual, material, intellectual and emotional expressions of the community'.[109] In turn, the CESCR has called on States to adopt positive measures to 'protect and promote the diversity of cultural expressions, and enable all cultures to express themselves and make themselves known'.[110]

Article 19(2) of the ICCPR also protects the right to freedom of expression, including the freedom to seek, receive and impart information and ideas of all kinds 'in the form of art'.[111] This protection is especially important for the

[103] Rama Mani and Thomas G Weiss, 'Can Culture Prevent Massacres?' (2011) 17(4) *Global Governance* 417, 421.

[104] Report of the Special Rapporteur in the Field of Cultural Rights, UN Doc A/HRC/37/55 (4 January 2018) para 10.

[105] Mani and Weiss, 'Can Culture Prevent Massacres?' (n 103) 421.

[106] Report of the Special Rapporteur in the Field of Cultural Rights (n 104) para 62.

[107] ICESCR (n 19), Art 15(3).

[108] CESCR, General Comment 21 (n 18) para 15(a).

[109] ibid para 15(c).

[110] ibid para 43.

[111] International Covenant on Civil and Political Rights (1966) 999 UNTS 171, Art 19.

expression of art in post-conflict and divided societies, where artistic and cultural interventions are more likely to be controversial and could invite considerable resistance from governments, institutions, and other stakeholders.[112] Similarly, Article 27(1) of the Universal Declaration of Human Rights ('UDHR') further provides for the right of everyone to enjoy the arts.[113]

Minorities and Indigenous Peoples are entitled to additional protections with regard to their right to cultural and artistic expression. The Declaration on the Rights of Persons Belonging to National or Ethnic, Religious and Linguistic Minorities ('UNDM') recommends that States should take measures to enable persons belonging to minorities to 'express their characteristics and develop their culture'.[114] Furthermore, Article 31 of the UNDRIP provides that 'Indigenous peoples have the right to maintain, control, protect and develop their … traditional cultural expressions'.[115] In addition to the human rights standards, a cultural rights-respecting approach is guided by UNESCO standard-setting in the area of cultural expression, including the UNESCO Universal Declaration on Cultural Diversity (2001)[116] and the UNESCO Convention on the Protection and Promotion of the Diversity of Cultural Expressions (2005), which affirms that cultural diversity can only be safeguarded if human rights and fundamental freedoms, including artistic expression, are fully respected.[117]

5.1 Gustavo Germano's *Ausencias*

During Argentina's military dictatorship from 1974 to 1983, almost 30,000 people were forcibly disappeared.[118] This became the defining crime of the dictatorship, one that left families without answers, forced to endure the pain of unresolved loss for decades. Thus, the absence of the disappeared continues to be a defining element of Argentina's collective trauma. Photographer, Gustavo Germano, was intimately familiar with this trauma. During the dictatorship, when Germano was aged 11, his 18-year-old brother Eduardo

[112] Report of the Special Rapporteur in the Field of Cultural Rights (n 104) para 20.
[113] Univeral Declaration of Human Rights (1948) Art 27.
[114] UN Declaration on the Rights of Person Belonging to National or Ethnic, Religious and Linguistic Minorities, adopted by General Assembly resolution 47/135 (18 December 1992), Art 4(2).
[115] UNDRIP (n 82) Art 31.
[116] UNESCO Declaration on Cultural Diversity (2 November 2001), Arts 6–8.
[117] UNESCO Convention on the Protection and Promotion of the Diversity of Cultural Expressions (20 October 2005).
[118] Antonius Robben, *Argentina Betrayed: Memory, Mourning, and Accountability* (University of Pennsylvania Press 2018) 11.

was disappeared.[119] Germano's photography exhibit *Ausencias* (Absences) emerged from his own personal experience and the broader struggle for memory and recognition in Argentina.

Ausencias consists of a series of paired photographs (seven pairs, fourteen photographs in total) that make the absence of the disappeared powerfully visible through art. Each pair features an original black-and-white photograph taken before 1976, showing the disappeared person alongside family or friends. The second photograph faithfully recreates the same setting and composition (except in full colour), but without the disappeared individual(s).[120] In some cases, no one from the original group remains, leaving an empty scene—a striking testament to the void left by State violence.[121]

The simplicity of *Ausencias* has evoked powerful emotions. The recreated photos emphasize the passage of time, showing the lives that victims could have lived, the decades their families have endured without them, and the void that cannot be filled.[122] This visualization of absence makes the pain and injustice tangible. By visually reconstructing absence, the project makes the disappeared visible, challenges collective amnesia, and restores dignity to victims and their families. Through the deliberate recreation of past photographs, *Ausencias* makes absence visible and forces viewers to confront the human cost of political violence.

Cultural mediums such as photography have been employed in transitional justice contexts in furtherance of grappling with difficult histories.[123] These can complement, facilitate, and even challenge formal transitional justice processes, such as criminal trials or truth commissions.[124] While *Ausencias* was not affiliated with any formal post-conflict justice mechanism in Argentina, it illustrated how culture can further the objectives of transitional justice in powerful ways. A cultural rights-based approach to transitional justice encourages such initiatives and requires States to adopt positive measures in furtherance of them and to refrain from taking any action that would unnecessarily impede or limit such interventions.

119 Lucas Bietti, '"Piercing Memories": Empty Spaces in the Histories of Argentinean Families—Personal Reflections' (2011) 4(1) Memory Studies 83, 84.

120 ibid 83–84.

121 Eduardo González Cueva and M Florencia Librizzi, 'Photography and Transitional Justice: Evidence, Postcard, Placard, Token of Absence' in Clara Ramirez-Barat (ed), *Transitional Justice, Culture, and Society: Beyond Outreach* (Social Science Research Council 2014) 448.

122 ibid; see also Simic, 'They Say That Justice Takes Time' (n 97) 151.

123 Sonya de Laat, 'Memory and Photographs of Unrepresentable Trauma in Rwandan Transitional Justice' in Stephanie Wolfe, Matthew Kane, and Tawia Ansah (eds), *In the Shadow of Genocide* (Routledge 2022) 228.

124 Gabriela Martínez, 'Photography as a Platform for Transitional Justice: Peru's Case' in Sandra Ristovska and Monroe Price (eds), *Visual Imagery and Human Rights Practice* (Springer 2018) 165.

5.2 Political murals in Northern Ireland

Of course, not all artistic and cultural initiatives are necessarily rights-respecting or further the goals of transitional justice.[125] Creative interventions have the potential to foster more violence, jeopardize peace, retraumatize victims, and denigrate the cultural practices and traditions of others.[126] Upsetting or controversial artistic expressions have the same rights protections afforded to more palatable forms; however, Article 20 of the ICCPR prohibits any expressions that could be considered propaganda for war or 'advocacy for national, racial or religious hatred that constitutes incitement to discrimination, hostility or violence'.[127] This is a risk that is particularly salient in post-conflict and divided societies, often trying to turn the page on identity-based conflicts fuelled by hatred and violence.

Writer Adrienne Maree Brown contests the neutrality of art, claiming that '[i]t either upholds or disrupts the status quo, advancing or regressing justice'.[128] There are many historical examples of how art and culture have been weaponized to further wrongdoing. Joseph Goebbels notoriously developed and promoted anti-Semitic films as propaganda for the Nazi regime in Germany.[129] Music (replete with hate-fuelled lyrics) by popular Rwandan singer Simon Bikindi contributed to ethnic hatred and ultimately incited genocide in that country, according to the ICTR.[130] The *Bikindi* case has been cited at the UN as an example of when art and culture can encourage ethnic hatred and genocide.[131] A cultural rights-based approach to transitional justice condemns the use of art and culture to sow division, oppress groups, degrade cultural identities, and potentially incite further hostility and division—all of which is antithetical to the full and equal realization of cultural rights.

These dilemmas are not always so straightforward. The political murals in Northern Ireland present a rather thorny case involving artistic and cultural expressions. There is a robust body of literature studying the long history of political murals in Northern Ireland.[132] Their use intensified during the

[125] Report of the Special Rapporteur in the Field of Cultural Rights (n 104) para 6.

[126] Cohen, 'Reimagining Transitional Justice' (n 98) 2.

[127] ICCPR (n 111) Art 20.

[128] Adrienne Maree Brown, *Emergent Strategy: Shaping Change, Changing Winds* (AK Press 2017) 197.

[129] RC Raack, 'Nazi Film Propaganda and the Horrors of War' (1986) 6(2) Historical Journal of Film, Radio and Television 189.

[130] Kristin Doughty, 'Language and International Criminal Justice in Africa: Interpretation at the ICTR' (2017) 11(2) International Journal of Transitional Justice 239, 239.

[131] Report of the Special Rapporteur in the Field of Cultural Rights (n 104) para 33.

[132] Andrew Hill and Andrew White, 'Painting Peace? Murals and the Northern Ireland Peace Process' (2012) 27(1) Irish Political Studies 71, 71 (noting the 'extensive literature' on the topic).

thirty-year conflict known as the 'Troubles'; and even today, nearly thirty years after the Good Friday Peace Agreement formally ended the conflict, many murals are still peppered across cities in Northern Ireland, particularly in Belfast and Derry.[133] How to engage with these cultural expressions has been one of the principal contestations in Northern Ireland's broader transitional justice landscape.[134]

There is great diversity in the murals, but many align with the binary unionist/loyalist versus nationalist/republican narratives at the heart of the Troubles.[135] They historically served as key expressions of identity, particularly among these communities. Many glorify and celebrate paramilitary figures or commemorate past battles. This tends to invoke strong emotions at each end of the spectrum. These murals serve not only as historical and territorial markers but also as reminders of unresolved grievances amongst these groups. Bill Rolston calls them 'tantamount to carving tombstones, a sign of political hopelessness, anathema in a society seeking political transformation'.[136]

Some research suggests that rather than celebrating heritage and strengthening cultural identities, the murals have contributed to division and exacerbated the conflict.[137] The Northern Ireland government has attempted to address the painful legacies of the murals, including through the 'Re-Imaging Communities' programme, which sought to replace several divisive murals with more neutral and positive images.[138] Under this programme, many murals, in conjunction with the help of local people and communities, were replaced with depoliticized imagery. However, such initiatives have often faced resistance, with local communities perceiving them as attempts to erase their histories and censor them.[139] Some communities have even perceived the initiative as an attempt to erase or delegitimize their historical narratives and cultural symbols.[140]

133 Fiona McGaughey, 'A Law unto Themselves: Murals in the Northern Ireland Conflict' in Jani McCutcheon and Fiona McGaughey (eds), *Research Handbook on Art and Law* (Edward Elgar Publishing 2020)

134 Mark Callaghan, 'Painting Over the Past: Political Palimpsests in Northern Ireland and the Complexities of the "Whitewash" Initiative', in Danielle Schaub and others (eds), *Topography of Trauma: Fissures, Disruptions and Transfigurations* (Brill 2019) 210.

135 Vikki Bell, 'Contemporary Art and Transitional Justice in Northern Ireland: The Consolation of Form' (2011) 10(3) Journal of Visual Culture 324, 332-33.

136 Bill Rolston, '"Trying to Reach the Future through the Past": Murals and Memory in Northern Ireland' (2010) 6(3) Crime, Media, Culture 285, 286.

137 McGaughey, 'A Law unto Themselves' (n 133).

138 Callaghan, 'Painting over the Past' (n 134) 208.

139 Bill Rolston, 'Re-imaging: Mural Painting and the State in Northern Ireland' (2012) 15(5) International Journal of Cultural Studies 447, 456.

140 Evaluation of the Building Peace through the Arts: Re-Imaging Communities Programme, Final Report (January 2016) <https://niopa.qub.ac.uk/bitstream/NIOPA/3594/1/BPttA_Final_Programme_Evaluation.pdf> accessed 1 February 2025.

While efforts to neutralize the divisive legacy of these murals continue, their persistence underscores the deep-rooted tensions that remain in Northern Ireland's post-conflict landscape. The murals serve as both cultural heritage and contested symbols, reflecting the enduring struggle over historical narratives, identity, and memory that many post-conflict societies must grapple with. Art that is co-opted for political purposes risks undermining healing and reconciliation rather than fostering it.[141] The challenge for a cultural rights-based approach, then, lies in finding ways to engage with cultural and artistic interventions that acknowledge their cultural significance and respect cultural identities, while promoting a more inclusive and peaceful society.

6. Memorialization

Culture is an essential part of memorialization, and hence cultural rights have significant relevance to memory work. To one degree or another, the memorialization of past atrocities is now a fixture in most transitional justice strategies.[142] Its centrality to the project is perhaps exemplified by the fact that it has been described as the field's fifth pillar, alongside the right to truth, right to justice, right to reparations, and guarantees of non-recurrence.[143] More than ever before, societies are responding to mass violence and systematic human rights abuses with demands that these events, along with their victims, be officially recognized and remembered by the State through post-conflict memory work. As a result, public memorials have been created in almost every corner of the world to confront and remember large-scale past harm.[144]

Memorialization plays a crucial role in transitional justice by providing spaces to acknowledge past atrocities and honour victims. Drawing on concepts of truth-telling, reparations, and reconciliation, memorialization has shown the potential to recognize victims and promote healing in fractured societies. Yet memory work is complex, especially when conducted in the fragile,

[141] Rama Mani, 'Women, Art and Post-Conflict Justice' (2011) 11 International Criminal Law Review 543, 551.

[142] Ereshnee Naidu, 'Memorialisation in Post-Conflict Societies in Africa: Potentials and Challenges' in Susanne Buckley-Zistel and Stefanie Schäfer (eds) *Memorials in Times of Transition* (Cambridge University Press 2014) 142.

[143] Report of the Special Rapporteur on the Promotion of Truth, Justice, Reparation and Guarantees of Non-recurrence, 'Memorialization Processes in the Context of Serious Violations of Human Rights and International Humanitarian Law: The Fifth Pillar of Transitional Justice', UN Doc A/HRC/45/45 (9 July 2020).

[144] Louis Bickford, 'Memoryworks/Memory Works' in Clara Ramirez-Barat (ed), *Transitional Justice, Culture, and Society: Beyond Outreach* (Social Science Research Council 2014) 517.

highly politicized environments that transitional justice typically operates in. Unfortunately, memorials are also used to solidify existing political power structures, create victim hierarchies, and sow divisions of hate.

Memorials have long served as reminders of great military victories and brave conquests across the world. For most of history, memorialization was limited to such archetypes. At the same time, people have long sought to memorialize human loss and suffering.[145] The past fifty years has seen a significant shift in the memory landscape, away from memorials of great victories and towards memorials aimed at remembering victims of mass atrocity.[146] This insistence that past atrocities and their victims be sufficiently recognized and remembered complements demands that perpetrators of human rights abuses be held accountable for their crimes and victims be compensated for their losses.[147] At least in theory, then, memory work is intended to operate alongside the more traditional forms and objectives of transitional justice in an interconnected and complementary way.[148]

The most common justifications for memorialization initiatives in post-conflict and divided societies fall into four general categories: (1) nation-building, (2) victim mourning, (3) public education, and (4) identity strengthening.[149] There are certainly other goals and benefits of post-conflict memorialization and these initiatives are also capable of serving more than one purpose simultaneously.[150] However, these four objectives seem to lend insight into how memory work most often operates in post-conflict and divided societies. They all implicate cultural rights, but the capacity to reconstruct and strengthen cultural identities presents unique opportunities and challenges for transitional justice to interact with culture and promote a cultural rights-based approach in the scope of memorialization.

Several principles have been developed at the UN which are relevant for memory work in post-conflict and divided societies. The Joinet/Orentlicher Principles provide for the inalienable right of all people to know the truth about past events concerning perpetration of heinous crimes.[151] The duty to preserve memory is also relevant, emphasizing the duty of States in connection with memory and their responsibility for transmitting history with a view

145 ibid.
146 ibid.
147 Klaus Neumann and Dan Anderson, 'Introduction: Violence, Justice and the Work of Memory' (2014) 8(1) International Journal of Conflict and Violence 5, 7.
148 Naidu, 'Memorialisation in Post-Conflict Societies in Africa' (n 142).
149 *See* Bickford, 'Memoryworks/Memory Works' (n 144).
150 Naidu, 'Memorialisation in Post-Conflict Societies in Africa' (n 142).
151 Joinet/Orentlicher Principles (n 34), principle 2.

to 'preserving the collective memory from extinction'.[152] Moreover, the Basic Principles and Guidelines state that reparations could take the form of public apologies, commemorations, and victim tributes, among other forms.[153] Based on the foregoing principles, post-conflict memorialization was initially categorized as a form of symbolic reparations within the transitional justice paradigm.[154] However, there is a growing consensus that memorialization represents a distinct tool of transitional justice praxis.[155]

The legal framework concerning cultural rights and memorialization is deeply rooted in the right to cultural identity. A recognized objective behind post-conflict memory work is remembering, reconstructing, and strengthening the identities of sub-national groups that were jeopardized in the underlying conflict or during periods of colonialism and/or oppression.[156] The right to cultural identity is recognized in several international human rights instruments, including in the ICESCR. In its authoritative interpretation of Article 15(1)(a) of the ICESCR, the CESCR stated that the right to participate in cultural life involved, *inter alia,* the right 'to act freely, to choose his or her own identity, to identify or not with one or several communities or to change that choice'.[157] In the context of individuals belonging to minority groups, States are further called upon to protect minority identities and encourage conditions for the promotion of that identity.[158]

Most memorials also constitute forms of cultural heritage. There is broad agreement that access to cultural heritage is essential for individuals and communities in relation to developing and maintaining their cultural identity.[159] Although no binding, international human rights instrument provides for a universal right to access cultural heritage, there are references to cultural heritage in various human rights instruments and in the practice of treaty monitoring bodies, especially the CESCR.[160] For example, the CESCR has made clear that States are obligated to adopt measures aimed at respecting the right

152 ibid principle 3.

153 Basic Principles and Guidelines (n 28), para 22.

154 Maria Chiara Campisi, 'From a Duty to Remember to an Obligation to Memory? Memory as Reparation in the Jurisprudence of the Inter-American Court of Human Rights' (2014) 8(1) International Journal of Conflict and Violence 61.

155 Report of the Special Rapporteur on the Promotion of Truth, Justice, Reparation and Guarantees of Non-recurrence, *Memorialization Processes* (n 143); see also Naidu, 'Memorialisation in Post-Conflict Societies in Africa' (n 142).

156 Bickford, 'Memoryworks/Memory Works' (n 144).

157 CESCR, General Comment No. 21 (n 18) para 88.

158 UNDM (n 114) Art 2.

159 Report of the Special Rapporteur in the Field of Cultural Rights (n 104) paras 9–17.

160 See, eg, UNDRIP (n 82) Art. 31; CESCR, General Comment No 21 (n 18) paras 15(b), 49(d).

of everyone '[t]o have access to their own cultural and linguistic heritage and to that of others'.[161]

The freedom of cultural and artistic expression is another key cultural right in memorialization. In the context of post-conflict memory work, former UN SRCR Farida Shaheed stated that '[a]rtists should be able to articulate their voices; the right to freedom of artistic expression and creativity must be fully respected and protected'.[162] As discussed earlier, Article 15(3) of the ICESCR and Article 19(2) of the ICCPR are essential for safeguarding cultural and artistic expressions, including in memory projects. Linking memorialization to this standard-setting helps to ensure that memory work operates in a way that protects and promotes cultural rights, especially for subnational groups whose cultural identities remain vulnerable in post-conflict and divided societies. Moreover, a cultural rights-based approach ensures the freedom for individuals and groups to articulate their cultural narratives through memory work is respected.

6.1 Memorialization in Guatemala

Post-conflict Guatemala serves as a unique case study to interrogate the parameters of a cultural rights-based approach to memorialization. First, it is one of only a handful of countries where conventional transitional justice mechanisms have explicitly endorsed memorialization as a form of symbolic reparations. Accordingly, memorialization, at least in theory, became a significant component of Guatemala's transitional justice programming.[163] At the same time, and for a variety of reasons, Guatemala's memory practice has remained relatively dormant over the past three decades.[164] Unlike other post-conflict societies, there has been a lack of commitment on behalf of Guatemala's transitional governments to memorialize the conflict in a meaningful way. This is especially true for memory projects that have been initiated by the State, as opposed to civil society, victims' groups, and spontaneous memorials erected by the relatives and loved ones of victims.[165] Guatemala's relative lack of

[161] CESCR, General Comment No. 21 (n 18) 49(d).

[162] Report of the Special Rapporteur in the Field of Cultural Rights, Farida Shaheed, *Memorialization Processes*, UN Doc A/HRC/25/49 (23 January 2014) para 48.

[163] Naidu, 'Memorialisation in Post-Conflict Societies in Africa' (n 142).

[164] Michael Steinberg and Matthew Taylor, 'Public Memory and Political Power in Guatemala's Postconflict Landscape' (2003) 933(4) Geographical Review 449.

[165] This is not meant to imply that the government has failed to engage in memory work. Among other measures, Guatemala has erected a number of monuments, declared 25 February as a Day for the Dignification of the Victims of the Armed Conflict, and conducted a number of commemorations and tributes. Denis Martinez (ed), 'Guatemala Resists Forgetting: Post-Conflict Memory

post-conflict memorialization practice mirrors a more general failure by the State to hold perpetrators accountable and sufficiently compensate victims for the harms they suffered during the internal conflict.

Additionally, cultural rights violations were ubiquitous during the Guatemalan Civil War. The internal conflict was exemplified by brutal attacks against the livelihoods of Indigenous Mayan communities.[166] Not only were they disproportionately murdered, raped, tortured, and displaced, but there was also a deliberate State campaign to destroy the cultural values, traditions, and ways of life of the Mayan people.[167] Their distinct cultural identities were repeatedly targeted and attacked during the decades-long civil war, leading the Historical Clarification Commission to conclude that Guatemala committed acts of genocide against Mayan community members between 1981 and 1983.[168] The three memory projects discussed below—(1) the Monument to Peace, (2) *Casa de la Memoria*, and (3) the Rabinal Achi Community Museum—demonstrate the extent to which Guatemala's post-conflict memorialization practice embraces a cultural rights-based approach.

The Monument to Peace is a bronze sculpture established by the Guatemalan government to commemorate the peace agreement reached in 1996.[169] It is prominently located in the courtyard of the National Palace in downtown Guatemala City. The centrepiece of the monument is a set of intertwined hands, which sits atop a base of sixteen interwoven arms. The two hands represent each side of the conflict reaching up and making peace with each other. The sixteen arms are then intended to symbolize the strength of the Guatemalan people.[170] The Monument to Peace provides a classic example of a memorial that is exclusively concerned with nation-building in the aftermath of violent conflict. There is no description of the conflict or representations of the victims, nor their suffering. Its sole objective is to celebrate a peace that was reached and to promote a narrative of a strong, united Guatemala. Indeed, the Guatemalan government has erected a number of monuments dedicated

Initiatives', *Impunity Watch* (2012) <https://www.impunitywatch.org/wp-content/uploads/2022/08/ResearchReport_Guatemala_Resists_Forgetting_Memory_Initiatives_2012_eng-1.pdf> accessed 1 February 2025.

[166] Guatemala Memory of Silence, 'Report of the Commission for Historical Clarification: Conclusions and Recommendations' (1999) <https://hrdag.org/wp-content/uploads/2013/01/CEHreport-english.pdf> accessed 1 February 2025.

[167] ibid.

[168] ibid.

[169] Katherine Bailey, *'So that all shall know': Memorialising Guatemala's Disappeared* (Dissertation, Lancaster University 2018).

[170] ibid 102–05.

generally to the peace agreement.[171] These are seen by many as hollow gestures not designed to meet the needs of victims and survivors.[172] From a cultural rights angle, the Monument to Peace does not recognize Indigenous Mayan people as being the primary victims of the conflict, nor does it acknowledge their unique cultural identities, which the government sought to eliminate during the conflict and which they are obligated to uphold.

Casa de la Memoria is a public memorial museum that opened in 2014. Similar to the Monument to Peace, it is located in Guatemala City's historical centre, which makes it readily available to Guatemala's city dwellers and tourists, but not as accessible to the majority of Mayan people. The museum contains numerous exhibits concerning the history and context behind the war in Guatemala.[173] In contrast to the Monument to Peace, *Casa de la Memoria* is focused on public education and the idea of non-recurrence, seeking to educate people about the human rights violations that occurred during the war, in furtherance of the non-repetition of such atrocities in the future. Despite some background information about Mayan civilization and the persistent attacks against Mayan people during the civil war, the strengthening of Mayan identity does not feature in the museum and there is little by way of a cultural exchange. This is exemplified by the fact the materials are only presented in Spanish, as opposed to the multiple indigenous Mayan languages. At the same time, the museum does take some strides in promoting alternative narratives regarding Mayan people in Guatemala. For example, some of the exhibits contain information regarding Mayan resistance to the violence, thus moving away from the notion that Mayans were helpless, passive victims.[174]

The Rabinal Achi Community Museum in Rio Negro is located in the municipality of Rabinal, an area of extreme violence perpetrated on behalf of the Guatemalan State, with the majority of the victims being Indigenous Mayans.[175] The museum was founded by a number of civil society organizations in 1999, including the Association for the Maya Achi Victims of Violence.[176] Its mission was to recover and disseminate the historical memory of the Maya Achi

171 Steinberg and Taylor, 'Public Memory and Political Power in Guatemala's Postconflict Landscape' (n 164).

172 Ruth Gidey and Hannah Roberts, 'Setting the Truth in Stone: Guatemala's Monuments to the Dead' (2003) 19(2) Medicine, Conflict and Survival 148, 149.

173 Bailey, 'So that all shall know' (n 169) 235–45.

174 ibid.

175 *The Case of the Río Negro Massacres v Guatemala*, Judgment (Preliminary objection, merits, reparations and costs) Inter-American Court of Human Rights Series C No 105 (4 September 2012) para 61.

176 Heidi McKinnon, 'Proposing a Museum of Memory: Reparations and the Maya Achí Genocide in Guatemala' in Annette B Fromm, Per B Rekdal, and Viv Golding (eds), *Museums and Truth* (Cambridge Scholars Publishing 2014).

people.[177] Critically, it represented the first memory project to focus on the local impact of the war, as well as the first memorial to be dedicated specifically to Mayan culture.[178] In stark contrast to the Monument to Peace and the *Casa de la Memoria*, the Rabinal Achi Community Museum actively seeks to reconstruct, strengthen, and celebrate Mayan cultural identity.[179] Significantly, a portion of the museum is dedicated to Mayan history, including multiple displays that depict local cultural practices.[180] The creators of the museum have made the conscious choice to promote Mayan cultural identity through this memory work. This is congruent with a cultural rights-based approach, including the CESCR's guidance for States to adopt measures to enable all cultures to make themselves known.[181]

Like many post-conflict societies, Guatemala struggles with how to properly memorialize a conflict embedded with so many different memories and histories.[182] As the above examples demonstrate, the government's memorialization initiatives tend to shy away from directly confronting the cultural violence that devasted so many Mayan communities. This may reveal a larger problem in Guatemalan society—a general reluctance to acknowledge the government's role in destroying Mayan culture.[183] Yet initiatives such as the Rabinal Achi Community Museum show the potential for successful projects that incorporate a cultural rights-based approach to memorializing mass cultural harm, including by celebrating and working to reconstruct cultural identities.

7. Cultural Reparations

In many post-conflict and divided societies, cultural loss weighs heavily on the hearts, minds, and souls of people. Cultural reparations can be an important tool to address and redress cultural loss and an important element of a cultural rights-based approach to transitional justice.[184] Such an approach

177 Rigoberto Ajcalón Choy, Aileen Ford, and Irma A Velásquez Nimatuj, 'Racism and Maya Achi Resistance within the Contradictions of Neoliberal Multiculturalism' in Juliet Hooker (ed), *Black and Indigenous Resistance in the Americas: From Multiculturalism to Racist Backlash* (Lexington 2020) 145.

178 Bailey, 'So that all shall know' (n 169).

179 McKinnon, 'Proposing a Museum of Memory' (n 176).

180 Bailey, 'So that all shall know' (n 169).

181 CESCR, General Comment 21 (n 18) para 43.

182 Steinberg and Taylor, 'Public Memory and Political Power in Guatemala's Postconflict Landscape' (n 164).

183 ibid.

184 Cultural reparations is not a term of art or a defined legal term; rather, it is used broadly herein to describe reparative measures taken to restore, revive, or compensate for the loss, suppression, or destruction of a community's cultural heritage, traditions, language, and identity.

to reparations would acknowledge cultural wrongs and position them as serious violations of human rights worthy of remedy and repair through an extraordinary justice process. A cultural rights-based approach to reparations also respects the cultural practices, protocols, and traditions of victims in the reparations process, regardless of the underlying harm being remedied.

Cultural reparations are not novel in the transitional justice landscape. As discussed in Chapter 1, reparative measures recommended and court-ordered in Guatemala were specifically aimed at rectifying cultural loss, restoring cultural identities, revitalizing cultural traditions, and supporting cultural heritage. Although largely unimplemented, these set an important precedent for integrating culture into reparations. Moreover, we are also increasingly seeing cultural reparations in the form of restituting stolen cultural heritage from governments and institutions in former colonial powers to origin States and communities.[185]

Under international law, reparations aim to wipe out the consequences of the harm and place the injured party in a position that would have existed if the wrong had never occurred in the first place.[186] The Basic Principles and Guidelines outline several forms of reparations and state that they should aim to promote justice in the face of 'gross violations of international human rights law or serious violations of international humanitarian law' and should be 'proportional to the gravity of the violations and the harm suffered'.[187] However, the document only makes a cursory reference to culture in connection with adhering to cultural practices in the scope of recovering, identifying, and reburying bodies.[188]

The Basic Principles and Guidelines further call on States to ensure a victim's right to a remedy under international law, including '[a]dequate, effective and prompt reparation for harm suffered' as well as access to justice and relevant information.[189] Thus, in transitional settings, States have a duty to offer reparations to victims negatively impacted by past large-scale violations of their human rights.[190] The Basic Principles and Guidelines further define 'victims' broadly to include persons who have suffered individual or

[185] See, eg, Charlotte Joy, *Heritage Justice* (Cambridge University Press 2020); Dan Hicks, *The Brutish Museums: The Benin Bronzes, Colonial Violence and Cultural Restitution* (Pluto Press 2020).

[186] *Factory at Chorzów, Germany v Poland*, Jurisdiction, Judgment, PCIJ Series A No 9, ICGJ 247 (26 July 1927) 21.

[187] Basic Principles and Guidelines (n 28) paras 15, 18–22.

[188] ibid para 22(c).

[189] ibid para 11.

[190] OHCHR, Rule-of-Law Tools for Post-Conflict States: Reparations Programs, HR/PUB/08/1 (2008) <https://www.ohchr.org/documents/publications/reparationsprogrammes.pdf> accessed 1 February 2025.

collective harm, including through substantial impairment of their fundamental rights.[191] While not explicitly referencing cultural loss, the recognition of collective harm and substantial impairment of fundamental rights extends victimhood to individuals and groups who have incurred large-scale violations of their collective cultural rights.

The legal basis for reparations is further enshrined in numerous human rights instruments.[192] For instance, Article 6 of the International Convention on the Elimination of All Forms of Racial Discrimination requires States to assure effective remedies through institutions and tribunals for any violations of the Convention.[193] The ICCPR further provides that any person suffering a violation of their rights under the Convention, including the right of minorities to enjoy their culture, must have an effective remedy determined by judicial, administration, or legislative authorities.[194]

Cultural reparations can take many forms, including the five (5) internationally recognized forms of reparations: (1) restitution, (2) compensation, (3) rehabilitation, (4) satisfaction, and (5) guarantees of non-repetition.[195] In recent transitional justice practice we have seen cultural reparations by way of repatriation of tangible cultural heritage stolen from colonized people (e.g. Germany's return of cultural objects housed in the Berlin Ethnological Museum to Namibia),[196] recommendations for language recognition and revitalization programmes (e.g. recommendation by Peru's Truth and Reconciliation Commission for Indigenous languages to receive equal status),[197] and state apologies acknowledging mass cultural wrongdoing (e.g. Canada Prime Minister Justin Trudeau apologizing for cultural genocide against Indigenous Peoples),[198] among other forms. More generally, reparations claims are increasingly incorporating cultural dimensions.

[191] Basic Principles and Guidelines (n 28) para 8.

[192] See, eg, Univeral Declaration of Human Rights (n 113) Art 8; ICCPR (n 111) Art 2; Convention against Torture and Other Cruel, Inhuman, Degrading Treatment or Punishment (1987) 1465 UNTS 85, Art 14; CRC (n 24) Art. 39.

[193] ICERD (n 21) Art 6.

[194] ICCPR (n 111) Art 2.3.

[195] Basic Principles and Guidelines (n 28) para 15.

[196] Rikke Gram and Zoe Schoofs, *Germany's History of Returning Human Remains and Objects from Colonial Contexts: An Overview of Successful Cases and Unsettled Claims between 1970 and 2021* (Deutsches Zentrum Kulturgutverluste 2022).

[197] Peru's Truth and Reconciliation Commission, Final Report of the Truth and Reconciliation Commission, Volume IX (2004) <http://www.cverdad.org.pe/ingles/ifinal/index.php> accessed 1 February 2025.

[198] Jasper Friedrich, 'Settling Accounts at the End of History: A Nonideal Approach to State Apologies' (2022) 50(5) Political Theory 700, 701 (recounting at least ten official apologies offered by Trudeau).

An interesting example can be found in the work of the Caribbean Community (CARICOM) Reparations Commission. The Commission was created to establish the 'moral, ethical and legal case' for the payment of reparations by former colonial powers to Caribbean nations. In 2014, the CARICOM States approved the Reparations Commission's *Ten Point Plan for Reparatory Justice*.[199] The goal of the Ten Point Plan was to reach settlements with former colonial powers (UK, France, and the Netherlands) and to achieve some degree of reparations for 'the Crimes against Humanity of Native Genocide, the Trans-Atlantic Slave Trade and a racialized system of chattel Slavery'.[200]

While genocide and slavery commonly denote physical harms, the Reparations Commission's Ten Point Plan has a notable focus on culture. Point 4 is centred on cultural institutions, noting the disparity regarding the museums and research centres that exist in Europe to help citizens understand native genocide, the transatlantic slave trade, and chattel slavery, compared to the lack of such institutions in the Caribbean.[201] The Reparations Commission contextualized this point by plainly stating:

> Part of the devastation of European colonisation was the deliberate attempt to destroy the cultures and languages of the indigenous peoples, enslaved Africans, and the indentured workers. Generations later, this has left a gap in the knowledge of some of these groups about the history of their ancestors as well as an inability to deeply appreciate ... the full and complete lives and cultures they had before European colonization.[202]

In calling for the creation of museums and research centres in the Caribbean, the Reparations Commission went on to comment on how a lack of cultural institutions in the Caribbean has resulted in a 'sense of rootlessness' for communities.[203] Notably, the availability of museums, libraries, and other cultural institutions is a necessary condition for the full realization of the right of everyone to take part in cultural life under the ICESCR.[204]

The Reparations Commission's Ten Point Plan further calls for an 'African knowledge programme' to fund cultural exchanges between Caribbean

[199] CARICOM Reparation Commission, CARICOM Ten Point Plan for Reparatory Justice <https://caricom.org/caricom-ten-point-plan-for-reparatory-justice/> accessed 1 February 2025.

[200] Amy Strecker, 'Indigenous Land Rights and Caribbean Reparations Discourse' (2017) 30(3) Leiden Journal of International Law 629, 629.

[201] CARICOM Reparation Commission, CARICOM Ten Point Plan for Reparatory Justice (n 199).

[202] CARICOM Reparation Commission, 10-Point Reparation Plan <https://caricomreparations.org/caricom/caricoms-10-point-reparation-plan/> accessed 1 February 2025.

[203] ibid.

[204] CESCR, General Comment No 21 (n 18) para 16(a).

nations and people and their homelands in Africa.[205] The purpose of the programme would be to address the knowledge gap caused by colonialism, the forced transfer of African people, and the resulting 'cultural and social alienation from identity and existential belonging'.[206] The Reparations Commission explicitly linked colonialism and the transatlantic slave trade to culture by stating that European countries 'deliberately tried to distance people from the sources of their culture and belonging' in an effort to 'destroy African heritage'.[207] Reparative measures aimed at facilitating access to culture and knowledge both acknowledge underlying cultural loss and help to ensure the right to know one's culture (as well as the cultures of others) and the right to engage in cultural exchange.[208]

Inspired by the CARICOM Reparations Commission,[209] the Movement for Black Lives has also formulated a policy demand for cultural reparations. The Movement for Black Lives is a broad social movement in the US with an overarching aim of defunding the police, abolishing prisons, amplifying the voices of marginalized individuals and communities, and advocating for reparations for Black people.[210] Much of its work revolves around challenging policies that negatively affect Black people and making policy proposals in furtherance of the above-referenced objectives. Social movements such as the Movement for Black Lives, as well as the broader decentralized Black Lives Matter movement, have prompted much introspection on the need for transitional justice to be implemented in response to the legacies of colonialism and slavery.[211]

The Movement for Black Lives has demanded reparations in connection with all past and continuing harm perpetrated against Black people, including stolen culture, and calls for measures that would confer agency to Black people over their culture.[212] In addition to its general reparations toolkit,

[205] ibid. paras 49(d), 56–59.
[206] CARICOM Reparation Commission, CARICOM Ten Point Plan for Reparatory Justice (n 199) Point 7.
[207] CARICOM Reparation Commission, 10-Point Reparation Plan (n 202).
[208] CESCR, General Comment No 21 (n 18) para 15(b).
[209] Movement for Black Lives, Case Study Two: CARICOM Reparations Commission <https://m4bl.org/wp-content/uploads/2020/11/Case-Study-Two.pdf> accessed 1 February 2025.
[210] Krystal Strong et al, 'Learning from the Movement for Black Lives: Horizons of Racial Justice for Comparative and International Education' (2023) 67(S1) Comparative Education Review S1, S4.
[211] See, eg, Zinaida Miller, 'Transitional Justice, Race, and the United States' *Just Security* (30 June 2020) <https://www.justsecurity.org/71040/Transitional-Justice-Race-and-the-United-States/> accessed 1 February 2025; Colleen Murphy, 'Transitional Justice in the United States' Just Security (16 July 2020)<https://www.justsecurity.org/71236/transitional-justice-in-the-united-states/> accessed 1 February 2025; Joshi Yuvraj, 'Does Transitional Justice Belong in the United States?' Just Security (13 July 2020) <https://www.justsecurity.org/71372/does-transitional-justice-belong-in-the-united-states/> accessed 1 February 2025.
[212] Movement for Black Lives, *Reparations Now Toolkit*, pp 36–38 <https://m4bl.org/wp-content/uploads/2020/05/Reparations-Now-Toolkit-FINAL.pdf?> accessed 1 February 2025.

the Movement for Black Lives has published an individual policy demand for cultural reparations specifically, stating that '[w]e need cultural reparations to publicly acknowledge the history of mass violence in the U.S. in order to begin to heal from the trauma'.[213] Part of the demand focuses on the inclusion of critical perspectives on slavery and colonialism in mandatory public school curriculum in order to address the 'cultural and educational exploitation, erasure, and extraction of [Black] communities'.[214] It also calls for funding for 'cultural assets and sacred sites' which 'speak to the triumphant quest of a determined people to create a new African community in this hostile land'.[215]

The reparations policies articulated by the Movement for Black Lives also rely upon and incorporate key international law standards underpinning their reparations demands, including by drawing explicitly from the language of the Basic Principles and Guidelines.[216] They elicit inspiration from the work of UN experts, including a statement by the UN's Working Group of Experts on People of African Descent after its official visit to the US in 2016, wherein it linked the legacies of colonialism, enslavement, and racism to ongoing deprivations of 'civil, political, economic, social and cultural rights of African Americans today'.[217]

The reparations demands articulated by both the CARICOM Reparations Commission and the Movement for Black Lives recognize the significance of underlying cultural harm and the need for cultural remedies for victims of the most overtly violent atrocities in human history—genocide and chattel slavery. This is reflective of the fact that cultural loss can loom large over the lives of victims, especially in the case of intergenerational harm. Cultural reparations play a vital role in addressing this deep and enduring harm. By recognizing cultural harms as serious human rights violations, and providing a remedy for such violations, States and institutions can foster deeper healing, strengthen cultural resilience, and ensure that past atrocities do not erase the histories, languages, and traditions of those who endured them.

[213] Movement for Black Lives, *Reparations for the Cultural and Educational Exploitation, Erasure, and Extraction of Our Communities in the Form of Mandated Public School Curriculums That Critically Examine the Political, Economic, and Social Impacts of Colonialism and Slavery and Funding to Support, Build, Preserve and Restore Cultural Assets and Sacred Sites to Ensure the Recognition and Honoring of Our Collective Struggles and Triumphs* <https://m4bl.org/wp-content/uploads/2020/05/CulturalReparations-OnePager.pdf> accessed 1 February 2025.

[214] ibid.

[215] ibid.

[216] Movement for Black Lives, Reparations Now Toolkit (n 212) 25–26.

[217] Statement to the Media by the United Nations' Working Group of Experts on People of African Descent, on the Conclusion of Its Official Visit to USA, 19–29 January 2016 (29 January 2016) <https://www.ohchr.org/en/statements/2016/01/statement-media-united-nations-working-group-experts-people-african-descent> accessed 1 February 2025.

6
INDIGENOUS PEOPLES' CULTURAL RIGHTS IN TRANSITIONAL JUSTICE

1. Introduction

In the late nineteenth century, Canada's first Prime Minister, John Macdonald, implemented a solution to the country's so-called Indian Problem. The Indian Problem was framed by Canadian politicians with reference to the need to integrate Indigenous Peoples into mainstream Euro-Canadian society.[1] The real problem, however, lay in the mere existence of Indigenous Peoples in Canada, and the obstacle they posed to the absolute control and possession of the territories and vast resources spread across the country.[2] The solution to such a problem ultimately manifested in a residential school system, a network of boarding schools funded and administered by the government and run primarily by Christian churches.[3] Many Indigenous children were forced to attend these schools, often located far from their families and communities. Justifying the establishment of the residential schools system before the House of Commons, Macdonald famously said:

> When the school is on the reserve, the child lives with its parents, who are savages, and though he may learn to read and write, his habits and training mode of thought are Indian. He is simply a savage who can read and write. It has been strongly impressed upon myself, as head of the Department, that Indian children should be withdrawn as much as possible from the parental influence, and the only way to do that would be to put them in central training

[1] David Newhouse and Yale Belanger, 'Beyond the Indian Problem: Aboriginal Peoples and the Transformation of Canada' in John Courtney and David Smith (eds), *The Oxford Handbook of Canadian Politics* (Oxford University Press 2010) 344.

[2] Gregory Younging, 'Inherited History, International Law, and the UN Declaration' in Gregory Younging, Jonathon Dewar, and Mike DeGagne (eds), *Response, Responsibility, and Renewal: Canada's Truth and Reconciliation Journey* (Aboriginal Healing Foundation 2009) 329.

[3] Jeff Corntassel, 'Indigenous Storytelling, Truth-telling, and Community Approaches to Reconciliation' (2009) 35(1) English Studies in Canada 137, 138.

Cultural Rights and Wrongs in Transitional Justice. Colin Luoma, Oxford University Press. © Colin Luoma 2025.
DOI: 10.1093/oso/9780198911371.003.0006

> industrial schools where they will acquire the habits and modes of thought of white men.[4]

Over the course of approximately 150 years, more than 150,000 Indigenous children attended these institutions.[5]

While most of these schools provided basic academic education, they were principally designed to separate Indigenous children from their families, break their cultural bonds with land and community, erase their languages and cultural practices, and assimilate them into mainstream Canadian society. In 1920, Duncan Campbell Scott, Canada's Deputy Minister of Indian Affairs, plainly stated the assimilative mission of the residential schools policy before Parliament, remarking that 'our object is to continue until there is not a single Indian in Canada that has not been absorbed into the body politic, and there is no Indian question, and no Indian Department'.[6]

The residential schools system was not designed to physically eliminate Indigenous Peoples (although thousands of children did die prematurely in these institutions); rather, its objective was to kill them culturally. Through forced schooling, Indigenous children were to be stripped of their Indigenous identities, languages, dress, practices, and worldviews. This was complemented by a series of further government policies designed to destroy Indigenous culture and identities, including prohibitions of Indigenous traditions, ceremonies, and practices, such as potlaches and the Indian Sun Dance.[7] The ultimate goal was to dispossess Indigenous Peoples of the lands, territories, and resources coveted by the government and settler Canadians.[8]

The violence of the residential school system in Canada has reverberated across generations, with lasting and deleterious impacts on survivors, families, and Indigenous communities, including through mass cultural loss, weakened family and community bonds, intergenerational trauma, ongoing structural

[4] Prime Minister Sir John A Macdonald, Official report of the debates of the House of Commons of the Dominion of Canada, 9 May 1883, 1107–08.

[5] Prime Minister Stephen Harper, Statement of Apology—to former students of Indian Residential Schools (11 June 2008) <http://www.aadnc-aandc.gc.ca/eng/1100100015644/110010001564> accessed 1 February 2025.

[6] Duncan Campbell Scott, then Canada's Deputy Minister of Indian Affairs, spoke these words in 1920 to the Special Committee on the Indian Act in support of an amendment to the Indian Act that would make Indigenous children's attendance at residential schools mandatory. Library and Archives Canada, RG10, volume 6810, file 470-2-3, volume 7, Evidence of DC Scott to the Special Committee of the House of Commons Investigating the Indian Act amendments of 1920, (L-2)(N-3).

[7] Katherine Pettipas, *Severing the Ties that Bind: Government Repression of Indigenous Religious Ceremonies on the Prairies* (University of Manitoba Press 1994).

[8] Truth and Reconciliation Commission of Canada, *Honouring the Truth, Reconciling for the Future: Summary of the Final Report of the Truth and Reconciliation Commission of Canada* (2015) 3.

violence, and long-term social problems.[9] Many Indigenous individuals in Canada have been raised with only attenuated connections to their culture as a direct result of the residential schools. Empirical research has further found that there are close links between familial attendance in residential schools and various negative health, economic, and social outcomes among descendants of residential school survivors and victims.[10] It is a past harm that very much remains in the memories and everyday lives of Indigenous survivors, descendants, and communities.

Approximately a century after John Macdonald first designed and Duncan Campbell Scott later institutionalized the residential school system as Canada's primary tool of assimilation, these schools became the subject of the most robust formalized attempt to address large-scale cultural wrongdoing through a transitional justice response. Canada's Truth and Reconciliation Commission was established in 2009 as a result of a class-action settlement, the Indian Residential School Settlement Agreement, reached by survivors, the government of Canada, and various religious organizations, among others.[11] The Canadian TRC was tasked with compiling a historical record of the Indian residential school system and legacy, including systematic harms, intergenerational consequences, and the impact on human dignity.[12] In 2015, the Canadian TRC released its landmark report and, in its most striking finding, concluded that Canada committed cultural genocide against Indigenous Peoples through its operation of the Indian residential schools.[13] The Commission's finding of cultural genocide sent shockwaves through Canadian society, challenging the dominant national narrative of a peaceful and human rights-abiding State.[14]

In many ways, the Canadian TRC put a spotlight on other established democracies' relationships with Indigenous Peoples and prompted these States to consider how to reckon with their own legacy of colonial wrongdoing.[15]

[9] Augustine SJ Park, 'Settler Colonialism, Decolonization and Radicalizing Transitional Justice' (2020) 14(2) International Journal of Transitional Justice 260, 261.

[10] Amy Bombay, Kimberly Matheson, and Hymie Anisman, 'The Intergenerational Effects of Indian Residential Schools: Implications for the Concept of Historical Trauma' (2014) 51(3) Transcultural Psychiatry 320; see also David K Androff, 'Adaptations of Truth and Reconciliation Commissions in the North American Context: Local Examples of a Global Restorative Justice Intervention' (2012) 13 Advances in Social Work 408, 414.

[11] Indian Residential Schools Settlement Agreement, Schedule N <http://www.residentialschoolsettlement.ca/settlement.html> accessed 1 February 2025.

[12] ibid.

[13] Truth and Reconciliation Commission of Canada (n 8) 1.

[14] Alissa Macoun and Elizabeth Strakosch, 'The Ethical Demands of Settler Colonial Theory' (2013) 3(4) Settler Colonial Studies 426, 433.

[15] Eduardo González, 'Standards and Policies for Conflict Resolution, Truth, Transitional Justice and Reconciliation', expert paper presented at the international expert group meeting: 'Truth, transitional justice and reconciliation processes, PFII/2022/EGM (15-17 November 2022) <https://social.desa.

In the decade since the Canadian TRC's final report, there have been several transitional justice initiatives—at national, provincial, and local levels—with the specific objective of addressing large-scale past harm committed against Indigenous Peoples. Most of these mechanisms are explicitly mandated to investigate and report on assimilationist policies and other forms of cultural harm that have been committed against Indigenous Peoples and certain minority groups.[16] This general momentum towards using the frameworks and tools of transitional justice to confront wrongdoing against Indigenous Peoples provides the impetus to examine to what extent these initiatives adopt a cultural rights-based approach in the scope of their work.

Indigenous Peoples have long sought increased recognition and protection of their distinct cultures—traditions, practices, values, worldviews, and ways of life that form their collective identity.[17] The primacy of culture in Indigenous life is widely acknowledged in the human rights field.[18] While Indigenous Peoples have diverse aspirations and traditions, they share a common goal of preserving their unique cultures.[19] Siegfried Wiessner notes that the '[t]he safeguarding and flourishing of their cultures is thus the preeminent basis of indigenous peoples' claims'.[20] Indigenous Peoples also tend to conceive of culture in its broadest sense, encompassing all aspects of life, including traditional knowledge, beliefs, values, customs, morals, law, art, literature, religion, and science and technology.[21] Thus, it is not uncommon to talk about cultural rights primarily in the context of Indigenous Peoples.[22]

Accordingly, the marginalization of cultural rights in transitional justice is inextricably intertwined with the field's historical marginalization of Indigenous Peoples. While Indigenous Peoples endure the full spectrum of human rights violations, much of the harm they sustain is directed at their unique cultural

un.org/sites/default/files/inline-files/Eduardo-Gonzalez-Transitional-Justice-and-Indigenous-Peoples.pdf> accessed 1 February 2025.

[16] See section 2.1 in Chapter 1 of this book.

[17] Elsa Stamatopoulou, 'Taking Cultural Rights Seriously: The Vision of the UN Declaration on the Rights of Indigenous Peoples' in Stephen Allen and Alexandra Xanthaki (eds), *Reflections on the UN Declaration on the Rights of Indigenous Peoples* (Hart Publishing 2011) 387.

[18] In the UNDRIP, for example, five articles explicitly protect indigenous cultural rights and 17 concern cultural rights. UN Declaration on the Rights of Indigenous Peoples, adopted by the UN General Assembly, UN Doc A/RES/61/295 (13 September 2007) Arts 11, 12, 13, 15, 34.

[19] Siegfried Wiessner, 'The Cultural Rights of Indigenous Peoples: Achievements and Continuing Challenges' (2011) 22 European Journal of International Law 121, 122.

[20] Siegfried Wiessner, 'Culture and the Rights of Indigenous Peoples' in Ana Vrdoljak (ed), *The Cultural Dimension of Human Rights* (Oxford University Press 2013) 118.

[21] Patrick Thornberry, *International Law and the Rights of Minorities* (Oxford University Press 1991) 188.

[22] Julie Ringelheim, 'Cultural Rights' in Daniel Moeckli and others (eds), *International Human Rights Law* (Oxford University Press, 3rd edn 2018) 280.

identities and practices. Forced removals of Indigenous children, the banning of Indigenous languages and dress, restrictions on cultural and spiritual practices, and various assimilationist policies have all been pursued by States to culturally eliminate Indigenous Peoples. In many countries, Indigenous cultural identities and practices continue to be denigrated and denied, with majority societies relying on their own sense of cultural superiority to push anti-Indigenous ideologies and policies into the present day.[23] This constitutes its own form of harm, and also contributes to much of the physical and structural violence that negatively shapes modern life for Indigenous communities.[24] This cultural wrongdoing is often latent, yet insidious and pervasive, working to fracture the social and communal bonds that allow Indigenous Peoples to exist and flourish as culturally distinct groups. In the wake of this violence, Indigenous Peoples consistently prioritize approaches that seek to reckon with a loss of culture.[25] Thus, a cultural rights-based approach to transitional justice is most likely to take root in cases of large-scale harm perpetrated against Indigenous Peoples.

This chapter charts the evolution of transitional justice's interaction with Indigenous Peoples, ranging from wholesale neglect to the current moment, where there is an emerging consensus that historical and contemporary wrongdoing against Indigenous Peoples can and should be addressed through some sort of transitional justice response. It also briefly grapples with some of the contestations around applying the logics and tools of transitional justice in response to Indigenous harm. A cultural rights-based lens is then applied to three distinct transitional justice initiatives in the context of large-scale wrongdoing against Indigenous Peoples: (1) Canada's National Inquiry into Missing and Murdered Indigenous Women and Girls, (2) Victoria's Yoorrook Justice Commission, and (3) the Peruvian theatre collective *Yuyachkani*. These diverse cases provide insights into the ways in which transitional justice programming has already begun to embrace a cultural rights-based approach in the case of Indigenous Peoples.

[23] Sheryl R Lightfoot, 'Emerging International Indigenous Rights Norms and "Over-Compliance" in New Zealand and Canada' (2010) 62(1) Political Science 84, 94, 98.

[24] See National Inquiry into Missing and Murdered Indigenous Women and Girls, *Reclaiming Power and Place: The Final Report of the National Inquiry into Missing and Murdered Indigenous Women and Girls* (2019) 327.

[25] See, eg, Gerald Taiaiake Alfred, 'Colonialism and State Dependency' (2009) 5(2) International Journal of Indigenous Health 42, 43; Kyle Powys Whyte, 'On Resilient Parasitisms, or Why I'm Skeptical of Indigenous/Settler Reconciliation' (2018) 14 Journal of Global Ethics 277, 277.

2. The Historic Invisibility of Indigenous Peoples in Transitional Justice

Until quite recently, transitional justice did not concern itself with Indigenous Peoples' violent experiences.[26] In every region of the world, Indigenous Peoples suffer from large-scale human rights abuses, including, *inter alia*, mass physical violence;[27] dispossession, degradation, and exploitation of their lands, territories, and resources;[28] and targeted attacks against their cultural identities and practices.[29] In spite of this, Indigenous harm has traditionally been omitted from transitional justice considerations.[30] By all accounts, transitional justice has been defined and theorized broadly enough to address the injustices suffered by Indigenous Peoples, including large-scale acts of cultural wrongdoing; overwhelmingly, however, these have fallen outside the direct purview of nearly all transitional justice projects.[31]

Historically, Indigenous Peoples were also not consulted when transitional justice mechanisms were designed and implemented. As a result, these mechanisms tended to overlook wrongdoing against Indigenous Peoples or only 'stumbled upon' it.[32] Restrictive mandates have also commonly prevented measures from confronting the full scope of violence perpetrated against Indigenous Peoples, particularly abuses that reach beyond recent memory. The underlying sentiment in this historical treatment is that wrongs committed against Indigenous Peoples are perceived as less grave and less egregious than those perpetrated against others.

This is counterintuitive given that Indigenous Peoples have suffered some of the world's most serious human rights violations,[33] and are arguably the

[26] Harry Hobbs, 'Locating the Logic of Transitional Justice in Liberal Democracies: Native Title in Australia' (2016) 39 University of New South Wales Law Journal 512, 523.

[27] Deborah J Yashar, 'Indigenous Rights and Truth Commissions: Reflections for Discussion' in ICTJ (ed), *Strengthening Indigenous Rights through Truth Commissions: A Practitioner's Resource* (ICTJ 2012) 7.

[28] Joshua Castellino, 'Colonial Crime, Environmental Destruction and Indigenous Peoples: A Roadmap to Accountability and Protection' in Morten Bergsmo, Wolfgang Kaleck, and Kyaw Yin Hlaing (eds), *Colonial Wrongs and Access to International Law* (Torkel Opsahl Academic EPublisher 2020) 577–602.

[29] Stamatopoulou, 'Taking Cultural Rights Seriously' (n 17) 388.

[30] ICTJ, *Strengthening Indigenous Rights through Truth Commissions: A Practitioner's Resource* (International Center for Transitional Justice 2012).

[31] Jennifer Balint, Julie Evans, and Nesam McMillan 'Rethinking Transitional Justice, Redressing Indigenous Harm: A New Conceptual Approach' (2014) 8(2) International Journal of Transitional Justice 194, 194.

[32] International Center of Transitional Justice, Indigenous Voices and Truth Commissions, Summary Materials: International Seminar (22–23 March 2010) <https://www.ictj.org/sites/default/files/IPTC-March-2010-Meeting-Summary-Materials.pdf> accessed 1 February 2025.

[33] Mauro Barelli, *Seeking Justice in International Law: The Significance and Implications of the UN Declaration on the Rights of Indigenous Peoples* (Routledge 2016) 9.

most marginalized of all groups in society.[34] A significant percentage of transitional justice settings have involved large-scale human rights abuses against Indigenous Peoples.[35] They often occupy resource-rich territories that are exploited during conflict, inflicting serious and continuing human rights violations.[36] Beyond the context of armed conflict, various forms of discrimination, structural violence, assimilationist policies, and land dispossession have eroded Indigenous self-determination and lie at the root of ongoing violence against these communities.[37] That is perhaps why the International Center for Transitional Justice contends that Indigenous Peoples 'live at a precarious intersection between unresolved historic injustices and the contemporary incursion of industry and political violence'.[38]

2.1 Indigenous neglect

Indigenous histories and perspectives have been neglected in many of the signature transitional justice cases. For example, one-third of the Indigenous Twa population in Rwanda was killed during the 1994 genocide against the Tutsi, with another one-third of the Twa population forced to flee as refugees.[39] The ensuing transitional justice policy in Rwanda did not include the Twa's suffering in the dominant account of the genocide.[40] They were prevented from adequately participating in transitional justice measures like the *gacaca*[41] and to this day have yet to be properly included in post-genocide commemoration and memorialization processes.[42] Barred from recognition or participation in transitional justice initiatives, their violent histories were completely

[34] International Center for Transitional Justice, 'Holding a Mirror to Society: Acknowledgment and the Struggle for Indigenous Peoples Rights' (August 2018) <https://www.ictj.org/news/holding-mirror-society-acknowledgment-and-struggle-indigenous-peoples-rights> accessed 1 February 2025.

[35] Chris Chapman, 'Transitional Justice and the Rights of Minorities and Indigenous Peoples' in Paige Arthur (ed), *Identities in Transition: Challenges for Transitional Justice in Divided Societies* (Cambridge University Press 2010) 251.

[36] Belkis V Izquierdo and Lieselotte Viaene, 'Decolonizing Transitional Justice from Indigenous Territories' *Peace in Progress*, No 38 (June 2018) <<https://www.icip.cat/perlapau/en/article/decolonizing-transitional-justice-from-indigenous-territories/>> accessed 24 June 2025.

[37] International Center for Transitional Justice, 'Holding a Mirror to Society' (n 34).

[38] International Center for Transitional Justice, 'Strengthening Indigenous Rights through Truth Commissions' (n 30) 1.

[39] Unrepresented Nations and Peoples Organization ('UNPO'), 'Batwa: Exclusion from Genocide Commemorations' (15 April 2019) <https://unpo.org/article/21462> accessed 1 February 2025.

[40] Laura A Young and Korir Sing'Oei, 'Access to Justice for Indigenous Peoples in Africa' in Wilton Littlechild and Elsa Stamatopoulou (eds), *Indigenous Peoples' Access to Justice, Including Truth and Reconciliation Processes* (Institute for the Study of Human Rights, Columbia University 2014) 108–09.

[41] ibid 109.

[42] UNPO, 'Batwa: Exclusion from Genocide Commemorations' (n 39).

written out of the historical narrative, furthering entrenching the Twa as 'invisible members of Rwandan society'.[43] This invisibility is replicated in the discourse, with the Twa being relegated to a 'mere footnote' in the story about the genocide.[44]

Rather than respect and protect their cultural rights, transitional justice policy in Rwanda has largely worked to deny the Twa's unique Indigenous identities. Indeed, the African Peer Review Mechanism determined that Rwanda's post-genocide policies towards the Twa were 'based on a policy of assimilation' with a 'desire to obliterate distinctive identities and to integrate all into some mainstream socio-economic fabric of the country'.[45] The post-genocide government banned civil society organizations advocating on behalf of the Twa and denied their Indigenous status, instead referring to them as historically marginalized peoples. Research into the Twa experience in post-genocide Rwanda confirms their neglect in transitional justice processes and the ongoing denial of their identity in furtherance of a reimagined, new Rwandan national identity.[46]

Similarly, transitional justice mechanisms in South Africa, and the wealth of accompanying scholarship, overwhelmingly exclude any reference to the indigenous Khoi-San peoples—the country's first inhabitants.[47] Apartheid policy in South Africa had devastating impacts on Khoi-San peoples, whose lands were stolen and cultures denigrated.[48] Yet, the South African Truth and Reconciliation Commission gave no individualized analysis to apartheid's impact on Indigenous Peoples. In the Commission's work, the term 'indigenous' was not applied to groups such as the Khoi-San, but instead was used to distinguish all black South Africans from white settlers.[49] Laura Young and Korir Sing'Oei argue that this 'appropriated Indigenous identity away from the Khoe-San'.[50] Transitional justice policymakers in South Africa were further

[43] Susan M Thomson, 'Ethnic Twa and Rwandan National Unity and Reconciliation Policy' (2009) 21(3) Peace Review 313, 313.

[44] Ezechiel Sentama, 'Transitional Justice and Redress for Racial Injustices against Marginalized Minorities: Lessons from Indigenous Twa People in Post-Genocide Rwanda' (2024) 18(1) The International Journal of Transitional Justice 66, 70.

[45] African Peer Review Mechanism, Country Review Report of the Republic of Rwanda (June 2005) para 153 <https://www.aprmtoolkit.saiia.org.za/documents/country-reports-and-exper/82-atkt-rwanda-aprm-country-review-report-2005-en/file> accessed 1 February 2025.

[46] Sentama, 'Transitional Justice and Redress for Racial Injustices' (n 44) 77.

[47] Young and Sing'Oei, 'Access to Justice for Indigenous Peoples in Africa' (n 40) 109.

[48] Report of the Special Rapporteur on the Situation of Human Rights and Fundamental Freedoms of Indigenous People, Rodolfo Stavenhagen: Mission to South Africa, UN Doc E/CN.4/2006/78/Add.2 (15 December 2005) 2.

[49] Young and Sing'Oei, 'Access to Justice for Indigenous Peoples in Africa' (n 40) 109–10.

[50] ibid 110.

accused of excluding Indigenous participation in the country's truth and reconciliation process.[51]

The cases of the Twa in Rwanda and the Khoi-San in South Africa exemplify the historic invisibility of Indigenous Peoples in transitional justice agendas globally, especially in the paradigmatic post-conflict and post-authoritarian contexts. In both countries, nation-building was advanced to the detriment and denial of racial, ethnic, and Indigenous identities.[52] These cases also demonstrate how transitional justice policy can often contribute to the denial of Indigenous Peoples' rights, including their right to cultural identity, rather than advancing such rights or redressing their violation. Other transitional justice mechanisms have followed similar trajectories, failing to sufficiently focus on Indigenous Peoples in the overall project of reckoning with large-scale past harm. In Nepal, for example, Indigenous Peoples were excluded from the post-war negotiation and drafting process associated with the 2015 Constitution, contributing to a further erosion of Indigenous rights under its domestic law.[53]

Indigenous neglect is committed not only through the nation-building aspirations of transitional justice, but also through overly restrictive mandates which adhered to the narrow, time-bound conception of violence in dominant theory and practice. For example, multiple truth commissions in Chile were tasked with documenting and uncovering State violence during the dictatorship of Augusto Pinochet.[54] At the same time, these bodies were prohibited from addressing much of the fundamental harm perpetrated against Indigenous Peoples in Chile due to temporal limitations that excluded the mass violence and land dispossession experienced by Mapuche and other Indigenous communities beginning in the nineteenth century.[55] In the collective memory of these groups, violence did not commence with authoritarian rule in the 1960s, but with the long history of colonialism in Chile. Chile's transitional justice

[51] Stavenhagen, 'Mission to South Africa' (n 48) para 32.

[52] Will Kymlicka, 'Transitional Justice, Federalism, and the Accommodation of Minority Nationalism' in Paige Arthur (ed), *Identities in Transition: Challenges for Transitional Justice in Divided Societies* (Cambridge University Press 2011) 304.

[53] See Submission of Asia Indigenous Peoples Pact (AIPP) and its member organizations for the report of the Expert Mechanism on the Rights of Indigenous Peoples on Recognition, Reparations and Reconciliation <https://www.ohchr.org/Documents/Issues/IPeoples/EMRIP/StudyRRR/AIPP_submission_EMRIP_RRR.pdf> accessed 1 February 2025.

[54] Rettig Commission, *Comisión Nacional de Verdad y Reconciliación, Informe de La Comisión Nacional de Verdad y Reconciliación* (1993) <https://bibliotecadigital.indh.cl/handle/123456789/170> accessed 1 February 2025; Valech Commission, Comisión Nacional Sobre Prisión Política y Tortura, Informe de La Comisión Nacional Sobre Prisión Política y Tortura (2004) <https://bibliotecadigital.indh.cl/handle/123456789/455> accessed 1 February 2025.

[55] Daniela Jara and others, 'Tracing Mapuche Exclusion from Post-dictatorial Truth Commissions in Chile: Official and Grassroots Initiatives' (2018) 12(3) International Journal of Transitional Justice 479, 491.

policy not only failed to focus on violations against Indigenous Peoples, but also arguably silenced their perspectives in the process.[56]

A further Chilean commission—the Historical Truth and the New Deal with Indigenous Peoples Commission—was initiated to specifically focus on the relationship between the State and Indigenous Peoples within it. The Commission found that Indigenous Peoples were the first inhabitants of Chile and that the Chilean government sought to assimilate them through violence and denial of their Indigenous identities.[57] However, the majority of measures recommended by the Commission were not initiated.[58] The New Deal with Indigenous Peoples was also widely criticized by Indigenous leaders for failing to address mass land dispossession and the political repression of the Mapuche people and for adopting an assimilationist approach that did not respect Indigenous Peoples' right to self-determination.[59] Notwithstanding, Chile's Historical Truth and the New Deal with Indigenous Peoples Commission was a breakthrough of sorts, being the first formal truth commission dedicated to the specific experiences of Indigenous Peoples.[60]

In Brazil, approximately 8,000 Indigenous community members were killed during the military dictatorship in the country between 1964 and 1985, rendering them the largest category of victims.[61] Thousands more had their livelihoods and rights violated through development projects, mass incarceration, and land dispossession.[62] Notwithstanding, Brazil's National Truth Commission was restricted to addressing 'serious human rights violations' defined as arbitrary imprisonment, torture, execution, and enforced disappearance.[63] This excluded a large proportion of violations against

[56] ibid 498.

[57] M. Florencia Librizzi, 'Challenges of the Truth Commissions to Deal with Injustice Against Indigenous Peoples' in Wilton Littlechild and Elsa Stamatopoulou (eds), *Indigenous Peoples' Access to Justice, Including Truth and Reconciliation Processes* (Institute for the Study of Human Rights, Columbia University 2014) 188.

[58] Jara and others, 'Tracing Mapuche Exclusion from Post-dictatorial Truth Commissions in Chile' (n 55) 482.

[59] Maria Cecilia Espinoza, 'A "New Deal" for Indigenous Groups' *Inter Press Service* (29 November 2003) <http://ipsnews.net/2003/11/rights-chile-a-new-deal-for-indigenous-groups/?utm_source=rss&utm_medium=rss&utm_campaign=rights-chile-a-new-deal-for-indigenous-groups> accessed 1 February 2025.

[60] González, 'Standards and Policies for Conflict Resolution, Truth, Transitional Justice and Reconciliation' (n 15).

[61] Gisele Iecker de Almeida, *From Dictatorship to Democracy: Confronting the Authoritarian Past in Brazil* (Liverpool University Press 2024) 95; see also Juliana Neuenschwander Magalhães, 'Political Transition, Continuities and Permanences: The Rights of Indigenous Peoples and Political Transition in Brazil' in Cristiano Paixão and Massimo Meccarelli (eds), *Comparing Transitions to Democracy. Law and Justice in South America and Europe* (Springer 2021) 31.

[62] Fabricio Teló and others, 'Land and Transitional Justice in Brazil' (2021) 15(1) International Journal of Transitional Justice 190.

[63] ibid 191.

Indigenous Peoples, including land dispossession and cultural rights violations. Transitional justice in Brazil, like elsewhere, followed the dominant model, privileging individualized accountability for egregious acts of recent physical violence while sidelining underlying issues of cultural harm and cultural loss that constituted equally, if not more, devastating forms of violence for many Indigenous communities.[64]

2.2 Transitional justice's slow creep towards engaging with indigenous harm

Transitional justice's wholesale reluctance to engage with Indigenous harm has gradually waned in recent years. This slow creep towards acknowledgement of Indigenous injustice has its genesis in Latin America, where early truth commissions in Guatemala and Peru addressed large-scale human rights abuses against Indigenous Peoples in more meaningful ways. In both countries, Indigenous communities suffered disproportionately from sustained periods of armed conflict, and ensuing truth commissions began to recognize the distinct harms perpetrated against Indigenous Peoples, albeit in limited ways.

Peru's internal conflict between the government and various insurgent groups disproportionately impacted Indigenous Peoples as well as poor rural communities.[65] The mandate of Peru's Truth and Reconciliation Commission explicitly put 'violations against the collective rights of the country's Andean and Native communities' within the truth commission's remit.[66] The Commission ultimately concluded that 75 per cent of the 70,000 casualties in the conflict were speakers of Indigenous languages.[67] At the same time, it did not take an Indigenous-centred approach in its work. None of the Commissioners were Indigenous and only one spoke Quecha, the most used Indigenous language in Peru.[68] The final report also failed to substantively

[64] Frank Haldemann and Rachelle Kouassi, 'Transitional Justice without Economic, Social, and Cultural Rights?' in Eibe Riedel and others (eds), *Economic, Social, and Cultural Rights in International Law: Contemporary Issues and Challenges* (Oxford University Press 2014) 498.

[65] The International Center for Transitional Justice, 'Ten Years after Peru's Truth Commission' (19 August 2013) <https://www.ictj.org/news/ten-years-after-peru-truth-commission> accessed 1 February 2025.

[66] Eduarrdo González, *Justice and Indigenous Peoples in Latin America: Lessons Learned from Case Studies of Guatemala, Peru and Colombia* (Global Initiative for Justice Truth and Reconciliation 2021) 23.

[67] *Comision de la Verdad y Reconciliacion, Informe Final de la Comision de la Verdad y Reconciliacion* (2004) <http://www.cverdad.org.pe/ingles/ifinal/index.php> accessed 1 February 2025.

[68] González, *Justice and Indigenous Peoples in Latin America* (n 66) 24.

address violations of collective rights, including cultural rights, even though a chapter in the Commission's final report relates to collective rights.[69]

Similarly, Guatemala's Historical Clarification Commission concluded that the government committed acts of genocide against Mayan communities, who constituted 83 per cent of the victims to the internal conflict.[70] While it was not specifically mandated to focus on wrongdoing perpetrated against Indigenous Peoples, it reported specifically on patterns of violence against Mayan communities, including with respect to their rights to cultural identity.[71] The Commission ultimately made clear that Mayan communities 'bore the full brunt of the institutionalized violence' in Guatemala's conflict.[72]

Truth-seeking in Peru and Guatemala took strides to expose long-standing violence and marginalization directed towards Indigenous communities. They also made recommendations for collective reparations flowing to these groups.[73] Yet, in both cases, they were designed and implemented without consulting Indigenous groups and failed to incorporate their worldviews and justice processes—itself a violation of these groups' fundamental cultural rights.[74] According to the ICTJ, they were created 'in some sort of culturally blind logic', without discussion with and participation from Indigenous Peoples themselves.[75] Among other things, this is counter to numerous decisions from the Inter-American human rights system, which has repeatedly affirmed Indigenous Peoples' participation and consultation rights in connection with any measures that impact them.[76]

Other transitional justice mechanisms have arguably only 'stumbled upon' the violent experiences of Indigenous Peoples.[77] In Kenya, for instance,

[69] ibid.

[70] Guatemala Memory of Silence, Report of the Commission for Historical Clarification: Conclusions and Recommendations (1999) <https://hrdag.org/wp-content/uploads/2013/01/CEHreport-english.pdf> accessed 1 February 2025.

[71] Memory of Silence, Report of the Commission for Historical Clarification, Volume 3 (1999) 171–206.

[72] Guatemala Memory of Silence (n 70) 1.

[73] ICTJ, 'Indigenous Voices and Truth Commissions' (n 32).

[74] Luke Moffett and James Gallen, 'From Truth to Repair—Implementing Truth Commissions' Recommendations on Reparations' (January 2020) <https://reparations.qub.ac.uk/assets/uploads/QUB-TRCs_Report_UPDATED130120.pdf> accessed 1 February 2025; see also Hobbs, 'Locating the Logic of Transitional Justice' (n 26) 523.

[75] ICTJ, 'Transitional Justice and the Struggle for Indigenous Rights' (8 February 2013) <https://www.ictj.org/news/transitional-justice-and-struggle-indigenous-rights> accessed 1 February 2025.

[76] See, eg, *Saramaka People v Suriname* (Preliminary Objections, Merits, Reparations, and Costs) Inter-American Court of Human Rights Series C No 172 (28 November 2007) para 134; *Kaliña and Lokono Peoples v Suriname* (Merits, Reparations and Costs), Inter-American Court of Human Rights Series C No 309 (25 November 2015) para 204; *Kichwa Indigenous People of Sarayaku v Ecuador* (Merits and Reparations), Inter-American Court of Human Rights Series C No 245, 201, 215, and 217 (27 June 2012) para 194.

[77] ICTJ, 'Indigenous Voices and Truth Commissions' (n 32).

the Truth, Justice and Reconciliation Commission ('Kenya TJRC') implemented in the wake of the post-2007 election violence was empowered with a broad mandate. Among other things, it was charged with inquiring into and establishing 'the reality or otherwise of perceived economic marginalization of communities and make recommendations on how to address the marginalization'.[78] The TJRC plainly concluded that Indigenous Peoples 'have suffered gross violations of human rights on account of their membership in these communities'.[79] It also found that Indigenous groups suffered from systematic discrimination, as well as violations of the rights to land and development.[80] Yet, despite steps to improve outreach to and participation of Indigenous Peoples in Kenya,[81] the TJRC's engagement with violations against these groups was extremely limited and, similar to truth commissions in Chile, Indigenous representatives criticized the TJRC's inability to account for the much of the land-grabbing and mass atrocities that occurred prior to and after the mandated period of 12 December 1963–28 February 2008.[82]

Undoubtedly, the application of transitional justice to Indigenous Peoples has gained it strongest footing so far in the CANZUS countries. Like other contexts, the violent experiences of Indigenous Peoples in the CANZUS countries were not historically addressed through any sort of extraordinary justice measures.[83] The genocidal campaigns that were integral to settler colonialism were not met with the same public reckoning that accompanied mass atrocities committed against other communities in other parts of the world.[84] While justice for Indigenous Peoples in such contexts is complicated by the historical nature of colonial-era violence, there is also a perception that the wrongdoing perpetrated against Indigenous Peoples was not as urgent or grave as atrocities committed against others.[85]

The considerable expansion of transitional justice programming in the CANZUS nations was highlighted by three signature mechanisms: Canada's

[78] Government of Kenya, The Truth, Justice and Reconciliation Commission Act, No. 6 of 2008 at para 6(p).
[79] Kenya Truth, Justice and Reconciliation Commission, 'Report of the Truth, Justice and Reconciliation Commission' Vol 2C (3 May 2013) v.
[80] ibid Vol 1, vii.
[81] Young and Sing'Oei, 'Access to Justice for Indigenous Peoples in Africa' (n 40) 110–11.
[82] Report on the African Commission's Working Group on Indigenous Populations/Communities Research and Information Visit to Kenya (1–19 March 2010) 73.
[83] Jennifer Balint, Julie Evans, and Nesam McMillan, 'Rethinking Transitional Justice, Redressing Indigenous Harm' (n 31) 194–95.
[84] Sarah Maddison and Laura J Shepherd, 'Peacebuilding and the Postcolonial Politics of Transitional Justice' (2014) 2(3) Peacebuilding 253, 262.
[85] Eric Palmer and Krushil Watene, 'Introduction: New Paths in Reconciliation, Transitional and Indigenous Justice' (2018) 14(2) Journal of Global Ethics 133, 134.

TRC; Australia's National Inquiry into the Separation of Aboriginal and Torres Strait Islander Children from Their Families; and the Waitangi Tribunal in New Zealand. While their impact and effectiveness have been routinely questioned, each of these mechanisms has been groundbreaking in its own right and has set important precedents for transitional justice's engagement with contemporary and historical wrongdoing committed against Indigenous Peoples.

2.3 An Indigenous era of transitional justice?

Part of transitional justice's considerable expansion includes the specific attention the field now affords to certain groups or categories of victims, including Indigenous Peoples.[86] Indigenous groups, activists, and organizations are increasingly invoking the language and tools of transitional justice in the context of their broader justice demands. In response, transitional justice has started to acknowledge, consider, and address the unique situations, needs, and demands of Indigenous Peoples in relationship to past large-scale harm.

In the current moment, the field is undoubtedly embracing its role as a framework for addressing the difficult and violent histories behind Indigenous harm, especially as it relates to colonial-era abuses. We are arguably experiencing an 'Indigenous era' of transitional justice, whereby the field is taking Indigenous claims of wrongdoing more seriously, mechanisms are being marshalled in response, and Indigenous communities are increasingly governing and consulting on how these mechanisms operate. This is further evidenced by a growing body of scholarly literature[87] and NGO advocacy[88] which regularly interrogates the role of transitional justice in response to large-scale wrongdoing committed against Indigenous Peoples.

[86] González, 'Standards and Policies for Conflict Resolution, Truth, Transitional Justice and Reconciliation' (n 15) 5.

[87] See, eg, Courtney Jung, 'Canada and the Legacy of the Indian Residential Schools: Transitional Justice for Indigenous Peoples in a Non-Transitional Society' in Paige Arthur (ed), *Identities in Transition: Challenges for Transitional Justice in Divided Societies* (Cambridge University Press 2010); Rosemary Nagy, 'The Scope and Bounds of Transitional Justice and the Canadian Truth and Reconciliation Commission' (2013) 7(1) International Journal of Transitional Justice 52; Balint, Evans, and McMillan, 'Rethinking Transitional Justice, Redressing Indigenous Harm: A New Conceptual Approach' (n 31); Park, 'Settler Colonialism, Decolonization and Radicalizing Transitional Justice' (n 9); Hobbs, 'Locating the Logic of Transitional Justice' (n 26); Maddison and Shepherd, 'Peacebuilding and the Postcolonial Politics of Transitional Justice' (n 84).

[88] González, *Justice and Indigenous Peoples in Latin America* (n 66); Usani Odum and Hari Tesfaye, *Transitional Justice and Indigenous Peoples: Lessons Learned from the Cases of Kenya, Morocco, Nigeria, Rwanda and Sierra Leone* (Global Initiative for Justice Truth and Reconciliation 2021); Yashar, 'Indigenous Rights and Truth Commissions' (n 27).

Likewise, at the UN, the relationships between transitional justice and Indigenous harm are now explicitly discussed. The EMRIP has published reports concerning recognition, reparations, and reconciliation in the context of implementing the UNDRIP, as well as Indigenous Peoples' access to justice, both of which discussed the application of transitional justice to Indigenous Peoples.[89] The EMRIP has stated that '[w]hile the application of transitional justice has traditionally centred on post-conflict or post-dictatorship contexts, its objectives and precepts provide a framework to address reparation and reconciliation for Indigenous Peoples'.[90] Moreover, the former UN Special Rapporteur on the rights of Indigenous Peoples, Victoria Tauli-Corpuz, said that 'indigenous justice systems can also play a role in transitional justice processes following armed conflicts'.[91] Former UN SRTJ Fabián Salvioli also discussed numerous Indigenous-centred transitional mechanisms in his thematic report on transitional justice in colonial contexts.[92]

As discussed briefly in Chapter 2, the signature transitional justice mechanisms in the CANZUS nations have spurred a host of measures aimed at addressing the unjust and violent treatment of Indigenous Peoples across multiple contexts. National truth commissions in the Arctic[93] and Canada,[94] along with regional truth commissions in the United States[95] and

[89] EMRIP, Efforts to Implement the United Nations Declaration on the Rights of Indigenous Peoples: Recognition, Reparation and Reconciliation, UN Doc A/HRC/EMRIP/2019/3/Rev.1 (2 September 2019); EMRIP, Access to Justice in the Promotion and Protection of the Rights of Indigenous Peoples, UN Doc A/HRC/EMRIP/2013/2 (29 April 2013).

[90] EMRIP, Access to Justice in the Promotion and Protection of the Rights of Indigenous Peoples (n 89) para 44.

[91] Special Rapporteur on the Rights of Indigenous Peoples, Promotion and Protection of All Human Rights, Civil, Political, Economic, Social and Cultural Rights, Including the Right to Development, UN Doc A/HRC/42/37 (2 August 2019) para 66.

[92] Report of the Special Rapporteur on the Promotion of Truth, Justice, Reparation and Guarantees of Non-Recurrence, Fabián Salvioli, Transitional Justice Measures and Addressing the Legacy of Gross Violations of Human Rights and International Humanitarian Law Committed in Colonial Contexts, UN Doc A/76/180 (19 July 2021).

[93] Commission to Investigate the Norwegianisation Policy and Injustice against the Sámi and Kvens/Norwegian Finns (1 June 2023) <https://www.stortinget.no/globalassets/pdf/sannhets--og-forsoningskommisjonen/rapport-til-stortinget-fra-sannhets--og-forsoningskommisjonen.pdf> accessed 24 December 2024; Truth and Reconciliation Commission for Kvens, Tornedalians and Lantalaiset (15 November 2023); Truth and Reconciliation Commission Concerning the Sámi People <https://sdtsk.fi/en/home/> accessed 31 December 2024; Truth Commission for the Sámi People <https://sanningskommissionensamer.se/en/about-the-commision/#:~:text=The%20Truth%20Commission%20for%20the%20Sami%20People&text=The%20Commission%20will%20survey%20and,consequences%20for%20the%20Sami%20people.> accessed 31 December 2024; Greenland's Reconciliation Commission, *We Understand the Past; We Take Responsibility for the Present; We Are Working for a Better Future* (December 2017).

[94] National Inquiry into Missing and Murdered Indigenous Women and Girls, *Reclaiming Power and Place* (n 24).

[95] Beyond the Mandate, Continuing the Conversation: Report of the Maine Wabanaki-State Child Welfare Truth and Reconciliation Commission (14 June 2015); see also State of California, Executive Order N-15-19 (establishing the California Truth and Healing Council) (18 June 2019) <https://

Australia,[96] have all been tasked with looking at specific aspects of wrong-doing vis-à-vis Indigenous Peoples. These official bodies are complemented by a growing list of political apologies[97] and broader reconciliation initiatives[98] aimed at improving the relations between Indigenous Peoples and mainstream societies. These measures are increasingly adopted and pursued even if they are not explicitly denominated as forms of transitional justice.

Even transitional justice measures that are not Indigenous-specific are engaging with Indigenous Peoples in more meaningful ways. In Colombia, for instance, Indigenous individuals were disproportionately victimized during the country's decades-long civil conflict, endangering both their physical and cultural survival.[99] Despite this, Indigenous Peoples were excluded from the peace process negotiations until the very last moment, when the 'Ethnic Chapter' of the peace accords were formulated.[100] The Ethnic Chapter accounts for special measures for Indigenous Peoples and minorities, but it is far from comprehensive and does not meet the majority of demands among Colombia's Indigenous groups.[101] This is observable by comparing the Ethnic Chapter to the National Peace Agenda of the Indigenous Peoples, an outcome document created by 300 Indigenous leaders participating in the National Forum for Peace of the Indigenous Peoples in 2014.[102] Among other things, the National Peace Agenda called for the creation of an Indigenous Peoples' Tribunal charged with handling cases of human rights violations and violations of international

tribalaffairs.ca.gov/wp-content/uploads/sites/10/2020/02/Executive-Order-N-15-19.pdf> accessed 1 February 2025.

[96] Letters Patent dated 14 May 2021 (establishing the Yoorrook Justice Commission) <https://yoorrookjusticecommission.org.au/wp-content/uploads/2023/03/Yoo-rrook-Justice-Commission-Letters-Patent-14-05-21-1.pdf> accessed 1 February 2025.

[97] See, eg, Office of the President, Republic of China (Taiwan),'President Tsai Apologizes to Indigenous Peoples on Behalf of Government' (1 August 2016) <https://english.president.gov.tw/NEWS/4950> accessed 1 February 2025; Parliament of Australia, Apology to Australia's Indigenous Peoples (13 February 2008) <https://www.aph.gov.au/Visit_Parliament/Art/Icons/Apology_to_Australias_Indigenous_Peoples#:~:text=On%2013%20February%202008%2C%20Prime,for%20voting%20to%20the%20Chamber > accessed 24 June 2025; Prime Minister Stephen Harper, Statement of Apology (n 6).

[98] Uluru Statement from the Heart <https://ulurustatement.org/the-statement> accessed 1 February 2025.

[99] Constitutional Court of Colombia, Order No 004 (2009) 35.

[100] Begoña Dorronsoro and Lieselotte Viaene, 'Indigenous Peoples and Transitional Justice in Colombia: Challenges, Risks and Lessons Learned' (9 March 2017) <https://ces.uc.pt/en/agenda-noticias/agenda-de-eventos/2017/indigenous-peoples-and-transitional-justice-in-colombia> accessed 1 February 2025.

[101] The Swedish Foundation for Human Rights, *Indigenous Peoples' Participation in Transitional Justice—Opportunity for Change? Lesson from Colombia* (July 2020) 22 < https://mrfonden.se/wp-content/uploads/2020/12/indigenous-peoples-participation-in-transitional-justice.pdf> accessed 1 February 2025.

[102] ibid 26.

humanitarian law against Indigenous Peoples, an Indigenous-led truth commission focused on abuses against Indigenous Peoples, and the establishment of an Indigenous Centre for Historic Memory.[103]

Notwithstanding these limitations, Colombia's transitional justice programming has had important implications for Indigenous Peoples. The Commission for the Clarification of Truth, Coexistence, and Non-Repetition found that Indigenous Peoples were victimized in Colombia's internal conflict, not just through bodily integrity violations, but also through territorial occupation, land dispossession, and violence against land.[104] Their cultural rights were also violated, including through the 'misrepresentation of their ancestral practices'.[105] Moreover, Colombia' Special Jurisdiction for Peace has adjudicated several Indigenous rights cases, including the recognition of various Indigenous territories.[106]

Of course, political winds tend to be fickle, and transitional justice's current preoccupation with Indigenous issues may ultimately lack longevity. For example, in Australia, the Queensland Truth Telling and Healing Inquiry was created in 2024 through the Path to Treaty Act, legislation passed by the provincial Queensland government in May 2023.[107] The Queensland Truth Telling and Healing Inquiry was initially mandated 'to conduct inquiries into and document the individual, familial, cultural and societal impacts and effects of colonization on Aboriginal peoples and Torres Strait Islander people' in Queensland.[108] However, a new provincial government in Queensland repealed the Path to Treaty Act in 2024 and effectively scrapped the Truth Telling and Healing Inquiry—a mere five months after it was created.[109] This came on the heels of the public's rejection of the 2023 Australia Voice Referendum, which would have amended the national constitution to explicitly recognize Aboriginal and Torres Strait Islander people and created a formal Aboriginal and Torres Strait Islander body within the Australian parliament.

[103] ONIC, 'Agenda Nacional de Paz de los Pueblos Indígenas' <https://www.onic.org.co/canastadesaberes/118-cds/publicaciones/conflicto-armado-y-paz/1820-agenda-nacional-de-paz-de-los-pueblos-indigenas> accessed 1 February 2025.

[104] Carlos Arturo Gutiérrez-Rodríguez, 'Beyond Liberal Justice? Decolonising Colombian Transitional Justice through Victims' Participation and Indigenous Rights' (2024) 28(10) The International Journal of Human Rights 1569, 1575.

[105] ibid.

[106] ibid 1579.

[107] Queensland, Path to Treaty Act 2023 <https://www.legislation.qld.gov.au/view/pdf/repealed/2024-04-26/act-2023-012> accessed 1 February 2025.

[108] ibid para 66(a).

[109] Australian Human Rights Commission, 'Ending QLD Truth-telling and Healing Inquiry Is Harmful and Divisive' (1 November 2024) <https://humanrights.gov.au/about/news/ending-qld-truth-telling-and-healing-inquiry-harmful-and-divisive> accessed 1 February 2025.

Transitional justice has gradually moved from wholesale Indigenous neglect to considering Indigenous impacts and perspectives in the implementation of mechanisms specifically targeting State wrongdoing against Indigenous Peoples. The case of the Queensland Truth Telling and Healing Inquiry demonstrates both this expansion and the ongoing uncertainty of the transitional justice enterprise in these contexts. Moreover, the opportunities, limitations, and incongruencies between transitional justice and Indigenous grievances have not been comprehensively studied. Questions certainly remain regarding the suitability of transitional justice in the context of Indigenous Peoples affected by large-scale past harm.

2.4 (In)compatibilities

Transitional justice has often been described as an unsuitable avenue for confronting the violence and injustice impacting Indigenous Peoples.[110] A number of authors contend that transitional justice, as traditionally theorized, is incompatible with Indigenous claims for justice.[111] Indigenous scholars, in particular, have expressed reluctance towards relying on conventional transitional justice approaches, especially when mechanisms are centred on promoting some form of reconciliation between Indigenous Peoples and the State.[112] They argue that transitional justice measures are largely 'symbolic',[113] a 'distraction',[114] an 'affective mess',[115] and 'window dressing'[116] to broader Indigenous demands for land restitution, cultural revitalization, and structural reforms.[117]

[110] Jennifer Matsunaga, 'Two Faces of Transitional Justice: Theorizing the Incommensurability of Transitional Justice and Decolonization in Canada' 5(1) Decolonization: Indigeneity, Education & Society 24, 30.

[111] Jeff Corntassel and Cindy Holder, 'Who's Sorry Now? Government Apologies, Truth Commissions, and Indigenous Self-Determination in Australia, Canada, Guatemala, and Peru' (2008) 9 Human Rights Review 465, 465–66; Glen Sean Coulthard, *Red Skin, White Masks: Rejecting the Colonial Politics of Recognition* (2018) 108–09; Matsunaga, 'Two Faces of Transitional Justice' (n 110) 30; Park, 'Settler Colonialism, Decolonization and Radicalizing Transitional Justice' (n 9) 261.

[112] See, eg, Gerald Taiaiake Alfred, 'Restitution Is the Real Pathway to Justice for Indigenous Peoples' in Gregory Younging and others (eds), *Response, Responsibility, and Renewal: Canada's Truth and Reconciliation Journey* (Aboriginal Healing Foundation 2009) 181–87; Jeff Corntassel, 'Re-envisioning Resurgence: Indigenous Pathways to Decolonization and Sustainable Self-Determination' (2012) 1(1) Decolonization: Indigeneity, Education & Society 86, 93–94; Whyte, 'On Resilient Parasitisms' (n 25); Leanne Betasamosake Simpson, 'Land and Reconciliation: Having the Right Conversations' *Watershed Sentinel* (23 November 2017) <https://watershedsentinel.ca/article/land-reconciliation/> accessed 1 February 2025.

[113] Whyte, 'On Resilient Parasitisms' (n 25) 280.

[114] Corntassel and Holder, 'Who's Sorry Now?' (n 111) 472.

[115] Billy Ray Belcourt, 'Political Depression in a Time of Reconciliation' Active History: History Matters (15 January 2016) <http://activehistory.ca/2016/01/political-depression-in-a-time-of-reconciliation/> accessed 1 February 2025.

[116] Simpson, 'Land and Reconciliation' (n 112).

[117] Alfred, 'Restitution Is the Real Pathway to Justice for Indigenous Peoples' (n 112) 196.

We see this resistance in debates regarding transitional justice's relationship to decolonization. Several scholars have recently pushed to incorporate decolonization as a desired goal of transitional justice.[118] They argue that transitional justice needs to do more to disrupt the pervasive inequalities produced by colonization, and which continue to persist in the lives of Indigenous Peoples. For instance, while critical of the power of traditional reconciliation initiatives to engage with decolonization, Rosemary Nagy optimistically maintains that transitional justice can better embrace decolonizing efforts by engaging with structural violence.[119] Augustine Park further argues that a primary goal of transitional justice in the context of settler colonialism must be decolonization and suggests that it can pursue this through recognizing Indigenous life as 'grievable'[120] and by relying on Indigenous cultural practices in transitional justice work.[121] Jeff Corntassel and Cindy Holder agree that decolonization should be a necessary element of reconciliation, but stress that whatever mechanisms are employed must recognize Indigenous sovereignty and right to land.[122]

Park further argues that while paradigmatic transitional justice cannot engage in decolonization, a radicalized form of transitional justice could.[123] This is perhaps theoretically true, but no transitional justice measure can be said to have achieved this. In response, critics argue that transitional justice is an inappropriate avenue for such an unsettling task. Jennifer Matsunaga, drawing on the inherent limitations of the dominant model, suggests that 'the foundations, goals, and discourses of transitional justice are major impeding factors that block decolonisation'.[124] Decolonization is about 'dismantling colonialist power in all its forms',[125] a burden no transitional justice policy can possibly bear. But while transitional justice is unlikely to bring about decolonization, perhaps it can make a modest contribution to decolonizing efforts in more consequential ways. This book does not seek to weigh in on the decolonization debate in any definitive way; rather, it just demonstrates the ongoing

[118] See, eg, Augustine SJ Park, 'Settler Colonialism and the Politics of Grief: Theorising a Decolonising Transitional Justice for Indian Residential Schools' (2015) 16(3) Human Rights Review 273.

[119] Nagy, 'The Scope and Bounds of Transitional Justice' (n 87) 54.

[120] Park, 'Settler Colonialism and the Politics of Grief' (n 118).

[121] Augustine SJ Park, 'Remembering the Children: Decolonizing Community-based Restorative Justice for Indian Residential Schools' (2016) 19(4) Contemporary Justice Review 424.

[122] Corntassel and Holder, 'Who's Sorry Now?' (n 111) 467.

[123] Park, 'Settler Colonialism, Decolonization and Radicalizing Transitional Justice' (n 9).

[124] Matsunaga, 'Two Faces of Transitional Justice' (n 110) 26.

[125] Bill Ashcroft, Gareth Griffiths, and Helen Tiffin, *Post-Colonial Studies: The Key Concepts* (Routledge 2000) 63.

contestations that exist with respect to the intersections between transitional justice and Indigenous Peoples.

Regardless, Indigenous Peoples themselves continue to invoke the language and tools of transitional justice in framing and pursuing their justice demands. In much the same way as human rights have been historically deployed, transitional justice can be a powerful form of advocacy and redress for Indigenous Peoples. The full scope and extent of potential incongruencies between transitional justice and Indigenous Peoples has yet to be fully interrogated, and only time will tell whether the host of recent and ongoing initiatives will have an appreciable impact on the lives of Indigenous victims.

3. A Cultural Rights-based Approach to Indigenous Harm

A cultural rights-based approach, rooted in international human rights standards, can be used to hold States legally and politically accountable for cultural wrongdoing against Indigenous Peoples and can also protect, strengthen, and promote Indigenous cultural rights more broadly. This chapter concludes by examining three transitional justice initiatives that intersect with Indigenous Peoples' cultural rights in very different ways. Canada's National Inquiry into Missing and Murdered Indigenous Women and Girls, Victoria's Yoorrook Justice Commission, and the Peruvian theatre collective *Yuyachkani* illustrate the diverse ways in which transitional justice practice can address, respect, and promote the cultural rights of Indigenous Peoples suffering from legacies of large-scale harm.

3.1 Canada's national inquiry into missing and murdered indigenous women and girls

Canada's National Inquiry into Missing and Murdered Indigenous Women and Girls (the 'MMIWG Inquiry') took an expansive and holistic approach to engaging with culture in the scope of its mandate. The MMIWG Inquiry released its final report in 2019, highlighting the alarming and disproportionate levels of violence experienced by Indigenous women, girls, and 2SLGBTQQIA (two-spirit, lesbian, gay, bisexual, transgender, queer, questioning, intersex, and asexual) individuals.[126] In a landmark determination, the MMIWG Inquiry

[126] National Inquiry into Missing and Murdered Indigenous Women and Girls, *Reclaiming Power and Place* (n 24).

concluded that this widespread violence constitutes an ongoing, race-based genocide against Indigenous Peoples, with women, girls, and 2SLGBTQQIA individuals being particularly targeted. While the genocide conclusion grabbed headlines, it has also eclipsed another significant achievement of the Inquiry—namely its groundbreaking recognition of cultural rights violations and cultural harm within a transitional justice framework.[127]

The MMIWG Inquiry was granted one of the broadest mandates ever given to a truth-seeking body. According to its terms of reference, it was tasked with investigating and reporting on:

> The systemic causes of all forms of violence—including sexual violence—against Indigenous women and girls in Canada, including the underlying social, economic, cultural, institutional, and historical factors contributing to the ongoing violence and specific vulnerabilities faced by Indigenous women and girls in Canada.[128]

With a mandate to address the 'systemic causes of all forms of violence', the MMIWG Inquiry was empowered to explore violence against Indigenous women, girls, and 2SLGBTQQIA individuals from a holistic perspective. By explicitly acknowledging the 'cultural' causes of harm, the MMIWG Inquiry was tasked with addressing Indigenous cultural rights violations and their connection to ongoing violence against Indigenous women and girls. The mandate left little room for the Commissioners to ignore, minimize, or relegate cultural harm to mere historical grievances.

Moreover, the MMIWG Inquiry was empowered to address distant violence in the form of historical cultural wrongs. As discussed, most truth commissions are limited to short periods immediately preceding the end of a conflict or oppressive regime, but the MMIWG Inquiry went beyond recent acts of violence to tackle cultural harms dating back to the colonial era.[129] This largely aligns with Indigenous worldviews, which perceive of colonial wrongs as continuous rather than isolated incidents.[130] Freed from the categorical and

[127] I have justified conceptualizing the MMIWG Inquiry as a form of transitional justice elsewhere. Colin Luoma, 'Closing the Cultural Rights Gap in Transitional Justice: Developments from Canada's National Inquiry into Missing and Murdered Indigenous Women and Girls' (2021) 39(1) Netherlands Quarterly of Human Rights 30, 39–43.

[128] Terms of Reference for the National Inquiry into Missing and Murdered Indigenous Women and Girls (Indigenous and Northern Affairs Canada, 12 December 2016) < https://www.rcaanc-cirnac.gc.ca/eng/1470141425998/1534527073231> accessed 1 February 2025.

[129] Luoma, 'Closing the Cultural Rights Gap' (n 127) 44.

[130] Eve Tuck and K Wayne Yang, 'Decolonization Is Not a Metaphor' (2012) 1 Decolonization: Indigeneity, Education & Society 1, 5.

temporal restrictions inherent in mainstream theorizations of violence in transitional justice, the MMIWG Inquiry was empowered to engage with culture in a unique and significant way.

The MMIWG Inquiry's expansive interpretation of violence incorporated 'cultural violence', referencing Johan Galtung's definition. It recognized that forms of cultural violence, such as racist ideologies and assimilationist policies, have deep roots in Canadian culture.[131] These State-sanctioned cultural attacks, which sought to erase Indigenous identities and cultures, were identified as some of the most severe forms of violence perpetrated against Indigenous Peoples.[132] In this vein, the MMIWG Inquiry embraced a broadened conception of violence to include its cultural dimensions.

With its expansive mandate, the MMIWG Inquiry devoted an entire chapter of its final report to the 'Right to Culture', detailing the cultural rights violations experienced by Indigenous Peoples and their lasting effects on Indigenous communities. The Inquiry highlighted how colonial policies and practices sought to suppress Indigenous cultures, regulating Indigenous identities and forcibly assimilating them into mainstream society. This cultural suppression disrupted family and community dynamics, creating a legacy that reverberated through generations.[133] By confronting cultural harm, the Inquiry moved beyond the direct physical violence inherent in the MMIWG epidemic and towards a richer and more holistic accounting of the wrongdoing experienced by Indigenous Peoples in Canada.

The MMIWG Inquiry also framed cultural violence against Indigenous Peoples in Canada as a key contributor of the physical violence perpetrated against Indigenous women, girls, and 2SLGBTQQIA individuals. Numerous testimonies from victims, victims' families, elders, and other participants emphasized the importance of respecting and protecting Indigenous cultures.[134] These testimonies linked the physical violence faced by Indigenous women and girls to violations of their cultural rights, asserting that access to culture, language, and land was key to safety, support, and healing.[135] In addressing the root causes of the MMIWG epidemic, the Inquiry framed attacks on Indigenous cultures as fundamental to the physical violence against

[131] National Inquiry into Missing and Murdered Indigenous Women and Girls, *Reclaiming Power and Place* (n 24) 77.

[132] ibid 327–408.

[133] ibid.

[134] ibid.

[135] National Inquiry into Missing and Murdered Indigenous Women and Girls, *Reclaiming Power and Place: Executive Summary of The Final Report of the National Inquiry into Missing and Murdered Indigenous Women and Girls* (2019) 50–51.

Indigenous women and girls. It directly tied it to past assimilationist policies that attacked cultural expression and the right to practice cultural traditions. The Commissioners asserted:

> Attacks on culture, which include residential schools, the Sixties Scoop, and other assimilatory policies, are the starting points for other forms of violence Indigenous women, girls, and 2SLGBTQQIA people experience today.[136]

In this way, the MMIWG Inquiry heeded the call to address the underlying root causes of large-scale harm. Testimonies before the Inquiry further reinforced the indivisibility and interdependence of cultural rights vis-à-vis other rights. Past cultural wrongdoing made Indigenous women, girls, and 2SLGBTQQIA individuals more vulnerable to other forms of violence and deepened their economic and social marginalization.[137]

Notably, the MMIWG Inquiry went beyond viewing cultural harm as merely a contributing factor to other rights violations. Witnesses shared not only their experiences of losing loved ones to violence but also how the erosion of their culture constituted a distinct form of violence in itself. They recounted how colonial policies inflicted deep trauma on Indigenous communities by dismantling their cultural systems.[138] The Inquiry found that Indigenous women, girls, and 2SLGBTQQIA individuals have been denied their right to learn, practice, and sustain their cultures; experienced genocide through the disruption of cultural transmission; received an education that excludes their language, history, and traditions; and faced systemic barriers to cultural belonging.[139]

By emphasizing cultural rights, the MMIWG Inquiry elevated these violations to the same level as other human rights abuses prioritized in transitional justice's dominant model. Unlike past truth commissions that have confined cultural rights violations to historical context, the Inquiry recognized them as central to the MMIWG crisis. In doing so, it made these harms more visible and arguably set a stronger foundation for more inclusive and holistic post-transition policies regarding Indigenous cultural rights. Not only did the MMIWG Inquiry address cultural harm, but it did so through the lens of international human rights law. The final report emphasized that Canada

[136] ibid 23.
[137] National Inquiry into Missing and Murdered Indigenous Women and Girls, *Reclaiming Power and Place* (n 24) 329.
[138] ibid 327–408.
[139] ibid 407–08.

must respect, protect, and fulfil Indigenous cultural rights, including the right to practice and revitalize cultural traditions, languages, and ways of life. The Inquiry also highlighted Canada's failure to uphold its international obligations, which have been ratified or endorsed by the State, including protections under the ICCPR, the ICESCR, and the CEDAW. The UNDRIP, in particular, was a key framework used by the Inquiry to analyse Canada's responsibility for the MMIWG crisis.[140] The Declaration sets out the minimum cultural rights standards for Indigenous peoples, including their right to maintain, develop, and practice their cultural traditions and to protect their cultural heritage.[141] The Inquiry directly linked these rights to State action and non-action and found that Canada had failed to adequately protect Indigenous cultural rights, contributing to the ongoing violence.[142]

Cultural rights also feature prominently in the MMIWG Inquiry's recommendations. Section 2 of the Inquiry's Calls for Justice is explicitly dedicated to culture, wherein the Commissioners called upon the federal and provincial governments in Canada to protect a host of cultural and language rights, including the right to access culture and the right to education in one's Indigenous language. It was further demanded that resources and measures be put in place for the preservation of language and traditional knowledge, including Indigenous-led initiatives for access to cultural knowledge. Recommendations were also made for measures to be implemented in culturally appropriate ways and in accordance with the cultural needs of Indigenous Peoples.[143]

The MMIWG Inquiry's direct and relatively robust treatment of cultural rights represents a significant deviation from mainstream transitional justice practice. Rather than respond to the MMWIG crisis under a familiar transitional justice paradigm, the Inquiry challenged the status quo by conceiving of violence in a way that includes not just the physical violations brought upon Indigenous women and girls, but the underlying cultural harm that permeates Indigenous life. Cultural wrongdoing was treated as its own form of violence, rather than merely a driver of bodily integrity violations. By linking and framing this cultural harm as violative of international human rights law, the Inquiry removed this cultural wrongdoing from the realm of policymaking and situated it in that of its legal commitments under international law.[144]

[140] ibid 200–01.
[141] UNDRIP (n 18) Arts 11, 12, 13, 15, 34.
[142] National Inquiry into Missing and Murdered Indigenous Women and Girls, Executive Summary (n 135) 60.
[143] ibid 65.
[144] See Lisa Laplante, 'Transitional Justice and Peace Building: Diagnosing and Addressing the Socioeconomic Roots of Violence through a Human Rights Framework' (2008) 2 International Journal of Transitional Justice 331, 342.

While these represent some of the direct recommendations aimed at the redress of cultural rights violations through a transitional justice response, it is yet to be determined whether they will be implemented. As with all rights violations, the implementation of a truth commission's recommendations to address cultural rights violations depends on the political will of the State. To date, little progress has been made in Canada in this regard, with the Commissioners marking the one-year anniversary of the final report by decrying 'deafening silence and unacceptable inaction from most governments'.[145] Thus, whether the MMIWG Inquiry's cultural recommendations are translated into concrete reforms remains highly uncertain.

3.2 The Yoorrook Justice Commission

The Yoorrook Justice Commission in Australia's state of Victoria provides an ongoing positive example of an Indigenous-governed transitional justice mechanism that is embracing an expanded conception of justice to include cultural elements. Established after years of Indigenous activism, the Commission is in the process of investigating and reporting on a wide array of historical injustices suffered by Indigenous Peoples in Victoria since colonization. These include abuses associated with mass atrocities, child removal policies, the criminal justice system, child protection services, health care, and land and water rights, among other areas.[146]

Violence against Indigenous Peoples in Australia has been ubiquitous since the British invasion in 1788. This violence has taken many forms across space and time. Indigenous Peoples have suffered frontier wars and mass physical atrocities, child removal policies and other formalized assimilationist methods, and pervasive discrimination and racism in all aspects of public life. Each of these has worked to deprive Indigenous Peoples in Australia of their cultural identities, practices, and worldviews. The forced separation of Indigenous children from their families and communities over several generations until 1969 (the 'Stolen Generations'), in particular, has produced mass

[145] 'Statement Marking the One-Year Anniversary of the Final Report of the National Inquiry into Missing and Murdered Indigenous Women and Girls' (3 June 2020) <https://www.canada.ca/en/crown-indigenous-relations-northern-affairs/news/2020/06/statement-from-minister-bennett-minister-monsef-minister-lametti-minister-miller-minister-guilbeault-and-minister-blair-marking-the-one-year-annive.html> accessed 1 February 2025.

[146] UN Special Rapporteur on the promotion of truth, justice, reparation and guarantees of non-recurrence, Transitional Justice Measures and Addressing the Legacy of Gross Violations of Human Rights and International Humanitarian Law Committed in Colonial Contexts (n 92) 51.

cultural dislocation and intergenerational trauma that continues to negatively impact Indigenous Peoples in Australia today.[147]

In Australia, the issue of how to reconcile with Indigenous Peoples, including reckoning with the Stolen Generations, has been at the forefront of the broader political landscape. Australia has also not been a stranger to transitional justice programming, even though the government does not refer to any measures as such. For instance, Australia's National Inquiry into the Separation of Aboriginal and Torres Strait Island Children from Their Families was formed to investigate the Stolen Generations, including the State-sanctioned removal of approximately 100,000 Indigenous Australian children from their families and communities between 1910 and 1970.[148] In 2008, Prime Minister Kevin Rudd formally apologized to Indigenous Peoples in Australia, calling the Stolen Generations the 'blemished chapter in our nation's history'.[149] Notwithstanding, the apology was largely symbolic and was criticized for not being linked to concrete plans for restitution and reparation.[150]

In 2021, the Victorian government created the Yoorrook Justice Commission. Pursuant to its terms of reference, the Commission is vested with the powers of a Royal Commission and is tasked with inquiring into and reporting on a wide array of injustices perpetrated against Indigenous Peoples, including the causes and consequences of such injustices.[151] From the vantage point of culture, this includes 'cultural violations', 'theft, misappropriation and destruction of cultural knowledge and property', and 'protectionist and assimilationist policies, including forced removals of children and attempts to eradicate language, culture and identity'.[152]

In contrast to previous State initiatives, the Yoorrook Justice Commission is Indigenous-led and governed. Four of its five Commissioners are Indigenous and from the state of Victoria.[153] It is perhaps the only formal truth-seeking body empowered to broadly investigate the impact of colonialism, but which is also Indigenous-designed and led. Transitional justice processes in settler-colonial States such as Australia have traditionally been initiated by the centralized government. These processes become national institutions that are

[147] Karen Menzies, 'Understanding the Australian Aboriginal Experience of Collective, Historical and Intergenerational Trauma' (2019) 62(6) International Social Work 1522, 1527.

[148] Report of the National Inquiry into the Separation of Aboriginal and Torres Strait Islander Children from Their Families (1997).

[149] Parliament of Australia, Apology to Australia's Indigenous Peoples (n 97).

[150] Corntassel and Holder, 'Who's Sorry Now?' (n 111) 478.

[151] Letters Patent dated 14 May 2021 (n 96) para 3.

[152] ibid.

[153] UN SRTJ, Transitional Justice Measures and Addressing the Legacy of Gross Violations of Human Rights and International Humanitarian Law Committed in Colonial Contexts (n 92) para 51.

designed by the State, with the assistance of transitional justice professionals and, in most instances at least, some consultation with Indigenous victims of large-scale human rights abuses. Initiatives that purport to be bottom-up often fail to relinquish sufficient decision-making authority to Indigenous Peoples themselves. This can further delegitimize transitional justice efforts in the eyes of Indigenous communities, especially if they divert power and attention away from the work of local and grassroots activists and movements.

In this case, the Commission's terms of reference were designed by Victoria's First People's Assembly[154] after consultations with Indigenous communities.[155] This has arguably enabled it to set priorities better aligned with Indigenous worldviews and demands. For instance, the Commission's methodology sets out a number of thematic priorities, including one centred on culture, language, and heritage. These priorities are explicitly derived from the UNDRIP and other human rights standards applicable to Indigenous Peoples. Indigenous governance over transitional justice processes has the potential to lead to a more serious engagement with Indigenous cultural rights, namely because cultural rights are of such critical importance for these groups.

Theoretically, the Commission's broad mandate empowers it to address a wide range of cultural wrongdoing, including both contemporary and distant wrongs. The terms of reference further acknowledge and incorporate human rights standards as part of the Commission's mandate, with explicit references to both the UNDRIP and the ICESCR.[156] According to the Commission, these instruments 'directly shape the Commission's inquiry into and understanding of historic and ongoing systemic injustices and how these can be addressed and/or redressed.'[157] Even though the Commission's work is still ongoing, it has begun to address Indigenous cultural harm in substantive ways, including with reference to core cultural rights standards under international law.[158] For example, in its comprehensive, 445-page report into Victoria's Child Protection and Criminal Justice Systems, the Commission positioned the lack of otherwise mandatory cultural plans for Indigenous children in care as potentially

154 The First Peoples' Assembly of Victoria is the independent and democratically elected body to represent Aboriginal and Torres Strait Islander peoples in Victoria.

155 Jeremie Bracka, 'Reckoning with Colonial Legacies of Harm: Victoria's Yoorrook Justice Commission' (2024) 18(2) International Journal of Transitional Justice 325, 332.

156 Letters Patent dated 14 May 2021 (n 96) para 1.

157 Yoorrook Justice Commission, *Yoorrook with Purpose: Interim Report* (June 2022) para 6 <https://yoorrookjusticecommission.org.au/wp-content/uploads/2022/07/Yoorrook-Justice-Commission-Interim-Report.pdf> accessed 1 February 2025.

158 Yoorrook Justice Commission, Yoorrook for Justice: Report into Victoria's Child Protection and Criminal Justice Systems (August 2023) 109–10 <https://yoorrookjusticecommission.org.au/wp-content/uploads/2023/09/Yoorrook-for-justice-report.pdf> accessed 1 February 2025.

violative of the right to culture.[159] More broadly, the Commission called on the Victorian government to

> recognise that the human and cultural rights of First Peoples children in permanent care to have, express, develop and maintain their culture, and to maintain contact with their Aboriginal family, kin and community.[160]

The Yoorrook Justice Commission has also embedded 'cultural justice' into its approach. In addition to investigating and reporting on various forms of cultural harm committed against Indigenous Peoples, it has also intentionally incorporated culture into its methodology and processes. The first listed value guiding and informing its work is 'culture and connection', including the recognition of 'the diversity of First Peoples' history, cultures, languages, and ways of knowing, being and doing'.[161] In this vein, it agreed to 'observe and uphold cultural values of the First Peoples of Victoria in the way it operates'.[162] In its General Guidelines on Information Gathering and Evidence, the Commission commits itself to 'centre First Peoples' ways of knowing, being and doing'.[163] The Commission further published a set of cultural protocols guiding its work. These include upholding Indigenous systems and decision-making processes and respecting Indigenous knowledge.[164] One of the Commission's defining features is its acknowledgement of and deferral to the cultural authority of elders in the scope of its work.[165] Jeremie Bracka contends that this integration of cultural values and protocols into the Commission's practices has rendered it 'culturally autonomous'.[166]

The Commission has also emphasized the importance of providing a culturally appropriate truth-telling forum, including respecting different languages and practices and recognizing 'cultural legal practices of story-telling and witnessing as legitimate and valid sources of evidence'.[167] In recognition

[159] ibid 186–200.
[160] ibid 34.
[161] Yoorrook Justice Commission, *Guiding the Path to Yoorrook* <https://yoorrookjusticecommission.org.au/wp-content/uploads/2022/11/Guiding-the-Path-to-Yoorrook-v2.pdf> accessed 1 February 2025.
[162] ibid.
[163] Yoorrook Justice Commission, *General Guidelines on Information Gathering and Evidence*, para 5. https://yoorrookjusticecommission.org.au/wp-content/uploads/2022/11/Yoorrook-General-Guidelines.pdf> accessed 1 February 2025.
[164] Yoorrook Justice Commission, *Guiding the Path to Yoorrook* (n 161).
[165] Bracka, 'Reckoning with Colonial Legacies of Harm' (n 155) 333.
[166] ibid.
[167] Yoorrook Justice Commission, *General Guidelines on Information Gathering and Evidence* (n 163), para 5(b), (e).

of this, the Commission has adopted Indigenous-centred methods, including 'yarning circles' and various cultural activities such as art, dance, song, and ceremonies, and has put these methods into practice.[168] The Commission was first launched with a smoking ceremony and a cultural performance by a Djirri Djirri dancer.[169] Indigenous art is also used in the work and branding of the Commission, including in its logo.[170]

Respect for Indigenous cultural traditions and practices in transitional justice is required under existing international law. Fulfilling the right to take part in cultural life under Article 15(1)(a) of the ICESCR requires that the right be realized in a way 'that is pertinent and suitable to a given cultural modality or context, that is, respectful of the culture and cultural rights of individuals and communities, including minorities and indigenous peoples'.[171] Article 34 of the UNDRIP provides for Indigenous Peoples' 'right to promote, develop and maintain their institutional structures and their distinctive customs, spirituality, traditions, procedures, practices and, in the cases where they exist, juridical systems or customs, in accordance with international human rights standards'.[172] Moreover, Article 40 of UNDRIP gives Indigenous Peoples the right to seek a resolution of conflicts and effective remedies for infringements on their individual or collective rights, with due consideration to the customs, traditions, rules, and legal systems of the indigenous peoples concerned.[173] By integrating Indigenous customs, traditional practices, and art into truth-telling, the Yoorrook Commission is embracing a more inclusive, cultural rights-based form of transitional justice.

3.3 Yuyachkani theatre collective

For decades, the *Yuyachkani* theatre collective (*Grupo Cultural Yuyachkani*) has been a leading theatre group in Peru in the realm of political theatre and social activism. *Yuyachkani* is a Quecha word meaning 'I am thinking, I am remembering'.[174] The name is perhaps apropos given the role it would later play

[168] ibid para 6.
[169] Yoorrook Justice Commission, *Yoorrook with Purpose* (n 157) 13.
[170] ibid 14.
[171] CESCR, General Comment No 21, Right of Everyone to Take Part in Cultural Life (Art 15, para 1a of the Covenant on Economic, Social and Cultural Rights), UN Doc E/C.12/GC/21 (December 2009) para 16(e).
[172] UNDRIP (n 18) Art 34.
[173] ibid Art 40.
[174] Francine Mary A'Ness, 'Resisting Amnesia: Yuyachkani, Performance, and the Postwar Reconstruction of Peru' (2004) 56(3) Theatre Journal 395, 401.

in the broader project of social remembrance in post-conflict Peru. But it also signifies the group's commitment and engagement with Indigenous Peoples.[175] The group is composed of several permanent actors as well as a director.[176] Founded in 1971, the Lima-based collective has been a fixture in the Peruvian arts society. Initially, it focused on engaging with political and cultural issues in Peru, with a commitment to grassroots activism, social issues, and advocacy. However, after the cessation of Peru's internal conflict in 2000, *Yuyachkani* became intimately involved in the country's truth-telling process through its collaboration with Peru's Truth and Reconciliation Commission.

As briefly discussed in Chapter 1, Peru's Truth and Reconciliation Commission was tasked with investigating serious human rights violations, including extra-judicial killings, forced disappearances, torture, massacres, and sexual violence, during the internal armed conflict in Peru between 1980 and 2000. The overwhelming majority of victims of Peru's internal conflict were either Indigenous or mixed-race (*mestizo*) peasants living in poverty.[177] Salomon Lerner Febres, former President of the Commission, explicated the disproportionate levels of violence committed against Indigenous Peoples during the conflict:

> The heaviest, most aggressive expressions of violence befell these indigenous peoples, at the hands of both the armed insurgents and the state forces. The color of their skin, their culture and language, their material poverty, clearly marked their membership in a group supposedly unfit to rule themselves, whose constituents could therefore be treated as means and never as ends in themselves.[178]

Indigenous Peoples are part of the cultural fabric of Peru, one of the most ethnically diverse countries in Latin America. This is a complexity that *Yuyachkani* has consistently engaged with through performance over the course of several decades.[179] It is in this 'imperfect' context that the theatre group made a crucial contribution to transitional justice in Peru through a cultural rights-based approach.[180]

[175] Diana Taylor, *The Archive and the Repertoire: Performing Cultural Memory in the Americas* (Duke University Press 2003) 311.
[176] Jane Turner and Patrick Campbell, 'Radical Care: Performative Generosity and Generativity in Third Theatre' (2018) 23(6) Performance Research 58, 59.
[177] A'Ness, 'Resisting Amnesia' (n 174) 396.
[178] Salomón Lerner Febres, 'Memory of Violence and Drama in Peru: The Experience of the Truth Commission and Grupo Cultural Yuyachkani—Violence and Dehumanization' (2020) 14(1) International Journal of Transitional Justice 232, 236.
[179] A'Ness, 'Resisting Amnesia' (n 174) 399
[180] Turner and Campbell, 'Radical Care' (n 176) 80.

Shortly after the Truth and Reconciliation Commission began its work, it reached an agreement with *Yuyachkani* for the group to conduct outreach to Indigenous and rural communities in the Andes. The purpose of the collaboration was for the theatre collective to essentially act as an intermediary between the Commission and these communities.[181] The idea was that, through public performance, *Yuyachkani* could raise awareness of the Commission's work and encourage people to participate in the hearings.[182] This was a challenging matter, in part because of linguistic and cultural barriers, but also because many of the abuses incurred by these groups were perpetrated by agents of the government—either through colonialism or in the course of the armed conflict.[183] *Yuyachkani* performed in public spaces where the Commission was conducting public hearings, to raise awareness but also to engage in what Francine A'Ness called the 'arduous task of reconstructing and remembering the traumas of the war.'[184]

The role of theatre and performance in transitional justice has been studied in the discourse, albeit sparingly.[185] *Yuyachkani* has been analysed in the transitional justice literature, including in an article penned by Lerner for a special issue of the International Journal of Transitional Justice in 2020 on the contributions of arts and culture to transitional justice.[186] Lerner argued that *Yuyachkani* was an essential complement to the work of the Truth and Reconciliation Commission because '[p]erformance heightens the senses and opens our imaginations to the deep truths that have been lost among the facts'.[187] However, the work of *Yuyachkani* in post-conflict Peru has yet to be analysed with a cultural rights lens.

One of the primary ways in which the work of *Yuyachkani* embodied a cultural rights-based approach was by bringing Indigenous characters and histories to life, and in this way, engaging in a sort of identity recognition.[188] Performances incorporated Indigenous stories and traditions, including folk dances and Quecha-language songs. This worked to foreground the value and richness of Indigenous culture, but also to recognize the broader diverse landscape of post-conflict Peru.[189] The collective's cultural interventions also

[181] Information presented by the Northern Ireland Human Rights Commission to the Human Rights Council, UN Doc A/HRC/25/NI/5 (27 February 2014) para 42.
[182] A'Ness, 'Resisting Amnesia' (n 174) 398.
[183] ibid.
[184] ibid 397.
[185] Tine Destrooper, 'Performative Justice? The Role of Theatre and Performance in Facilitating Transitional Justice' (2019) 32(3) *South African Theatre Journal* 199.
[186] Lerner, 'Memory of Violence and Drama in Peru' (n 178).
[187] ibid 239.
[188] ibid 240.
[189] Turner and Campbell, 'Radical Care' (n 176) 61.

helped to bring Indigenous Peoples into the post-conflict truth-seeking and reconciliation process and implicitly reinforced Indigenous identities and their unique place in the narrative of the conflict.[190]

Yuyachkani's theatre productions were critical cultural expressions that facilitated a dialogue between the Truth and Reconciliation Commission and Indigenous and rural peasant communities. It also played a significant role in bringing Indigenous perspectives and histories to the forefront of the collective remembering process principally facilitated by Peru's Truth and Reconciliation Commission. Under international human rights law, everyone has the right to know one's culture as well as the cultures of others.[191] Theatre was used in this case to educate Peruvians about each other and to celebrate their immense diversity.[192] *Yuyachkani* is not an Indigenous theatre collective, but it has embraced Indigenous performance and story-telling and promoted the cultures of Indigenous Peoples in Peru through its various performances and creations. *Yuyachkani* does not attempt to speak for Indigenous Peoples in a paternalistic way that would infringe on their inherent right to self-determination; instead, it incorporates, celebrates, and elevates Indigenous culture for all Peruvians to benefit from.[193] Perhaps more importantly, it had engaged with Indigenous issues prior to its work with the Commission, giving it a degree of legitimacy and credibility with affected communities.[194]

Through cultural expression, *Yuyachkani* connected with Indigenous communities, incorporating their experiences into a collective healing and remembering process that was more inclusive of Indigenous groups in Peru.[195] It represents just one example of how artistic and cultural interventions can contribute to the goals of transitional justice in ways that also respect cultural rights. They can be important cultural tools to remember past injustices, reinforce core values in societies (such as ethnic and cultural diversity), preserve collective memory, and encourage healing and reconciliation.

The cases of the MMIWG Inquiry, the Yoorrook Justice Commission, and the *Yuyachkani* theatre collective represent ways in which transitional justice is already moving towards a more serious engagement with culture, and hence cultural rights. They are representative of a broader momentum in the field to grapple with Indigenous injustices in more holistic and culturally relevant

[190] Information presented by the Northern Ireland Human Rights Commission (n 181) para 42.
[191] CESCR, General Comment 21 (n 171).
[192] A'Ness, 'Resisting Amnesia' (n 174) 400.
[193] Taylor, *The Archive and the Repertoire* (n 175) 311.
[194] *The Derry/Londonderry Report on Upholding the Human Right to Culture in Post-Conflict Societies* (Northern Ireland Human Rights Commission 2014) para 3.2.
[195] ibid.

ways. This is quite a departure from the wholesale neglect of Indigenous Peoples in the vast majority of the paradigmatic cases of the 1980s and 1990s. It is not clear to what extent the cultural rights-respecting approach embodied in these three examples will move from exception to norm in transitional justice programming impacting Indigenous Peoples, but lessons and best practices can be drawn from these cases in developing a cultural rights-based approach to transitional justice.

CONCLUSION

> To be rooted is perhaps the most important and least recognized need of the human soul.[1]
>
> —*Simone Weil*

1. Introduction

In Northern Uganda, a former child soldier abducted from his family returns to his village and approaches the entrance of his ancestral home. Dozens, if not hundreds, of community members are gathered around as the boy approaches. Elders have placed a stick and a raw egg at the entrance of the home. The boy proceeds to step on the egg, while at the same time being brushed with green grass by the elders. The crowd erupts in jubilation as the raw egg is crushed under the boy's foot. Through this ritual, the boy is reintegrated back into his community and cleansed of the evil spirits that he may have encountered during his absence.[2]

At the Gila Crossing Community School in Arizona, US President Joe Biden is escorted to a stage overlooking several hundred people sitting on white folding chairs scattered across a football field. Traditional song and drums are heard playing in the background as President Biden, wearing dark aviator sunglasses, waits to address the crowd. After a few minutes of perfunctory introductions and acknowledgements, the sitting US president proceeds to formally apologize for the US government's role in running more than 150 Indian boarding schools, what he calls a 'blot on American history'. He proceeds to lament the '[l]ost generations, culture and language, lost trust', calling the boarding school system a 'sin on our soul'.[3]

[1] Simone Weil, *The Need for Roots: Prelude to a Declaration of Duties Towards Mankind* (Routledge 2002) 40.

[2] This is a fictional account depicting a real traditional reconciliation practice in Northern Uganda called *Nyono Tong Gweno*. Catherine Jendia, 'The Cultural Factor in Conflict Management/Resolution: A Case Study of the Acholi of Northern Uganda' (2019) 11(2) African Journal of History and Culture 15, 22.

[3] Full speech: Biden apologizes for forced Native American boarding school policy, *NBC News* (24 October 2024) <https://www.nbcnews.com/video/full-speech-biden-apologizes-for-forced-native-american-boarding-school-policy-222701125937> accessed 1 February 2025.

In Brussels, a ceremony is being held at the ornate Palais d'Egmont. Men in suits carry an empty casket to the front of the room. After relinquishing the casket, the men position a photograph of the assassinated Congolese independence leader Patrice Lumumba atop it. Lumumba's daughter, Juliana, then addresses the small gathering of people in the room, all of whom are assembled to witness the return of a single golden tooth to Juliana and Lumumba's other descendants. Once in the illicit possession of a Belgian policeman, the only known remains of Patrice Lumumba are returned to their rightful custodians to bring home to the Democratic Republic of the Congo.[4]

These seemingly unrelated stories share a common thread, namely the relevance of culture in the overall project of reckoning with past large-scale harm. In every corner of the world, culture and transitional justice are intersecting in diverse and dynamic ways. Transitional justice work is constantly negotiating cultural landscapes, even if the field is not self-aware enough to directly acknowledge it. Culture, as a complex and omnipresent phenomenon, influences and affects human life in every conceivable way.[5] It is perhaps only natural that it would shape and inform all facets of transitional justice.

Today, mass wrongdoing is now almost always met with some form of transitional justice. In the three decades since transitional justice emerged as a conceptual framework to address past episodes of large-scale harm, we are still trying to strike the right balance between the myriad issues facing post-conflict and divided societies. However, cultural rights have not been sufficiently integrated into transitional justice policymaking or programming. It is within this context that this book sought to intervene, arguing that the field of transitional justice can and should increasingly engage with cultural rights in more meaningful ways.

2. Summary of Arguments

The first goal of this book was to interrogate the issue of culture, and hence cultural rights, in the field of transitional justice. The critique around the 'cultural rights blind spot' articulated in Chapter 1 built off the work of authors who have challenged the traditional parameters of the transitional justice field, but whose analysis did not extend to the treatment of cultural rights. The field's tendency to

[4] Annélie Delescluse and Emmanuel Murhula A Nashi, 'A Note on the Return of Patrice Lumumba's Tooth: Restitution, Politics, and Media' (2023) 3(4) Cahiers d'études Africaines 859.

[5] Noelle Higgins and Katie Donnellan, 'Ireland's Cultural Policy and the Protection and Promotion of the Cultural Rights of Migrants' (2023) 32(2) Cultural Trends 171, 175.

sideline cultural rights, and issues of culture more generally, is readily apparent. Transitional justice authors and policymakers remain concerned primarily with the redress of civil and political rights violations, especially those that rise to the level of international crimes. Although economic and social rights have been pushed to the forefront of transitional justice discussions and debates in recent years, cultural rights have overwhelmingly been omitted, treated as historical context, or considered only in the context of other rights violations. This blind spot runs across the field's discourse, as well as its core practical mechanisms.

The marginalization of cultural rights has undermined efforts to address the full spectrum of harm experienced by victims in post-conflict and divided societies. It also reinforces the subordination of cultural rights and diminishes their importance in the hierarchy of human rights. Such treatment is not only incompatible with the fundamental principles of human rights law—which emphasize the indivisibility, interrelation, and interdependence of all rights—but also weakens the transformative potential of transitional justice. By neglecting cultural rights, transitional justice mechanisms fail to achieve a truly holistic vision of justice, limiting their ability to foster reconciliation, restore dignity, and acknowledge the deep cultural and identity-based harms suffered by affected individuals and communities.

Significant developments have undoubtedly pushed cultural rights more squarely into the remit of transitional justice, especially in relation to cultural heritage protection and restitution, as well as truth commissions tasked with addressing historical wrongdoing against Indigenous Peoples. This represents a shifting tide of sorts, a significant step towards treating cultural rights as integral rather than auxiliary to the transitional justice project. Notwithstanding, instances where transitional justice mechanisms genuinely grapple with the complexities of cultural harm remain comparatively rare and the ones that do tend to be sporadic and often fail to address cultural rights abuses as independent harms. Moreover, in most of these cases, cultural harm is also not framed as violative of State obligations under the international human rights framework, reinforcing their status as a 'remnant category' of rights.[6]

The genesis of this book can be fairly traced to a lingering question in my mind regarding why some wrongs seem to matter in transitional justice while others do not. Chapter 2 wrestled with this question. It argued that the marginalization of cultural rights remains principally rooted in dogmatic and inflexible interpretations of what constitutes a transition, justice, and violence under

[6] Asbjørn Eide, 'Cultural Rights as Individual Human Rights' in Asbjørn Eide, Catarina Krause, and Allan Rosas (eds), *Economic, Social and Cultural Rights* (1st edn, Martinus Nijhoff Publishers 1995) 229.

conventional transitional justice theory. Narrow understandings of these core concepts have undoubtedly restricted the field's application and kept cultural rights on the margins. These conceptual constraints were formed through an early coalescence around the idea that transitional justice was primarily a tool of democratization, facilitating the transition of violent repressive regimes' towards peaceful liberal democracies.[7] In turn, a dominant model developed and was replicated across a wide range of disparate transitional settings, largely to the exclusion of cultural rights. In many ways, the dominant model has determined the field's subjects, problems, and solutions and has significantly shaped its overall trajectory away from considerations of culture. While important advancements and developments have been made to chip away at this conceptual rigidity, many of the field's preoccupations, biases, and predispositions have been difficult to disrupt.

Chapter 2 demonstrated how the field's entrenched and intransigent approach to transition, justice, and violence has significantly sidelined issues of cultural wrongdoing, culturally appropriate justice processes, and cultural interventions. Dominant understandings of where a society must be transitioning from and to have been dominated by the field's paradigmatic cases—transitions from dictatorship to liberal democracy and/or transitions from armed conflict to peace. Transitional justice policy and programming was not originally designed to address the contemporary or historical wrongs experienced by victims in established democracies or other contexts that exist outside of post-conflict and post-authoritarian settings. This effectively placed these societies and their wrongdoing, including large-scale cultural harm, outside the scope of the field. Despite an expansion in the settings in which transitional justice is employed, its application in such contexts remains relatively uncertain.

Dominant forms of justice have coalesced around the specific modalities thought to be most effective in moving societies towards peace or liberal democracy. This invariably includes judicial or quasi-judicial mechanisms employing some form of Western justice with an overarching aim of nation-building in the wake of large-scale human rights abuses. An overriding focus on individual criminal accountability permeates the field to the point that it has become synonymous with transitional justice itself. Despite efforts to rebuke top-down, blueprint approaches, many of the same justice modalities continue

[7] Will Kymlicka, 'Transitional Justice, Federalism, and the Accommodation of Minority Nationalism' in Paige Arthur (ed), *Identities in Transition: Challenges for Transitional Justice in Divided Societies* (Cambridge University Press 2011) 328.

to be replicated, without sufficient consideration of and deference to local priorities, laws, systems, or solutions.[8] This has provided very little space for transitional justice to accommodate cultural practices, protocols, customary laws, and worldviews that significantly diverge from Western thought.

Lastly, cultural rights are marginalized because the dominant model construes violence quite narrowly, privileging recent acts of physical violence and violations of civil and political rights more broadly. Reckoning with mass physical violence has long been seen as the most apt way to move societies to the endpoints of the paradigmatic transitions. Inheriting biases from the parent field of human rights and adhering to a 'gross violations' standard, transitional justice treats these bodily integrity violations as more serious and more urgently in need of extraordinary redress. By prioritizing civil and political rights violations as the only types of violence worthy of our collective attention, the dominant model pushes cultural wrongs—both contemporary and historical—to the sidelines.

Despite notable deviations, the dominant model has largely persisted, even when transitional justice is increasingly applied in contexts far afield from the paradigmatic settings. While the field of transitional justice has begun to acknowledge some of its limitations and is showing signs of evolving, the fundamental shift necessary to meaningfully incorporate cultural rights remains elusive. A modest alternative theorization is necessary for the field to move beyond the engrained characteristics which tend to evade culture and towards a more context-specific approach, capable of embracing a cultural rights-based approach to transitional justice.

Unmoored from its initial conceptual boundaries, transitional justice has the flexibility to confront cultural wrongdoing, respect culturally diverse justice traditions, and accommodate cultural and artistic responses to large-scale harm. However, this 'thicker' version is only possible if the field begins to shed some of the principal assumptions, biases, and preoccupations embedded in the prevailing way that transitional justice is understood and operationalized. Without a theoretical shift in how we think about doing justice in times of transition, it is predictable that cultural rights will largely remain outside the remit of the field.

In Chapter 3, transitional justice's conventional theory was rethought in order to promote and facilitate a more meaningful engagement with cultural rights. A single dominant theory of transitional justice is increasingly

[8] Makau Mutua, 'What Is the Future of Transitional Justice?' (2015) 9 International Journal of Transitional Justice 1, 5.

problematic as the field has expanded into various settings.[9] The challenges faced by victims and survivors are diverse and complex, necessitating nuanced, thoughtful, and flexible approaches, even if they deviate significantly from what we have traditionally understood to be transitional justice under conventional theory.

Transitions justifying a transitional justice intervention can be broadened to include less obvious but still significant transitions, including those occurring in established democracies. There is no persuasive conceptual or practical rationale for why the field should be beholden to the original, paradigmatic transitions. Not extending transitional justice to established democracies perpetuates the neocolonial character of the field, whereby Western nations are seemingly immune from the same type of historical reckoning that is expected of other States. Rigid interpretations of transition further overlook the need for these States to reckon with their own legacies of violence and systemic human rights abuses, which are disproportionately cultural in nature. Conversely, conceiving of a transition more broadly to include, *inter alia*, moves from 'unjust relations to just relations'[10] extends the logic of transitional justice to large-scale cultural harm perpetrated against subnational groups in established democracies.[11] These States can be treated as transitional justice cases in the same way as post-conflict and post-authoritarian States, without defeating the concept of a transition.[12]

Conventional forms of 'justice' can also be rethought to better respect and address cultural rights. Mainstream approaches transposing standardized formulas have proven ineffective when extended beyond the paradigmatic cases. At the outset, transitional justice must discard unfettered nation-building aspirations in exchange for inclusive models that respect everyone's right to cultural identity, with special protections for minorities, Indigenous Peoples, and other groups whose cultures remain marginalized and threatened. The modalities of justice should be increasingly owned, governed, and controlled by Indigenous and local communities. Consulting with these communities may ultimately dictate that overly legalistic or individualistic justice approaches be

[9] Thomas Obel Hansen, 'Transitional Justice: Toward a Differentiated Theory' (2011) 13 Oregon Review of International Law 1, 3.

[10] Jennifer Balint, Julie Evans, and Nesam McMillan, 'Rethinking Transitional Justice, Redressing Indigenous Harm: A New Conceptual Approach' (2014) 8(2) International Journal of Transitional Justice 194, 214.

[11] See generally Harry Hobbs, 'Locating the Logic of Transitional Justice in Liberal Democracies: Native Title in Australia' (2016) 39 University of New South Wales Law Journal 512.

[12] Matt James, 'Uncomfortable Comparisons: The Canadian Truth and Reconciliation Commission in International Context' (2010) 5(2) The Ethics Forum 23, 24.

cast off in favour of more cultural rights-friendly models aligned with local customs, traditions, protocols, and worldviews.

Finally, dominant conceptions of violence can be challenged and expanded to include violence against cultures. The harms incurred by victims are multifaceted, extending far beyond the narrow confines of bodily integrity harms. Cultural wrongs can be complex, layered, and intersecting. They can also be historical or contemporary, structural or discrete, individual or collective. Often, cultural harm is subtle and insidious, characterized by efforts to render minorities or Indigenous Peoples unworthy of the full measure of human dignity guaranteed for other groups. This harm lives in the historical memory of victims, but it also manifests itself in modern policies and practices that continue to effect violence on these communities. The field must endeavour to move beyond a narrow understanding of violence to fully recognize the enduring forms of cultural harm that shape societies in negative ways.

While the field of transitional justice is demonstrating signs of evolution and increased awareness of its limitations, a fundamental shift in thinking is necessary to meaningfully incorporate cultural rights. The path forward necessitates a reframing of transitional justice through the lens of cultural rights. This involves challenging dominant theory, acknowledging its inherent limitations, and embracing a more comprehensive and inclusive understanding of what constitutes a transition, justice, and violence in ways that enable transitional justice to address the full spectrum of harms inflicted on human cultures.

While there is now widespread acceptance of the idea that transitional justice must grapple with a broader range of issues and in more diverse ways, these debates have yet to be meaningfully extended to cultural rights. The propriety of incorporating cultural rights into transitional justice has yet to be given considerable individualized attention in the existing discourse. Chapter 4 thus attempted for the first time to tease out some of the justifications for why transitional justice should embrace a cultural rights-based approach and increasingly engage with cultural rights on an equal plane with other rights categories.

One of the central tenets of a human rights-based approach is the principle that all rights are important and should be given equal treatment. However, despite a theoretical consensus concerning the universality, indivisibility, interconnectedness, and interrelatedness of all human rights, cultural rights are notoriously neglected and underdeveloped. Adhering to this principle means treating cultural rights as equally important in the larger project of transitional justice. While mechanisms cannot possibly afford equal attention to all rights violations in all circumstances, the harms that are ultimately addressed should not be decided based on arbitrary distinctions between rights categories. A careful and balanced approach would disregard hierarchal divisions and instead analyse context-specific factors to determine which harms to address. In a number of cases, this would inevitably result in increased attention being paid to large-scale cultural harm.

Cultural wrongdoing not only constitutes its own form of violence, but also serves as the root causes of other forms of violence. Addressing cultural rights violations through transitional justice not only helps to close an impunity gap around cultural violations, but can also account for underlying drivers of physical and structural violence. At the same time, respecting and incorporating cultural rights in transitional justice programming is critical for fostering dialogue and ensuring the non-recurrence of violations. It is also imperative that transitional justice strategies are responsive to the needs and expectations of victims. Victims stress the need to address cultural wrongdoing that accompanies conflict and societal divisions. Indigenous victims, in particular, consistently structure their justice claims around revitalizing their languages, cultural practices, and distinct ways of life. Initiatives that fall short of engaging with cultural harm can fail to respond to the needs and demands of victims, thus risking the legitimacy of the transitional justice project.

The final rationale advanced for engaging with cultural rights in transitional justice centres on its ability to promote an accurate narrative of violence, conflict, and/or division and its potential to promote longer-term structural reforms. By framing underlying violence as cultural, transitional justice programming can put pressure on governments to engage in more meaningful reforms aimed at the protection and revitalization of cultures and the reform of national policies and laws that infringe on culture. Fortunately, a robust engagement with cultural rights is eminently achievable with the requisite political will. The redress of cultural rights violations does not implicate broad-based development in the same way that socioeconomic reforms might. Thus, concerns over the feasibility of expanding transitional justice are mitigated when it seeks to confront cultural rights violations. To overlook cultural harm is far more costly, both in terms of reconciling with the past and moving towards a more peaceful future.

Chapter 5 of this book sought to take the re-theorized version of transitional justice and situate it in practice to flesh out the contours of a cultural rights-based approach. There is now a relatively robust legal framework to guide transitional justice programming in its engagement with cultural rights. This includes a host of fundamental cultural rights protections under international human rights law. A cultural rights-based approach incorporates and respects local and Indigenous justice traditions, customs, and protocols, recognizing that justice is often experienced and understood differently within diverse cultural contexts. This involves a move away from top-down, externally imposed models of transitional justice towards more bottom-up, community-led initiatives that incorporate customary justice process and encourage victims and survivors to define what wrongdoing should be confronted.

Transitional justice mechanisms have the capacity to increasingly recognize and address cultural rights violations as an integral part of their mandate, ensuring a more comprehensive approach to justice. Good practice in this regard can be derived from the evolving approach of the ICC, where the OTP has explicitly committed to considering the destruction of intangible cultural heritage in future prosecutions, signalling a significant expansion in the recognition of cultural harm within the scope of international justice frameworks. This development underscores the potential for transitional justice mechanisms to address cultural rights violations in more meaningful ways, both in legal accountability and in broader truth-seeking and reparative processes.

Cultural rights standards also protect cultural and artistic initiatives in transitional justice, including the right to cultural expression. Creative interventions, whether at grassroots levels or incorporated into formal transitional justice mechanisms, can be powerful tools for engaging in truth-telling, challenging dominant narratives, facilitating dialogue among stakeholders, and encouraging victim participation. As illustrated by the example of Germano Gustavo's photography exhibit *Ausencias*, art can also make the 'invisible, visible',[13] giving a voice to the marginalized, amplifying the experiences of victims, and contributing to a broader societal understanding of past trauma.

A cultural rights-based approach is also highly relevant to memorialization, often described as the fifth pillar of transitional justice.[14] The creation and preservation of memorials must respect and reflect the cultural values and traditions of the communities affected, allowing them to shape their own narratives of memory and remembrance. Examples from Guatemala illustrate both the potential and the limitations of memorialization initiatives in post-conflict and divided societies. While State-initiated projects can provide important symbolic recognition and public education, community-led initiatives often

[13] Pablo de Greiff, 'Preface: On Making the Invisible Visible: The Role of Cultural Interventions in Transitional Justice Processes' in Clara Ramirez-Barat (ed), *Transitional Justice, Culture, and Society: Beyond Outreach* (Social Science Research Council 2014) 1.

[14] Report of the Special Rapporteur on the promotion of truth, justice, reparation and guarantees of non-recurrence, Memorialization Processes in the Context of Serious Violations of Human Rights and International Humanitarian Law: The Fifth Pillar of Transitional Justice, UN Doc A/HRC/45/45 (9 July 2020).

prove more successful in strengthening marginalized cultural identities and centring local perspectives.

Cultural reparations are an essential and increasingly recognized component of transitional justice and an important element of a cultural rights-based approach. By acknowledging cultural violations as serious human rights abuses, reparative measures can restore cultural identities, revitalize traditions, and support communities in reclaiming their histories. The reparations demands of the CARICOM Reparations Commission and the Movement for Black Lives highlight the devastating and far-reaching cultural loss incurred through colonialism and the transatlantic slave trade. They also emphasize that reparations must go beyond material compensation to include measures that reaffirm cultural agency, restore historical narratives, and prevent further cultural marginalization.

This book concludes by studying the potential for a cultural rights-based approach to transition justice in the specific case of Indigenous Peoples. The marginalization of culture and the potential for cultural rights engagement in transitional justice cannot be understood without understanding how transitional justice has intersected with Indigenous Peoples. This is principally because culture tends to permeate all aspects of Indigenous life and Indigenous Peoples have been arguably the primary victims of large-scale cultural rights violations. Despite this, Indigenous perspectives and harms were historically overlooked in transitional justice. This has had a knock-on effect for the marginalization of cultural rights. Fortunately, Indigenous Peoples are no longer wholly neglected, as transitional justice has migrated squarely into the realm of Indigenous injustice, including through numerous truth-seeking bodies mandated to investigate and report on large-scale cultural wrongdoing.

Chapter 6 interrogated the relationship between Indigenous Peoples and transitional justice before proceeding to think through what a cultural rights-based approach might look like in the Indigenous context. It drew on best practices from three diverse transitional justice measures—the MMIWG Inquiry, the Yoorrook Justice Commission, and the *Yuyachkani* theatre collective. Each of these initiatives contributes to our understanding of how cultural rights can be addressed, used, and respected in post-conflict and divided societies.

The MMIWG Inquiry challenged dominant theory by redefining violence to encompass not only the physical harm inflicted on Indigenous women and girls but also the deeper cultural harm that pervades Indigenous life in Canada. It recognized cultural wrongdoing as a distinct form of violence rather than merely a component or driver of bodily integrity violations. Additionally, the Inquiry framed this cultural harm as violative of international human rights law, shifting Canada's cultural transgressions from the sphere of policymaking to its legal obligations under international law. Ultimately, it marks one of the most significant and comprehensive engagements with cultural rights violations within a transitional justice framework.

The Yoorrook Justice Commission highlights the importance of Indigenous governance in transitional justice processes, ensuring that the needs and perspectives of Indigenous Peoples shape the inquiries into historical injustices. Its focus on cultural violations as part of its mandate represents a decisive step toward integrating cultural rights into transitional justice frameworks. In this context, the Commission's methodologies—grounded in Indigenous traditions and community engagement—are vital for creating trust and ensuring that the narratives of Indigenous communities are accurately represented and validated.

Finally, the work of the *Yuyachkani* theatre collective adds yet another dimension, emphasizing the power of art and performance as mediums for truth-telling and remembrance. By actively engaging with Indigenous stories and traditions, *Yuyachkani* contributes to a broader discourse on cultural rights and identity recognition, fostering inclusivity in the transitional justice process. Through its performances, the collective not only preserves Indigenous narratives but also educates others, promoting a shared understanding that reflects the complexities of Peru's diverse cultural landscape.

It is worth noting that transitional justice is a relatively new field, whose full story has yet to be written.[15] In a remarkably brief period, it has undergone numerous evolutions, embraced an increasingly wide range of issues, and in the process moved to the centre of post-conflict peacebuilding agendas. Encounters between transitional justice and cultural rights seem only likely to expand, especially with a renewed sense of urgency in many States, including politically stable Western democracies, to begin grappling with legacies of colonial harm. To the extent transitional justice measures continue to come to fruition in these contexts, transitional justice will increasingly be faced with opportunities to address mass cultural harm and corresponding violations of cultural rights.

Thus, the opportunities for interaction between transitional justice and cultural rights have arguably never been greater. With the growth and development of these two fields, it is inevitable that transitional justice scholars, policymakers, and practitioners will be increasingly thinking through how to

[15] Frank Haldemann and Rachelle Kouassi, 'Transitional Justice without Economic, Social, and Cultural Rights?' in Eibe Riedel and others (eds), *Economic, Social, and Cultural Rights in International Law: Contemporary Issues and Challenges* (Oxford University Press 2014) 500.

navigate their intersections. The many tensions, challenges, and opportunities associated with using the tools and logic of transitional justice to address large-scale cultural harm only begin to be teased out in this book. While transitional justice has embraced its critical turn, there is certainly scope for further study in this area, with a myriad of issues and dilemmas yet to be examined and likely to come to the surface in future praxis.

BIBLIOGRAPHY

Books

Ashcroft B, Griffiths G, and Tiffin H, *Post-Colonial Studies: The Key Concepts* (Routledge 2000)
Barelli M, *Seeking Justice in International Law: The Significance and Implications of the UN Declaration on the Rights of Indigenous Peoples* (Routledge 2016)
Bass G, *Stay the Hand of Vengeance: The Politics of War Crimes Tribunals* (Princeton University Press 2014)
Bird AR, *US Foreign Policy on Transitional Justice* (Oxford University Press 2015)
Borrows J, *Freedom and Indigenous Constitutionalism* (University of Toronto Press 2016)
Brown AM, *Emergent Strategy: Shaping Change, Changing Winds* (AK Press 2017)
Chow PYS, *Cultural Rights in International Law and Discourse: Contemporary Challenges and Interdisciplinary Perspectives* (Brill Nijhoff 2018)
Churchill W, *Kill the Indian, Save the Man: The Genocidal Impact of American Indian Residential Schools* (City Lights 2004)
Collier P, *Economic Causes of Civil Conflict and Their Implications for Policy* (Oxford University 2006)
Cooper J, *Raphael Lemkin and the Struggle for the Genocide Convention* (Palgrave Macmillan 2008)
Coulthard GS, *Red Skin, White Masks: Rejecting the Colonial Politics of Recognition* (University of Minnesota Press 2014)
De Almeida GI, *From Dictatorship to Democracy: Confronting the Authoritarian Past in Brazil* (Liverpool University Press 2024)
Donders D, *Towards a Right to Cultural Identity?* (Intersentia 2003)
Ehlert C, *Prosecuting the Destruction of Cultural Property in International Criminal Law: With a Case Study on the Khmer Rouge's Destruction of Cambodia's Heritage* (Martinus Nijhoff Publishers 2013)
Elster J, *Closing the Books: Transitional Justice in Historical Perspective* (Cambridge University Press 2004)
Engle K, *The Elusive Promise of Indigenous Development: Rights, Culture, Strategy* (Duke University Press 2010)
Galtung J and Fischer D, *Johan Galtung: Pioneer of Peace Research* (Springer 2013)
Hayner PB, *Unspeakable Truths: Transitional Justice and the Challenge of Truth Commissions* (2nd edn, Routledge 2010)
Henderson J and Wakeham P (eds), *Reconciling Canada: Critical Perspectives on the Culture of Redress* (University of Toronto Press 2013)
Hicks D, *The Brutish Museums: The Benin Bronzes, Colonial Violence and Cultural Restitution* (Pluto Press 2020)
Huntington S, *The Third Wave: Democratization in the Late Twentieth Century* (University of Oklahoma Press 1991)
Hutton AR, *Phil Sheridan and His Army* (University of Nebraska Press 1985)
Joy C, *Heritage Justice* (Cambridge University Press 2020)
Kritz N, *Transitional Justice: How Emerging Democracies Reckon with Former Regimes* (US Institute of Peace Press 1995)
Krug E and others (eds), *World Report on Violence and Health* (World Health Organization 2002)

Kouame HFA, *Reconciliation in Côte d'Ivoire: A Case Study of the Implementation of Transitional Justice in Post-conflict States* (Ethics International Press 2024)
Lightfoot S, *Global Indigenous Politics: A Subtle Revolution* (Routledge 2016)
Lixinski L, *Legalized Identities: Cultural Heritage Law and the Shaping of Transitional Justice* (Cambridge University Press 2021)
Lynch G, *Performances of Injustice: The Politics of Truth, Justice and Reconciliation in Kenya* (Cambridge University Press 2018)
Macklem P, *The Sovereignty of Human Rights* (Oxford University Press 2015)
Maddison S and others (eds), *The Limits of Settler Colonial Reconciliation: Non-Indigenous People and the Responsibility to Engage* (Springer 2016)
Mani R, *Beyond Retribution: Seeking Justice in the Shadows of War* (Polity Press 2002)
McAuliffe P, *Transformative Transitional Justice and the Malleability of Post-conflict States* (Edward Elgar Publishing 2017)
McEvoy K and McGregor L (eds), *Transitional Justice from Below: Grassroots Activism and the Struggle for Change* (Bloomsbury Publishing 2008)
Minow M, *Between Vengeance and Forgiveness: Facing History after Genocide and Mass Violence* (Beacon University Press 1998)
Murphy C, *The Conceptual Foundations of Transitional Justice* (Cambridge University Press 2017)
Nozick R, *Anarchy, State and Utopia* (Blackwell 1794)
Olsen T, Payne L, and Reiter A, *'Transitional Justice in Balance': Comparing Processes, Weighing Efficacy* (US Institute of Peace 2010)
Pettipas K, *Severing the Ties that Bind: Government Repression of Indigenous Religious Ceremonies on the Prairies* (University of Manitoba Press 1994)
Power S, *'A Problem from Hell': America and the Age of Genocide* (Basic Books 2002)
Ramirez-Barat C (ed), *Transitional Justice, Culture, and Society: Beyond Outreach* (Social Science Research Council 2014)
Rawls J, *A Theory of Justice* (Harvard University Press 1971)
Regan P, *Unsettling the Settler Within: Indian Residential Schools, Truth Telling, and Reconciliation in Canada* (UBC Press 2010)
Robben A, *Argentina Betrayed: Memory, Mourning, and Accountability* (University of Pennsylvania Press 2018)
Rush PD and Simic O (eds), *The Arts of Transitional Justice* (Springer 2014)
Said E, *Orientalism* (Routledge and Kegan Paul 1978)
Sands P, *East West Street: On the Origins of Genocide and Crimes Against Humanity* (Knopf 2016)
Schmid E, *Taking Economic, Social and Cultural Rights Seriously in International Criminal Law* (Cambridge University Press 2015)
Sharp DN, *Re-Thinking Transitional Justice for the 21st Century* (Cambridge University Press 2018)
Sharp DN (ed), *Justice and Economic Violence in Transition* (Springer 2014)
Shaw R, Waldorf L, and Hazan P (eds), *Localizing Transitional Justice: Interventions and Priorities after Mass Violence* (Stanford University Press 2010)
Stamatopoulou E, *Cultural Rights in International Law: Article 27 of the Universal Declaration of Human Rights and Beyond* (Brill 2007)
Taylor D, *The Archive and the Repertoire: Performing Cultural Memory in the Americas* (Duke University Press 2003)
Teitel RG, *Transitional Justice* (Oxford University Press 2000)
Thornberry P, *International Law and the Rights of Minorities* (Oxford University Press 1991)
Torpey J, *Making Whole What Has Been Smashed: On Reparations Politics* (Harvard University Press 2006)
Uvin P, *Human Rights and Development* (Kumarian Press 2004)
Weil S, *The Need for Roots: Prelude to a Declaration of Duties Towards Mankind* (Routledge 2002)
Williams R, *Keywords: A Vocabulary of Culture and Society* (Oxford University Press 1983)
Wolfe A, *An Intellectual in Public* (University of Michigan Press 2005)

Xanthaki A, *Indigenous Rights and United Nations Standards: Self-Determination, Culture and Land* (Oxford University Press 2007)
Zunino M, *Justice Framed: A Genealogy of Transitional Justice* (Cambridge University Press 2019)

Journal Articles

A'Ness FM, 'Resisting Amnesia: Yuyachkani, Performance, and the Postwar Reconstruction of Peru' (2004) 56(3) Theatre Journal 395
Akech JG, 'Rethinking Transitional Justice in South Sudan: Critical Perspectives on Justice and Reconciliation' (2020) 14(3) International Journal of Transitional Justice 585
Alfred GT, 'Colonialism and State Dependency' (2009) 5(2) International Journal of Indigenous Health 42
An-Na'im AA, 'Editorial Note: From the Neocolonial "Transitional" to Indigenous Formations of Justice' (2013) 7 The International Journal of Transitional Justice 197
Anaya SJ, 'Divergent Discourses about International Law, Indigenous Peoples, and Rights over Lands and Natural Resources: Toward a Realist Trend' (2005) 16 Colorado Journal of International Environmental Law and Policy 237
Andrieu K, 'Transitional Justice: A New Discipline in Human Rights' (2010) Online Encyclopedia of Mass Violence 18
Andrieu K, 'Civilizing Peacebuilding: Transitional Justice, Civil Society and the Liberal Paradigm' (2010) 41(5) Security Dialogue 537
Androff DK, 'Adaptations of Truth and Reconciliation Commissions in the North American Context: Local Examples of a Global Restorative Justice Intervention' (2012) 13(2) Advances in Social Work 408
Arbour L, 'Economic and Social Justice for Societies in Transition' (2007) 40 New York University Journal of International Law and Politics 1
Arthur P, 'How "Transitions" Reshaped Human Rights: A Conceptual History of Transitional Justice' (2009) 31 Human Rights Quarterly 321
Babo-Soares D, 'Nahe Biti: The Philosophy and Process of Grassroots Reconciliation and Justice in East Timor' (2004) 5 The Asia Pacific Journal of Anthropology 15
Baines E, 'Spirits and Social Reconstruction after Mass Violence: Rethinking Transitional Justice' (2010) 190 (436) African Affairs 409
Balasco LM, 'The Transitions of Transitional Justice: Mapping the Waves from Promise to Practice' (2013) 12(2) Journal of Human Rights 198
Balint J, Evans J, and McMillan N, 'Rethinking Transitional Justice, Redressing Indigenous Harm: A New Conceptual Approach' (2014) 8(2) International Journal of Transitional Justice 194
Barker AJ, 'The Contemporary Reality of Canadian Imperialism: Settler Colonialism and the Hybrid Colonial State' (2009) 33(3) The American Indian Quarterly 325
Bell C, 'Transitional Justice, Interdisciplinarity and the State of the "Field" or "Non-Field"' (2009) 3(1) International Journal of Transitional Justice 5
Bell C and O'Rourke C, 'Does Feminism Need a Theory of Transitional Justice? An Introductory Essay' (2007) 1(1) The International Journal of Transitional Justice 23
Bell V, 'Contemporary Art and Transitional Justice in Northern Ireland: The Consolation of Form' (2011) 10(3) Journal of Visual Culture 324
Bietti L, '"Piercing Memories": Empty Spaces in the Histories of Argentinean Families—Personal Reflections' (2011) 4(1) Memory Studies 83
Bilsky L and Klagsbrun R, 'The Return of Cultural Genocide?' (2018) 29(2) European Journal of International Law 373
Bishop-Burney US, 'Prosecutor v. Ahmad Al Faqi Al Mahdi' (2017) 111(1) American Journal of International Law 126
Blake JE, 'Taking a Human Rights Approach to Cultural Heritage Protection' (2011) 4(2) Heritage & Society 199

Boerefijn I, 'A Human-Rights Based Approach of Violence Against Women' (2007) 4 International Studies Journal 181
Bombay A, Matheson K, and Anisman H, 'The Intergenerational Effects of Indian Residential Schools: Implications for the Concept of Historical Trauma' (2014) 51(3) Transcultural Psychiatry 320
Boyle K, 'Reconceptualising Socio-economic Rights in the Transitional Justice Discipline' (2016) 20(2) Law, Social Justice and Global Development Journal 1
Bracka J, 'Reckoning with Colonial Legacies of Harm: Victoria's Yoorrook Justice Commission' (2024) 18(2) International Journal of Transitional Justice 325
Brammertz S and others, 'Attacks against Cultural Heritage as a Weapon of War: Prosecutions at the ICTY' (2016) 14(5) Journal of International Criminal Justice 1143
Cahill-Ripley A, 'Foregrounding Socioeconomic Rights in Transitional Justice: Realising Justice for Violations of Economic and Social Rights' (2014) 32(2) Netherlands Quarterly of Human Rights 183
Campisi MC, 'From a Duty to Remember to an Obligation to Memory? Memory as Reparation in the Jurisprudence of the Inter-American Court of Human Rights' (2014) 8(1) International Journal of Conflict and Violence 61
Carranza R, 'Plunder and Pain: Should Transitional Justice Engage with Corruption and Economic Crimes?' (2008) 2(3) International Journal of Transitional Justice 310
Ceia EM, 'The Contributions of the Inter-American Court of Human Rights to the Development of Transitional Justice' (2015) 14 Law and Practice of International Courts and Tribunals 457
Chechi A, 'The Return of Cultural Objects Displaced during Colonialism. What Role for Restorative Justice, Transitional Justice and Alternative Dispute Resolution?' (2023) 6(1) International Journal of Restorative Justice 95
Chechi A, 'Repairing Historic Injustice: The Return of Indigenous Peoples' Ancestral Human Remains Through Transitional Justice' (2023) 30(4) International Journal of Cultural Property 419
Clark JN, 'Re-thinking Memory and Transitional Justice: A Novel Application of Ecological Memory' (2021) 14(4) Memory Studies 695
Coakley S and McAuliffe P, 'Picking Up the Pieces: Transitional Justice Responses to Destruction of Tangible Cultural Heritage' (2022) 40(3) Netherlands Quarterly of Human Rights 311
Cohen C, 'Reimagining Transitional Justice' (2020) 14(1) International Journal of Transitional Justice 1
Corntassel J, 'Re-envisioning Resurgence: Indigenous Pathways to Decolonization and Sustainable Self-Determination' (2012) 1(1) Decolonization: Indigeneity, Education & Society 86
Corntassel J and Holder C, 'Who's Sorry Now? Government Apologies, Truth Commissions, and Indigenous Self-Determination in Australia, Canada, Guatemala, and Peru' (2008) 9(4) Human Rights Review 465
Corntassel J, Chaw-win-is, and T'lakwadzi, 'Indigenous Storytelling, Truth-Telling, and Community Approaches to Reconciliation' (2009) 35(1) English Studies in Canada 137
Cunneen C, 'Colonialism and Historical Injustice: Reparations for Indigenous Peoples' (2005) 15(1) Social Semiotics 59
Davidovic M, 'Transform or Perish? The Crisis of Transitional Justice' (2020) 20(2) Conflict, Security and Development 293
De Greiff P, 'Theorizing Transitional Justice' (2012) 51 Nomos 31
Delescluse A and Nashi EMA, 'A Note on the Return of Patrice Lumumba's Tooth: Restitution, Politics, and Media' (2023) 3(4) Cahiers d'études Africaines 859
Destrooper T, 'Performative Justice? The Role of Theatre and Performance in Facilitating Transitional Justice' (2019) 32(3) South African Theatre Journal 199
Doughty K, 'Language and International Criminal Justice in Africa: Interpretation at the ICTR' (2017) 11(2) International Journal of Transitional Justice 239
Duthie R, 'Toward a Development-Sensitive Approach to Transitional Justice' (2008) 2(3) International Journal of Transitional Justice 292

Ellis MS, 'The ICC's Role in Combatting the Destruction of Cultural Heritage' (2017) 49 Case Western Reserve Journal of International Law 23
Engle K, 'On Fragile Architecture: The UN Declaration on the Rights of Indigenous Peoples in the Context of Human Rights' (2011) 22(1) European Journal of International Law 141
Erueti A, 'The Politics of International Indigenous Rights' (2017) 67(4) University of Toronto Law Journal 569
Evans M, 'Structural Violence, Socioeconomic Rights, and Transformative Justice' (2016) 15(1) Journal of Human Rights 1
Febres SL, 'Memory of Violence and Drama in Peru: The Experience of the Truth Commission and Grupo Cultural Yuyachkani–Violence and Dehumanization' (2020) 14(1) International Journal of Transitional Justice 232
Fletcher LE and Weinstein HM, 'Violence and Social Repair: Rethinking the Contribution of Justice to Reconciliation' (2002) 24(3) Human Rights Quarterly 573
Fletcher LE and Weinstein HM, '"North-South" Dialogue: Bridging the Gap in Transitional Justice-Workshop Transcript' (2018) 36(2) Berkeley Journal of International Law 218
Forsyth M, 'Casualties of War: The Destruction of Iraq's Cultural Heritage as a Result of US Action During and After the 1991 Gulf War' (2004) 14 DePaul-LCA Journal of Art and Entertainment Law 73
Friedrich J, 'Settling Accounts at the End of History: A Nonideal Approach to State Apologies' (2022) 50(5) Political Theory 700
Galbraith J, 'The Trump Administration Revokes the ICC Prosecutor's US Visa Shortly Before the ICC Pre-Trial Chamber Declines to Authorize an Investigation into War Crimes in Afghanistan' (2019) 113(3) The American Journal of International Law 625
Galtung J, 'Violence, Peace, and Peace Research' (1969) 6(3) Journal of Peace Research 167
Galtung J, 'Cultural Violence' (1990) 27(3) Journal of Peace Research 291
Garcia B and Lixinski L, 'Beyond Culture: Reimagining the Adjudication of Indigenous Peoples' Rights in International Law' (2020) 15 Intercultural Human Rights Law Review 127
Gerstenblith P, 'The Destruction of Cultural Heritage: A Crime Against Property or a Crime Against People?' (2016) 15(336) John Marshall Review of Intellectual Property Law 337
Gidey R and Roberts H, 'Setting the Truth in Stone: Guatemala's Monuments to the Dead' (2003) 19(2) Medicine, Conflict and Survival 148
Gready P, 'Analysis: Reconceptualising Transitional Justice: Embedded and Distanced Justice' (2005) 5(1) Conflict, Security & Development 3
Gready P, 'Culture, Testimony, and the Toolbox of Transitional Justice' (2008) 20(1) Peace Review 41
Gready P and Robins S, 'From Transitional to Transformative Justice: A New Agenda for Practice' (2014) 8(3) International Journal of Transitional Justice 339
Gready P and Robins S, 'Rethinking Civil Society and Transitional Justice: Lessons from Social Movements and "New" Civil Society' (2017) 21(7) The International Journal of Human Rights 956
Gready P and Robins S, 'Transitional Justice and Theories of Change: Towards Evaluation as Understanding' (2020) 14(2) International Journal of Transitional Justice 280
Green R, 'Unsettling Cures: Exploring the Limits of the Indian Residential School Settlement Agreement' (2012) 27(1) Canadian Journal of Law and Society 129
Grover L, 'Transitional Justice, International Law and the United Nations' (2019) 88 Nordic Journal of International Law 359
Gunn BL, 'Engaging a Human Rights Based Approach to the Murdered and Missing Indigenous Women and Girls Inquiry' (2017) 2(2) Lakehead Law Journal 90
Gutiérrez-Rodríguez CA, 'Beyond Liberal Justice? Decolonising Colombian Transitional Justice through Victims' Participation and Indigenous Rights' (2024) 28(10) The International Journal of Human Rights 1569
Hansen TO, 'Transitional Justice: Toward a Differentiated Theory' (2011) 13 Oregon Review of International Law 1

Henry N, 'From Reconciliation to Transitional Justice: The Contours of Redress Politics in Established Democracies' (2015) 9(2) International Journal of Transitional Justice 199
Higgins N and Donnellan K, 'Ireland's Cultural Policy and the Protection and Promotion of the Cultural Rights of Migrants' (2023) 32(2) Cultural Trends 171
Hill A and White A, 'Painting Peace? Murals and the Northern Ireland Peace Process' (2012) 27(1) Irish Political Studies 71
Hobbs H, 'Locating the Logic of Transitional Justice in Liberal Democracies: Native Title in Australia' (2016) 39 University of New South Wales Law Journal 512
Jamar A, 'Accounting for Which Violent Past? Transitional Justice, Epistemic Violence, and Colonial Durabilities in Burundi' (2022) 14(1) Critical African Studies 73
James M, 'Uncomfortable Comparisons: The Canadian Truth and Reconciliation Commission in International Context' (2010) 5(2) The Ethics Forum 23
James M and Bonner M, 'The Three R's of Seeking Transitional Justice: Reparation, Responsibility, and Reframing in Canada and Argentina' (2011) 2(3) The International Indigenous Policy Journal 1
Jara D and others, 'Tracing Mapuche Exclusion from Post-Dictatorial Truth Commissions in Chile: Official and Grassroots Initiatives' (2018) 12(2) International Journal of Transitional Justice 479
Jendia C, 'The Cultural Factor in Conflict Management/Resolution: A Case Study of the Acholi of Northern Uganda' (2019) 11(2) African Journal of History and Culture 15
Jung C, 'Reconciliation: Six Reasons to Worry' (2018) 14(2) Journal of Global Ethics 252
Kravchenko A and others, 'Crime against Memory or Cultural Genocide? On the Destruction of the Cultural Heritage of Ukraine during Russian Aggression in the XXI Century' (2022) 10(2) European Journal of Transformation Studies 206
Kuokkanen R, 'Reconciliation as a Threat or Structural Change? The Truth and Reconciliation Process and Settler Colonial Policy Making in Finland' (2020) 21 Human Rights Review 293
Lambourne W, 'Transitional Justice and Peacebuilding after Mass Violence' (2009) 3(1) International Journal of Transitional Justice 28
Laplante LJ, 'On the Indivisibility of Rights: Truth Commissions, Reparations, and the Right to Develop' (2007) 10 Yale Human Rights and Development Law Journal 141
Laplante LJ, 'Transitional Justice and Peace Building: Diagnosing and Addressing the Socio-economic Roots of Violence Through a Human Rights Framework' (2008) 2(3) The International Journal of Transitional Justice 331
Lawrence B and Dua E, 'Decolonizing Antiracism' (2005) 32(4) Social Justice 120
Leebaw BA, 'The Irreconcilable Goals of Transitional Justice' (2008) 30 Human Rights Quarterly 95
Lightfoot S, 'Emerging International Indigenous Rights Norms and "Over-Compliance" in New Zealand and Canada' (2010) 62(1) Political Science 84
Lixinski L, 'Cultural Heritage Law and Transitional Justice: Lessons from South Africa' (2015) 9(2) International Journal of Transitional Justice 278
Lixinski L, 'Confederate Monuments and International Law' (2017) 35 Wisconsin International Law Journal 549
Logan W, 'Cultural Diversity, Cultural Heritage and Human Rights: Towards Heritage Management as Human Rights-based Cultural Practice' (2012) 18(3) International Journal of Heritage Studies 231
Lostal M, 'The Misplaced Emphasis on the Intangible Dimension of Cultural Heritage in the Al Mahdi Case at the ICC' (2017) 1(2) Inter Gentes—The McGill Journal of International Law & Legal Pluralism 45
Lundy P and McGovern M, 'Whose Justice? Rethinking Transitional Justice from the Bottom Up' (2008) 35 Journal of Law and Society 265
Luoma C, 'Closing the Cultural Rights Gap in Transitional Justice: Developments from Canada's National Inquiry into Missing and Murdered Indigenous Women and Girls' (2021) 39(1) Netherlands Quarterly of Human Rights 30

MacGinty R, 'Indigenous Peace-making versus the Liberal Peace' (2008) 43(2) Cooperation and Conflict 139

Macoun A and Strakosch E, 'The Ethical Demands of Settler Colonial Theory' (2013) 3(4) Settler Colonial Studies 426

Maddison S and Shepherd L, 'Peacebuilding and the Postcolonial Politics of Transitional Justice' (2014) 2 Peacebuilding 253

Mamdani M, 'Amnesty or Impunity? A Preliminary Critique of the Report of the Truth and Reconciliation Commission of South Africa (TRC)' (2002) 32 (2) Diacritics 33

Mani R, 'Dilemmas of Expanding Transitional Justice, or Forging the Nexus Between Transitional Justice and Development' (2008) 2(3) International Journal of Transitional Justice 253

Mani R, 'Women, Art and Post-Conflict Justice' (2011) 11 International Criminal Law Review 543

Mani M and Weiss TG, 'Can Culture Prevent Massacres?' (2011) 17 Global Governance: A Review of Multilateralism and International Organizations 417

Mapulanga-Hulston JK, 'Examining the Justiciability of Economic, Social and Cultural Rights' (2002) 6(4) The International Journal of Human Rights 29

Matsunaga J, 'Two Faces of Transitional Justice: Theorizing the Incommensurability of Transitional Justice and Decolonization in Canada' 5(1) Decolonization: Indigeneity, Education & Society 24

McAuliffe P, 'From Molehills to Mountains (and Myths?): A Critical History of Transitional Justice Advocacy' (2011) 22 Finnish Yearbook of International Law 1

McAuliffe P, 'Transitional Justice's Expanding Empire: Reasserting the Value of the Paradigmatic Transition' (2012) 2(2) Journal of Conflictology 32

McAuliffe P, 'Rhetoric and Realpolitik: Interrogating the Relationship between Transitional Justice and Socio-economic Justice' (2016) 23 Finnish Yearbook of International Law 239

McAuliffe P, 'Complicity or Decolonization? Restitution of Heritage from "Global" Ethnographic Museums' (2021) 15(3) International Journal of Transitional Justice 678

McEvoy J, 'Managing Culture in Post-conflict Societies' (2011) 6(1) Contemporary Social Science 55

McEvoy K, 'Beyond Legalism: Towards a Thicker Understanding of Transitional Justice' (2007) 34(4) Journal of Law and Society 411

McGill D, 'Different Violence, Different Justice? Taking Structural Violence Seriously in Post-conflict and Transitional Justice Processes' (2017) 6(1) State Crime Journal 79

McGregor D, 'Reconciliation and Environmental Justice' (2018) 14(2) Journal of Global Ethics 222

Menzies K, 'Understanding the Australian Aboriginal Experience of Collective, Historical and Intergenerational Trauma' (2019) 62(6) International Social Work 1522

Meral Z, 'A Duty to Remember? Politics and Morality of Remembering Past Atrocities' (2012) 5(1) International Political Anthropology 29

Mieder W, '"The Only Good Indian Is a Dead Indian": History and Meaning of a Proverbial Stereotype' (1993) 106 Journal of American Folklore 38

Mihlar F, 'Contending with Identity and Minority Rights in Transitional Justice: The Case Study of Sri Lanka' (2024) 28(1) The International Journal of Human Rights 1592

Millar G, 'Local Evaluations of Justice through Truth Telling in Sierra Leone: Postwar Needs and Transitional Justice' (2011) 12(4) Human Rights Review 515

Miller Z, 'Effects of Invisibility in Search of the "Economic" in Transitional Justice' (2008) 2(3) International Journal of Transitional Justice 266

Miller Z, 'Temporal Governance: The Times of Transitional Justice' (2021) 21(5) International Criminal Law Review 848

Moffett L, Rose DV, and Hickey R, 'Shifting the Paradigm on Cultural Property and Heritage in International Law and Armed Conflict: Time to Talk about Reparations?' (2019) 26(7) International Journal of Heritage Studies 1

Moses AD, 'Official Apologies, Reconciliation, and Settler Colonialism: Australian Indigenous Alterity and Political Agency' (2011) 15(2) Citizenship Studies 145

Moyo K, 'Mimicry, Transitional Justice and the Land Question in Racially Divided Former Settler Colonies' (2015) 9 International Journal of Transitional Justice 70
Mullen M, 'Reassessing the Focus of Transitional Justice: The Need to Move Structural and Cultural Violence to the Centre' (2015) 28(3) Cambridge Review of International Affairs 462
Murdock EG, 'Unsettling Reconciliation: Decolonial Methods for Transforming Social-Ecological Systems' (2018) 27 Environmental Values 513
Murdock EG, 'Storied with Land: Transitional Justice on Indigenous Lands' (2018) 14(2) Journal of Global Ethics 232
Mutua M, 'What Is the Future of Transitional Justice?' (2015) 9 International Journal of Transitional Justice 1
Muvingi I, 'Sitting on Powder Kegs: Socioeconomic Rights in Transitional Societies' (2009) 3(2) International Journal of Transitional Justice 163
Naidu E, 'Symbolic Reparations and Reconciliation: Lessons from South Africa' (2012) 19 Buffalo Human Rights Law Review 251
Nagy R, 'Transitional Justice as Global Project: Critical Reflections' (2008) 29 Third World Quarterly 275
Nagy R, 'Truth, Reconciliation and Settler Denial: Specifying the Canada–South Africa Analogy' (2012) 13(3) Human Rights Review 349
Nagy R, 'The Scope and Bounds of Transitional Justice and the Canadian Truth and Reconciliation Commission' (2013) 7(1) International Journal of Transitional Justice 524
Neumann K and Anderson D, 'Introduction: Violence, Justice and the Work of Memory' (2014) 8(1) International Journal of Conflict and Violence 5
Ní Aoláin F and Campbell C, 'The Paradox of Transition in Conflicted Democracies' (2015) 27 Human Rights Quarterly 172
O'Donnell T, 'The Restitution of Holocaust Looted Art and Transitional Justice: The Perfect Storm or the Raft of the Medusa?' (2011) 22(1) European Journal of International Law 49
O'Keefe R, 'The "Right to Take Part in Cultural Life" under Article 15 of the ICESCR' (1998) 47 International and Comparative Law Quarterly 904
Ochoa-Sánchez JC, 'Economic and Social Rights and Transitional Justice: A Framework of Analysis' (2019) 18 Journal of Human Rights 522
Ohgushi K, 'A Critical Note on "Hypercritical" Studies of Transitional Justice' (2015) 79 The Journal of Social Science 83
Orakhelashvili A, 'The Interaction between Human Rights and Humanitarian Law: Fragmentation, Conflict, Parallelism, or Convergence?' (2008) 19(1) European Journal of International Law 161
Orford A, 'Commissioning the Truth' (2006) 15(3) Columbia Journal of Gender and Law 851
Palmer E and Watene K, 'Introduction: New Paths in Reconciliation, Transitional and Indigenous Justice' (2018) 14(2) Journal of Global Ethics 133
Paquette E, 'Reconciliation and Cultural Genocide: A Critique of Liberal Multicultural Strategies of Innocence' (2020) 35(1) Hypatia 143
Park ASJ, 'Settler Colonialism and the Politics of Grief: Theorising a Decolonising Transitional Justice for Indian Residential Schools' (2015) 16(3) Human Rights Review 273
Park ASJ, 'Remembering the Children: Decolonizing Community-Based Restorative Justice for Indian Residential Schools' (2016) 19(4) Contemporary Justice Review 424
Park ASJ, 'Settler Colonialism, Decolonization and Radicalizing Transitional Justice' (2020) 14(2) International Journal of Transitional Justice 260
Pasipanodya T, 'A Deeper Justice: Economic and Social Justice as Transitional Justice in Nepal' (2008) 2 International Journal of Transitional Justice 378
Paterson RK, 'Protecting Taonga: The Cultural Heritage of the New Zealand Maori' (1999) 8(1) International Journal of Cultural Property 108
Posner EA and Vermeule A, 'Transitional Justice as Ordinary Justice' (2004) 117(3) Harvard Law Review 761
Quijano A, 'Coloniality and Modernity/Rationality' (2007) 21(2) Cultural Studies 168
Quinn JR, 'Whither the Transition of Transitional Justice' (2014) 8 Interdisciplinary Journal of Human Rights 63

Raack RC, 'Nazi Film Propaganda and the Horrors of War' (1986) 6(2) Historical Journal of Film, Radio and Television 189

Rigney S, 'The Hopes and Discontents of Indigenous-Settler Reconciliation' (2017) 11(2) International Journal of Transitional Justice 359

Robins S, 'Whose Voices? Understanding Victims' Needs in Transition: Nepali Voices: Perceptions of Truth, Justice, Reconciliation, Reparations and the Transition in Nepal by the International Centre for Transitional Justice and the Advocacy Forum, March 2008' (2009) 2(1) Journal of Human Rights Practice 320

Rolston B, '"Trying to reach the future through the past': Murals and Memory in Northern Ireland' (2010) 6(3) Crime, Media, Culture 285

Rolston B, 'Re-imaging: Mural Painting and the State in Northern Ireland' (2012) 15(5) *International Journal of Cultural Studies* 447

Rolston B and Aoláin FN, 'Colonialism, Redress and Transitional Justice: Ireland and Beyond' (2018) 7 State Crime Journal 329

Russell L, 'Settler Colonial Studies: Eliminating the Native and Creating the Nation' (2020) 23(1) Postcolonial Studies 153

Sarkin J and Davi T, 'Examining the Criticisms Levelled Against Transitional Justice: Towards an Understanding of the State of the Field' (2017) 11(1) Human Rights and International Legal Discourse 7

Schimmel N, 'A Postcolonial Reflection on the Rwandan Genocide against the Tutsi and Statement of Solidarity with Its Survivors' (2021) 4(2) Journal of Victimology and Victim Justice 179

Schmid E, 'War Crimes related to Violations of Economic, Social and Cultural Rights' (2011) 71(3) Heidelberg Journal of International Law 523

Schmid E, 'Socio-Economic and Cultural Rights and Wrongs after Armed Conflicts: Using the State Reporting Procedure before the United Nations Committee on Economic, Social and Cultural Rights More Effectively' (2013) 31(3) Netherlands Quarterly of Human Rights 241

Schmid S and Nolan A, '"Do No Harm"? Exploring the Scope of Economic and Social Rights in Transitional Justice' (2014) 8(3) International Journal of Transitional Justice 362

Sentama E, 'Transitional Justice and Redress for Racial Injustices against Marginalized Minorities: Lessons from Indigenous Twa People in Post-Genocide Rwanda' (2024) 18(1) The International Journal of Transitional Justice 66

Sharp DN, 'Addressing Economic Violence in Times of Transition: Toward a Positive-Peace Paradigm for Transitional Justice' (2011) 35 Fordham International Law Journal 780

Sharp DN, 'Interrogating the Peripheries: The Preoccupations of Fourth Generation Transitional Justice' (2013) 26 Harvard Human Rights Journal 149

Sharp DN, 'Addressing Dilemmas of the Global and the Local in Transitional Justice' (2014) 29 Emory International Law Review 71

Sharp DN, 'Emancipating Transitional Justice from the Bonds of the Paradigmatic Transition' (2015) 9(1) International Journal of Transitional Justice 150

Sharp DN, 'What Would Satisfy Us? Taking Stock of Critical Approaches to Transitional Justice' (2019) 13(3) International Journal of Transitional Justice 570

Shefik S, 'Reimagining Transitional Justice through Participatory Art' (2018) 12(2) International Journal of Transitional Justice 314

Short D, 'Reconciliation, Assimilation, and the Indigenous Peoples of Australia' (2003) 24(4) International Political Science Review 491

Simor J, 'Tackling Human Rights Abuses in Bosnia and Herzegovina: The Convention Is Up to It; Are Its Institutions?' (1997) European Human Rights Law Review 644

Stamatopoulou E, 'Monitoring Cultural Human Rights: The Claims of Culture on Human Rights and the Response of Cultural Rights' (2012) 34(4) Human Rights Quarterly 1170

Steinberg M and Taylor M, 'Public Memory and Political Power in Guatemala's Postconflict Landscape' (2003) 933(4) Geographical Review 449

Strong K and others, 'Learning from the Movement for Black Lives: Horizons of Racial Justice for Comparative and International Education' (2023) 67(S1) Comparative Education Review S1

Symonides J, 'Cultural Rights: A Neglected Category of Human Rights' 50(158) International Social Science Journal 559
Szoke-Burke S, 'Not Only Context: Why Transitional Justice Programs Can No Longer Ignore Violations of Economic and Social Rights' (2015) 50 Texas International Law Journal 465
Teitel RG, 'Transitional Justice Genealogy' (2003) 16 Harvard Human Rights Journal 69
Teitel RG, 'Transitional Justice: Postwar Legacies' (2006) 27 Cardozo Law Review 1615
Teló F and others, 'Land and Transitional Justice in Brazil' (2021) 15(1) International Journal of Transitional Justice 190
Theidon K, 'Editorial Note' (2009) 3(3) The International Journal of Transitional Justice 1
Thielen-Wilson L, 'Troubling the Path to Decolonization: Indian Residential School Case Law, Genocide, and Settler Illegitimacy' (2014) 29(2) Canadian Journal of Law & Society/La Revue Canadienne Droit et Société 181
Thoms ONT and Ron J, 'Do Human Rights Violations Cause Internal Conflict' (2007) 29 Human Rights Quarterly 674
Thomson SM, 'Ethnic Twa and Rwandan National Unity and Reconciliation Policy' (2009) 21(3) Peace Review 313
Tuck E and Yang KW, 'Decolonization Is Not a Metaphor' (2012) 1(1) Decolonization: Indigeneity, Education & Society 1
Turner J and Campbell P, 'Radical Care: Performative Generosity and Generativity in Third Theatre' (2018) 23(6) Performance Research 58
Viaene L and Brems E, 'Transitional Justice and Cultural Contexts: Learning from the Universality Debate' (2010) 28(2) Netherlands Quarterly of Human Rights 199
Vielle S, 'Transitional Justice: A Colonizing Field?' (2012) 4(3) Amsterdam Law Forum 58
Vinck P and Pham P, 'Ownership and Participation in Transitional Justice Mechanisms a Sustainable Human Development Perspective from Eastern DRC' (2008) 2(3) International Journal of Transitional Justice 398
Wakeham P, 'The Slow Violence of Settler Colonialism: Genocide, Attrition, and the Long Emergency of Invasion' (2022) 24(3) Journal of Genocide Research 337
Walasek H, 'Cultural Heritage and Memory after Ethnic Cleansing in Post-Conflict Bosnia-Herzegovina' (2019) 101 International Review of the Red Cross 273
Waldorf L, 'Anticipating the Past: Transitional Justice and Socio-Economic Wrongs' (2012) 21(2) Social and Legal Studies 171
Waldorf L, 'Cuddled, Loved and Mutilated: Transitional Justice as Transitional Object' (2019) 2 Responsibility to Protect Student Journal 6
Walsh J, 'The National Inquiry into the Missing and Murdered Indigenous Women and Girls of Canada: A Probe in Peril' (2012) 8 Indigenous Law Bulletin 1
Wartenberg M, 'Cultural Heritage—An Overlooked Component in Transitional Justice?' (2021) 12(12) International Journal on Rule of Law, Transitional Justice and Human Rights 59
Whelan D, 'Indivisible Human Rights' (2010) 69 Global Issues Series 3
Whitbeck LB and others, 'Conceptualizing and Measuring Historical Trauma Among American Indian People' (2004) 33(4) American Journal of Community Psychology 119
Whyte KP, 'On Resilient Parasitisms, or Why I'm Skeptical of Indigenous/Settler Reconciliation' (2018) 14(2) Journal of Global Ethics 277
Wiessner S, 'The Cultural Rights of Indigenous Peoples: Achievements and Continuing Challenges' (2011) 22 European Journal of International Law 121
Winter S, 'Towards a Unified Theory of Transitional Justice' (2013) 7(2) International Journal of Transitional Justice 224
Wolfe P, 'Settler Colonialism and the Elimination of the Native' (2006) 8(4) Journal of Genocide Research 387
Woolford A, 'Transition and Transposition: Genocide, Land and the British Columbia Treaty Process' (2011) 4(2) New Proposals: Journal of Marxism and Interdisciplinary Inquiry 67
Yupsanis A, 'The Concept and Categories of Cultural Rights in International Law: Their Broad Sense and the Relevant Clauses of the International Human Rights Treaties' (2009) 37 Syracuse Journal of International Law and Commerce 207

Yusuf H, 'Colonialism and the Dilemmas of Transitional Justice in Nigeria' (2018) 12(2) International Journal of Transitional Justice 257

Xanthaki A, 'Indigenous Cultural Rights in International Law' (2000) 2 European Journal of Law Reform 343

Xanthaki A, 'Multiculturalism and International Law: Discussing Universal Standards' (2010) 32(1) Human Rights Quarterly 21

Xanthaki A, 'When Universalism Becomes a Bully: Revisiting the Interplay Between Cultural Rights and Women's Rights' (2019) 41(3) Human Rights Quarterly 701

Chapters in Edited Collections

Alfred GT, 'Restitution Is the Real Pathway to Justice for Indigenous Peoples' in Younging G, Dewar J, and DeGagne M (eds), *Response, Responsibility, and Renewal: Canada's Truth and Reconciliation Journey* (Aboriginal Healing Foundation 2009)

Arthur P, 'Introduction: Identities in Transition' in Arthur P (ed), *Identities in Transition: Challenges for Transitional Justice in Divided Societies* (Cambridge University Press 2010)

Bickford L, 'Memoryworks/Memory Works' in Ramirez-Barat C (ed), *Transitional Justice, Culture, and Society: Beyond Outreach* (Social Science Research Council 2014)

Boven TV, 'Categories of Rights' in Moeckli D and others (eds), *International Human Rights Law* (Oxford University Press, 3rd edn 2018)

Buckley-Zistel S and others, 'Transitional Justice Theories: An Introduction' in Buckley-Zistel S and others (eds), *Transitional Justice Theories* (Routledge 2014)

Callaghan M, 'Painting Over the Past: Political Palimpsests in Northern Ireland and the Complexities of the "Whitewash" Initiative', in Schaub D and others (eds), *Topography of Trauma: Fissures, Disruptions and Transfigurations* (Brill 2019)

Castellino J, 'Colonial Crime, Environmental Destruction and Indigenous Peoples: A Roadmap to Accountability and Protection' in Bergsmo M, Kaleck W, and Hlaing KY (eds), *Colonial Wrongs and Access to International Law* (Torkel Opsahl Academic EPublisher 2020)

Cavallaro J and Albuja S, 'The Lost Agenda: Economic Crimes and Truth Commissions in Latin America and Beyond' in McEvoy K and McGregor L (eds), *Transitional Justice from Below: Grassroots Activism and the Struggle for Change* (Hart Publishing 2008)

Chapman C, 'Transitional Justice and the Rights of Minorities and Indigenous Peoples' in Arthur P (ed), *Identities in Transition: Challenges for Transitional Justice in Divided Societies* (Cambridge University Press 2010)

Rigoberto Ajcalón Choy RA, Ford A, and Nimatuj IAV, 'Racism and Maya Achi Resistance within the Contradictions of Neoliberal Multiculturalism' in Hooker J (ed), *Black and Indigenous Resistance in the Americas: From Multiculturalism to Racist Backlash* (Lexington 2020)

Cueva EG and Librizzi MF, 'Photography and Transitional Justice: Evidence, Postcard, Placard, Token of Absence' in Ramirez-Barat C (ed), *Transitional Justice, Culture, and Society: Beyond Outreach* (Social Science Research Council 2014)

De Greiff P, 'Preface: On Making the Invisible Visible: The Role of Cultural Interventions in Transitional Justice Processes' in Ramirez-Barat C (ed), *Transitional Justice, Culture, and Society: Beyond Outreach* (Social Science Research Council 2014)

De Greiff P, 'Transitional Justice and Development' in Currie-Alder B and others (eds), *International Development: Ideas, Experience & Prospects* (Oxford University Press 2014)

Donders Y, 'Foundations of Collective Cultural Rights in International Human Rights Law' in Jakubowski A (ed), *Cultural Rights as Collective Rights: An International Law Perspective* (Brill 2016)

Eide A, 'Cultural Rights as Individual Human Rights' in Eide A and others (eds), *Economic, Social and Cultural Rights* (2nd edn, Martin Nijhoff Publishers 2001)

Gibson J, 'Community Rights to Culture' in Allen S and Xanthaki A (eds), *Reflections on the UN Declaration on the Rights of Indigenous Peoples* (Hart Publishing 2011)

Greenland F and Göçek FN, 'Introduction' in Greenland F and Göçek FM (eds), *Cultural Violence and the Destruction of Human Communities New Theoretical Perspectives* (Routledge 2020)
Haldemann F and Kouassi R, 'Transitional Justice without Economic, Social, and Cultural Rights?' in Riedel E and others (eds), *Economic, Social, and Cultural Rights in International Law: Contemporary Issues and Challenges* (Oxford University Press 2014)
Jung C, 'Canada and the Legacy of the Indian Residential Schools: Transitional Justice for Indigenous Peoples in a Non-Transitional Society' in Arthur P (ed), *Identities in Transition: Challenges for Transitional Justice in Divided Societies* (Cambridge University Press 2010)
Kent L, 'Engaging with "The Everyday": Towards a More Dynamic Conception of Hybrid Transitional Justice' in Wallis J and others (eds), *Hybridity on the Ground in Peacebuilding and Development: Critical Conversations* (ANU Press 2018)
Kirmayer LJ, Brass GM, and Valaskakis GG, 'Conclusion: Healing/Invention/Tradition' in Kirmayer LG and Valaskakis GG (eds), *Healing Traditions: The Mental Health of Aboriginal Peoples in Canada* (UBC Press 2014)
Kymlicka W, 'Transitional Justice, Federalism, and the Accommodation of Minority Nationalism' in Arthur P (ed), *Identities in Transition: Challenges for Transitional Justice in Divided Societies* (Cambridge University Press 2011)
Laat SD, 'Memory and Photographs of Unrepresentable Trauma in Rwandan Transitional Justice' in Wolfe S, Kane M, and Ansah T (eds), *In the Shadow of Genocide* (Routledge 2022)
Lambourne W, 'Transformative Justice, Reconciliation and Peacebuilding' in Buckley-Zistel S and others (eds), *Transitional Justice Theories* (Routledge 2013)
Lebaron M, 'Culture and Conflict' in Burgess G and Burgess H (eds), *Beyond Intractability* (Conflict Information Consortium 2003)
Lenzerini F, 'Reparations for Indigenous Peoples in International and Comparative Law: An Introduction' in Lenzerini F (ed), *Reparations for Indigenous Peoples: International and Comparative Perspectives* (Oxford University Press 2008)
Lenzerini F, 'Intentional Destruction of Cultural Heritage' in Francioni F and Vrdoljak AF (eds) *The Oxford Handbook on International Cultural Heritage Law* (Oxford University Press 2020)
Librizzi MF, 'Challenges of the Truth Commissions to Deal with Injustice Against Indigenous Peoples' in Littlechild W and Stamatopoulou E (eds), *Indigenous Peoples' Access to Justice, Including Truth and Reconciliation Processes* (Institute for the Study of Human Rights, Columbia University 2014)
Lutz E, 'Transitional Justice: Lessons Learned and the Road Ahead' in Roht-Arriaza N (ed), *Transitional Justice in the Twenty-first Century: Beyond Truth versus Justice* (Cambridge University Press 2006)
Mair T, 'Transforming Transitional Justice to Address Colonial Crime: the Nama's and Herero's Claim for Justice for Germany's Colonial Genocide in Namibia in Weiß N (ed), Transitional *Justice: Theoretical and Practical Approaches* (Universitätsverlag Potsdam 2022)
Magallanes CJI, 'Reparations for Maori Grievances in Aotearoa New Zealand' in Lenzerini F (ed), *Reparations for Indigenous Peoples: International and Comparative Perspectives* (Oxford University Press 2008)
Magalhães JN, 'Political Transition, Continuities and Permanences: The Rights of Indigenous Peoples and Political Transition in Brazil' in Paixão C and Meccarelli M (eds), *Comparing Transitions to Democracy. Law and Justice in South America and Europe* (Springer 2021)
Martínez G, 'Photography as a Platform for Transitional Justice: Peru's Case' in Ristovska S and Price M (eds), *Visual Imagery and Human Rights Practice* (Springer 2018)
McAuliffe P, 'Structural Causes of Conflict and the Superficiality of Transition' in Corradetti C and others (eds), *Theorizing Transitional Justice* (Ashgate Publishing 2015)
McGaughey F, 'A Law unto Themselves: Murals in the Northern Ireland Conflict' in McCutcheon J and McGaughey F (eds), *Research Handbook on Art and Law* (Edward Elgar Publishing 2020)
McGoldrick D, 'Culture, Cultures, and Cultural Rights' in Baderin MA and McCorquodale R (eds), *Economic, Social and Cultural Rights in Action* (Oxford University Press 2007)

McKay E, 'If They Read What You Are Writing, This Is the Teachings, This Is Some of the Teachings that We Want Them to Read About' in McCaskill P and others (eds), *In the Words of Elders: Aboriginal Cultures in Transition* (University of Toronto Press 1999)

McKinnon H, 'Proposing a Museum of Memory: Reparations and the Maya Achí Genocide in Guatemala' in Fromm AB, Rekdal PB, and Golding V (eds), *Museums and Truth* (Cambridge Scholars Publishing 2014)

Moses AD, 'Rafael Lemkin, Culture and the Concept of Genocide' in Bloxham D and Moses AD (eds), *The Oxford Handbook of Genocide Studies* (2012)

Naidu E, 'Memorialisation in Post-Conflict Societies in Africa: Potentials and Challenges' in Buckley-Zistel S and Schäfer S (eds) *Memorials in Times of Transition* (Cambridge University Press 2014)

Newhouse D and Belanger Y, 'Beyond the Indian Problem: Aboriginal Peoples and the Transformation of Canada' in Courtney J and Smith D (eds), *The Oxford Handbook of Canadian Politics* (Oxford University Press 2010)

Nicholas G and Smith C, 'Considering the Denigration and Destruction of Indigenous Heritage as Violence' in Apaydin V (ed), *Critical Perspectives on Cultural Memory and Heritage: Construction, Transformation and Destruction* (UCL Press 2020)

Phillips M, 'Justice-Seeking in Settler States: A Model for Thinking about "Justice" in Transitional Societies' in Corradetti C, Eisikovits N, and Rotondi JV (eds), Theorizing Transitional Justice (Ashgate Publishing 2015)

Pineschi L, 'Cultural Diversity as a Human Right? General Comment No. 21 of the Committee on Economic, Social and Cultural Rights' in Borelli S and Lenzerini F (eds), *Cultural Heritage, Cultural Rights, Cultural Diversity: New Developments in International Law* (Martinus Nijhoff Publishers 2012)

Powderly J, 'Prosecuting Heritage Destruction' in Cuno J and Weiss TG (eds) *Cultural Heritage and Mass Atrocities* (Getty Publications 2022)

Radzik L and Murphy C, 'Reconciliation' in Zalta EN and Nodelman U (eds), *Stanford Encyclopedia of Philosophy* (2003)

Reiter AG, 'The Development of Transitional Justice' in Simic O (ed), *An Introduction to Transitional Justice* (2nd edn, Routledge 2021)

Ringelheim J, 'Cultural Rights' in Moeckli D and others (eds), *International Human Rights Law* (Oxford University Press, 3rd edn 2018)

Rodríguez-Garavito C and Lam Y, 'Addressing Violations of Indigenous Peoples' Territory, Land, and Natural Resource Rights During Conflicts and Transitions' in ICTJ (ed), *Strengthening Indigenous Rights through Truth Commissions: A Practitioner's Resource* (ICTJ 2012)

Roht-Arriaza N, 'The New Landscape of Transitional Justice' in Roht-Arriaza, N and Mariezcurrena, J (eds), *Transitional Justice in the Twenty-First Century: Beyond Truth versus Justice* (Cambridge University Press 2014)

Roht-Arriaza N, 'Reparations and Economic, Social, and Cultural Rights' in Sharp DN (ed), *Justice and Economic Violence in Transition* (Springer 2014)

Roht-Arriaza N, 'Measures of Non-repetition in Transitional Justice: The Missing Link?' in Gready P and Robins S (eds), *From Transitional to Transformative Justice* (Cambridge University Press 2019)

Sands P and Rai A, 'After the Dust Settles: Transitional Justice and Identity in the Aftermath of Cultural Destruction' in Cuno J and Weiss TG (eds), *Cultural Heritage and Mass Atrocities* (Getty Publications 2022)

Simic O, '"They say that justice takes time": Taking Stock of Truth Seeking in Peru, Argentina and Serbia' in Kent L and Demian M (eds), *Transitional Justice in Law, History and Anthropology* (Routledge 2020)

Skaar E, 'The Nordic Truth and Reconciliation Commissions: A New TRC Model for Resolving Historic and Ongoing Violations of Indigenous Rights' in Aldred R, Klaasen J, and Skum LM (eds) *Cultivating Transformative Reconciliation* (Pickwick 2024)

Stamatopoulou E, 'Taking Cultural Rights Seriously: The Vision of the UN Declaration on the Rights of Indigenous Peoples' in Allen S and Xanthaki A (eds), *Reflections on the UN Declaration on the Rights of Indigenous Peoples* (Hart Publishing 2011)

Toki V, 'The Issues of the Criminal Justice System and of Resources in Aoteoroa/New Zealand' in Littlechild W and Stamatopoulou E (eds), *Indigenous Peoples' Access to Justice, Including Truth and Reconciliation Processes* (Institute for the Study of Human Rights, Columbia University 2014)

Torpey J, 'Introduction' in Torpey J (ed), *Politics and the Past: On Repairing Historical Injustices* (Rowman & Littlefield Publishers 2004)

Vrdoljak AF, 'Reparations for Cultural Loss' in Lenzerini F (ed) *Reparations for Indigenous Peoples: International and Comparative Perspectives* (Oxford University Press 2008)

Vrdoljak AF, 'The Criminalisation of the Intentional Destruction of Cultural Heritage' in Bergin T and Orlando E (eds), *Forging a Socio-Legal Approach to Environmental Harms* (Routledge 2017)

Whittaker R, 'Cultural Property and Identity: Reconceptualising Restitution as a Form of Transitional Justice' in Fabiani MD, Burmon K, and Hufnagel S (eds), *Cultural Property Crime and the Law* (Routledge 2024)

Wiessner S, 'Culture and the Rights of Indigenous Peoples' in Vrdoljak AF (ed), *The Cultural Dimension of Human Rights* (Oxford University Press 2013)

Wilson M, 'The Truth and Reconciliation Commission of Canada' in Littlechild W and Stamatopoulou E (eds) *Indigenous Peoples' Access to Justice, Including Truth and Reconciliation Processes* (Institute for the Study of Human Rights, Columbia University 2014)

Xanthaki A, 'The UN Declaration on the Rights of Indigenous Peoples and Collective Rights: What's the Future for Indigenous Women?' in Allen S and Xanthaki A (eds), *Reflections on the UN Declaration on the Rights of Indigenous Peoples* (Hart Publishing 2011)

Waldorf L, 'Between Transition and Transformation Legal Empowerment as Collective Reparations' in Gready P and Robins S (eds), *From Transitional to Transformative Justice* (Cambridge University Press 2019)

Waldorf L, 'Expanding Transitional Justice' in Simic O (ed), *An Introduction to Transitional Justice* (2nd edn, Routledge 2021)

Yashar DJ, 'Indigenous Rights and Truth Commissions: Reflections for Discussion,' in ICTJ (ed), *Strengthening Indigenous Rights through Truth Commissions: A Practitioner's Resource* (ICTJ 2012)

Young LA and Sing'Oei K, 'Access to Justice for Indigenous Peoples in Africa' in Littlechild W and Stamatopoulou E (eds), *Indigenous Peoples' Access to Justice, Including Truth and Reconciliation Processes* (Institute for the Study of Human Rights, Columbia University 2014)

Younging G, 'Inherited History, International Law, and the UN Declaration' in Younging G, Dewar J, and DeGagne M (eds), *Response, Responsibility, and Renewal: Canada's Truth and Reconciliation Journey* (Aboriginal Healing Foundation 2009)

Yusuf HO, 'Transitional Justice and Colonialism' in Lawther C, Moffett L, and Jacobs D (eds), *Research Handbook on Transitional Justice* (Edward Elgar 2023)

Reports

African Peer Review Mechanism, Country Review Report of the Republic of Rwanda (June 2006)

Arthur P, Indigenous Self-Determination and Political Rights: Practical Recommendations for Truth Commissions (International Center for Transitional Justice 2014)

Barsalou JM and Baxter V, The Urge to Remember: The Role of Memorials in Social Reconstruction and Transitional Justice (United States Institute of Peace 2007)

Beyond the Mandate, Continuing the Conversation: Report of the Maine Wabanaki-State Child Welfare Truth and Reconciliation Commission (2015)

Chega! The Final Report of the Timor-Leste Commission for Reception, Truth and Reconciliation (November 2013)

Chinkin C, 'The Protection of Economic, Social and Cultural Rights Post-Conflict' Report Commissioned by the Office of the High Commissioner for Human Rights (2007)

Comisioín de la Verdad y Reconciliacioín, Informe Final de la Comisioín de la Verdad y Reconciliacioín (2004) <http://www.cverdad.org.pe/ingles/ifinal/index.php> accessed 1 February 2025

Comisión Nacional de Verdad y Reconciliación, Informe de La Comisión Nacional de Verdad y Reconciliación (1993) <https://bibliotecadigital.indh.cl/handle/123456789/170> accessed 1 February 2025

Comisión Nacional Sobre Prisión Política y Tortura, Informe de La Comisión Nacional Sobre Prisión Política y Tortura (2004) <https://bibliotecadigital.indh.cl/handle/123456789/455> accessed 1 February 2025

Commission to Investigate the Norwegianisation Policy and Injustice against the Sámi and Kvens/Norwegian Finns (1 June 2023) <https://www.stortinget.no/globalassets/pdf/sannhets--og-forsoningskommisjonen/rapport-til-stortinget-fra-sannhets--og-forsoningskommisjonen.pdf> accessed 5 February 2025

The Derry/Londonderry Report on Upholding the Human Right to Culture in Post-Conflict Societies (Northern Ireland Human Rights Commission 2014) <https://nihrc.org/publication/detail/upholding-the-human-right-to-culture-in-post-conflict-societies> accessed 1 February 2025

Evaluation of the Building Peace through the Arts: Re-Imaging Communities Programme, Final Report (January 2016) <https://niopa.qub.ac.uk/bitstream/NIOPA/3594/1/BPttA_Final_Programme_Evaluation.pdf> accessed 1 February 2025

Gram R and Schoofs Z, Germany's History of Returning Human Remains and Objects from Colonial Contexts: An Overview of Successful Cases and Unsettled Claims between 1970 and 2021 (Deutsches Zentrum Kulturgutverluste 2022)

Greenland's Reconciliation Commission, We Understand the Past; We Take Responsibility for the Present; We Are Working for a Better Future (December 2017)

González E, 'Standards and Policies for Conflict Resolution, Truth, Transitional Justice and Reconciliation', Expert paper presented at the International Expert Group Meeting: 'Truth, transitional justice and reconciliation processes, PFII/2022/EGM (15–17 November 2022) <https://social.desa.un.org/sites/default/files/inline-files/Eduardo-Gonzalez-Transitional-Justice-and-Indigenous-Peoples.pdf> accessed 1 February 2025

González E, Justice and Indigenous Peoples in Latin America: Lessons learned from cases studies of Guatemala, Peru and Colombia (Global Initiative for Justice Truth and Reconciliation 2021)

Guatemala Memory of Silence, Report of the Commission for Historical Clarification ('CEH'): Conclusions and Recommendations (1999) <https://hrdag.org/wp-content/uploads/2013/01/CEHreport-english.pdf> accessed 1 February 2025

Human Rights Watch, 'Repression of Kurdish Political and Cultural Rights in Syria' (26 November 2009) <https://www.hrw.org/report/2009/11/26/group-denial/repression-kurdish-political-and-cultural-rights-syria> accessed 1 February 2025

Information presented by the Northern Ireland Human Rights Commission to the Human Rights Council, UN Doc. A/HRC/25/NI/5 (27 February 2014)

International Center of Transitional Justice, *Strengthening Indigenous Rights through Truth Commissions: A Practitioner's Resource* (ICTJ 2012)

Kenya Truth, Justice and Reconciliation Commission, 'Report of the Truth, Justice and Reconciliation Commission' (3 May 2013)

Library and Archives Canada, RG10, volume 6810, file 470-2-3, volume 7, Evidence of D. C. Scott to the Special Committee of the House of Commons Investigating the Indian Act amendments of 1920, (L-2)(N-3)

Lostal M and Cunliffe E, 'The Aftermath of Destruction of Cultural Heritage: Factoring In Cultural Rights in Post-Conflict Recovery Processes' UN Human Rights Office of the High Commissioner Submission to Study on Intentional Destruction of Cultural Heritage (2016) <https://www.ohchr.org/Documents/Issues/CulturalRights/DestructionHeritage/NGOS/M.Lostal_E.Cunliffe.pdf> accessed 1 February 2025

Martinez D (ed), Guatemala Resists Forgetting: Post-Conflict Memory Initiatives (Impunity Watch 2012) <https://www.impunitywatch.org/wp-content/uploads/2022/08/ResearchReport_Guatemala_Resists_Forgetting_Memory_Initiatives_2012_eng-1.pdf> accessed 1 February 2025

Moffett L and Gallen J, 'From Truth to Repair—Implementing Truth Commissions' Recommendations on Reparations' (January 2020) <https://reparations.qub.ac.uk/assets/uploads/QUB-TRCs_Report_UPDATED130120.pdf> accessed 1 February 2025

Naidu-Silverman E, The Contribution of Art and Culture in Peace and Reconciliation Processes in Asia (Centre for Culture and Development 2015)

National Inquiry into Missing and Murdered Indigenous Women and Girls, Reclaiming Power and Place: The Final Report of the National Inquiry into Missing and Murdered Indigenous Women and Girls (2019)

Nunca Más: The Report of the Argentine National Commission on the Disappeared (1986) <http://www.desaparecidos.org/nuncamas/web/english/library/nevagain/nevagain_001.htm> accessed 1 February 2025

Pham P and others, When the War Ends: a Population-based Survey on Attitudes about Peace, Justice, and Social Reconstruction in Northern Uganda (December 2007)

Prime Minister Sir John A. Macdonald, Official report of the debates of the House of Commons of the Dominion of Canada, 9 May 1883, 1107–08

Report on the African Commission's Working Group on Indigenous Populations/Communities Research and Information Visit to Kenya (1–19 March 2010)

Report of the National Inquiry into the Separation of Aboriginal and Torres Strait Islander Children from Their Families: Bringing Them Home (1997)

Report of the Truth and Justice Commission of Mauritius (November 2011) <https://www.usip.org/sites/default/files/ROL/TJC_Vol1.pdf> accessed 1 February 2025

Robins S, Kenya: 'To live as other Kenyans do': A Study of the Reparative Demands of Kenyan Victims of Human Rights Violations (International Center for Transitional Justice 2011)

Rubio-Marín R and others, 'Indigenous Peoples and Reparations Claims: Tentative Steps in Peru and Guatemala' ICTJ Research Brief (International Center for Transitional Justice 2009)

Sarr-Savoy Report on the Restitution of African Cultural Heritage, Toward a New Relational Ethics (November 2018) <https://www.about-africa.de/images/sonstiges/2018/sarr_savoy_en.pdf> accessed 5 February 2025

Solomon Islands Truth and Reconciliation Commission, *Confronting the Truth for a Better Solomon Islands: Final Report* (February 2012)

Terms of Reference for the National Inquiry into Missing and Murdered Indigenous Women and Girls (Indigenous and Northern Affairs Canada, 12 December 2016) <https://www.mmiwg-ffada.ca/wp-content/uploads/2018/10/terms-of-reference.pdf> accessed 1 February 2025

The Gambia Truth, Reconciliation and Reparations Commission, <https://www.justiceinfo.net/en/86069-trrc-final-report-gambia-between-prosecutions-and-amnesties.html#Gambia-TRRC-final-report> accessed 1 February 2025

The Office of the Prosecutor of the International Criminal Court, *Policy on Cultural Heritage* (June 2021) <https://www.icc-cpi.int/sites/default/files/itemsDocuments/20210614-otp-policy-cultural-heritage-eng.pdf> accessed 1 February 2025

The Swedish Foundation for Human Rights, Indigenous Peoples' Participation in Transitional Justice—Opportunity for Change? Lesson from Colombia (July 2020) <https://mrfonden.se/wp-content/uploads/2020/12/indigenous-peoples-participation-in-transitional-justice.pdf> accessed 1 February 2025

The Taranaki Report Kaupapa Tuatahi, Waitangi Tribunal Report (1996) 274–75 <https://forms.justice.govt.nz/search/Documents/WT/wt_DOC_68453721/Taranaki%201996.compressed.pdf> accessed 1 February 2025

Truth and Reconciliation Commission of Canada, Honouring the Truth, Reconciling for the Future: Summary of the Final Report of the Truth and Reconciliation Commission of Canada (2015)

Truth and Reconciliation Commission of South Africa Report (1999) <https://www.justice.gov.za/trc/report/> accessed 1 February 2025

Truth and Reconciliation Commission Concerning the Sámi People <https://sdtsk.fi/en/home/> accessed 1 February 2025

Truth and Reconciliation Commission for Kvens, Tornedalians and Lantalaiset (15 November 2023)

Truth Commission for the Sámi People <https://sanningskommissionensamer.se/en/about-the-commision/#:~:text=The%20Truth%20Commission%20for%20the%20Sami%20People&text=The%20Commission%20will%20survey%20and,consequences%20for%20the%20Sami%20people> accessed 1 February 2025

UN and World Bank, *Pathways for Peace: Inclusive Approaches to Preventing Violent Conflict* (World Bank 2018)

UN OHCHR, Rule-of-Law Tools for Post-Conflict States: Prosecution Initiatives, HR/PUB/06/4 (2006) <https://www.Ohchr.Org/Documents/Publications/RuleoflawProsecutionsen.Pdf> accessed 1 February 2025

UN OHCHR, Rule-of-Law Tools for Post-Conflict States: Reparations Programs, HR/PUB/08/1 (2008) <https://www.Ohchr.Org/Documents/Publications/ReparationsProgrammes.Pdf> accessed 1 February 2025

UN OHCHR, Rule-of-Law Tools for Post-Conflict States: National Consultations on Transitional Justice, HR/PUB/09/2 (2009) <https://www.Ohchr.Org/Documents/Publications/NationalConsultationsTJ_EN.Pdf> accessed 1 February 2025

UN OHCHR, Transitional Justice and Economic, Social and Cultural Rights, HR/PUB/13/5 (2014)

UN OHCHR, 'Principles and Guidelines for a Human Rights Approach to Poverty Reduction Strategies', HR/PUB/06/12 <https://www.ohchr.org/Documents/Publications/PovertyStrategiesen.pdf> accessed 1 February 2025

UNESCO, 'The Role of Culture in Peace and Reconciliation' (April 2013) (on file with author)

Odum U and Tesfaye H, Transitional Justice and Indigenous Peoples: Lessons Learned from the Cases of Kenya, Morocco, Nigeria, Rwanda and Sierra Leone (Global Initiative for Justice Truth and Reconciliation 2021)

Yoorrook Justice Commission, Yoorrook with Purpose: Interim Report (June 2022) para 6 <https://yoorrookjusticecommission.org.au/wp-content/uploads/2022/07/Yoorrook-Justice-Commission-Interim-Report.pdf> accessed 1 February 2025

Yoorrook Justice Commission, Yoorrook for Justice: Report into Victoria's Child Protection and Criminal Justice Systems (August 2023) 109–10 <https://yoorrookjusticecommission.org.au/wp-content/uploads/2023/09/Yoorrook-for-justice-report.pdf> accessed 1 February 2025

Yoorrook Justice Commission, Guiding the Path to Yoorrook <https://yoorrookjusticecommission.org.au/wp-content/uploads/2022/11/Guiding-the-Path-to-Yoorrook-v2.pdf> accessed 1 February 2025

Yoorrook Justice Commission, General Guidelines on Information Gathering and Evidence, para 5. <https://yoorrookjusticecommission.org.au/wp-content/uploads/2022/11/Yoorrook-General-Guidelines.pdf> accessed 1 February 2025

Newspaper Articles

D'Silva B, 'The Battle for Ukraine's Cultural Gems', *BBC News* (22 August 2023) <https://www.bbc.com/culture/article/20230821-the-fight-to-save-ukraines-cultural-spaces-and-heritage#:~:text=Today%2C%20intentional%20targeting%20of%20cultural,protocol%20drawn%20up%20in%201999> accessed 1 February 2025

Diskin E, 'Sweden to Return the Skulls of 25 Sami People to Their Proper Resting Place', *Matador Network* (8 August 2019) <https://matadornetwork.com/read/sweden-return-skulls-sami-people/> accessed 1 February 2025

Espinoza MC, 'A "New Deal" for Indigenous Groups', *Inter Press Service* (29 November 2003) <https://www.mapuche-nation.org/english/html/news/n-65.htm> accessed 1 February 2025

Finne A, 'Abuse and Colony Era Still Marks Greenlanders', *High North News* (25 October 2018) <https://www.highnorthnews.com/en/abuse-and-colony-era-still-marks-greenlanders> accessed 1 February 2025

Websites and Blogs

Amnesty International, 'Landmark ICC Verdict against Al-Mahdi Must Be First Step to Broader Justice in Mali Conflict' (27 September 2016) <https://www.amnesty.org/en/latest/news/2016/09/landmark-icc-verdict-against-almahdi-must-be-first-step-to-broader-justice-in-mali-conflict-2/> accessed 1 February 2025

Annan K, 'The Age of Human Rights', *Project Syndicate* (26 September 2000) <https://www.project-syndicate.org/commentary/the-age-of-human-rights-2000-09> accessed 1 February 2025

Andersen AN, 'Lessons from the Greenlandic Reconciliation Process', JusticeInfo.Net (5 March 2020) <https://www.justiceinfo.net/en/43949-lessons-from-the-greenlandic-reconciliation-process.html> accessed 1 February 2025

Australian Human Rights Commission, 'Ending QLD Truth-telling and Healing Inquiry Is Harmful and Divisive' (1 November 2024) <https://humanrights.gov.au/about/news/ending-qld-truth-telling-and-healing-inquiry-harmful-and-divisive> accessed 1 February 2025

Belcourt BR, 'Political Depression in a Time of Reconciliation', *Active History: History Matters* (15 January 2016) <http://activehistory.ca/2016/01/political-depression-in-a-time-of-reconciliation/> accessed 1 February 2025

Canadian Public Opinion on Aboriginal Peoples, Indian Residential Schools and the Truth and Reconciliation Commission <https://www.environicsinstitute.org/docs/default-source/project-documents/public-opinion-about-aboriginal-issues-in-canada-2016/indian-residential-schools-and-the-trc.pdf?sfvrsn=25b66577_2#:~:text=Awareness%20of%20the%20TRC%20varies,education%20level%20and%20household%20income> accessed 1 February 2025

CARICOM Reparation Commission, CARICOM Ten Point Plan for Reparatory Justice <https://caricom.org/caricom-ten-point-plan-for-reparatory-justice/> accessed 1 February 2025

CARICOM Reparation Commission, 10-Point Reparation Plan <https://caricomreparations.org/caricom/caricoms-10-point-reparation-plan/> accessed 1 February 2025

Dorronsoro B and Viaene L, 'Indigenous Peoples and Transitional Justice in Colombia: Challenges, Risks and Lessons Learned' (9 March 2017) <https://ces.uc.pt/en/agenda-noticias/agenda-de-eventos/2017/indigenous-peoples-and-transitional-justice-in-colombia> accessed 1 February 2025

FIDH, 'Mali: The Hearing of Al Mahdi before the ICC Is a Victory, But Charges Must Be Expanded' (30 September 2015) <https://www.fidh.org/en/issues/international-justice/international-criminal-court-icc/mali-the-hearing-of-abou-tourab-before-the-icc-is-a-victory-but> accessed 1 February 2025

Frogameni E, 'Cameroon's Anglophone Crisis: The Dangers of Language Conflict on Display', *Oxford Political Review* (14 August 2024) <https://oxfordpoliticalreview.com/2024/08/14/cameroons-anglophone-crisis-the-dangers-of-language-conflict-on-display/> accessed 5 February 2025

Full speech: Biden Apologizes for Forced Native American Boarding School Policy, *NBC News* (24 October 2024) <https://www.nbcnews.com/video/full-speech-biden-apologizes-for-forced-native-american-boarding-school-policy-222701125937> accessed 1 February 2025

International Commission of Jurists, 'Sri Lanka: New Bill to Establish "Commission for Truth, Unity and Reconciliation" Lacks Credibility and Unlikely to Bring Accountability (12 January 2024) <https://www.icj.org/sri-lanka-new-bill-to-establish-commission-for-truth-unity-and-reconciliation-lacks-credibility-and-unlikely-to-bring-accountability/> accessed 5 February 2025

International Center of Transitional Justice, 'Indigenous Voices and Truth Commissions', Summary Materials: International Seminar (22–23 March 2010) <https://www.ictj.org/sites/default/files/IPTC-March-2010-Meeting-Summary-Materials.pdf> accessed 1 February 2025

International Center of Transitional Justice, 'Transitional Justice and the Struggle for Indigenous Rights' (8 February 2013) <https://www.ictj.org/news/transitional-justice-and-struggle-indigenous-rights> accessed 1 February 2025

International Center of Transitional Justice, 'Ten Years After Peru's Truth Commission' (19 August 2013) <https://www.ictj.org/news/ten-years-after-peru-truth-commission> accessed 1 February 2025

International Center of Transitional Justice, 'Holding a Mirror to Society: Acknowledgment and the Struggle for Indigenous Peoples Rights' (2018) <https://www.ictj.org/news/holding-mirror-society-acknowledgment-and-struggle-indigenous-peoples-rights> accessed 1 February 2025

Izquierdo BV and Viaene L, 'Decolonizing Transitional Justice from Indigenous Territories' *Peace in Progress*, No. 38 (June 2018) <https://www.icip.cat/perlapau/en/article/decolonizing-transitional-justice-from-indigenous-territories/> accessed 1 February 2025

JusticeInfo.Net, 'Hour of Reckoning for Colonial Crimes' <https://www.justiceinfo.net/en/78778-hour-of-reckoning-for-colonial-crimes.html> accessed 1 February 2025

Miller Z, 'Transitional Justice, Race, and the United States', *Just Security* (30 June 2020) <https://www.justsecurity.org/71040/transitional-justice-race-and-the-united-states/> accessed1 February 2025

Movement for Black Lives, Case Study Two: CARICOM Reparations Commission <https://m4bl.org/wp-content/uploads/2020/11/Case-Study-Two.pdf> accessed 1 February 2025

Movement for Black Lives, Reparations for the Cultural and Educational Exploitation, Erasure, and Extraction of Our Communities in the Form of Mandated Public School Curriculums That Critically Examine the Political, Economic, and Social Impacts of Colonialism and Slavery and Funding to Support, Build, Preserve and Restore Cultural Assets and Sacred Sites to Ensure the Recognition and Honoring of Our Collective Struggles and Triumphs <https://m4bl.org/wp-content/uploads/2020/05/CulturalReparations-OnePager.pdf> accessed 1 February 2025

Movement for Black Lives, Reparations Now Toolkit, <https://m4bl.org/wp-content/uploads/2020/05/Reparations-Now-Toolkit-FINAL.pdf?> accessed 1 February 2025

Murphy C, 'Transitional Justice in the United States', *Just Security* (16 July 2020) <https://www.justsecurity.org/71236/transitional-justice-in-the-united-states/> accessed 1 February 2025

Northern Ireland, Independent Commission for Reconciliation and Information Recovery <https://icrir.independent-inquiry.uk/> accessed 5 February 2025

Office of the President, Republic of China (Taiwan),'President Tsai Apologizes to Indigenous Peoples on behalf of Government' (1 August 2016) <https://english.president.gov.tw/NEWS/4950> accessed 1 February 2025

ONIC, 'Agenda Nacional de Paz de los Pueblos Indígenas' <https://www.onic.org.co/canastadesaberes/118-cds/publicaciones/conflicto-armado-y-paz/1820-agenda-nacional-de-paz-de-los-pueblos-indigenas> accessed 1 February 2025

Parliament of Australia, Apology to Australia's Indigenous Peoples (13 February 2008) <https://www.aph.gov.au/Visit_Parliament/Art/Icons/Apology_to_Australias_Indigenous_Peoples#:~:text=On%2013%20February%202008%2C%20Prime,for%20voting%20to%20the%20Chamber> accessed 1 February 2025

Pillai P, 'Truth Commissions and Colonial Atrocities: Moving the Needle Further Towards State Responsibility?', *OpinioJuris* (27 April 2019) <http://opiniojuris.org/2019/04/27/truth-commissions-and-colonial-atrocities-moving-the-needle-further-towards-state-responsibility/> accessed 1 February 2025

Sheria KC, 'Summary of The Truth, Justice and Reconciliation Commission (TJRC) Report' (2014) <https://kituochasheria.or.ke/wp-content/uploads/2022/09/TJRC-Report-2013-GS-with-isbn1.pdf> accessed 1 February 2025

Simpson LB, 'Land and Reconciliation: Having the Right Conversations', *Watershed Sentinel* (23 November 2017)

Statement of the Prosecutor of the International Criminal Court, Fatou Bensouda, following the transfer of the first suspect in the Mali investigation: 'Intentional Attacks against Historic Monuments and Buildings Dedicated to Religion Are Grave Crimes' (26 September 2015) <https://www.icc-cpi.int/news/statement-prosecutor-international-criminal-court-fatou-bensouda-following-transfer-first> accessed 1 February 2025

Statement to the Media by the United Nations' Working Group of Experts on People of African Descent, on the conclusion of its official visit to USA, 19–29 January 2016 (29 January 2016). <https://www.ohchr.org/en/statements/2016/01/statement-media-united-nations-working-group-experts-people-african-descent> accessed 1 February 2025

Statement Marking the One-Year Anniversary of the Final Report of the National Inquiry into Missing and Murdered Indigenous Women and Girls (3 June 2020) <https://www.canada.ca/en/crown-indigenous-relations-northern-affairs/news/2020/06/statement-from-minister-bennett-minister-monsef-minister-lametti-minister-miller-minister-guilbeault-and-minister-blair-marking-the-one-year-annive.html> accessed 1 February 2025

The Waitangi Tribunal: Te Roopu Whakamana i te Tiriti o Waitangi <https://waitangitribunal.govt.nz> accessed 1 February 2025

The World Bank Group, 'GDP (Current US$)—World Bank Open Data' <https://data.worldbank.org/indicator/NY.GDP.MKTP.CD> accessed 5 February 2025

Uluru Statement from the Heart <https://ulurustatement.org/the-statement> accessed 1 February 2025

UN OHCHR, 'Applying a Human-Rights Based Approach to Climate Change Negotiations, Policies and Measures' <https://www.uncclearn.org/wp-content/uploads/library/infonotehrba1.pdf> accessed 1 February 2025

UN OHCHR, 'Human Rights: A Basic Handbook for UN Staff' <www.ohchr.org/documents/publications/hrhandbooken.pdf> accessed 1 February 2025

UN OHCHR, 'Integrating Cultural Rights in Transitional Justice Strategies in Post-conflict Societies' <https://www.ohchr.org/EN/NewsEvents/Pages/Integratingculturalrightsinpost-conflictsocieties.aspx> accessed 1 February 2025

UN OHCHR, 'Key Concepts on ESCRs—Can Economic, Social and Cultural Rights Be Litigated at Courts?' <https://www.ohchr.org/EN/Issues/ESCR/Pages/CanESCRbelitigatedatcourts.aspx> accessed 1 February 2025

UN Press Release, '"We Can Love What We Are, Without Hating What—And Who—We Are Not," Secretary-General Says in Nobel Lecture', UN Doc. SG/SM/8071 (10 December 2001) <https://press.un.org/en/2001/sgsm8071.doc.htm> accessed 1 February 2025

University of Birmingham, 'Aboriginal Remains Returned to Ancestral Home' (18 October 2016) <https://www.birmingham.ac.uk/news-archive/2016/aboriginal-remains-returned-to-ancestral-home> accessed 5 February 2025

Unrepresented Nations and Peoples Organization, 'Batwa: Exclusion from Genocide Commemorations' (15 April 2019) <https://unpo.org/article/21462> accessed 1 February 2025

United States Senate Committee on Armed Services, Summary of the Fiscal Year 2023 – National Defense Authorization Act <https://www.armed-services.senate.gov/imo/media/doc/fy23_ndaa_agreement_summary.pdf> accessed 1 February 2025

Yuvraj J, 'Does Transitional Justice Belong in the United States?' (13 July 2020) <https://www.justsecurity.org/71372/does-transitional-justice-belong-in-the-united-states/> accessed 1 February 2025

Conference Papers and Other Documents

Arbour L, 'Economic and Social Justice for Societies in Transition', Second Annual Transitional Justice Lecture hosted by the Center for Human Rights and Global Justice at New York University School of Law and by the International Center for Transitional Justice (New York University Law School, 25 October 2006)

Balint J and Evans J, 'Transitional Justice and Settler States', The Australian and New Zealand Critical Criminology Conference (2011)

Bell C, 'The Fabric of Transitional Justice: Binding Local and Global Political Settlements' University of Edinburgh School of Law, Research Paper Series No 2016/22 (2016) 19 <https://www.politicalsettlements.org/wp-content/uploads/2016/10/Bell-Transitional-Justice-Ch-1-2016.pdf> accessed 1 February 2025

Indian Residential Schools Settlement Agreement, <http://www.residentialschoolsettlement.ca/settlement.html> accessed 1 February 2025

Bailey K, 'So that all shall know': Memorialising Guatemala's Disappeared (Dissertation, Lancaster University 2018)

Submission of Asia Indigenous Peoples Pact (AIPP) and its member organizations for the report of the Expert Mechanism on the Rights of Indigenous Peoples on Recognition, reparations and reconciliation <https://www.ohchr.org/Documents/Issues/IPeoples/EMRIP/StudyRRR/AIPP_submission_EMRIP_RRR.pdf> accessed 1 February 2025

Vrdoljak AF, 'Minorities, Cultural Rights and the Protection of Intangible Cultural Heritage' (Contemporary Issues, ESIL Research Forum on International Law 2005)

INDEX

For the benefit of digital users, indexed terms that span two pages (e.g., 52–53) may, on occasion, appear on only one of those pages.

The manufacturer's authorised representative in the EU for product safety is Oxford University Press España S.A. of el Parque Empresarial San Fernando de Henares, Avenida de Castilla, 2 – 28830 Madrid (www.oup.es/en or product.safety@oup.com). OUP España S.A. also acts as importer into Spain of products made by the manufacturer.

www.ingramcontent.com/pod-product-compliance
Ingram Content Group UK Ltd.
Pitfield, Milton Keynes, MK11 3LW, UK
UKHW020926180926
475595UK00035B/193/J
9780198911371